Presidential Campaign Discourse

SUNY Series, Human Communication Processes
Donald P. Cushman and Ted J. Smith, III, Editors

PRESIDENTIAL CAMPAIGN DISCOURSE

Strategic Communication Problems

Edited by Kathleen E. Kendall

Kathleen E. Kendall

STATE UNIVERSITY OF NEW YORK PRESS

Published by
State University of New York Press, Albany

© 1995 State University of New York

Chapter 2 "The Problem of Getting on the Media Agenda: A Case Study in
Competing Logics of Campaign Coverage" © 1995 Joshua Meyrowitz

Printed in the United States of America

For information, address State University of New York Press,
State University Plaza, Albany, N.Y., 12246

Production by Cathleen Collins
Marketing by Fran Keneston

Library of Congress Cataloging in Publication Data

Presidential campaign discourse : strategic communication problems /
    edited by Kathleen E. Kendall.
        p.   cm. — (SUNY series, human communication processes)
    Includes bibliographical references (p.   ) and index.
    ISBN 0-7914-2681-5 (alk. paper). — ISBN 0-7914-2682-3 (pb : alk.
paper)
        1. Presidents—United States—Election—1992.   2. Communication in
politics—United States.   3. Rhetoric—Political aspects—United
States.   4. Mass media—Political aspects—United States.   5. United
States—Politics and government—1989–1993.   I. Kendall, Kathleen
E., 1937-   .   II. Series: SUNY series in human communication
processes.
E884.P73   1995
324.973'0928—dc20   95-14650
                                                                 CIP

10 9 8 7 6 5 4 3 2

For
Zachary Richard Kendall

Contents

Preface

Election campaigns are very noisy affairs, with each candidate struggling to be heard. Who is listening? What, and whom, do potential voters really hear?

While reaching voters by appealing to what may interest them in a special way, presidential candidates strive to balance intense coverage from the local media with a strategy of projecting their candidature to a national audience. They must win the financial backing and endorsement of prominent individuals and groups. With strategies that inevitably change during the early, middle, and late phase of the campaign, they must adopt positions on complex policy questions and emotional moral issues, promote an image, react to bad news, and communicate a program. Many of these campaign problems, though appearing to be unique or arising in a daily "crisis," are recurrent in every election. As illustrated in this book, scholars have traced campaign patterns and recurrent strategies that candidates have used to find solutions to these communication problems.

Presidential campaign discourse is diverse in setting and complex in scope. Conversations with voters in a diner in New Hampshire may be illuminated by the klieg lights of a network camera crew. Speeches, interviews, debates, direct mail, and ads carry the campaign messages. But unless the media decide to report this discourse, candidates have to rely on their own means of reaching the public, and the number of people who hear their messages is thus reduced. Strategies for securing media coverage are a vital part of presidential campaign discourse. Political communication is an interactive process, involving candidates, media, and citizens. The essays in this collection concentrate mainly on the role of the candidates and media in this process.

The book focuses on communication problems in the 1992 presidential campaign, and the strategies candidates used to solve them. The authors develop theoretical explanations for the relative success or failure of the strategies adopted. But the book is about more than one campaign. All of the problems discussed here transcend time, affecting candidates of the past and future alike.

The unique contribution of the book is its analysis of strategies for solving communication problems, rather than focusing upon individual candidates, or particular issues, or the media's role. These factors are considered—the individuals, the issues, the media—but the search for answers in this book deals with the choices and decisions the candidates make in the face of communication problems so basic they have come to be part of the innate structure of presidential campaigns. Thus, the book begins with the New Hampshire primary (Kendall, chapter 1), where the candidates and media struggle to control the script of the electoral drama. The author presents an interpretive perspective of this key primary and its role in defining who and how and what kinds of characters will take part in the drama to come.

Chapter 2 (Meyrowitz) examines the problem of getting on the media agenda, and the logics media employ for deciding whom to cover. A case study of Larry Agran's unsuccessful efforts to get on the media agenda and interviews with journalists provide evidence for analysis. Chapter 3 (Trent and Trent) examines the decisions made by George Bush, Bill Clinton, and Ross Perot about challenger and incumbent strategies, and the problem of adapting those strategies to the prevailing conditions of any given election.

Voters want a president to be a leader with a vision: this is the condition addressed in chapter 4, as Wendt and Fairhurt compare ways in which the 1992 candidates attempted to communicate a rhetoric of leadership. Chapter 5 (Stuckey and Antczak) also explores the language of political leadership, in the candidates' efforts to dominate and control the definition of issues and images. This involves the redefining and refiguring of political discourse to create the appearance of identification with, and thus representation of, the electorate.

Debates pose an important tactical challenge for presidential candidates, particularly as more voters are undecided late in campaigns, and claim that debates help them make their decisions. In chapter 6, Owen discusses the strategies candidates have developed to meet a new environment of media populism in which formats, timing, candidate performance, and public participation have all changed.

Certain values run deep in American society, and the candidate who can harness those values effectively commands wide interest. Perot's strategy of weaving these values into the narratives of his televised advertisements is the subject of chapter 7 (Kern). The focus on advertising continues in chapter 8 (Roberts), with a report on how voters used political advertising messages in 1992 to influence their thinking about the presidential candidates. The study sheds light on the role of the ads in forming general impressions, and in evoking comments about specific visual details, as well as on the influence of negative ads.

Gregg (in chapter 9) and Daughton (in chapter 10) continue the discussion of American values begun by Kern. Gregg examines the ways in which candidates dealt with the "culture war" of 1992, particularly the abortion issue, and Daughton analyzes the handling of gender-related issues in political convention speeches of the past and present.

Opinion polls are omnipresent in campaigns. In chapter 11, Bauman and Herbst examine the rhetorical strategies candidates employ to deal with news of polling data, particularly when they are losing, and the themes in journalistic discourse about polls.

Once the campaign is over and the winners and losers are known, there is an important ritual remaining: the concession speech. In chapter 12, Corcoran compares the 1992 concession speeches with those of the past, revealing the framework and content and rules for this occasion.

In the concluding chapter (13), Smith distills some of the common findings of the book, discussing the struggle for interpretive dominance over the electoral process, the struggle to mobilize a winning coalition, and the struggle for access to the agenda-setting process.

The goal of this book is to make a significant contribution to our understanding of political communication in presidential campaigns, particularly the role of political discourse. It has been written for the general, serious reader, to illuminate the choices and decisions made in political campaigns, and to take stock of the strategies developed over time to meet the practical communication problems facing candidates.

Acknowledgments

The editor wishes to thank the following:

Donald P. Cushman, series editor, of the Department of Communication, University at Albany, State University of New York, for suggesting that this book be written;

Pamela D. Alesky, Syracuse University; Moya Ann Ball, Trinity University; Thomas W. Benson, Pennsylvania State University; Jane Blankenship, University of Massachusetts; Paul E. Corcoran, University of Adelaide, South Australia; Robert V. Friedenberg, Miami University: Ellen Reid Gold, University of Kansas; Doris Graber, University of Illinois, Chicago; Bruce E. Gronbeck, University of Iowa; Anne Hildreth, University at Albany, State University of New York; Montague Kern, Rutgers University; James F. Klumpp, University of Maryland; Raymie E. McKerrow, University of Maine; Michael Pfau, University of Wisconsin–Madison; Laurinda W. Porter, St. Cloud State University; Vincent Price, University of Michigan; Craig A. Smith, University of North Carolina, Greensboro; John Splaine, University of Maryland; Judith S. Trent, University of Cincinnati; Theodore O. Windt, University of Pittsburgh; and David Zarefsky, Northwestern University—for the time and care they gave to the critical reading of chapters, in spite of the enormous press of other responsibilities;

Henry C. Kenski, University of Arizona, Tucson, and David L. Paletz, Duke University, for serving as respondents to earlier versions of these chapters presented at the Speech Communication Association and International Communication Association conventions;

the authors, all of you, for your skill and talent, of course (that's why I chose you in the first place), but also for working so hard and so fast on this project. You were a pleasure to work with. I was a lucky editor!

ONE

The Problem of Beginnings in New Hampshire

Control over the Play

KATHLEEN E. KENDALL

> The New Hampshire primary: "It's the closest thing we've
> got to political amniocentesis."
> —Dayton Duncan, Booknotes interview,
> C-SPAN, March 31, 1991

INTRODUCTION AND BACKGROUND

That the New Hampshire primary is a key event in American political campaigns has been well established. It is the first primary in the nation, as mandated by the New Hampshire legislature.[1] This chapter takes an interpretive perspective, based on direct observation of the candidates and media during the primary and on an analysis of the primary's messages. This single primary constructs a critical part of the quadrennial electoral drama, defining the characteristics of the protagonists. The candidates have an unusually broad array of communication strategies available to them in this state. The focus of this chapter is on the initial electoral struggle of the candidates and media to exert control over the discourse of the 1992 New Hampshire presidential primary, and through it, the campaign to follow.

New Hampshire's voter turnout is regularly among the highest in the nation for a primary: 67 percent of registered voters voted in 1992, when the average turnout in primaries was just over 30 percent of registered voters (Baker, 1993). Not only is voter interest and participation high, but "tidal shifts in preference have not been uncommon in the final days before primaries there" (John, 1989, p. 592), placing great pressure on the candidates to respond quickly to change and on the media to make sense of a volatile situation.

1

From 1952 through 1988 no candidate ever won the presidency without winning there. (Bill Clinton broke this pattern in 1992, coming in second in New Hampshire.) News coverage of this primary is often the heaviest of all the states (Adams, 1987; Lichter, Amundsen, and Noyes, 1988; Kerbel, 1994). Research on the 1992 primaries has established that voters in other states formed candidate perceptions based on network news coverage of the New Hampshire primary, extending its influence far beyond the Northeast (Pfau et al., 1993). And the winner in New Hampshire has regularly made significant gains in the opinion polls (Mayer 1987).

Much prior research has been done on this subject. We know that the candidates go through a frenzy of presidential surfacing in New Hampshire, introducing themselves and attempting to emerge as serious contenders for the nomination of a major party, their final chance before the first primary votes are cast (Trent, 1978; Kendall and Trent, 1989). In an age of television and computers, this frenzy is only heightened. As Meyrowitz says, "action and reaction collapse into a co-constructed reality once possible only in face-to-face communication," with groups reacting "to each other's reactions to each other—in real time" (1992, p. 470). Voters at this early stage are just beginning to focus on the campaign; they tend to be so uninformed and uncertain about who the candidates are and which one they prefer that the candidates have an unparalleled opportunity to influence their knowledge and feelings (Patterson, 1980; Kennamer and Chaffee, 1982; Popkin, 1991).

We know that the majority of media coverage of the primary deals with the horse race, the question of who is winning (Patterson, 1980, 1993; Robinson and Sheehan, 1983), and with the candidates' viability, or "the relative chances of candidates winning the nomination." These questions about winning include the media's "fascination with [the] momentum" of the candidates (Brady and Johnston, 1987, p. 132). Matthews (1978) has established that the early primaries have a winnowing effect, as candidates who have done poorly withdraw from the race because they no longer seem to be viable.

Finally, we know that the voters and media are looking at the candidates' character, for signs that they have the presidential leadership traits to solve the nation's problems (Brady and Johnston, 1987; Bartels, 1988). This focus explains the heavy attention given to such presumed revelations of inner character as Senator Edmund Muskie's crying while defending his wife from an editorial attack in the 1972 New Hampshire primary. Candidates work to convey image traits effectively through their messages, both interpersonally and through the media. But the task is complex and difficult, because images are not only multifaceted and to some extent affected by the particular campaign context, but also co-constructed among the candidates, the media, and the voters. According to Louden (1990), image is "an evaluation negotiated and constructed by candidates and voters in a cooperative venture" (p. 1). Certainly that is true, but the media also play a role in this construction.

Voters have an ideal image of a candidate in their minds, and some of the traits in that profile have reappeared across campaigns: honesty, competence (including experience), empathy, and strength and decisiveness (Nimmo and Savage, 1976; Hellweg and King, 1983; Hellweg, King, and Williams, 1988; Trent et al., 1993). In a study of New Hampshire citizens attending candidate events during the 1992 primary, respondents said the most important candidate characteristics (4 or above on a 5-point scale) were (in this order): honesty, talks about the nation's problems (tied), has solutions to problems, good moral character, calm and cautious, energetic and aggressive leader, forceful public speaker, and experience in office (Trent et al., 1993).

These research findings have been valuable in aiding our understanding of the nature and significance of communication in the early primaries. However, the overall picture may be lost sight of when we focus on these pieces of the whole. The metaphor of the dramatic ritual advocated by Nimmo and Combs (1990) allows us to examine the whole event. They define ritual as "a series of acts that, for the most part, people regularly and faithfully perform time and time again"; a dramatic ritual exists "when the elements of a drama repeatedly relate to one another in a ritualistic fashion" (p. 54). Rituals are much more powerful than ceremonies, because they transform, appealing to the emotions; they "tap, reflect, and intensify deeply held values, ideals, and desires" (p. 69).

The presidential election is such a structured, rule-governed ritual, they argue, consisting of "dramatic confrontations, each side fantasizing an ideal America either lost but to be regained, or one yet to be found." In this ritual, the incumbent generally defends the *status quo*, arguing that his administration has brought gains and there will be more to come. The challenger attacks the *status quo* and argues for changes to bring about a brighter future, presenting himself as the one most capable of effecting these changes. The campaign renews the belief "that the story will have a happy ending (that is, that the contest can be won and greatness can be found or regained")" (pp. 54–55). The dramatic ritual of the campaign places a premium on hope: if it makes a difference who is going to be president, and if the choice is important to voters—a concept underlined by the campaign ritual—then the candidates "must enunciate a rhetorical vision of hope" (p. 68). Examples of such visions have been John F. Kennedy's promise to "get America moving again" and Jimmy Carter's theme of restoring trust and providing a "government as good as its people."

This metaphor of the dramatic ritual seemed particularly appropriate for examining the New Hampshire primary, after my immersion in that primary in 1988 and 1992. My perspective both years was that of a participant observer, a communication professor with media credentials,[2] traveling with the journalists and observing them and the candidates every day. All appeared to be engaged in a quest and a struggle: a quest to find out what the campaign (or play) was going to be about, and a struggle to shape the way the play was written. The concern with surfacing and the horse race and viability and winnowing and character were all there. but the main goal was to grasp and shape the presidential campaign story.

Nimmo and Combs say that "each phase of the presidential election coverage . . . is a minidrama" (p. 55), and identify the primary and caucus phase as one of those minidramas. In this view, New Hampshire would be a small part of the overall minidrama of thirty-eight primaries and thirteen caucuses in 1992. But the view from within the New Hampshire primary seemed bigger than that. At this early point in the campaign, when public opinion was so unformed (Patterson, 1980; Kennamer and Chaffee, 1982; Popkin, 1991), there was an obvious opportunity for a substantial part of the election drama to be constructed. The New Hampshire primary received almost undivided attention from the media and candidates during the February 11–19 period. Never again would there be such a concentrated focus; after New Hampshire, as Renee Loth of the *Boston Globe* wrote (Feb. 19, 1992, p. 1), the presidential campaign would split "like a band of refracted light, flashing attention on the 27 states that will hold primaries or caucuses in the next 30 days." The media focused heavily on the matter of electability, on who could win, not just in New Hampshire, but also in the fall election. In effect, they were trying to foresee the end of the play.

With these impressions of the large scope and influence of New Hampshire in mind, I examined the efforts of the candidates and media to shape answers to the following questions, which are inherent in the electoral drama, and the evidence of their success:

1. Who were the protagonists, and who were the minor characters in the play? Indicators of such position included endorsements, pictures, press attention, claims of important accomplishments, poll standings, crowd size, and titles.

2. What was the content of the character of the protagonists? Who had the traits of honesty, competence, compassion, and strength most closely approximating the ideal image of a presidential candidate? Character was conveyed through word choice, pictures, and the selection of representative anecdotes supposedly revealing of character.

3. What visions did the protagonists project, and who best projected the vision of hope? Language and pictures were instrumental in creating these visions.

For the candidates, it was vital that the construction of answers to these questions would please the voters, first in New Hampshire, and because New Hampshire influenced national perceptions, voters in the rest of the nation (Pfau et al., 1993). The media, as interpreters of the action to the public, also had to make decisions about these questions. The candidates struggled among themselves to make their answers prevail, and they also struggled with the media. All were well aware of the record of this primary in selecting a winner and dooming most of the candidates to life as a historical footnote. (Note: Other scholars are doing important work focusing upon voter involvement in this process during the primaries. See Kern and Just, 1994; Kern and Just, forthcoming, 1995; West, Kern, and Alger, 1992; Neuman, Just, and Crigler, 1992).

New Hampshire is a small state (in 1992 its population was only 1,110,801; *World Almanac,* 1994). The main way voters learn about the candidates is through mass communication—the candidates' television ads, and newspapers and television news—and the primary emphasis of this study is on those media. But "retail politics" remain vitally important in New Hampshire. Because the bulk of the population is clustered in the southern part of the state, the candidates can easily travel around and be seen by thousands of voters personally. They can meet with influential people who, with a phone call, can secure a vote. The state also has a long history of intense interest in primaries and high voter turnout. Thus, the chapter discusses three other avenues through which the candidates reached smaller numbers of the voters and the press: their campaign literature, their published daily schedules, and their speeches.

This chapter focuses on the two front-runners in each party in February 1992: Republicans George Bush and Pat Buchanan, and Democrats Paul Tsongas and Bill Clinton. The information is part of a larger study that will include Democrats Tom Harkin, Bob Kerrey, and Jerry Brown as well.

METHODS

In examining the candidates' input into the script, I reviewed the following: one major campaign leaflet from each candidate, secured at the campaign headquarters, as well as Tsongas's larger booklet; the first three or four of their television ads shown in New Hampshire; the video distributed door to door by the Clinton campaign; the candidate schedules distributed by the campaigns; and sample speeches I observed. I based my analysis of the campaign leaflets on the pictures, the language that appeared in bold or large type, and the captions. Important analysis of the New Hampshire television advertisements has been done by L. Patrick Devlin (1994), and I relied on that and added analysis of Clinton's video distributed to undecided voters. I read the candidates' schedules to see which groups they spoke to, and counted each person's public campaign appearances.

The discussion of speeches and speech events is based on those I saw myself, including six by Clinton, two each by Tsongas and Buchanan, and one by Bush; a debate involving all five leading Democrats; a Democratic dinner at which three of the Democrats spoke; and a Buchanan whistle-stop tour.

In describing the media's efforts to construct the script, I examined all front-page stories and pictures about the primary in the newspapers (150 stories and 58 pictures), and 25 television news broadcasts in the February 11–19, 1992 period (the primary was on Feb. 18). The national print sources examined were the *New York Times* and *USA Today*. Regional sources were the *Boston Globe* and the *Boston Herald*. Local sources were the *Manchester Union Leader*, *Concord Monitor* (Feb. 13, 14, 15, and 17 only), and *Nashua Telegraph*. These papers were selected because they were available in the Manchester-Concord-Nashua area where the majority of New Hampshirites live, and where the candidates and journalists clustered. The television broadcasts viewed were from NBC, CBS, and ABC nightly news, complete except for NBC, February 15 and 16. A more exhaustive study would have included coverage by CNN, WMUR (the New Hampshire television station), and several Boston stations.

The units of analysis for television were stories on the New Hampshire campaign. The coding scheme drew on Graber (1987), recording the date, network, anchor and reporter names, and topics covered, and then examined the way the story answered the three research questions. For each story the researcher asked: (1) which candidates were mentioned (to distinguish major and minor characters in the play); (2) what candidate characteristics were described or shown; and (3) what attention, if any, was given to the candidates' visions of the future.

The units of analysis for newspapers were the front-page stories and pictures on the primaries. These first-presented messages were selected because of their attention-getting position, because newspaper readers whether interested in politics or not generally scan the first page, and because this choice brought the volume of material down to a manageable size. The coding scheme followed for the newspaper stories was similar to that used for the televised news stories.

THE CANDIDATES' ATTEMPT TO CONSTRUCT THE PLAY

Campaign Literature

The candidates have complete control over the message in their literature, and therefore an examination of the contents was useful to discover how they chose to present themselves. It is not surprising that all the candidates used their literature to claim that they were major characters in the play. They were the stars of their leaflets pictorially: their faces always appeared on the cover, except for that of Tsongas, who appeared waving and smiling once the leaflet was opened. Bush emphasized his importance through the use of title—he was "President George Bush"—while the others chose a less hierarchical and more folksy approach, calling themselves Bill Clinton, Paul Tsongas, and Pat Buchanan.

Three of the four protagonists used their past records to support a claim to a major role, summarizing positions held, legislation initiated, proposals made. The exception to this pattern was Buchanan, whose leaflet made no claims to a past record of accomplishment; instead, it devoted the entire space to attacking the *status quo* and proposing a ten-point plan for change.

Two other strategies candidates used in their literature to convey an impression of viability and legitimacy were endorsements and accounts of how they had won against the odds before.

There was a sameness in the way the Democratic candidates constructed their images in the literature. The ideal image of the president, based on the Democrats' literature, was of a "fighter." Both used that word on the pamphlet cover: Clinton was "Fighting for the Forgotten Middle Class," and Tsongas told "How to fight for America's economic future and win."

The two Republicans displayed little common ground in their efforts to flesh out their images. The Buchanan character, according to his leaflet, was first of all patriotic: he favored "Putting and Keeping America First." The whole leaflet developed this theme, presenting ten steps for achieving these goals. Bush, in contrast, stressed his competence and decisiveness on the topic New Hampshirites were most concerned about: the economy. His pamphlet was "A Plan" for an "Economic Growth Agenda," and the pictures showed him in action, presumably promoting his plan.

A third question about the literature concerns the efforts of each candidate to project a vision of what he would do as president, a fantasy of "an ideal America either lost but to be regained, or one yet to be found" (Nimmo and Combs, 1990, pp. 54–55).

Clinton's pamphlet had a clear, dominant vision, called "Bill Clinton's Plan" to "Put America Back to Work." He offered an economic plan, a health care plan, and a plan to improve education; in each plan he envisioned the positive effects of his proposal. Positive, smiling pictures and language reinforced the vision.

The most original and ambitious print document in the 1992 New Hampshire primary was Tsongas's eighty-five-page booklet, "A Call to Economic Arms." He distributed it widely by mail and in person, autographing and giving away dozens of copies at every public appearance. It argued that

America was not prepared to do battle economically in world markets, that there was an economic crisis, and that the nation must take action to reemerge as the world's preeminent economic power. He discussed what must be done in education, the environment, energy, and foreign policy.

The booklet presented the Tsongas vision, stern about recognizing and facing problems, but inspirational in urging that "the spirit of the American people" should be unleashed so we could return to an ideal America, once again securing "our future and the future of our descendants" (p. 85). The weight and scope of the booklet were impressive at a glance, even daunting, and that impression alone may have served Tsongas's purpose. It is not clear how many recipients actually read this lengthy booklet.

The Tsongas campaign leaflet examined was larger and longer than those of other candidates—three 8 1/2 x 11 sheets, front and back—and the most informative. For those who took the time to penetrate the dense text, Tsongas's pamphlet presented a vision of a return to economic greatness, with him at the helm, summarizing the proposals in "A Call to Economic Arms." The tone was hopeful and optimistic, predicting that "America can once again be the world's number one economic power."

The Buchanan leaflet was short and modest in size (the front and back of an 8 1/2 x 11 page), picturing a smiling Buchanan. The vision he projected in his ten-point plan for "Putting and Keeping America First" was one of cutting programs and saying no. He would "phase out foreign aid," "play hardball in trade talks," "cut tax rates," "veto tax hikes," "freeze Federal spending," and "limit terms for politicians." The language was decisive and firm, conveying a no-nonsense, businesslike image. Buchanan predicted that tax cuts would bring America the "most attractive economic climate in the industrial world," with "millions of new jobs." For those already convinced that the *status quo* in American government was in urgent need of repair, his crisp list might well offer hope. Like Tsongas, he expressed a longing for an ideal America, pledging efforts to regain it: "With God's help, we can hand down to the next generation a country as great and grand and good as the one that our parents gave to us."

Bush's pamphlet, like Tsongas's, was large, covering both sides of three 8 1/2 x 11 sheets, and contained eight pictures. His vision or "Plan to Make New Hampshire and America Move" would "spur economic growth and create jobs for New Hampshire," "provide tax relief for the people of New Hampshire," and "strengthen New Hampshire families." The parts of the plan were highlighted by dark type and generous spacing, and they addressed specific audiences, of businesses and of families longing for tax relief. Bush sounded as though he understood the problems and knew what to do about them. His "Growth Agenda" would "stimulate the economy; help put more money in the pockets of taxpayers, restore consumer confidence, and keep interest rates and inflation down." Any reader would find these to be desirable goals: they described a return to happier times.

However, the credibility of the Bush message in evoking a vision of hope was undermined by two factors. First, the pictures did not reinforce the message effectively: he did not look optimistic. A second problem was that the carefully outlined and extensive vision of the future, while well suited to a challenger, seemed inappropriate for an incumbent entering his fourth year as president. Such a future-oriented agenda might well raise questions such as, "Where have you been?"

Candidate Schedules

In contrast to their literature, the candidates' daily schedules (called editors' advisories or press advisories) were targeted to the press. However, they were also published daily in the *Union Leader* (Manchester), thus reaching a much wider audience. The schedule was strictly factual, reporting on the events the candidate would be attending each day. But the selection of groups and subjects addressed and the scope of the campaign effort provided clues to the visions and character traits of the candidates. High numbers of appearances, for example, created an impression of high motivation to win, and of vigor and energy.

Perhaps the most striking finding regarding the schedules was that Tsongas made the fewest public appearances per day. The candidates' average daily number of public and press events was three; for Tsongas it was only two. Such evidence of low activity was not at all in Tsongas's interest. Questions about his health circulated constantly among the press, as he had had cancer and claimed to be fully recovered. But doubts lingered—was he strong enough and well enough to handle the responsibilities of the presidency? The members of the press I talked with interpreted his paucity of appearances as evidence that he had to conserve his strength.

Candidate Speeches

During my week in New Hampshire, I observed sixteen speeches or speech-type events, including debates, dinners, whistle-stop speeches, individual speeches, and rallies. Hundreds of voters a day heard the candidates personally (some of the rallies attracted close to one thousand people). New and personal information, even in small amounts, has been found to carry more weight with voters than abstract information (Popkin, 1991). In a primary in which the difference between the first- and second-place Democrats was only 14,116 votes, and the totals for Kerrey and Harkin differed by only 1,518 votes (*New York Times*, Feb. 20, 1992, p. A21), the thousands who attended speeches, with their networks of friends and family, could have affected the outcome. Speeches are part of the retail politics still thriving in New Hampshire.

In addition to the role speeches played in communicating directly with interested citizens, speeches by these four candidates were also heavily attended by the media. The television networks showed little of the actual speeches to the public, except for C-SPAN (Kendall, 1993). However, reporters observing the speeches had a chance to form personal impressions of the candidates and their abilities, and to see who came to hear the candidate, how the audience responded, and how the candidate dealt with their questions. These impressions often formed the nucleus of stories on television and in the print media.

The speeches provided excellent opportunities for the candidates to "write the play" their own way. First, the candidates had complete control over the content of the speeches, unlike press conferences or interviews, in which the press led with the questions. They had a chance to show their priorities, as when Buchanan explained his support of the voucher system for schools (Concord, Feb. 11), and Tsongas criticized the proposal for a middle-class tax cut, saying he wanted to be the "pathfinder," not "Santa Claus" (Nashua, Feb. 14). They had a chance to show how much (or how little) they knew, backing up their proposals with evidence, or telling the audience about their experience in solving the problem. They could introduce themselves to the press and the voters as people with unique human qualities and feelings, as when Tsongas joked about his lack of charisma, or Clinton showed his teaching skills, explaining the ramifications of the policies he advocated. They could also use the content of their speeches to stress the campaign themes found in leaflets, ads, and interviews.

Second, the candidates cast their speeches in their own language, making stylistic choices for such purposes as conveying their personal characteristics, or inspiring, or ridiculing. Buchanan's speech at Concord (Feb. 11) attempted all these things. He was tough—he would "play hardball" with countries that "give us a hard time"; we shouldn't be "trade wimps," he said. He was patriotic, calling for a "new patriotism": "Not only America first, but America second and third as well." He ridiculed the Democrats, especially Teddy Kennedy, who would sign a bill "if only he can find his pants." "How many fifty-nine-year-olds do you know," he asked, "who still go to Florida for spring break?" He appealed to deeply held values such as "shared sacrifice" (he would roll back the federal pay raise, turn in half of the president's pay, and call for reduction in the salaries of the boards of directors of automobile companies). He reminded his audience of the principles of the American Revolution; the federal bureaucracy was like the British, he said, spending 25 percent of the GNP. "I hope you will join me in a second American Revolution, and take America back," he concluded.

Vivid words can touch an audience's emotions, making them laugh, and applaud, and nod, and go away full of enthusiasm or anger. Clichés, such as the jokes about Senator Kennedy, a favorite butt of conservative humor, can give audiences a satisfying sense of participation. The candidates' words are at the heart of the campaign ritual, tapping and "intensifying deeply held values" (Nimmo and Combs, 1990, p. 69). Yet they are seldom present in media coverage of the events.

Third, the speeches gave the candidates free media exposure. Except for the cost of travel to the location and press releases distributed in advance, the speech event guaranteed some media attention at a nominal cost.

Fourth, the speeches gave the candidates a chance to make distinctions between themselves and their opponents. As Jamieson (1992) has pointed out, "the longer the statement, the more likely it is to compare and contrast candidates' positions," providing useful information to voters (p. 259). And speeches are long enough to make substantive distinctions. Clinton's speech to the American Association of Retired Persons (Concord, Feb. 13), for example, contrasted his position on health care with that of Bush, and proposed specific reforms, such as uniform billing, the establishment of more group centers, and an emphasis on promoting wellness.

Fifth, speeches gave the candidates a chance to move quickly to meet campaign developments, replying to charges of opponents or media claims immediately. Tsongas responded immediately to a February 13 attack by Harkin on his position on nuclear power (Seabrook); on February 14, Tsongas said, "Tom is playin' fast and loose right now," discussed his support by environmental groups, and proclaimed that if companies violated environmental standards he would "prosecute and prosecute hard" (Nashua). Buchanan built his campaign on attacks against Bush for breaking his promise about "no new taxes", and for being a distant and uncaring figure. Bush's whirlwind campaign day on February 15 could well have been interpreted as a response to Buchanan's attacks, as it was devoted mainly to defending his attempts to revive the economy through a seven-point economic plan. While references to Buchanan were only oblique, his surrogates, such as Senator Warren Rudman, fought off Buchanan's charges with sentences such as, "I've never known a man who suffers when you suffer more than George Bush" (Derry, Feb. 15).

Finally, speeches gave the candidates an opportunity to interact directly with the voters, showing their quickness and adaptability, their knowledge of issues voters inquired about, and, when there were hecklers (as there were with Clinton and Bush), their ability to react well under fire. For example, when Bush was heckled by an ACT-UP AIDS demonstrator shouting, "What about AIDS?", the heckler was quickly removed from the room. But Bush then departed from his text to say, "Understandably, they're upset, but sometimes their tactics hurt their effort. We are going to whip that disease . . . we're doing everything we can." He then cited figures to show the growth of AIDS research funding during his administration (Derry, Feb. 15).

Some of the candidates, especially Clinton and Tsongas, regularly engaged in long, substantive question periods with audiences, using the opportunity to develop their themes and further shape impressions of their character. Reporters I spoke with remarked on Clinton's ability to speak knowledgeably and at length on a wide variety of public policy issues; they were impressed with his competence. Tsongas, with his quick-witted humor, courage to criticize and reject the popular middle-class tax cut idea, and efforts to dissect and analyze complex issues, also won respect and admiration among the press.

Candidate Television Advertisements

The candidates used ads heavily in a traditional way in New Hampshire, to write the script themselves, uncensored by the media. They cast themselves as the experienced incumbents, as attractive alternatives to the *status quo*, or, in the case of Buchanan, battler against the representative of the *status quo*, Bush.

If the quantity of television advertising is used as a criterion, all of the candidates except Brown established themselves as major characters in the play. Brown spent only $60,000, but the others spent between $430,000 (Tsongas) and $1.4 million (Buchanan) on the New Hampshire primary. Clinton was the top spender on campaign ads among the Democrats in New Hampshire, using 18 ads for a cost of $950,000; Bush ran 4 ads, spending $700,000 (Devlin, 1994).

Specific ads by Clinton and Buchanan were notable for their effectiveness in the New Hampshire context: the twelve-minute videotape "American Dream" distributed door-to-door by the Clinton campaign, and Buchanan's "Read My Lips" ads. In addition, Clinton made unusual use of paid television in audience question formats.

During the last weekend before the primary, Clinton distributed twenty thousand free copies of a twelve-minute videotape to undecided households in New Hampshire. The Clinton campaign called recipients and reported that 60 percent to 70 percent had watched the tape (James Carville, comments to press, Feb. 16, 1992). Half of those who watched it reported that they had voted for Clinton (Ceaser and Busch, 1993). This tape made a vigorous effort to construct Clinton as an ideal candidate for New Hampshire. It painted him as a major character in the electoral play, and a character of strong and admirable image traits. But the dominant and most effective emphasis was on his vision of hope for the future.

He spoke constantly of change, of making life better, of the future. Through skillful use of synonyms and repetition, in words full of optimism and determination, he drove the point home. He advocated change (6 repetitions) in the future (4 repetitions), a vision (2 repetitions), a plan (3 repetitions), a dream (3 repetitions). It was a dream for us, for you in the middle class (5); it was your dream and our dream, to work with common purpose (2), to take the responsibility (3) and provide the leadership (6) to "bring this country together again." He would do it with us; we would win again (4), together.

There was tremendous emphasis on winning as a people; Clinton managed to equate *his* winning with *our* winning, taking over the game metaphor that so dominates media coverage of campaigns and changing it from the victory of an individual candidate into the victory of a group, the middle class, and even more specifically, the middle-class voters in New Hampshire, with Clinton as one of them.

In addition to these forms of paid advertising, Clinton also purchased two half hours of time on New Hampshire's largest television station, WMUR, on Thursday and Friday nights, February 13 and 14. He bought the time at the height of the controversy over his draft status during the Vietnam War, and used the first evening for questions from a small studio audience of uncommitted voters, and the second evening for a live call-in show. With these two programs, Clinton dominated television for three nights in a row, for on February 12 he had appeared on "Nightline" with Ted Koppel, discussing his 1969 letter regarding the draft. As a condition of appearing on "Nightline," he had insisted that the entire draft letter be shown on the screen, and Koppel agreed. The letter, which was over 1,200 words long, filled one screen after another, allowing viewers to read it in its entirety. He also paid to have the letter printed in full in the *Union Leader* the next day, and other papers, including the *Concord Monitor,* the *Boston Globe* (partial transcript), and the *New York Tames,* published it as news. The result was a blurring together of advertising and news in which voters were presented with Clinton's own construction of the script. Both the degree of candidate control over the language and the quantity of the language were unusual.

Buchanan's New Hampshire ads such as "Protect" and "Broken Promises" contained much large print about Bush's broken promises, and pictures of Bush, particularly the famous "Read my lips, no new taxes" scene from his 1988 acceptance address. "Can we afford four more years of broken promises?" asked the narrator. "Send Bush a message. Vote for Pat Buchanan for president." Symbolically these bold attacks on the president promoted Buchanan as a major character in the play, the only Republican to take on the president of the United States and offer an alternative. Focus groups reported that the "Read My Lips" ads made the biggest impression of all the ads in the primaries, that they resonated with the voters' anger about Bush; polls confirmed this effect (West, Kern, and Alger, 1992). But Buchanan did little to develop his own character or present a vision of hope. At the end of the ads voters saw Buchanan's smiling face on the screen, and heard his gravelly voice. But they learned nothing about this character in the play, except that he was "not Bush." Unlike his pamphlet, in which he proposed a plan for a presidency of "Putting and Keeping America First," especially through cutting taxes and spending and foreign aid, his television ads devoted themselves mainly to identifying and describing the villain in the play, George Bush. In this he was very successful.

On Election Day, 53 percent of the Republicans voted for Bush, 37 percent for Buchanan, 10 percent for others. The majority of Buchanan voters in exit polls reported that "they were trying to get through to Bush, not backing the challenger" (Richard Benedetto, *USA Today*, Feb. 13, 1992, p. 1). While Bush was still the clear winner of the primary, the anti-Bush vote was surprisingly large. In constructing himself as the antibush, Buchanan gave the Republicans a way to express their anger at the president. He also won favorable attention for having the courage to fight against the odds, in a context in which even prominent Democrats had refused to compete with Bush. But he was never able to gain this much support in other primaries, though he expressed the hope he would begin to win in the South. Instead, his vote percentages dwindled steadily. The Buchanan team's decision to write the script for his opponent's character and not to develop his own character or vision of the presidency was shortsighted for his own candidacy. There are limits to a candidacy cast simply as "not the incumbent." However, Clinton and Perot picked up some of Buchanan's themes and language and employed them effectively later in the campaign.

The Tsongas ad "Swim," in which he swam the difficult butterfly stroke, has been described as "one of the most memorable ads of the primary campaign year" for its visual uniqueness and skillful creation of a metaphor for Tsongas's whole life (Devlin, 1994, pp. 83–84). The ad emphasized his characteristics of strength and determination, describing his victories over corrupt politicians and cancer, the same fighting spirit portrayed in his literature. However, when the ad appeared around the country in ad watches, it worked against him. Instead of being impressed with his strength, viewers raised questions about his cancer and discussed the importance of health in a presidential candidate (West, Kern, and Alger, 1992).

Bush only ran four ads in New Hampshire, with the goals of showing that he cared about people's economic troubles, presenting his economic plan, demonstrating leadership, and asking for votes on Election Day (Devlin, 1994). As president and clear front-runner of the Republicans, Bush was *de facto* a major character in the play. His ads relied heavily on the incumbency strategies discussed by Trent and Trent in chapter 3 of this book, and in general maintained the themes found in his campaign literature. They ignored Buchanan and his attacks, and portrayed the enemy as the Democratic Congress.

THE MEDIA ATTEMPT TO CONSTRUCT THE PLAY

Television News Coverage of the Candidates

Kenneth Burke long ago pointed out the power of naming: "Naming . . . [is an] interpretive act," he said, and thus has the power not only to describe but also to shape events (1965, pp. 176–91). This power is clearly seen in the lead stories of television news, in which certain events are named as most deserving of our attention. In the February 11–19, 1992 period, 60 percent (15 out of 25) of the lead stories on ABC, CBS, and NBC were about the New Hampshire primary; two others were about the primaries in general. There is no doubt that the news professionals saw the dramatic potential of this story, which they selected over all the crimes and disasters of the day.

Network Choices of Major and Minor Characters. Previous research on media coverage of campaigns has found that the media measure candidates through a number of means: "opinion polls, assessments by experienced politicians and observers, the status of each candidate's campaign organization, who is supporting whom, the size of the contenders' financial war chests, even the amount of coverage the media themselves give respective candidates" (Nimmo and Combs, 1990, p. 56). We also know from prior research that the media are likely to convey these impressions with heavy use of metaphors, especially metaphors of violence and sports (Blankenship, 1976). These patterns emerged in this study as well.

Network news coverage of the 1992 New Hampshire primary in the February 11–19 period suggested that there were six individuals and two groups who were major or potentially major characters in the campaign play. The individuals were: Buchanan, Bush, Clinton, Harkin, Kerrey, and Tsongas. The groups were the citizen/voters and "Democratic leaders."

The networks gave these individuals and groups status as major characters by two means: by covering them in the news, and by discussing their viability or electability. Citizen/voters were mentioned explicitly or implicitly in every broadcast, usually as numbers. They were the numbers in the polls. Occasionally they were interviewed, and they were often shown meeting candidates or in crowds gathered to hear candidates. The chart below shows the number of days the candidates were mentioned by the networks.

Number of Days Networks Mentioned Candidate, Feb. 11–19
(Possible total: 25)

Clinton	24
Bush	20
Tsongas	19
Buchanan	17
Kerrey	16
Harkin	15
Democratic leaders	9
Cuomo	7
Brown	6
Nader, Ralph	1
Leynane, James	1

The main reason for this order of attention to the candidates seems to be tangled up in the question of candidate viability or electability, a major finding in previous studies (Patterson, 1980, 1993; Robinson and Sheehan, 1983). Network stories discussed everyone's electability; not a candidate was spared. Here at the very start of the campaign, the news focused on the ending: who would win the election? Who could win the election?

Electability also emerged as the most significant trait in the ideal Democrat sought by the Democratic leaders. As portrayed by the networks, these powerful leaders loomed in the wings; at any moment they might push a new candidate onto the stage, or rush onto the stage themselves (Bentsen and Gephardt were mentioned). They were "fearful," "worried," "uneasy," and "unhappy" about the chances of the announced candidates for election, afraid that no one would work out. Their chorus served to magnify the theme.

Network Descriptions of Character Traits.   In addition to developing a lineup of major and minor characters in the play, organized around the theme of electability, the networks sketched the personal traits of each candidate. The following summaries attempt to capture the recurring images of the candidates communicated by the words and pictures used by each network.

Buchanan: Buchanan emerged in the three ABC stories as a potentially strong character, powerful enough to embarrass the president, teasing the president by accusing him of stealing his lines (Feb. 12). He was shown fighting hard for votes, going on an ambitious whistle-stop bus tour of the state, and exuding confidence that he would give the president a "wake-up call" (Feb. 17). In the six CBS stories the image was similar but more developed. Buchanan was described as a strong and aggressive candidate, who attacked Bush for betraying the American middle class (Feb. 14). Shown actively campaigning at rallies, in ads, and during his long bus tour, he was described as having the power to hurt Bush by exposing his flaws (Feb. 17). The question was raised, however, about whether Buchanan had real power or was just a way for the voters to send a message to Bush (Feb. 14).

NBC's coverage was also quite favorable to Buchanan, emphasizing the energetic fighter who used hard-hitting ads and hammered at Bush (Feb. 14, 17).

Bush: The ABC image of President Bush was decidedly mixed, both positive and negative. In their five stories during this period, they showed him as an out-of-touch elitist, worried and fearful about a Buchanan protest vote, and lacking in charisma. Demonstrators were televised carrying signs saying, "Jobs not socks" and something about yachts. On the other hand, the ABC reports showed Bush in his presidential role, as he said that presidents have important things to do, and that elections are not about charisma. The CBS coverage was more negative. While they portrayed Bush as actively and aggressively working for reelection, and indicated that there was no doubt he would be the winner of the Republican primary, they also portrayed him as a worried, defensive player.

Finally, the NBC coverage portrayed a Bush of uncertain stature, a man who on the one hand was aggressively campaigning and fighting to keep Buchanan in the low numbers, and who was more statesmanlike than Buchanan. On the other hand, this was the same Bush who failed to command strong voter support and who never really caught fire with his audiences. In the end, even when he won the primary, the network raised the question of electability (Feb. 19).

Clinton: The networks constructed an ambivalent characterization of Clinton. On ABC there was the ever-present question of electability; he had fallen from the position of front-runner and the party's hope, and now was fighting to save his candidacy, even "scrambling" (Feb. 15). Party leaders said he had been wounded. But his fighting to save himself was shown as a mighty effort, displaying great energy and inventiveness. As he fought, the network selected words and pictures that emphasized his upbeat style and positive personality traits (Feb. 13, 14).

CBS developed a similar ambivalent picture of Clinton in the February 11–18 period. Their questions about his electability were more prominent than ABC's, as they reported his drop in the polls and gave a visible role to the Democratic leaders who doubted his survivability (Feb. 12, 14). As late as February 17, Dan Rather wondered if Clinton might be politically dead. Members of the public were shown coming to his defense, however, lamenting that there was so much "looking for dirt" (Feb. 11), and casting him as a kind of sympathy-evoking underdog figure. In general, CBS emphasized that he was an active, energetic campaigner.

Once the primary results were known, CBS gave Clinton important national attention and a platform for shaping perceptions of his character in a live interview with Dan Rather on the February 19 news broadcast. Considering that Clinton had come in second to Tsongas in New Hampshire, one could ask why this prime-time interview was not with Tsongas. In answer to Rather's questions, Clinton naturally seized the opportunity to portray himself as a strong, competent, honest, experienced candidate who understood what the people wanted.

NBC cast a pall over all the Democratic candidates in their early (Feb. 11) coverage, suggesting that none of the candidates was strong. They presented a mixed picture of Clinton, raising doubts almost nightly, which contributed to a more negative image than that of ABC or CBS. The question of his honesty received much more attention here than on the other networks, chiefly through the voices of citizens discussing the draft issue and marital infidelity (Feb. 11, 18). NBC questioned his electability by pointing to his fall in the polls (Feb. 11, 12) and suggested that his handling of the draft issue had wounded his chances for victory in the South (Feb. 19). On Election Day, anchor Tom Brokaw wondered if Clinton could survive (Feb. 18), just as Dan Rather had done on CBS (Feb. 17).

But NBC also had positive words and pictures for Clinton. They noted that he had a good campaign organization and was well funded (Feb. 11, 13), and that he was aggressively fighting to save his candidacy (Feb. 12). And they let him speak for himself in a vivid moment of his campaign, when he almost pleaded with New Hampshirites to give him a second chance. If they did, he said he would be there for them "'til the last dog dies" (Feb. 13).

Tsongas: Tsongas's front-runner status in New Hampshire, based on his standing in the polls, made him a major character in the play, and he was mentioned in nineteen of the twenty-four news broadcasts studied between February 11 and 19. But the networks seemed puzzled by Tsongas, trying out one description and then another. The only characteristic they discussed consistently was his lack of electability, expressing doubts that his success in New Hampshire would carry over to the rest of the country.

In spite of their doubts, they had to explain him to the voters, all the more so when he won the Democratic primary, gaining 34 percent of the votes in a field of five, including votes from many Republicans. This character had the following traits. He was witty (ABC and CBS showed him joking about his charisma, and about a T-shirt he had been given [Feb. 11]). He was a nice guy, who defended Clinton when the draft letter story broke (ABC, Feb. 13), in contrast to Harkin. He was knowledgeable and competent about economic issues (he was shown speaking about the economy, and opposing the middle-class tax cut, NBC, Feb. 14; ABC, Feb. 16). He was courageous, adopting an "I'm no Santa Claus" position on the popular middle-class tax cut. And clearly, as front-runner, he was powerful.

None of the candidates fit the image of the ideal presidential candidate, as they were portrayed by the media. But Tsongas, who had not held a major elective office for eight years, who had not been a dominant figure when he was in the Senate, and who rejected the popular middle-class tax break, deviated from the ideal image enough that the networks portrayed him as an unconventional and unlikely candidate. Tsongas fostered the idea himself at a rally the day before the election, saying, "This is so bizarre. This is so bizarre. I am such an unlikely candidate" (author's notes and NBC, Feb. 17). The networks suggested that Tsongas had simply been lucky in New Hampshire, benefiting from Clinton's problems, from a kind of protest vote against the economic *status quo* (CBS, Feb. 18), and from the advantage of his early entry and proximity to New Hampshire (NBC, Feb. 18). He had little money or backing from leading Democrats (ABC, Feb. 18; NBC, Feb. 19), and both are usually necessary for a successful campaign. And lurking in the background was the question of his health: Would his cancer recur? The question was not discussed openly, but suggested obliquely when Richard Threlkeld asked whether the Tsongas campaign had the "stamina" to last through the primaries (CBS, Feb. 19). Never was the campaign described as energetic or aggressive.

These doubts and qualifications seemed geared to prepare the viewer for an early failed candidacy. Tsongas was a major player now, but he would not last long.

Network Coverage of Candidates' Visions of Hope.   The candidates' efforts to project a vision of hope for the future, a positive visualization of what the nation would look like under their presidency, received little attention on network television news. A citizen wishing to determine what the candidates intended to do as president would find little evidence there. These messages were usually contained in candidate speeches, and the networks seldom used candidate language from the speeches. In a few cases they reported a candidate's main theme, such as Tsongas's "call to economic arms" (CBS, Feb. 18). Favorite issues or topics of candidates were sometimes mentioned, such as Clinton's proposal for lower middle-class taxes (NBC, Feb. 14), Tsongas's views of what needed to be done for the environment (NBC, Feb. 17), and Buchanan's opposition to the civil rights bill (NBC, Feb. 19). Perhaps the closest they came to presenting any candidate's vision was with Bush, when they let him speak for himself as he announced his candidacy, told of his goal to reduce the size and cost of government, and described his economic recovery plan (CBS and NBC, Feb. 12). But in general the rhetorical visions of hope enunciated by most of the candidates in their speeches, leaflets, and ads received little explicit attention on the network news.

Newspaper Coverage of the Candidates

The Leading Characters as Portrayed in the Papers. As the newspapers wrote the campaign play on their front pages during the February 11–19 period, Clinton, Tsongas, Bush, and Buchanan were the dominant characters, the same names leading the network stories.[3] But there were differences in the way the print media constructed the play. They paid less attention than the networks to the "Democratic leaders" with their gloomy remarks about electability, giving them front-page coverage in only five stories (*USA Today*, Feb. 19; *New York Times*, Feb. 16; *Boston Globe*, Feb. 12 and 18; *Union Leader*, Feb. 18). They made a clearer distinction between major and minor characters than the networks: only four candidates had regular front-page coverage. Television, though it devoted more time to the poll leaders than the others, mentioned and showed six of the seven candidates regularly. The nature of the medium is such that there is no clear front page, middle section or back page on television. When Harkin and Kerrey were shown almost as often as Tsongas and Clinton, for example, that created some equality in prominent coverage, even though Tsongas and Clinton received more time.

In addition, the national press and the regional and local press differed in the four candidates they covered most heavily. In the national papers, Clinton led in frequency of coverage (followed by Bush, Tsongas, and Buchanan), while in the regional and local papers, Bush led in number of stories (followed by Buchanan, Clinton, and Tsongas). On the following page are tables of frequency of front-page textual and pictorial coverage of the candidates during the February 11–19 period. Any mention of a candidate was considered to be coverage of that person, except for straight listing of poll figures.

These figures suggest that the "electability" rule followed in network coverage (electability as measured by the poll standings of the candidates) also governed the papers. For example, the Republican poll standings of February 12, according to the *Boston Globe*/WBZ-TV tracking poll, were: Bush, 50 percent; Buchanan, 29 percent; other, 9 percent; don't know, 12 percent. The Democratic ratings in the same poll were: Tsongas, 26 percent; Clinton, 20 percent; Harkin, 12 percent; Kerrey, 9 percent; Brown, 6 percent; Cuomo, 6 percent; other, 3 percent; don't know, 18 percent (*Boston Globe*, Feb. 23, 1992, p. 20). The front-runners received much more coverage than those who were low in the poll standings.

Candidate Characteristics Portrayed in the Newspapers. The newspapers developed the personal characteristics of the cast of characters through their word choice, pictures, and selection of representative anecdotes. This study examined the front-page coverage of the candidates in the 150 stories and 58 pictures of the February 11–19 period, thereby determining which candidate

Frequency of Front-Page Coverage, February 11–19

National press	Clinton	15
	Bush	13
	Tsongas	9
	Buchanan	6
	Harkin	2
	Kerrey	2
	Brown	2
	Cuomo	1
Regional press	Bush	19
	Buchanan	13
	Clinton	12
	Tsongas	10
	Harkin	3
	Kerry	2
	Cuomo	1
	Brown	0
Local press	Bush	36
	Buchanan	27
	Clinton	20
	Tsongas	20
	Kerry	12
	Harkin	11
	Brown	10
	Cuomo	4

Frequency of Front-Page Pictures

National press	Clinton	4
	Tsongas	3
	Bush	2
	Buchanan	2
Regional press	Buchanan	4
	Bush	3
	Tsongas	3
Local press	Bush	6
	Clinton	5
	Tsongas	4
	Kerrey	4
	Buchanan	3
	Harkin	1
	Cuomo	1

characteristics were given the most prominence. The extensive coverage inside the papers was not examined.

On the simplest level, the coverage was examined to determine whether the candidates were shown as happy and positive, or sad or angry. Each picture was coded as (1) smiling, (2) neither smiling nor frowning, or (3) glum or frowning. The assumption was that these expressions communicated an optimistic, positive outlook, or pessimistic outlook to the voters. Based on the pictures, the happiest candidates were Buchanan (7 smiling, 2 neutral) and Tsongas (6 smiling, 4 frowning), with a mixed portrayal of Clinton (2 smiling, 5 neutral, 2 frowning). Pictures of Bush were decidedly downbeat on the national and regional levels (none smiling, 5 frowning), with a more positive look on the local level (4 smiling, 2 frowning).

The tone of the language reporters chose to describe the candidates was also analyzed. Stories in which the candidate was described as pleased, winning, getting voter support, or improving his standing were counted as positive; stories in which the candidate was described as worried, slipping, scrambling, under attack, and the like, were counted as negative. Stories in which no clear position emerged, or a mixture of positive and negative factors emerged, were counted as neutral. Because there was only óne coder, I will report only the most obvious and clear-cut results.

The tone of coverage for Tsongas was positive in all three levels of newspapers, national, regional, and local (24 positive, 14 neutral, 1 negative). Just as clearly, the tone was predominantly negative for Bush on all three levels (12 positive, 18 neutral, 39 negative). Stories of sour and skeptical voters, and of Democratic leaders who thought the field should be broadened, contributed to a negative tone in general.

Bush: Of particular interest was the treatment of Bush, who received heavily negative coverage. If the New Hampshire primary established the characterizations of the candidates for the whole campaign to follow, the clear image drawn in New Hampshire may well have tarred Bush for the rest of the year. Throughout the primary campaign, the newspapers referred to Bush's campaign as "weak" or "weakening." This generally referred to his standing in the polls. The main reason for his weakness, according to the front-page stories, was that the voters doubted his competence to deal with the recession. Buchanan and the Democrats drove this point home, using "the ravaged economy as a club against President Bush in their campaigns" (Doina Chiacu, AP, *Telegraph*, Feb. 16).

The response of the Bush campaign to Buchanan's attacks and gains in the polls was also portrayed as weak; it was described as "limping" (Joe Battenfeld, *Boston Herald*, Feb. 16), "lackluster" (Michael Kranish, *Boston Globe*, Feb. 11), "frantic" (Walter V. Robinson, *Boston Globe*, Feb. 18), and "nervous" (John Distaso, *Union Leader*, Feb. 12). Stories noted that he had spent little time in New Hampshire, and was scrambling to add a few visits the last week.

The public's response to Bush's campaigning was described as weak too: there was no "real excitement" at his events (Tammy Annis, *Union Leader*, Feb. 17); crowds were small and there was more applause for Barbara Bush and Arnold Schwarzenneger than for Bush (Andrew Rosenthal, *New York Times*, Feb. 17).

Bush was charged with another kind of weakness, which dovetailed an issue with image traits. Buchanan addressed this point when he derided Bush for breaking his no-tax pledge, and for first proposing a middle-class tax exemption for children in his State of the Union Address, then withdrawing it from his budget proposal. The Democrats reinforced this attack in their debate, saying he was "indifferent to the suffering of those hurt by the recession" (Felice Belman, *Concord Monitor*, Feb. 17); Tsongas said that all five Democrats had "a stronger core" than Bush (Richard Benedetto, *USA Today*, Feb. 17). Bush's changes on particular issue positions were thus used to portray him as weak in honesty and empathy.

Bush aides contributed to this aura of weakness by entering into the numbers game with the press, discussing what percentage of the vote Bush needed to avoid being embarrassed by Buchanan. Considering the media's history of turning New Hampshire primary victories into defeats because candidates have not made a certain magic number (Edmund Muskie's 1972 campaign is the best example), one would expect that campaigns would avoid discussing percentages at all costs. When Bush received only 53 percent of the Republican vote and Buchanan 37 percent on Election Day, with 10 percent going to other candidates, the Bush campaign estimates proved too optimistic, and the outcome was portrayed as a stunning defeat for Bush.

One would hardly have known that Bush had won the New Hampshire primary. The beaming Republican "winner" on the February 19 front pages was Buchanan, not Bush. The headlines focused on the blow dealt to Bush: "Bush Jarred in First Primary" (*New York Times*); "Buchanan Grabs 40% in New Hampshire, Shocks Bush" (*USA Today*); "Bush Whacked!" (*Boston Herald*); "GOP Voters Signal Protest on Recession" (*Boston Globe*); "Bush Supporters: Presidency Weakened" (*Union Leader*); "Buchanan Fire Wounds Bush" (*Telegraph*).

Saussure (1916/1959) has argued that pairs of words (such as open/ closed) get their meaning from each other; that one term in the pair becomes meaningful because we associate the other term with it. It is in the antithesis of the terms that meaning arises (Corcoran, 1990). The words used to describe the state of the Bush campaign after the New Hampshire primary gained power from just such antithetical meaning. The media called the results a "wake-up call" (Judy Keen, *USA Today*, Feb. 19), implying that Bush had been asleep. A voter remarked that she voted for Buchanan so Bush would "sit up and take notice," implying that he had been lying down (asleep? tired?). "An absent Bush conceded Buchanan gave him a huge scare," said the *Telegraph* (Feb. 19, Kevin Landrigan); the opposites were much more positive, suggesting that a candidate who was present and brave would be a better choice. Finally there came the amazing suggestion that Bush might drop out of the race, introduced both through analogies to other incumbent presidents who had decided not to run after getting the primary results (such as Lyndon Johnson and Harry Truman), and through the loaded sentence, "The president himself has vowed to stay in the race," with the implication of its opposite, "get out of the race" (John Distaso, *Union Leader*, Feb. 13).

Although Saussure never talked about antithesis in relation to pictures, there is such a striking difference in the Bush and Buchanan pictures (and, in fact, between the Bush pictures and those of all the other candidates), that the idea of such opposites leaps to mind. Bush was older than Buchanan, and older than all the Democrats as well. In the pictures he looked worried, puzzled, and angry more than any of the other candidates. Pictures, of course, are much more ambiguous in meaning than words, and leave much to the viewer to fill in. But in a state that was hard hit economically, in a primary campaign requiring that voters choose among many candidates, six out of seven of whom were calling for change, it would be understandable if many voters concluded that this old, tired, worried-looking president should be replaced by someone younger and with more energy and fresh ideas.

There were positive Bush stories, of course. Much of the front-page coverage in the *Concord Monitor* and *Telegraph* (Nashua) was positive, with Bush and his spokespeople quoted frequently. But in general the visual and verbal portrayal by the newspapers was unflattering.

Buchanan: Buchanan was portrayed as the antibush; he was defined by what he said against Bush. Though stories often reported that voters were using him as a messenger, as a way "to get through to Bush," rather than seeing him as a serious candidate (Richard Benedetto, *USA Today*, Feb. 19), the frequency of Buchanan stories, pictures, and quotations established him as a major character in the play. He was "the challenger," the "rival."

The dominant qualities emphasized in the Buchanan stories were his energy and strength—energy in fighting against Bush and strength in driving Bush down in the polls. This image was in direct contrast to the weak image of Bush. Words such as "pugnacious" (Adam Nagourney, *USA Today*, Feb. 18), "fired up" (Wayne Woodlief, *Boston Herald*, Feb. 16), "upbeat" (Chris Black and Michael Kranish, *Boston Globe*, Feb. 18), and "aggressive" (Mark Travis, *Concord Monitor*, Feb. 17) characterized coverage on Buchanan.

The Buchanan quotations chosen for these stories were consistent with this fighter image. For example, he said he would "shock the world" by humbling Bush at the polls, that "the Buchanan brigades are going to run into the hollow army of King George and cut through it like butter" (Wayne Woodlief, *Boston Herald*, Feb. 16). The boldness in such statements was particularly striking considering that no major Democrat had been willing to run against Bush due to his popularity after the Persian Gulf War.

The stories also commented on Buchanan's effectiveness in producing changes in voter attitudes and behavior, a major sign of power. For example, his political advertising was reported to be effective: "significant numbers of voters" were repeating his advertising themes (R. W. Apple Jr., *New York Times*, Feb. 15). Polls showed him "closing fast on the president" (Wayne Woodlief, *Boston Herald*, Feb. 14), who was trying to "stave off an embarrassingly strong showing" by Buchanan (Robin Toner, *New York Times*, Feb. 17).

There was little suggestion in all this coverage that Buchanan was competent to be president. In fact, the *Boston Herald*, which endorsed him in a front-page editorial, confessed they did not know much about his leadership abilities, and focused on Bush's weaknesses. They urged a vote for Buchanan "to protest the state of the country" (Feb. 12). Buchanan's presumed incompetence was discussed by Bush, who wondered why anyone would vote for a man with so few qualifications for president, a former television commentator (Michael Kranish and Chris Black, Feb. 17, *Boston Globe*). But as a fighting antibush, running on a platform of change, Buchanan gave Republicans a way to express their dissatisfaction with Bush. Clinton was already adopting this refrain in New Hampshire and later Ross Perot did the same. In November, both candidates succeeded in converting voters from Bush; 12.2 percent of Clinton's 43.7 percent vote came from 1988 Bush voters; 11.3 percent of Perot's 19 percent vote came from Bush voters (Pomper, 1993, p. 141).

Tsongas: The coverage of Tsongas was generally positive on all levels, with the question of his electability raised occasionally. His dominant trait as portrayed by the newspapers was his front-runner status and his "growing lead" (Judy Keen, *USA Today*, Feb. 12). Many of Tsongas's traits were described in relation to his leadership in the polls. For example, he was shown as confident—that voters would "flock to his message" (Joe Battenfeld and Andrew Miga, *Boston Herald*, Feb. 18). He was "glowing"—about his new status as front-runner (Robin Toner, *New York Times*, Feb. 12). He had credibility—because he had bested Clinton in the primary (Curtis Wilkie, *Boston Globe*, Feb. 19).

The reporters of the *New York Times* and *Boston Globe* gave Tsongas stature as a serious, substantive, knowledgeable candidate in several front-page stories, and the *Boston Herald* did it with an editorial. Robin Toner referred to his "against-the-grain economic message," describing his positions on capital gains and the middle-class tax cut (*New York Times*, Feb. 12); Gwen Ifill described him as a serious, policy-oriented candidate who criticized policy issues instead of attacking fellow Democrats (*New York Times*, Feb. 15). Walter Robinson said he focused on his positions on the economy and the environment, contrasting him with Clinton, who was busy blaming the Republicans for dirty tricks (*Boston Globe*, Feb. 11). The *Boston Herald* editorial praised him for many qualities, including integrity, decency, strength of character, experience, knowledge, and moral leadership, not to mention his pro-business philosophy.

Tsongas was also portrayed as a man amazed by his success; he sounded "almost awed by the status he had achieved" (Robin Toner, *New York Times*, Feb. 16), and "labelled himself a 'most unlikely candidate'" (Walter V. Robinson, *Boston Globe*, Feb. 18). While these reactions gave him an aura of genuine humility, they also conflicted with the image of confidence and did little to rebut the question of his electability. This question was raised in several stories: Would he be able to translate a win in his own backyard into national credibility and the necessary financial support? (Richard Benedetto, *USA Today*, Feb. 19; Michael J. Birkner, *Concord Monitor*, Feb. 17; Tsongas picture text, *USA Today*, Feb. 19).

Clinton: The description of the Clinton character in the primary play was quite mixed in the newspapers. Like Bush, he was slipping in the polls during the February 11-19 period, and the words used to describe his status made him sound desperate and his campaign hopeless. On the other hand, he was fighting to save himself, and, just as with Buchanan, the press expressed its admiration for a tough, energetic fighter. The two events that precipitated his decline in the polls—the Gennifer Flowers story and the draft letter incident—were often alluded to in the coverage, and each carried with it a host of negative associations, about his honesty, faithfulness, courage, and patriotism. The national press gave Clinton more front-page coverage than all the other candidates of either party, while the regional and local press wrote the play a different way, focusing the script on the Bush-Buchanan struggle. But there, too, Clinton received as much or slightly more coverage than Tsongas, the Democratic front-runner.

There seemed to be two main reasons for this heavy coverage. First, the "falling front-runner" stories of Bush and Clinton played right to the reporters' dramatic instincts, for successful dramatic ritual requires both rising and falling action. A front-runner remaining steadily in the lead fails to meet these requirements. This finding is consistent with Nimmo and Combs' (1990) research on the 1988 preprimary campaigns where the front-runners also received the most coverage, and the most negative coverage. A second explanation for the attention to Clinton was that he created a story by fighting, vowing to "fight like hell," and beginning a "blitz" of door-to-door campaigning, rallies, call-in shows, and television ads (Richard Benedetto, *USA Today*, Feb. 17). His words emphasized his determination: "I want these people to see me out there working hard, reaching out to them and fighting until the last dog dies" (Robin Toner, *New York Times*, Feb. 16).

Clinton's image suddenly took a positive turn after he finished second to Tsongas. He had demonstrated his "resilience," said the *Boston Globe* (Curtis Wilkie, Feb. 19). More dramatically, he had been resurrected, as from the dead (Kevin Landrigan, "Clinton claims . . .," *Telegraph*, Feb. 19). Clinton's own words were, "New Hampshire tonight has made Bill Clinton the comeback kid" (Richard Benedetto, *USA Today*, Feb. 19).

Newspaper Coverage of Candidates' Visions of Hope.   The front-page newspaper coverage of the primary gave few insights into the vision of the individual candidates. The emphasis was heavily on electability, poll standings, and the characteristics of the candidates, not the ideal America and plans for the future envisioned by each candidate. Voters who read the front page would have little information on how the candidates' goals differed.

CONCLUSIONS

This chapter has focused on the struggle of the candidates and the media in the New Hampshire primary to construct the script for the presidential campaign drama. The primary is part of a dramatic ritual, a contest among candidates to try to win over the voters through a series of repeated acts, introducing themselves as major characters in the play, establishing the nature of their characters, and projecting their visions of the future. The media participate in the ritual by reconstructing these messages and transmitting them to the citizens, with a heavy overlay of horse race imagery.

Both candidates and the media go to New Hampshire with a sense of urgency. The candidates know, based on the primary's history, that the state has a remarkable record of selecting winners in the general election, and that most of them will be winnowed out of the contest soon after the primary. They play a dual role, as both playwrights and as characters in the play.

The media also have a sense of urgency. They must grasp a complicated story and communicate it to their audiences. The primary season will be long (there were thirty-eight primaries in 1992, occurring over almost four months), and it will require that they know something about many candidates. Like the voters, they, too, are not very familiar with some of the candidates. The outcome of the drama is uncertain, and they must decide how to cover it. Journalists from around the nation and world congregate in New Hampshire to "get a fix on" the contest. The script they construct there through their intensive coverage has the effect of introducing the electoral drama to much of the nation.

The findings of this research reveal that the candidates and media in 1992 sometimes co-constructed the script and sometimes wrote different scripts. Each candidate tried to present himself as a major character in the play, while the media were much more selective, relying chiefly on opinion polls to determine who the two front-runners were in each party and emphasizing them. The candidates constructed themselves as characters with many qualities, while the media focused chiefly on electability and winning.

On one image trait most of the candidates and media were in agreement: the presidential candidate must be a "fighter." Demonstrations of fighting against the odds by Clinton and Buchanan received heavy coverage, and Tsongas stressed his fighter image in ads and the booklet "A Call to Economic Arms." Bush and the *status quo* were the main objects of this fighting. The Saussurian concept of symbolic differentiation, in which words gain important meaning from their opposites (Saussure, 1959), played a crucial role in the construction of the primary. On the Republican side, Buchanan and the press portrayed Buchanan as strong, a fighter; Bush was weak, slipping in the polls, afraid. So pervasive was this verbal and visual image that Buchanan, the loser in the primary (by a 53–37 margin), received the triumphant front-page pictures.

On the Democratic side, the question of whether Clinton could survive the scandals, raised frequently by the media and Democratic leaders quoted by the national press, gave a special definition to the concept of strength. Here the issue was whether a campaign would be strong enough to survive, or would prove to be politically dead (Dan Rather, CBS, Feb. 17; Tom Brokaw, NBC, Feb. 18). The word "survive" suggests that one has continued to live in spite of a dangerous event such as a wreck; the dangerous events were the stories of Clinton's infidelity and draft evasion. In the context of a multi-candidate campaign, a survivor is stronger than those who have not survived; the word takes its meaning combined with its opposite, the dead. The result is hardly the image of a winner. But Clinton's burst of energy to save himself won admiration and positive coverage in the media, more coverage than all the other candidates in the national press. With their coverage of his strength and energy, they created an intriguing mosaic rather than the predictable, moralistic, negative images projected during the controversies over infidelity and the draft.

In addition to their claims to be protagonists and their efforts to project admired personal traits, the candidates also attempted to explain their vision for the future of the nation, their plans and priorities. In these efforts, however, they had to rely chiefly on themselves; the media gave little prominent attention to their goals or the language they used to express them. Unlike stories about winning and losing and fighting, which met the dramatic requisites for television and newspapers and were easily constructed in poll numbers and battle imagery, accounts of the candidates' visions took more discussion and explanation, and lent themselves less readily to dramatic portrayals. Pictures in the media may have conveyed some impressions of the candidates' outlook on a superficial level (optimistic, pessimistic, happy, sad), as a smile is a more hopeful expression than a frown. But little of what the candidates visualized or proposed came through on network television or front-page newspaper stories.

In most states, the media script would be the only script. How else would voters learn about the campaign in New York? Florida? Illinois? Thomas Patterson (1993) has made a persuasive case that the media have replaced the political parties as chief intermediaries between candidates and voters. Now the media, not the parties, he argues, outline the candidates' strengths and weaknesses and guide the voters in their choices. In their guidance, they have portrayed the candidates in a heavily negative light, souring the public on the process. But the evidence in the New Hampshire primary is somewhat different. There the candidates often found ways around the intermediaries, and got to the voters directly. They communicated in their own language, not the language of the media, in messages of sufficient length that they were able to explain their visions for the future.

Only through remarkably inventive, persistent, and often expensive means could the candidates compensate for the media's neglect of their goals. They reached the voters both interpersonally and through the paid media. Tsongas managed to communicate his message by giving speeches and meeting people in New Hampshire for almost a year before the primary, and through his booklet, *A Call to Economic Arms.* Clinton communicated his vision by giving the longest speeches, with the most extensive question-and-answer periods, having a rally every day the final week, buying two half hours of television for call-in questions, distributing twenty thousand videotapes, and publishing his full draft letter in the newspaper. Over one hundred Arkansan friends also descended on the state, meeting and greeting voters and telling them about "Bill and Hillary." Buchanan campaigned in New Hampshire for over two months (while Bush was absent), giving speeches and meeting voters, and bombarded the state with his advertisements, spending more than all the other candidates. Most of the candidates made heavy use of advertising, some of it to outline their vision of an ideal America. These efforts, rather than the media coverage, allowed the voters to hear the candidates discussing their goals.

In contrast to the other candidates, Bush violated the New Hampshire "rules," spending little time there—only twelve hours until the final week (Michael Kranish, *Boston Globe*, Feb. 11, p. 1). He gave a few short speeches, but chose a largely nonverbal personal style. He passed through malls, shook hands, waved and smiled, providing good pictures but avoiding the microphone. His ads, leaflets, and surrogate speakers carried his message. Yet he won, and decisively. He won in spite of heavily negative media coverage, steady attacks from all the Democrats, and an opponent who campaigned vigorously and conveyed the image of a "fighter." One can only surmise that the reservoir of reputation he had built up as the Republican president in a state that favored Republicans was sufficient to protect him against the onslaught. His winning percentage of the vote was far smaller than his campaign had predicted, however, and smaller than most incumbent presidents had received. The image of weakness and ineptitude constructed of him by Buchanan, the Democrats, and the media haunted him for the next nine months.

Rituals are emotionally satisfying because they engage people in repetitive acts that remind them of deeply held values. A major part of most important rituals is their language, as people repeat the age-old marriage vows, or catechism, or slogans, drawing sustenance and a sense of worth from the words. The dramatic ritual of political campaigns *can* reinforce deeply held values, but without language, the satisfaction from participation is very limited. In many states, the only candidate language citizens hear is in ads, and though ads appeal to the emotions through the language of values and feelings (Kern, 1989), their brevity makes it difficult to develop and sustain political messages in the way a speech or a prolonged discussion can.

In New Hampshire, candidates have found ways to reach the voters with their own political language, expressing their visions and plans for the future, in spite of media obstacles. Perhaps the high voter participation in that state is in part due to the satisfaction of the citizens with a dramatic ritual that engages them so fully through its language.

The words and pictures from New Hampshire, and the votes that give them credence, establish who and how and what kind of characters will perform in the electoral drama. This primary is the critical beginning of the drama, but far more than a chronological beginning. It is a definitional beginning, whose character constructions will dominate the rest of the play.

NOTES

1. The Iowa caucuses precede the New Hampshire primary, and also claim attention as "first in the nation." They have played pivotal roles in several presidential campaigns, starting in 1976. Their record as predictor of the campaign to come has not been impressive, however. In 1988 the winners there were soon winnowed out in early primaries; in 1992, candidates abandoned the Iowa caucuses to favorite son Senator Tom Harkin.

2. In February 1988 and 1992, I spent 8–9 days before the primary travelling with the media and attending public events of the candidates in New Hampshire. I received press credentials from WAMC in Albany, New York, a National Public Radio affiliate, and called in several stories during the trip.

3. The newspapers, like the networks, gave substantial coverage to the citizen/voters, both by reporting their preferences in poll standings, and through interviews and quotations. The "New Hampshire voters" were characterized as "cantankerous," "crotchety," "unpredictable," "savvy," "skeptical," and "difficult to please." On top of that, they were sour about the economy and not happy with the candidates chosen—all in all a tough bunch. More research is needed on their role in the electoral drama.

REFERENCES

Adams, William C. (1987). As New Hampshire goes . . . In Gary R. Orren and Nelson W. Polsby, eds., *Media and momentum: The New Hampshire primary and nomination politics.* Chatham, N.J.: Chatham House, pp. 42–59.

Baker, Ross K. (1993). Sorting out and suiting up: The presidential nominations. In Gerald M. Pomper, ed., *The election of 1992.* Chatham, N.J.: Chatham House, pp. 39–73.

Bartels, Larry M. (1988). *Presidential primaries and the dynamics of public choice.* Princeton, N.J.: Princeton University Press.

Blankenship, Jane (1976). The search for the 1972 Democratic nomination: A metaphorical perspective. In Jane Blankenship and Hermann G. Stelzner, eds., *Rhetoric and communication: Studies in the University of Illinois tradition.* Urbana, Ill.: University of Illinois Press, pp. 236–60.

Boot, William (1989, Jan.–Feb.). Campaign '88: TV overdoses on the inside dope. *Columbia Journalism Review,* 23–29.

Brady, Henry E., and Richard Johnston (1987). What's the primary message: Horse race or issue journalism? In Gary R. Orren and Nelson W. Polsby, eds., *Media and momentum: The New Hampshire primary and nomination politics.* Chatham, N.J.: Chatham House, pp. 127–86.

Buchanan, Pat (1992, Feb.). Putting and keeping America first. Leaflet.

Burke, Kenneth (1965). *Permanence and change: An anatomy of purpose.* Indianapolis, Ind.: Bobbs-Merrill.

Bush, George (1992, Feb.). A plan to make New Hampshire and America move . . . and keep moving. Leaflet.

Castle, David S. (1992, Jan.). Media coverage of presidential primaries. *American Politics Quarterly, 19,* 33–42.

Ceaser, James, and Andrew Busch (1993). *Upside down and inside out: The 1992 elections and American politics.* Boston: Littlefield Adams.

Clinton, Bill (1992a, Feb.). America Dream. Great American Media, Inc. Videotape.

Clinton, Bill (1992b, Feb.). Fighting for the forgotten middle class. Leaflet.

Corcoran, Paul E. (1990). Language and politics. In David Swanson and Dan Nimmo, eds., *New directions in political communication.* Newbury Park, Calif.: Sage, pp. 51–85.

Crouse, Timothy (1972). *The boys on the bus.* New York: Ballantine Books.

Devlin, L. Patrick (1994, Jan.–Mar.). Television advertising in the 1992 New Hampshire presidential primary election. *Political Communication, 11,* 81–99.

Duncan, Dayton (1991a). *Grassroots.* New York: Viking.

Duncan, Dayton (1991b, Mar. 31). Interview on Booknotes, C-SPAN.

Graber, Doris A. (1987). Framing election news broadcasts: News context and its impact on the 1984 presidential election. *Social Science Quarterly, 69*, 552–67.

Hellweg, Susan A., and Stephen W. King (1983). Comparative evaluation of political candidates: Implication for the voter decision-making process. *Central States Speech Journal, 34*, 134–38.

Hellweg, Susan A., Stephen W. King, and Steve E. Williams (1988). Comparative candidate evaluation as a function of election level and candidate incumbency. *Communication Reports, 1*, 76–85.

Jamieson, Kathleen Hall (1992). *Dirty politics: Deception, distraction, and democracy*. New York: Oxford University Press.

John, Kenneth E. (1989). The polls—A report. 1980–1988 New Hampshire presidential primary polls. *Public Opinion Quarterly, 53*, 590–605.

Kendall, Kathleen E. (1993, Nov.–Dec.). Public speaking in the presidential primaries through media eyes. *American Behavioral Scientist, 37*, 240–51.

Kendall, Kathleen E., and Judith S. Trent (1989, Fall). Presidential surfacing in the New Hampshire primary. *Political Communication Review, 14*, 1–29.

Kennamer, J. D. and S. H. Chaffee (1982). Communication of political information during early presidential primaries: Cognition, affect, and uncertainty. In M. Burgoon (Ed.), *Communication Yearbook 5* (pp. 627–650). New Brunswick, NJ: Transaction.

Kerbel, Matthew Robert (1994). *Edited for television: CNN, ABC, and the 1992 presidential campaign*. Boulder, Colo.: Westview.

Kern Montague (1989). *30-second politics: Political advertising in the eighties*. New York: Praeger.

Kern, Montague, and Marion Just (1994, April). How voters construct images of political candidates: The role of political advertising and televised news. Research Paper R-10, The Joan Shorenstein Barone Center, Harvard University.

Kern, Montague, and Marion Just (1995, forthcoming, June). The focus group method, political advertising, campaign news and the construction of candidate images. *Political Communication, 12*.

Lichter, S. Robert, Daniel Amundson, and Richard Noyes (1988). *The Video Campaign: Network Coverage of the 1988 Primaries*. Washington, DC: American Enterprise Institute for Public Policy Research.

Louden, Allan Dean (1990). Image construction in political spot advertising: The Hunt/Helms Senate campaign 1984 (Ph.D. diss., University of Southern California).

Matthews, Donald R. (1978). Winnowing. In James D. Barber, ed., *Race for the presidency*. Englewood Cliffs, N.J.: Prentice Hall, pp. 55–78.

Mayer, William G. (1987). The New Hampshire primary: A historical overview. In Gary R. Orren and Nelson W. Polsby, eds., *Media and momentum: The New Hampshire primary and nomination politics.* Chatham, N.J.: Chatham House, pp. 9–41.

Meyrowitz, Joshua (1992, June). The power of television news. *The World and I,* 6(7), 452–73.

Neuman, W. Russell, Marion R. Just, and Ann N. Crigler (1992). *Common knowledge.* Chicago: University of Chicago Press.

Nimmo, Dan, and Robert L. Savage (1976). *Candidates and their images: Concepts, methods, and findings.* Pacific Palisades, Calif.: Goodyear.

Nimmo, Dan, and James E. Combs (1990). *Mediated political realities.* 2nd ed. New York: Longman.

Orren, Gary R., and Nelson W. Polsby, eds. (1987). *Media and momentum: The New Hampshire primary and nomination politics.* Chatham, N.J.: Chatham House.

Patterson, Thomas E. (1980). *The mass media election: How Americans choose their president.* New York: Praeger.

Patterson, Thomas E. (1993). *Out of order.* New York: Alfred A. Knopf.

Pfau, Michael, Tracy Diedrich, Karla M. Larson, and Kim M. Van Winkle (1993, Summer). The influence of communication modalities on voters' perceptions of candidates during presidential primary campaigns. *Journal of Broadcasting and Electronic Media, 37,* 275–92.

Pomper, Gerald M. (1993). *The election of 1992: Reports and Interpretations.* Chatham, N.J.: Chatham House.

Popkin, Samuel L. (1992). Decision making in presidential primaries. In Shanto Iyengar and William J. McGuire, eds., *Explorations in political psychology.* Durham, N.C., and London: Duke University Press, pp. 361–79.

Popkin, Samuel L. (1991). *The reasoning voter: Communication and persuasion in presidential campaigns.* Chicago: University of Chicago Press.

1992 Presidential Primary Commercials. Purdue University Public Affairs Video Archives, # 91-04-30-0000-4 5660-24630.

Ridout, Christine F. (1991). The role of media coverage of Iowa and New Hampshire in the 1988 Democratic nomination. *American Politics Quarterly, 19,* 43–58.

Robinson, Michael J. and Margaret A. Sheehan (1983). *Over the wire and on tv.* New York: Russell Sage Foundation.

Rosenstiel, Tom (1993). *Strange bedfellows: How television and the presidential candidates changed American politics, 1992.* New York: Hyperion.

Saussure, Ferdinand de (1959). *Course in general linguistics.* Trans. W. Baskin. New York: Philosophical Library. (Original work published 1916).

Trent, Judith S. (1978). Presidential surfacing: The ritualistic and crucial first act. *Communication Monographs, 45*, 281–92.

Trent, Judith S., Paul A. Mongeau, Jimmie D. Trent, Kathleen E. Kendall, and Ronald B. Cushing (1993, Nov.). The ideal candidate: A study of the desired attributes of the public and the media across two presidential campaigns. *American Behavioral Scientist, 37*, 225–39.

Tsongas, Paul E. (n.d.) *A call to economic arms: Forging a new American mandate.* Boston, Mass.: The Tsongas Committee.

Tsongas, Paul (1992, Feb.). How to fight for America's economic future and win. Leaflet.

West, Darrell M., Montague Kern, and Dean Alger (1992, Sept.). Political advertising and ad watches in the 1992 presidential nominating campaign. Paper presented at the American Political Science Association, Chicago, Ill.

Newspapers (Feb. 11–19, 1992):

Boston Globe, Boston Herald, Concord Monitor (Feb. 12, 13, 15, 17), *New York Times, The Telegraph* (Nashua), *Union Leader* (Manchester), *USA Today*

Television news (Feb. 11–19, 1992, 6:30 or 7:00 P.M.)

ABC World News Tonight, CBS Evening News, NBC Nightly News (missing Feb. 15–16)

TWO

The Problem of Getting on the Media Agenda

A Case Study in Competing Logics of Campaign Coverage

JOSHUA MEYROWITZ

Studies of political campaign coverage generally focus on variables such as the balance of personality versus issue coverage, the themes and narratives in the coverage, possible bias toward or against a party or candidate, length of sound bites on TV news, those aspects of a candidate's policies and rhetoric that receive the most and least coverage in the press, and so on.[1]

Such explorations assume, of course, that candidates receive a significant amount of news coverage in the first place. Yet most of the candidates for the presidency in 1992, as in other years, received very little or no national press coverage. Of the more than sixty candidates who entered the first primary in New Hampshire, only eight were routinely covered in the national news media: George Bush and Pat Buchanan of the Republican Party, and Bill Clinton, Bob Kerrey, Tom Harkin, Douglas Wilder, Paul Tsongas, and Jerry Brown of the Democratic Party. The only other candidate to receive extensive national news coverage during the campaign was independent Ross Perot.

This chapter will explore the patterns of coverage and noncoverage of U.S. presidential political campaigns through a case study of one of the candidates who received very little national press coverage: Democrat Larry Agran. Although there were thirty-six candidates for the Democratic nomination in the New Hampshire primary, Agran's campaign is an unusually good lens through which to observe competing logics of campaign coverage. As a former mayor of a city of 110,000 people, Agran, who was forty-seven years old during the campaign, did not have the customary background and experience to be considered a "major candidate" by the national press; but, unlike virtually all the other so-called fringe candidates, he was not easy to dismiss out of hand. He was a respected member of one of the two major parties, had an impressive twelve-year track record as an elected public official, had some foreign policy experience, was a Harvard Law School graduate and book author, had basic components of a serious campaign with a formal announcement speech and position papers, had a sufficiently large and competent national staff to have his name placed on most primary and caucus ballots (the stumbling block for most of the other ballots was his failure to meet the criterion of "significant national press coverage"), had measurable showings in some early polls, was sometimes included in forums with the "major" candidates, garnered some small newspaper endorsements, outlasted most of the "major" candidates, eventually qualified for federal matching funds, and even won a few delegate votes at the Democratic convention. Further, although Agran received nowhere near the amount of news coverage that would have allowed his name to be recognized by most voters, he did receive a fair amount of coverage in the local media (especially during the New Hampshire primary), as well as a continual smattering of coverage in major national news outlets such as the "MacNeil/Lehrer NewsHour," *New York Times, Washington Post, Los Angeles Times, Boston Globe,* CBS News, CNN, C-SPAN, and National Public Radio.[2] Moreover, in most of the handful of forums in which he was allowed to participate with "major" candidates, there is, as described below, at least some credible evidence that he outshone several or all of his better-known rivals.

Agran's campaign often approached the threshold between minor and major, but there was almost nothing he could do to cross it. He was barred from most of the televised debates, and most national news organizations ignored his campaign most of the time. Generally, the national press did not attend his press conferences or campaign events; made little or no mention of him in the press coverage of forums in which he was allowed to participate, regardless of how well the audience responded to him; rarely showed pictures of him, even when he was standing or sitting next to widely covered candidates; and played down or ignored his results in early polls, even when he tied or passed one of the "major" candidates.

The purpose of this chapter is to analyze the coverage and noncoverage of the Agran campaign for what it tells us about U.S. presidential campaign coverage in general. Agran's anomalous status—as "less than a 'major' candidate" but "more than a 'fringe' candidate"—helps expose different ways of thinking about whether and how a presidential campaign should receive coverage. After summarizing Agran's campaign experiences, this chapter describes three competing "logics" for how presidential campaigns should be covered: national journalistic logic, local journalistic logic, and public logic.

THE AGRAN CAMPAIGN

On August 22,1991 Larry Agran launched his campaign for the presidency from his home town of Irvine, in Orange County, California. His announcement speech offered a detailed plan for a "New American Security" that put "human need at home ahead of military overkill abroad" (Agran, 1991). That same day, the Orange County edition of the *Los Angeles Times* carried a 1,200-word story on the announcement on the first page of Section B, with part of the headline reading: "He May Not Win, But He Vows to Make Voice of Liberalism Heard" (Willman, 1991a). Several follow-up articles appeared in the Orange County edition the next day, including one titled "Why Agran Could Be a Primary Figure" (Parsons, 1991). But the main edition of the *Los Angeles Times*, which is distributed nationally, was less encouraging. It carried only one brief, three-hundred-word story on the announcement, referring to Democrat Agran's quest as "the longest-shot candidacy of all" within a party that had only a long shot chance of winning the White House in the first place (Willman, 1991b). The story ran on page 46, the obituary page.

Thus, the general pattern that would repeat itself throughout the campaign was established early: respectful local coverage contrasted with marginalized national coverage that suggested that the Agran campaign was dead on arrival.

In early September 1991 Agran was one of only two declared U.S. presidential candidates to address five hundred party members at the Sioux City Democratic Party Unity Dinner in Iowa, the first Democratic event of the presidential campaign season. A fleeting image appeared on Cable News Network of Agran being greeted by candidate Paul Tsongas and soon-to-declare candidates Senator Tom Harkin and Governor Bill Clinton. But when the same encounter appeared in an Associated Press (AP) photo published by the lasting "newspaper of record," the *New York Times*, Agran was nowhere to be seen. Tsongas and Harkin are shown oriented toward some unseen figure beyond the right margin of the photograph. (Agran is mentioned in the text of the 1,100-word article, but not until the third-to-last paragraph, where he is described briefly as "a dark horse candidate" who also addressed the group; Toner, 1991.)

Over the next weeks and months, as other well-known politicians declared their candidacies, the national press spent a considerable amount of time on them, as well as speculating at length over whether two prominent noncandidates—the Rev. Jesse Jackson and New York Governor Mario Cuomo—would run. But the national media gave little or no attention to the Agran campaign. In the relatively rare instances when his name did appear, he was described as a "fringe candidate," a "dark horse," or "an obscure contender." Agran was barred from most of the televised debates on the basis of criteria that shifted as he tried to meet them.[3] With Catch-22 logic, news media executives told Agran that he had not earned the right to media exposure, because, among other things, he had not received enough media exposure.

Much of the mainstream national press rejected Agran before a single vote was cast and even before the public had a chance to learn who the candidates were. The national press placed him in the same category with candidates who merely paid $1,000 to be put on the ballot only in New Hampshire and had little else in the way of background, experience, or campaign organization and activities. Agran was grouped, for example, with a recovering alcoholic and the bicycle-riding candidate who proposed having sheep and goats tend the front lawn of the White House.

To be fair to those making such news judgments, thirty-six candidates entered the Democratic primary in New Hampshire. Further, Agran certainly had unconventional credentials as a presidential contender. Although he had devoted twenty years to public service, he had never held statewide or national office. He had served for a dozen years as an elected official in Irvine, California, America's largest master-planned city. Virtually all the national journalists I interviewed dismissed him based on his having held only local office, just as they once would have dismissed anyone who was "only" a congressman (who represents a local district rather than a state) or was only a former senator or governor (Dennis, 1992). As journalist Roger Mudd put it at the start of a rare national TV interview with Agran: "It does stretch credulity to think that a Jewish ex-mayor of a small suburban California town can make it" ("MacNeil/Lehrer NewsHour, Aug. 30, 1991).[4]

Agran's campaign staff and supporters, however, pointed out that, as Irvine's first directly elected mayor, Agran had initiated a series of progressive programs that received national acclaim (childcare, affordable housing, mass transportation, one of the nation's first curbside recycling programs, hazardous waste regulations, open-space preservation, and many others). They noted that, as executive director of the Center for Innovative Diplomacy (a progressive foreign policy think tank), Agran had played a unique role as a "global mayor," who pursued issues of international trade, arms reduction, and human rights, and earned his city a United Nations award for his pioneering legislation to eliminate ozone-depleting compounds—all from an unlikely base in deeply conservative Orange County, the county that had given Ronald Reagan and George Bush huge margins of victory. Agran's supporters pointed out that he had much more governing experience than Pat Buchanan and Ross Perot put together, and more foreign policy experience than Bill Clinton. And they described him as the most articulate presidential contender with some of the clearest plans for solving the country's problems, including the most specific blueprint for shifting cold war military spending to post-cold war domestic needs. They also said that the public's reaction to many of Agran's appearances was so positive that his ideas deserved to be heard—and allowed to influence the platforms of the "major" candidates—even if Agran himself had little chance of winning the nomination. Finally, Agran's supporters argued that, since his campaign had done the work to get his name on more than thirty-five primary and caucus ballots, the public deserved to be told something about him so as to be able to make an informed choice in the voting booth. (No other major-party candidate who was on that many primary ballots was being ignored by the press.)

It is no surprise that Agran's staff and supporters saw more in Agran than did most national journalists. What is surprising, however, is the extent to which Agran's campaign received similar encouragement from the coverage of the *local* New Hampshire press reporting on the first-in-the-nation primary, as well as from two nationally known columnists, Colman McCarthy and Sydney Schanberg. In New Hampshire, dozens of newspaper articles, editorials, columns, and letters to the editor described Agran's exclusion and/or supported his right to be heard in national debates. Publications with articles or editorials on Agran included the *Union Leader, Concord Monitor, Telegraph, Foster's Daily Democrat, Rockingham County Newspapers, Atlantic News, Portsmouth Press, Derry News, Keene Sentinel, Rochester Courier, Portsmouth Herald,* and *Country Town Ledger.* Sample headlines ran: "Agran Resents Campaign Trail Tolls" (Miller, 1991); "At Least Give Agran a Chance to Lose" (Field, 1991); "Agran's Struggle to Get Noticed" (Hilyard, 1991); "Larry Agran Deserves a Place in Democratic Primary Debates" (Merton, 1992); "Larry Agran Fights Label as Outsider" (Pritchard, 1992); and "Unlock the Process" (1992). Agran was also interviewed more than two hundred times by local New Hampshire radio stations, many inviting him back several times (Agran, 1993).

Beyond New Hampshire, Colman McCarthy (1992a) and Sydney Schanberg (1992) each wrote columns challenging Agran's designation as a "minor candidate" and endorsing his right to be heard and seen through debates and national news coverage. McCarthy's column asked "What's Minor about This Candidate?" and Schanberg argued that Agran was "A 'Minor Candidate' Worth a Listen."

Agran was also the highest-rated Democratic candidate in some progressive publications, including Maine's *Casco Bay Weekly* ("How to Caucus," 1992) and *Nuclear Times* ("*Nuclear Times*'s More-or-Less Nonpartisan Guide," 1991–92), the latter calling him "bright, earnest, and visionary" and saying he would "bring the right values to the White House." In addition, Agran's campaign was followed on progressive computer networks, such as PeaceNet.

As his campaign was greeted with national media silence, the normally soft-spoken and mild-mannered Agran felt forced to change his tactics. For example, in December 1991, when he was barred by the chairman of the state

Democratic Party from a televised health care forum with other presidential candidates in Nashua, New Hampshire, Agran stood up in the audience and demanded to know by what criteria he was being excluded. Responding to a signal from a state party official, security police began to remove Agran from the hall, but the crowd's shouts of "Freedom of speech!" and "Let us vote!" embarrassed the men at the dais into inviting him to join them. (New Alliance Party candidate Lenora Fulani, who was running in the New Hampshire primary as a Democrat, also took this opportunity to join the other candidates.) Agran's confrontation with party officials and his subsequent inclusion in the health forum was his first widely reported "campaign event"—but little mention was made of his innovative proposals for health care reform.

To prevent a public call for inclusion from happening again (the state party chair called it "intimidation"), the state Democratic Party organization moved its next debate to a high-security TV studio with no audience. Agran stood outside the studio, among a crowd of four hundred people who braved zero-degree temperatures to protest the exclusion of their candidates from the debates. (Most of the protesters were supporters of Lenora Fulani, but several other "fringe" candidates were also represented.) As reported in the local New Hampshire press, such as the *Union Leader*, the protest offered many dramatic moments, with the "major" candidates forced to pass "picket lines for democracy" as protesters shouted "Scab! Scab! Scab!" (Rapsis, 1992). Yet perhaps because there was no violence and the closed debate was not disrupted, the protest received almost no attention in the national news media.[5]

When local press coverage and protests had no impact on Agran's national media profile, his campaign staff became convinced that his status as a "fringe" candidate could be erased if he tied or passed one or more of the "major" candidates in the polls. They were wrong.

When Agran made his first measurable showing in a University of New Hampshire/WMUR-TV poll taken from January 6 to 11, the AP story on the poll grouped Agran's results into a total score for "minor candidates and write-ins," without mentioning his name ("Clinton Still Making Great Strides in Primary Polls," 1992). When a January 22 poll, conducted by the American Research Group (ARG), showed Agran tied with former California Governor Jerry Brown and Iowa Senator Tom Harkin, the polling group's press release suggested three headlines, including "Agran Appears in Democratic Race." But the Associated Press buried Agran's result in a single sentence two-thirds of the way through a story focusing on Clinton as the front-runner ("Polls Show Clinton ahead of President and the Democrats," 1992). When a follow-up ARG poll showed Agran doubling his support and moving ahead of Brown, the AP again focused on Clinton, but this time on the drop in his rating. Agran's tally was reported much further down in the story (after

Brown's lower score), and it was incorrectly referred to as Agran's "first measurable showing in the poll" ("Clinton Rating Falls in Poll," 1992). When the next ARG poll showed Agran still between Brown and Harkin, ABC's "World News Sunday"—perhaps to avoid the complexity of explaining the identity of a candidate they had not been covering—simply dropped Agran's tally from the middle of the reported poll results. Harkin's score was followed directly by Brown's. Other major news organizations solved the "problem" (of skipping over a higher score to report a lower one) by reporting only on the top three names.

ARG pollster Dick Bennett believed that had Agran's surprise strength in the polls been played up by news organizations, it might well have led to a further rise in the polls. Instead, "the press completely ignored the story, and he began to sink" (Bennett, 1992).

Agran's unusual appearance with four of the so-called major candidates at the U.S. Conference of Mayors in Washington, D.C., in January led to the first significant mention of his campaign in the *New York Times*, which in effect declared him the winner of the debate. The article, "Mayors Appear Unmoved by the Major Candidates," began by observing that "After hearing pitches from the Democratic Presidential contenders on how they would revive America's cities, dozens of mayors meeting here today seemed to agree on one thing: the single candidate who truly understands urban needs is Larry Agran" (Berke, 1992). Michael Brown, director of the U.S. Conference of Mayors, sent me the results of a news tracking agency's report of coverage of the conference, which revealed that Agran's positive reception, or at least his presence, was briefly mentioned in several other newspaper reports on the conference. Yet the most widely distributed news reports, those of the Associated Press, ABC radio news, and the satellite television All News Channel, did not even mention that Agran was there.

Similarly, when Agran and several of the "major" candidates participated via satellite in the Global Warming Leadership Forum in Tallahassee in early February, the audience, according to conference organizer Carole Florman, "was very enthusiastic about Larry Agran and less than enthusiastic about Bill Clinton and Bob Kerrey" (Florman, 1992). Agran's participation was mentioned in local newspaper stories. But the major national news organizations covering the event—ABC News, CBS News (through a local affiliate), and the AP—omitted any mention of Agran from their reports.

Agran's tying or passing well-known candidates in several polls and outperforming them at two forums—all within a ten-day period—could have been seen as a "major story" by the national news media. But that story was never constructed and never told.[6]

As the pattern of exclusion from national coverage built, there seemed to be nothing that Agran could do to register with the national media. Press language even excluded evidence of his and other "minor" candidates' existence. A TV news program would report: "Four out of the five Democratic presidential candidates were in Manchester, New Hampshire today," as if there were no other candidates. Or, a report would say: "Bill Clinton spoke in Nashua, New Hampshire today. The rest of the candidates were in other states"—while Agran was very much in New Hampshire and actively campaigning. Or a TV report focusing on only four candidates would conclude: "That's the reaction from the presidential hopefuls, with the exception of Bill Clinton." Even in reporting on the eve of the February 23 South Dakota debate, which had long been scheduled with six participants—including Agran, who had the added boost of recently being endorsed by South Dakota's *Lakota Times* (Giago, 1992)—"NBC Nightly News" reported "All five Democrats are in South Dakota for a debate."

Agran's strong performance in the South Dakota debate (especially his effective attacks on Jerry Brown for being only a very recent convert with respect to campaign finance reform) led to the most simultaneous national attention he had received at any point during his campaign. Agran's participation was featured late that night on some TV news programs (the debates took place after the evening news programs had aired), including CNN Headline News. The next day's *Los Angeles Times* called him "the showstopper of the evening" (Decker, 1992), and the *Boston Globe* wrote "One of the surprises of the debate was the solid performance turned in by Larry Agran" (Lehigh, 1992a). The same Globe reporter filed an article exclusively on Agran's performance at the debate titled, "Larry Agran: 'Winner' in Debate with Little Chance for the Big Prize" (Lehigh, 1992b). The *Washington Post* and the *New York Times* also reported on his participation. But by the day after the debate, his presence at the forum began to fade from national television. Of the nine reports on the debate on the network morning news shows, only three mentioned his participation. By that evening, he was gone. "NBC Nightly News," which had mentioned only five participants the night before, did not correct the number of participants and showed video only of Clinton speaking briefly, following by a clip of Harkin and Tsongas clashing at the debate. ABC's "World News Tonight" featured the same clash between Harkin and Tsongas. The "CBS Evening News" mentioned the South Dakota primary, but had no report on the debate.

Throughout the primary season, the national media would offer routine coverage of whatever the "major" candidates were doing. During the New Hampshire primary, for example, Bob Kerrey's visit to Weeks Restaurant in Dover, New Hampshire, where he interacted awkwardly with seemingly uncomfortable patrons, received national television coverage. But few journalists would attend Larry Agran's formal press conferences, and still fewer news reports would appear.

As the primary season wound on, Agran found that in most cases the best coverage he could hope for was a passing mention of his presence at an event. When he and former senator Eugene McCarthy were allowed to participate with Bill Clinton and Jerry Brown in a March debate held in Buffalo, New York, many national news reports mentioned that Agran and McCarthy were there, but did not report on a single thing that either of them said. Instead, they were used as a backdrop to the clashes between Clinton and Brown over Brown's previous attempts to block limits on campaign contributions. The *Washington Post*, for example, reported "Clinton's charges were made at the end of a candidates' forum here, where he and Brown appeared with former Minnesota senator Eugene McCarthy and Larry Agran, the former major of Irvine, Calif. Brown had no opportunity to respond beyond challenging Clinton to another debate" (Drehle, 1992). The seven-hundred-word article made no other reference to the other candidates (and no mention that the effective charges against Jerry Brown were made earlier by Larry Agran during the South Dakota debate). The emphasis of the six-hundred-word *Newsday* story matched its headline, "Top Two Tangle at Buffalo Debate," with only a single sentence on the participation of the two "minor candidates" (Clifford and Kasindorf, 1992). Television coverage was similar. ABC News, for example, introduced the report that included video of the Buffalo debate by saying, "Democratic front-runner Bill Clinton was out campaigning vigorously in New York and Connecticut today, hoping to keep his last remaining rival, Jerry Brown, from making inroads among former supporters of Paul Tsongas" (Mar. 21, 1992). Therefore, even when Agran's presence was mentioned or shown, only Brown and Clinton were allowed to "speak" to the public through national newspaper and television reports.

By the end of March 1992, Tom Harkin, Bob Kerrey, and Paul Tsongas had all joined Douglas Wilder in suspending their campaigns, but the narrowed Democratic field did not generate any increased attention to Agran. Even when Agran garnered more voter signatures to be placed on the New York ballot than Jerry Brown, only Jerry Brown was allowed to participate in New York City debates with Bill Clinton.[7] At the start of one debate on urban problems (Agran's specialty) at Lehman College in the Bronx, one of the five boroughs of New York City, Agran stood up in the audience and said, "I respectfully ask to be included in this forum." As he continued to speak, explaining his standing as the only other actively campaigning Democratic candidate on the ballot, he was quickly tackled to the floor by about six plainclothes police, dragged down a flight of stairs head first, handcuffed, thrown into a police paddy wagon until the debate was over, and then kept in custody at a Bronx jail for several more hours on charges of disorderly conduct, trespassing, and resisting arrest. The TV cameras did not even turn away from the debate stage to focus on any of this drama.[8] Agran's New York campaign manager, who was sitting next to Agran, was also roughed up and arrested.

Agran's arrest received some coverage in New York, including a brief mention in the *New York Times*. The *New York Post* covered it—in both senses of the word. At the end of a tiny story on protests outside the debate, the *Post* reported: "Two men were arrested inside the Lehman College auditorium when they started heckling the candidates, according to police" ("150 in Scuffle at Auditorium," 1992). The most significant national coverage of the incident was in Agran's home state paper, the *Los Angeles Times*, which printed a brief report on the arrest on April 1, and then condemned the police action in an editorial the next day arguing that "something's weird when the former mayor of perhaps the most orderly city in the country is busted for disorderly conduct in the most disorderly city in America" ("Busted Candidate," 1992). But beyond that, there was largely silence.

Early in the campaign, national journalists told me that one reason Agran was not worthy of coverage was that he had not qualified for federal matching funds, and was unlikely to do so. But in May, when Agran did qualify for matching funds—becoming only the tenth candidate of all parties to do so since the start of the campaign—there was little press coverage of this,[9] and no change in the attention level he received.

Agran did not win his party's nomination. But he did receive three delegate votes at the Democratic convention. They were listed on the TV screens as votes for "Other."

Agran's trial resulting from his request for inclusion in the Bronx, New York debate was delayed several times, and he remained under threat of imprisonment for ten months. All charges were finally dismissed on January 19, 1993. In spite of Agran's efforts to draw press attention to his legal woes and their implications for an open political system, neither the prolonged court proceedings nor the dismissal received any significant news coverage.

By some measures at least, Agran's seventeen months of struggling to be heard were filled with many "newsworthy events." Yet the national news media mostly ignored him. A computer search through the Nexis system reveals that Agran's name did not appear even once in the campaign stories of the major news magazines, *Time, Newsweek,* and *U.S. News & World Report.*[10]

COMPETING COVERAGE LOGICS

The sharp contrast between the reporting on the primary campaign in the national media and in the local media in New Hampshire (where I live) was one of the things that drew my attention to this topic. Even though New Hampshire was flooded with national reporters, the local coverage of Larry Agran's campaign had no discernable impact on national coverage.

To explore the patterns of inclusion and exclusion, I began collecting press clippings and telephoning local and national journalists to inquire about their reasoning in dealing with Agran and the other candidates. I also began to discuss the issue of campaign press coverage with my students, colleagues, and average citizens I met at campaign events for various candidates.

When I asked an editor at a major link to the national media—the Associated Press bureau in Concord, New Hampshire—about the lack of mention in their national releases of the local articles, letters, and editorials on Agran, I was told bluntly: "We don't report on editorials." I was also told that the instructions concerning which candidates should receive "blanket coverage" on the part of the local AP came from the national AP in Washington.

At first I thought that perhaps the national journalists simply had not heard of Larry Agran, that Agran's staff had been unsuccessful in calling the candidate's policies, or even his existence, to the attention of the national media. Yet virtually all the national journalists I spoke with at the *New York Times, Los Angeles Times, Washington Post, Boston Globe, Time, Newsweek, U.S. News & World Report,* NBC News, "Nightline," and other places knew about Larry Agran, but had decided to give him little or no coverage. (Later, I learned that during this campaign most national journalists had access via modem to the political news service, *Hotline,* which had about 150 stories that mentioned the Agran campaign between August 1991 and July 1992.) All the national journalists I interviewed also expressed little surprise over the press treatment that Agran received, and they offered similar explanations for it. At the same time, most of the local journalists I interviewed thought that Agran's campaign was worthy of coverage, as was also obvious from the local press treatment that he was receiving.

Indeed, in following the coverage and noncoverage of Agran's campaign and in interviewing journalists and in speaking to voters, I discerned three fairly distinct and competing "logics" for campaign coverage: (1) national journalistic logic; (2) local journalistic logic; and (3) public logic.

Broadly speaking, what I call *national journalistic logic* involves a set of justifications for restricting most coverage to a narrow set of largely predetermined "major" candidates. This stands in greatest contrast to *public logic,* which is the most open to "unknown" candidates. *Local journalistic logic* generally falls in between. For reasons analyzed below, "minor" candidates, at least some of them, receive respectful local press treatment, but most of the coverage is still focused on the "major" candidates, as defined by national media coverage.

These three categories are not as neatly bounded as their labels may suggest. That is, a handful of national journalists (Colman McCarthy and Sydney Schanberg, for example) expressed thinking that was closer to local journalistic logic and to public logic than to the logic expressed by most of their peers. Further, a few local journalists with whom I spoke (primarily *television* journalists) espoused some views that were close to national journalistic logic. And the views I heard in conversations with dozens of average citizens ranged widely. Further, some gatekeepers had split media personalities: Phil Donahue of the evening show "Pozner and Donahue" expressed public logic when he championed Agran's right to news coverage on a program featuring Agran (Feb. 14, 992), but Phil Donahue of the daytime "Donahue" show restricted his candidates' debate before the New York primary to Clinton and Brown. Nevertheless, the vast majority of the views I heard (and read in print) clustered surprisingly neatly within these three categories.[11]

At the same time, the three logics were not equidistant from each other along all dimensions of campaign coverage. As described below, both local and national journalistic logics were very similar with respect to some variables (concern with limited news-reporting resources, for example). In other respects, local journalistic logic and public logic were very close to each other. Below, I analyze the differences and similarities among these three logics along several different dimensions.

Perception of News Gathering Resources

To the public eye, seeing hordes of reporters surrounding candidates, news organizations appear to have ample resources to cover as many campaigns as they see fit. The general attitude I heard expressed in many informal conversations with voters was echoed in the response to a question in a written survey I gave to a class of University of New Hampshire undergraduates: 85 percent thought that the press had an obligation to give "significant" press coverage to "all" (60%) or "most" (25%) declared candidates.[12]

Virtually all the journalists I spoke with, however, on both the national and local levels, complained about the problem of lack of resources to cover campaigns. This led them to be concerned with narrowing the coverage of candidates, even as the public was demanding a widening of options.

What public logic may not take into account is that while there are thousands of journalists across the nation covering the campaign, each news organization wants to do its best in covering the candidates with its own individual resources. This news logic of "protective coverage"—covering what other news organizations are covering—leads to a great deal of redundant reporting on the part of hundreds of different news organizations. It also makes each news organization feel overloaded when there are more than a few candidates. Elizabeth Kolbert, a reporter at the *New York Times*, told me that "Even six candidates are a lot to cover if you give them equal time. We were barely covering Tsongas at one point" (Kolbert, 1993).

Most of the journalists I spoke with, both nationally and locally, also mentioned that the poor economy had led to reduced staff size, and that lower newspaper advertising revenues meant that there was also less space for news. Such factors, I was told, reduced the likelihood that "minor" candidates would be covered by national news organizations. Rod Doherty, executive editor of the New Hampshire newspaper *Foster's Daily Democrat*, said that the same pressures reduced local news coverage of "unique candidates such as Larry Agran" (Doherty, 1993). The concern for resource allocation, therefore, separated local journalistic logic from an inclusive public logic, even within those local news organizations that felt that Larry Agran deserved to be given more coverage nationally.[13]

When Governor Wilder abandoned his campaign early in the race, many ordinary citizens I spoke with felt that there was now "an empty chair" for another candidate. In a similar spirit, local newspapers not only reported on Agran's hope of taking Wilder's seat at upcoming debates; they also published editorials and columns advocating his right to do so. But national journalists had the opposite reaction: "We can't wait to winnow the race down even further," I was told by Tom Rosenstiel (1992), who is stationed in Washington as a writer on politics and media for the *Los Angeles Times*. He explained that it is difficult, expensive, and confusing for the media to have to contend with a lot of candidates. "Journalists don't sit around in newsrooms asking 'Whom else should we cover?' The big question is 'Whom can we *stop* covering?' We're asking 'Can we skip Jerry Brown, too?'" Another journalist for a major newspaper, who preferred not to be named, echoed the desire to narrow the field as quickly as possible and noted that for his publication "every extra candidate means another reporter and another $150-a-day hotel bill."

This last comment also points to one reason that local media may be more willing and able to cover more candidates. Unlike the national press, local news organizations do not have to spend time and money on travel. Although particular reporters may be primarily assigned to particular candidates, the local news organization is actually covering a territory rather than a group of candidates. National journalists must follow the candidates around the country, but the candidates—both "major" and "minor"—come to the local news organization's space. Local news media have more flexibility in assigning one reporter to cover more than one candidate and in sending different reporters to cover the same candidate. This leads to more coverage of more candidates with fewer resources than most national news organizations can manage.

At the same time, however, local reporters continue to have an obligation to cover other area events—school board meetings, town council meetings, the police blotter, fires, and so forth. And, as local journalists informed me, "minor" candidates are more likely to lose out in the competition among concurrent events. The pragmatics of local news resources, therefore, may allow for more coverage of "minor" candidates than in the national media, but the pressure to stretch limited resources to an expanded set of "local events" during the campaign season keeps local journalistic logic distinct from public logic.

For television, both local and national, another form of "limited resource" is airtime. A thirty-minute news program squeezed between two other programs, and shortened further by commercials, has no room to expand to accommodate a large number of candidates. This, along with the added complication of a limited number of video crews, makes it difficult for local television to cover many candidates at once. New Hampshire's local television stations also have intimate ties with national television networks, with whom they exchange video feeds. For all these reasons, perhaps, the local television news directors I spoke with worked with a relatively restrictive logic that was often closer to national journalistic logic than that of their print colleagues. Agran received some coverage on local TV (WGOT-TV, for example, did five reports on him between September 4 and December 27, according to Rhonda Mann, 1993, the station's news director), but relatively less than he received in local newspapers.

Ironically, part of the tension between public logic and the two journalistic logics may stem from the lack of coverage of most of the candidates. Many members of the public I spoke with simply did not know that there were so many declared candidates, and they therefore had given no thought to the pragmatic difficulties of trying to cover so many campaigns. If all the candidates received extensive coverage, the public might cry out for simplification and focus.

Best Ideas or Best Chance of Winning?

The problem of too few resources to cover too many candidates, however, does not fully explain the patterns of campaign coverage. If number of candidates were the only factor involved, then Agran would have received significant coverage when only he, Clinton, and Brown remained as the active Democratic candidates.

Another factor is the varying conception of "what a presidential campaign is all about." Generally, the public logic I heard expressed—at campaign events, in casual conversations, in newspaper reports on public polls and "the public mood," in letters to the editor, and in my classes—revealed voters hungry for candidates with new ideas for solving our country's problems. Public logic generally sees a presidential campaign as fostering a national dialogue on key issues. But the national journalists I spoke with mostly saw the campaign as a horse race. "An election is not a matter of who is the smartest, the most articulate, or who has the best ideas," said Tom Rosenstiel of the *Los Angeles Times*. "It's much more complicated than that. What it really comes down to is who can win the most votes." Ultimately, Rosenstiel notes, "if we think someone is not likely to win, then we do not think of them as someone to devote much time to" (Rosenstiel, 1992).

Similarly, Jonathan Alter, a senior editor at *Newsweek*, described the "fairly simple rules of the press pack: If we don't think that you have at least some chance of being elected, you just don't get any coverage. Perhaps it's not the way it should be, but that's the way it is" (Alter, 1992).

Of course, these responses beg the question. How do the journalists know who has a chance of winning if they do not give the public a chance to respond to the available candidates? Tom Rosenstiel (1992) suggests that national journalists use several criteria. For one thing, political reporters tend to cover those candidates who their sources—the party professionals—tell them are the major candidates. "Reporters ask them 'What are you hearing?' 'Who is lining up endorsements?' 'Who is doing fundraisers for whom?' If professional politicians don't take Larry Agran seriously, then reporters won't take him seriously either."

National journalists also look to each other to see who is being taken as a "serious" candidate. Bill Wheatley, an executive producer at NBC News, which excluded Agran from its televised debate, told me that press coverage was "certainly one of the factors." He continued: "A number of independent news organizations had made that judgment to exclude Agran. It's not a conspiracy. One needs to pay attention to one's colleagues' decisions." Yet while Wheatley saw press decisions as "independent," he admitted that "journalistic consensus in part reflects consensus of party professionals who have some experience knowing who is electable" (Wheatley, 1992).

Similarly, Alvin Sanoff, a senior editor at *U.S. News & World Report*, told me: "Journalists all talk to the same people, the same readers of tea leaves. We have similar kinds of input from similar sources. It takes a leap of faith to say, 'We're missing the story.' . . . We all read and talk to each other. We speak to similar experts and gurus and poll takers. We're influenced by the same influences" (Sanoff, 1992).

Colman McCarthy, a columnist for the *Washington Post* who advocated Agran's inclusion in debates, observed the same pattern, but with a more critical tone. He spoke of typical journalistic routines surrounding campaigns as a form of "incest" between journalists and party officials (McCarthy, 1992b).

In contrast, local journalists and editors were moved by what they saw as the strength of a candidate's ideas. "Agran impressed us with the quality of his thinking," said Rod Doherty (1993), executive editor of *Foster's Daily Democrat*, published in Dover, New Hampshire. Similarly, Phil Kincade, editorial page editor of the same newspaper, said that several editorial board meetings with Agran convinced the paper's staff that "Agran was not a fringe candidate" (Kincade, 1993). *Foster's* published editorials advocating Agran's inclusion in debates because, as Kincade told me, they perceived Agran as "a serious candidate, addressing a number of important issues." *Foster's* editorial noted that Agran did not have much of a chance of winning, "but then Jerry Brown and Paul Tsongas do not have much better chances" ("He's out with the In-crowd," 1992).

William B. Rotch, publisher of New Hampshire's *Milford Cabinet and Wilton Journal*, wrote a number of editorials praising Agran's ideas: "Ideas, Not Names," "Whose Ideas Are Best?," "N.H. Democracy," and "Ideas, a Campaign and a Faith in Democracy." Rotch was also unconcerned about Agran's chances of winning: "Agran offers a challenge, and even though he might not win, if he forces other candidates to take a more honest view of the issues, to explain more clearly their view of America's immediate future, he will have made a valuable contribution." Rotch concluded by reminding readers that he wasn't predicting that Agran "was going to lead the pack in the New Hampshire primary," only "that we might have a better government if he did" (Rotch, 1992b).

The focus on the quality of ideas was also apparent in the *Atlantic News*, published in Hampton, New Hampshire, which editorialized that "We owe Larry Agran an opportunity to participate in the election process. Our problems are no joke. His proposals may just include some of the cures we are looking to find" ("Welcome to New Hampshire, Larry Agran," 1991). Andrew Merton (1992), a columnist for "The New Hampshire Weekly" section of the *Boston Globe*, wrote that Agran deserved to be in primary debates "because he is not just any small-city mayor. . . . He is a small-city mayor whose vision of converting America from a crumbling Cold War fortress to a dynamic peace-time leader has met with national and international acclaim." And Tom Field (1991), managing editor of the *Portsmouth Press*, wrote, "Agran is one of the few . . . candidates to actually offer a tangible campaign platform. . . . Let the people, not the Democratic Party elite, decide whether Larry Agran is a legitimate candidate."

Although I focused primarily on the local press coverage in New Hampshire, the clippings collected by the Agran campaign revealed the same focus on ideas, rather than winning, in local coverage in other parts of the country. *Sacramento Bee* columnist William Endicott, for example, wrote that "Agran knows his chances of moving into the White House are slim to none. But he hopes to at least influence the campaign dialogue by getting his ideas before the voters, and that's probably a better reason to run for president than some of his better-known rivals have" (Endicott, 1991). Similarly, New Mexico's *Santa Fe Reporter* wrote, "Too bad it's left to candidates like [Agran] to say the things the 'real' candidates ought to be saying" (Aldrich, 1991). And South Dakota's *Rapid City Journal* editorialized that while "Agran has been described as radical," his "ideas are not so far from mainstream politics. In fact, these are ideas that many Americans favor" ("'The People' Aren't Making This Decision," 1992).

Local New Hampshire editors told me that they did not really care what party professionals in Washington thought about the chances of various candidates. "We're not as closed-minded as the national media," said Phil Kincade (1993). "We tried to cover as many candidates as we possibly could. . . . Because we are first in the nation, we assume that everyone is starting with a clean slate. We had no basis for eliminating people before they've had a chance."

Although local journalistic logic was in this regard much closer to public logic than to national journalistic logic, further questioning revealed that the local press also felt comfortable screening the candidates for voters, but based on its own set of criteria. For example, Rod Doherty (1993) of *Foster's Daily Democrat* indicated that if a candidate missed scheduled meetings or phone interviews with his paper's staff, then he felt comfortable with not giving much coverage to the candidate. Similarly, candidates whom local editors deemed to have "no serious political experience" or "narrow platforms" or who were perceived as "just running as a lark" were not necessarily offered to the readership for consideration.

Like national journalists, local editors also looked outward for at least some cues to a candidate's viability, but the "sources" of this information were quite different from the national journalists' sources: Rather than looking to national party leaders, local journalists said they tried to assess the local public's reaction to candidates, and they were also partially influenced in their decisions by the views of local politicians and local academic "experts" (including me).

Local journalistic logic had another particular component that separated it from the other two logics. Local journalists saw themselves as covering the campaign through the filter of "community events." This view blended with public logic when it allowed "minor" candidates, including Larry Agran, to receive significant local coverage compared with their exclusion from the national media. "A presidential candidate is appearing *here*," explained local editor Rod Doherty (1993). "That's a big deal." Similarly, correspondent Jerry Miller said that his paper, the *Union Leader*, tried to give "equitable coverage to every candidate, including non-big-name candidates." Coverage, said Miller, was determined less by who the candidate was than by "who was in my region, my beat area" (Miller, 1993). Local coverage reflected, at least generally, the local campaign events sponsored by local politicians and average citizens (such as "candidate coffees"). But the community-events filter also meant that to get coverage, a candidate—especially a "minor" candidate—had to have a local campaign event. Unlike the "major" candidates, Agran and other "minor" candidates could receive coverage only in one small part of the country at a time.

The local-events filter also meant that some "major" candidates, especially President Bush—whose presence itself was a "major local event"—would receive blanket local coverage. One local newspaper editor told me off the record: "If the president is here, we're there with him. Even if he's here five days a week. Even if he's not doing anything. I don't want to live the rest of my life being the editor of the local paper that missed the president getting shot in our town." Such coverage means, of course, that other simultaneous local events and other candidates get little or no coverage.

Whose Vote Counts?

Because national journalists turn to party insiders for clues to "who can win" (and therefore whom to cover), they often display a surprising disregard for the citizens who are supposed to determine the winners through their voting. Elizabeth Kolbert at the *New York Times*, for example, explained that "the unspoken consensus" at the *Times* was not to give the Agran campaign any significant coverage. "We were a little queasy about it, but it was a gut thing, and everybody made the same call." This decision had nothing to do with what the *Times* guessed would be the public's reaction to Agran, however. Indeed, Kolbert noted that "people would have loved him because he was so different" (Kolbert, 1993).

At the same time, my interviews with national journalists suggested that while journalists start out with more concern for what party insiders tell them, they are not entirely immune to voter reactions. *Newsweek*'s Jonathan Alter (1992) told me that national journalists began to take Paul Tsongas more seriously once they saw significant and prolonged evidence of enthusiastic volunteers. Similarly, as several national journalists told me, they would have been willing to give Larry Agran extensive coverage—had he won a primary, or placed second or third. While public logic and local journalistic logic suggested that Agran deserved national media attention in order to see if his message sparked the interest of the public, national journalistic logic suggested that he would somehow have to generate massive public interest *before* earning the right to national media attention. In contrast, Douglas Wilder was treated seriously from the start because he was a sitting governor whom party insiders considered a good alternative to the more radical black candidate Jesse Jackson, even though there was little evidence of public enthusiasm for Wilder.

National journalists' alignment with party insiders and insider candidates goes beyond issues of winning a political campaign. As Tuchman (1978, pp.

68–69) indicates, a journalist's own career rise is dependent on knowing the highest-placed sources. Journalists' desire for "prestige assignments" led them to focus on "the stars." From the very beginning, the Clinton campaign was seen as the premiere assignment, which led to more attention to him—both positive and negative—and defined him throughout as the key player.

Connections with a "major" candidate can be of long-term value to journalists even if the candidate loses a primary. Campaign coverage of a winner could lead to a near-term future filled with "inside scoops" and "exclusive interviews," perhaps a best-seller on the campaign, or even an offer to be a press secretary, a presidential adviser, or an ambassador-at-large. In short, national journalists had much more to gain from covering high-status candidates, win or lose, than they had to forfeit from ignoring Larry Agran. In contrast, local editors told me that they could always find one of their reporters who was eager to cover any presidential candidate.

Close relationships with official sources may have encouraged the national media to define "major" candidates not only in relation to what party officials *believed*, but also in relation to what party officials *wanted*. After describing how "major" candidate status is determined, for example, Tom Rosenstiel (1992) implicitly suggested that the press plays along with party insiders' perspective on whose candidacies should be buried for strategic reasons. "This year, especially," he said, "the last thing the Democratic leaders want is to have attention paid to someone like Larry Agran, which would reinforce the impression that they are putting forward a 'field of unknowns.'" Thus, the national press seemed willing to play a role in protecting the credibility of the "major" candidates by not reporting on other candidates.[14]

National journalistic thinking about party insiders and the public also led to a particular type of response to voter discontent. When, for example, the *New York Times* wrote that George Bush has no "blueprints for the future" of the United States, and that he has little competition among the major presidential contenders or in Congress (Rosenbaum, 1992), this seemed to reflect fairly accurately the skepticism of the public. But public logic dictated that one solution should be that the mainstream media look beyond the typical political spotlight for new ideas. National journalistic logic suggested otherwise. The national journalists I spoke with seemed to see this sad state of affairs as a reason to protect the "insiders" even more. Indeed, in some interviews, journalists expressed willingness to reject the significance of a "outsider" candidate even if he won the election! Tom Rosenstiel told me: "One of the problems that people in D.C. see in the presidential primary season is that anyone can run. There's a body of thought among insiders, including the media, that this is not necessarily a good thing." He pointed to former President Jimmy Carter as an example of someone who was too much of an outsider to know how to govern the country effectively. He noted that there is a "divisiveness" that comes from candidates attacking and running against "the institutions that run the country." This view also seemed to underlie the hostility toward Jerry Brown that I heard among many national journalists—even as he was winning caucuses and primaries. So while the public was clearly demanding change, national journalists seem closely aligned, perhaps more fiercely than ever, with the status quo.

Ironically, within national journalistic logic, the public's anti-mainstream mood was even more of a reason not to give "undue coverage" to "fringe" candidates. While the national journalists I interviewed seemed very sensitive to the possibility that giving Agran coverage might unduly *boost* his campaign, they were hesitant to admit that not covering him might unduly hurt his campaign.[15] Much of what I heard echoed what ABC political director Hal Bruno was quoted as saying in a *USA Today* article on candidates who were excluded from debates and press coverage: "It's pathetic to think that's the only reason their campaigns are not taking off. Their campaigns are not taking off because no reasonable person can take them seriously" (Phillips, 1992).

Interpreting the Signs

Early in the campaign, Agran and his staff had believed that at some point local press attention would build into national exposure. But several reporters and editors at national newspapers and magazines with whom I spoke admitted that the longer one has not covered a candidate, the harder it becomes to do so. "It's very hard to change the narrative in midstream," said Elizabeth Kolbert (1993) at the *New York Times.* "Once the ball got rolling, it was very hard to cover him. The press would have to go back and explain who this guy was." Kolbert added that even if an individual reporter decided to file a major story on Agran, the editors would likely decide not to run it or to delay it beyond the point that it would have much impact. Similarly, Alvin Sanoff at *U.S. News & World Report,* told me "The obvious question in such situations is 'Where have you been that you just discovered this person?'" He also noted, "It's always safer to stay with the pack and be wrong, than to risk going out on a limb and covering someone who then turns out to not be that important" (Sanoff, 1992).

When something happened that in the eyes of public logic was an indication of Agran's strength, national journalists—hesitant to shift narratives— generally "reframed" the event to maintain the belief in Agran's marginality. When Larry Agran passed Jerry Brown in some polls, for example, public logic dictated that this was an indication of the legitimacy of the Agran campaign. Local journalists I spoke with also saw it as vindication of their respectful treatment of his candidacy. But the national journalists I spoke with saw it as something else: further proof of Brown's fringe status. "It's just one marginal candidate passing another marginal candidate," said Tom Rosenstiel of the *Los Angeles Times.* Even after Brown's surprise strength with the electorate, national journalists tended to maintain the same dismissive attitude. In a March *New York Times* story, for example, Jeffrey Schmalz (1992) reported that "Although Mr. Brown was widely applauded at a candidates' forum in Buffalo on Saturday, he was also lumped in with two lesser-known candidates. . . . That format meant that the forum was Bill Clinton versus three lesser lights, of whom one was Mr. Brown." The narrative that Agran had more than held his own in a forum with "major" candidates could not pierce through such journalistic constructions.

National journalists' reporting decisions also seemed consistent with the desire to hide from the public the arbitrariness of news judgments and the impact of such judgments on the general outcome of campaigns. This led them to stick with their initial decisions not to give much coverage to Agran, regardless of what happened later. (This may also explain why journalists felt they had to cover no-party candidate Ross Perot as soon as he even hinted that he might enter the race. Since billionaire Perot had the money to buy direct access to the public through the media, not covering him would make the public aware of the media as "censors." In contrast, true third-party candidates, such as Lenora Fulani of the New Alliance Party and Libertarian André Marrou, were virtually ignored by the news media and were excluded from the nationally televised debates.)

Where the Testing Ground Is

In what arena is the presidential campaign waged? This question seems to be answered somewhat differently by each of the coverage logics. Implicit in many public-logic comments I heard was concern with what the candidates would do once in the imagined space of the White House. The candidates' performances in the real space of local campaign events figured prominently in local journalistic logic. National journalistic logic, however, seemed to be focused on the campaign as experienced through the "shared national arena" of television.

The primacy of television in the national view of the campaign lent weight to criteria that made sense to commercial TV network executives, such as keeping the debates short so as not to lose too much commercial time, and limiting the debates to celebrity candidates and celebrity journalists in order to maximize ratings (and flow through to subsequent commercial programs). Bill Wheatley of NBC News told me that it was important to keep the number of participants to a minimum since "it is not realistic to expect a commercial network to put aside two to three hours for a debate" (Wheatley, 1992).

Beside the concerns of the institutions that control television, there is also a basic difference between television and newspapers as forms of communication: Television is a medium of "aura." On television, the gestures and expressions of candidates are often as important as, if not more important than, the words and ideas expressed (Meyrowitz, 1985, 1992a). Further, on TV, one's aura is blended with the aura of whoever else is in the same image. This characteristic apparently led to the cancellation of several TV debates, according to several off-the-record descriptions by debate organizers. One planned two-night format, which was to split the candidates into two groups of three at a New Hampshire college, ran into trouble because none of the other candidates wanted to be among the two chosen to blend their auras with Jerry Brown's. Another New Hampshire television debate was canceled when several candidates refused to be on the same set with Pat Buchanan. Similarly, the "major" candidates were apparently much more sensitive to being matched against "fringe" candidates on television than they were concerned about being mentioned in the same newspaper article with them. Further, on TV, the moderator's status and aura are affected by who else is there in a way that the print reporter's status is not affected by whom he or she interviews "off camera." As I was told by debate organizers, the "star" moderators for some of the television debates were also hesitant to lower their own status and the status of the event by including "minor" candidates.

The primacy of television in the national campaign could not help but interact with local journalistic logic and public logic as well. Local journalists told me that they felt less concern about missing an Agran campaign event, because, practically speaking, his exclusion from TV debates meant that "he wasn't going to make a difference," as editor Rod Doherty (1993) put it. And many voters I spoke with at Agran campaign events seemed torn between their enthusiasm for Agran and his policies and their concern about "throwing away" their vote on a candidate whose existence and ballot tallies were not even going to be featured on national television. The "news judgments" of national television journalists, then, can easily become self-fulfilling prophecies.

Coverage of "Minor" Candidates at Major Events

Perhaps the largest gap between national journalistic logic and the other two logics concerns the reporting on minor candidates at major events. Although many of the nonjournalist citizens I spoke with accepted that some candidates do and should receive more coverage than others, most of them were also shocked to learn that a candidate articulating serious positions would be censored from reports of events in which he participated, especially when he was received very well by those at the event. In contrast, almost all the national journalists I spoke with were shocked that anyone would be shocked by this (and a few of them even started yelling at me for being so naive and stupid as to ask about such a thing).

As mentioned above, when Agran participated in the Global Warming Leadership Forum in Tallahassee, Florida, the audience was much more enthusiastic about him than about a few of the "major" candidates. The "public logic" I encountered in speaking about this event with average citizens was that Agran's positive reception should have been widely reported. (Again, students at my university echoed the views I heard among many average citizens: 78 percent of the students I surveyed believed that the press had an obligation to report on any candidate who participated in a covered event, even if the press had not been routinely covering that candidate. Typical comments were: "It's our right to know—plain and simple". "It would not be ethical to exclude a candidate," "It's the reporter's job to report what happened"; "Otherwise the news is slanted"; and "How could they not?")[16] The public had a "let the best person win" philosophy and was hungry for "good ideas" regardless of the source.

Yet all the national news organizations covering the event omitted all mention of Agran's presence. Further, several journalists who did not cover it told me they would have omitted mentioning him had they covered it, regardless of his performance relative to that of the others.

The national journalists I spoke with saw all such events as symbolic of the national campaign, and regardless of what happened in that particular forum in that particular place, Agran was not viewed by them as a contender in the national arena. Their concern was not with ideas or with the public's reaction to ideas or with the winning of a local debate, but with "who can win the presidency."

On this issue, local journalistic logic was very close to public logic. All the local New Hampshire journalists I spoke with said that they felt an obligation to mention all the candidates who participated in a covered campaign event. Indeed, many grew angry at the thought of any journalist leaving out the presence of a candidate at a forum. April Jacobs, who reported on the campaign for the *Portsmouth Herald*, said that leaving out a mention of Agran at an event in which he had participated was "not only inaccurate but unfair" (Jacobs, 1993). Deena Ferguson, associate news editor at *Rockingham County Newspapers*, thought it was "amazing" that journalists could omit the participation of a candidate from their reports (Ferguson, 1993). *Union Leader* correspondent Jerry Miller (1993) echoed these concerns about fairness and accuracy. And *Foster's Daily Democrat* editor Rod Doherty (1993) said: "I see our reports as a historical record. . . . Deleting a candidate's presence is deleting a part of history."

Although the local journalists I interviewed were adamant about reporting on all candidates participating in an event—as a universal ethical principle—this aspect of local journalistic logic may be related to the "community events" focus mentioned above. Local reporters and editors described the event partly as a symbolic "national" event, but also as one that happened "in our town" in real space and time. (The logic seemed to be: "Had you gone downtown to place X, this is what you would have seen.") Local newspaper accounts therefore generally mentioned when Agran was at an event and summarized his views, but they, too, often focused primarily on the "major" candidates. Much of the local excitement, after all, was over the presence of nationally recognized figures.

The idea that the national press would suppress a story about a "minor" candidate outperforming "major" candidates was something else that made many members of the public with whom I spoke very angry. Public logic perceived the outsider who outdebated an insider as someone who represented them and their distaste for the same old system and business as usual. (Hollywood's emotional cliché of the little guy winning also seemed to work its power here.) But national journalistic logic held a different view: Of course an outsider can outperform party insiders, several journalists told me. This is because outsiders have an unfair advantage over insiders in that outsiders do not have to please so many diverse constituencies, and outsiders also have a smaller stake than insiders, since they do not have the potential nomination to lose. (This same sort of reasoning about the explosive power of a "loose cannon" was used by several of the national journalists I interviewed to dismiss any positive reactions to Jerry Brown's speeches and debate performances.) In any case, it did not matter to the national journalists how well "minor" candidates performed, since they could not win.

Implicit in many of the comments of the national journalists I interviewed was a concern that giving attention to Larry Agran because he had good ideas—while it made some surface sense in 1992—might create massive coverage problems in future campaigns by encouraging numerous candidates with good ideas, but no chance of winning, to enter the race. The national journalists seemed to think that good ideas were a lot easier to find than public logic suggested. *Time*'s Washington bureau chief, Stanley Cloud, echoed what national journalists told me when he offered the following comments on "Pozner and Donahue": "An election . . . is a debate among people who have a chance of being elected. It's not a free-for-all. . . . I have neighbors in the Democratic Party who I think have better ideas than any of the leading candidates . . . but they aren't running. Why? Because they have no following" (Feb. 14, 1992).

Within national journalistic logic, excluding the mention of Larry Agran from coverage of a campaign event was a service to readers. One national journalist told me off the record: "The press has a responsibility to its readers. It has to decide what information is valuable to them. The press is not simply a stenographer. If readers aren't satisfied, they'll go elsewhere."

Similarly, Chris Black, who reported on the presidential campaign for the *Boston Globe*, described how citizens have very little time to pay attention to the news. "If we gave the same amount of coverage to all candidates, then ultimately we'd be doing a disservice to our readers. . . . Our responsibility to readers is to get them as much news as possible about the candidates who are performing." Black added that "Ultimately, we're in the news business: Who is going to win; who is generating support; who is affecting the debate. It's not Civics 101. Our role is to report the *news*, not just 'information.' It's the difference between doing a small, information story on Larry Agran in December and covering the war between Clinton and Tsongas. News is about the struggle to win, and what the candidates are saying to win" (1994).[17]

Within national journalistic logic, burdening readers with details about someone who cannot win was an unnecessary distraction. With "major" candidates, the news media's focus on "who can win" led to reporting on clashes with rivals and on strategies for success. Since Agran was not seen as electable, however, the national journalists had no decisive clashes or relevant strategies on which to report. And so even when Agran was mentioned, his candidacy was generally reduced to a word or a phrase—"fringe," "dark horse," "obscure," 'long-shot'—all of which "responsibly" communicated the national media's view of him: "He can't win—so forget about him."

CONCLUSION

The 1992 U.S. presidential election stood out as one where opinion polls suggested an unprecedented level of voter dissatisfaction with politics-as-usual. Polls showed disenchantment with both parties and with all the so-called major candidates. Voters expressed the wish that other candidates had entered the race. The national press dutifully reported on these polls. But a truly responsive democratic press would go further. It would widen the spotlight beyond the center stage that is the subject of public discontent.

Yet many factors converged to exclude "new voices" such as Agran's from national press coverage. These included routines for allocating limited press resources, a large number of declared candidates, national journalists' reliance on official sources, a desire for prestige assignments, the primacy of television in the campaign, and the concern with hiding the arbitrary nature of earlier coverage decisions. Combined, these factors made it appear to national journalists that giving Larry Agran significant news coverage would be "nonobjective" reporting because it would give an unmerited stimulus to his hopeless campaign, while ignoring him would be consistent with "objective" journalism.

Bill Wheatley of NBC News is no doubt correct that such coverage patterns are not the result of a "conspiracy." No conspiracy is necessary to reach general consistency of thought and action if journalists come to the situation with similar training, follow similar routines, interact with the same sources and with each other, and monitor each other's news judgments.

The national journalists I spoke with may be right that public logic is based on unrealistic assumptions. Even if this is the case, however, national journalists may owe the public some "education" on this topic, including a more explicit admission of how their "news judgments" are made. There is clearly a gap between the logics that needs to be addressed. While national journalists made me feel that my questions about the Agran campaign coverage were naive, the vast majority of the members of the public I spoke with about this case are clearly troubled by national journalistic logic.[18]

This research focused on only one candidate in one campaign. Further, my study of public and local journalistic logic was restricted largely to New Hampshire. Additional research is clearly needed to reach definitive conclusions. But this preliminary analysis suggests that we currently have a relatively closed national news system that is only slightly sensitive to high degrees of public dissatisfaction with the current functioning of our political system and with so-called major candidates. One could certainly argue that a true democracy deserves—and requires—something better.

NOTES

1. The author wishes to thank Larry Agran, Stephen C. Smith, Kathleen Kendall, and Mike Kaspar for their research assistance and David Paletz, Jane Harrigan, and Peter Schmidt for their comments on earlier drafts. The research for this project was supported in part by a faculty fellowship from the Graduate School of the University of New Hampshire. The earliest version of this project appeared as a brief article, "The Press Rejects a Candidate," in *Columbia Journalism Review*, March/April 1992, pp. 46–48. I thank *CJR* editor Gloria Cooper for insisting that I write about what I was observing during the New Hampshire primaries and for allowing Maria Peralta, a *CJR* intern, to help with tracking down some of the sources for that article. A shorter version of this chapter appeared in 1994 in *Political Communication, 11*, 145–164.

2. For my study of local media coverage of the Agran campaign in New Hampshire, I relied on three sources: (a) my own clippings of articles and monitoring of TV and radio news; (b) Agran's campaign staff, who gave me access to their clipping file, the candidate's interview schedule, and the results of their own monitoring of TV and radio news; and (c) selected interviews with news organizations, when I had questions about their past coverage and future coverage plans. For my study of national media coverage of the Agran campaign, I relied on five sources: (a) my own clippings of articles and monitoring of TV news; (b) a Nexis search of all mentions of Larry Agran

from August 1991 to December 1992; (c) the Agran campaign staff, which gave me access to the materials they had; (d) selected interviews with news organizations; and (e) the clippings and TV/radio transcripts provided by the organizers of several campaign events. Through the combination of these methods, I believe I was able to review the vast majority of the significant discussions of Agran's campaign in local New Hampshire newspapers and in major national news media. Although I no doubt have missed at least some significant coverage, I found the patterns throughout the coverage that I did review sufficiently consistent to make me very comfortable with the examples and claims outlined in this analysis. Since many of the clippings I copied from the Agran clipping file had no page numbers, I have not been able to provide page numbers in all the references at the end of this chapter.

3. To address the frustration of shifting criteria, Agran, who is now director of CityVote (a project sponsored by the U.S. Conference of Mayors to develop a national urban presidential primary for the 1995–96 election cycle), has outlined a set of specific objective criteria for inclusion in presidential preference ballots and televised debates. They are available from CityVote Project Office, 14978 Sand Canyon Avenue, Suite A, Irvine, CA 92718.

4. A few days after Agran's appearance on the show, Peggy Robinson, senior producer for politics, wrote Agran a letter (which Agran's staff gave me a copy of) indicating that "we have certainly gotten a lot of positive feedback to the Agran/Mudd interview. . . . The phones were ringing . . . with people calling and asking where they could get more information." Robinson expressed pride over a radio talk show host's praising of the "NewsHour" for "not being 'gatekeepers' deciding who was a 'legitimate candidate' and who was not." But a few months later, when "MacNeil/Lehrer" held its own candidates' debate, Agran was excluded based on what executive producer Lester Crystal described to me as "general news judgment" (personal communication, Jan. 1992).

5. Brief references to the protest in the national media were easily lost amid the thousands of words on the official event. The final edition of the *Washington Post*, for example, carried a 130-word "Debate Postscript" story on the protest (Schwartz, 1992). The *Los Angeles Times* had 65 words on the protest toward the end of a 1,295-word story on the debates. I could find no reference to the protest in the *New York Times*. CNN Headline News made passing mention of a protest—without pictures—as a tag line about every fourth time it presented its report on the debate, well-illustrated with images from inside the studio. The *Los Angeles Times* did publish a 505-word story on the protest, but only in its local Orange County edition (Berkman, 1992), Agran's home base. Ironically, that article distorted the event in favor of Agran, by mentioning no other "minor" candidates and reporting that the hundreds of protesters were all there to complain about his exclusion.

6. See Smith (1992) for a relevant analysis of the "dramatic" versus "empirical" logic of campaign coverage. In pursuing a dramatic form of story-telling, notes Smith, journalists are not in the habit of looking for facts that contradict their preconceived narratives. Further, since dramatic logic in campaign coverage focuses on the mythical "quest" for the nomination by powerful "heroes," journalists are more likely to question the suitability of "major" candidates for the hero status than to look beyond the majors to a "minor" candidate such as Larry Agran.

7. In descending order, the signatures collected for ballot inclusion in New York State were: Bill Clinton, 48,281; Tom Harkin, 38,803; Larry Agran, 21,423; Jerry Brown, 19,413; Bob Kerrey, 20,685; Paul Tsongas, 13,952; and Eugene McCarthy, 10,666 (Michelle Schweda, Public Information Services, New York State Board of Elections, personal communication, Nov. 8, 1993).

8. Agran notes that his only crime was to speak, that he had a ticket to the event, and that he offered no resistance to the men who tackled him, who neither identified themselves nor told him he was under arrest.

9. Even when Agran did receive coverage for winning matching funds, the story "angle" was often not very flattering. The *Washington Post* referred to him as the "winless Democrat" who would have to be in New York at the time of the Democratic convention anyway, since he "faces criminal charges, from his arrest during a Democratic debate last month" ("Agran Nears Matching Fund Mark," 1992). *USA Today*'s brief coverage echoed the same themes.

10. Between August 1, 1991 and December 7, 1992, Agran was mentioned in 567 stories listed by Nexis (many of these were redundant references in similar stories in different editions of the same newspaper or different versions of the same wire release, or noncampaign stories from the Orange County edition of the *Los Angeles Times*). In contrast, during the same period, the number of citations for some of the other candidates were: 4,527 for Wilder, 7,025 for Kerrey, 7,615 for Harkin, 9,266 for Buchanan, 11,476 for Tsongas, and 14,288 for Brown. The search for Clinton citations was halted at 82,229.

11. At first, I simply thought of the national press as "being biased" against Agran. What moved me to the conception of these "logics" was that during interviews I would try to capture the perspectives of those I interviewed by summarizing and repeating back to them what I understood their views to be. In numerous instances I found *my* whole way of thinking about the issue of press coverage of campaigns shifting in gestalt-like fashion during these talks, and then shifting back again when I spoke with local journalists or members of the public.

12. Sixty-seven students in an undergraduate mass communication course completed the survey on October 20, 1993. "Significant" press coverage was defined as "enough to allow interested voters to find out the names and

positions of candidates through normal attention to the news media." Twelve percent of the students selected "some." Only two students (3%) chose "a select few." A similar survey I gave to twenty-eight students in a smaller class in analysis of news in September 1993 yielded comparable results, with a slightly greater call for inclusive coverage.

13. An interesting additional variable was mentioned by Chris Black of the *Boston Globe*. She noted that a major space problem had come about not from a decline in ad revenues, but from the graphic redesign of the paper, which now has larger type and shorter stories (which she attributed to television's impact on newspapers). "You can rarely take a story to 900 words. You file 700, and editors take off 200 and make it a 500-word story." "In 1980," Black said, "a reporter could write a 1200-word article on a candidate going nowhere, but now 200 words would be a lot." The result is that "you have to focus on the big guys" (Black, 1994).

14. See Smith, 1994, for a fascinating analysis of how Democratic National Committee strategy may have influenced the national news media and debate organizers in their decisions not to give coverage or extend debate invitations to Larry Agran.

15. Academics are often equally unwilling to admit the impact of their research on the topics explored. To be honest, therefore, I should point out that I was aware that my interviews with journalists might lead them to give more coverage to Larry Agran, and indeed in several instances that seems to have been the case. Further, my earliest article on this topic in *Columbia Journalism Review* (Meyrowitz, 1992) led to an article in the *Village Voice* on Agran's exclusion (Baker, 1992).

16. An additional 10 percent thought that the press had an obligation to cover a candidate in such circumstances "in most cases." The remaining 11 percent answered "it depends" (9%), "usually not" (1%), and "never" (1%). In the written explanations of their answers it became clear that the word "obligated" was taken by the sole "never" respondent to mean "legally required," which he/she thought was a violation of the First Amendment, but he/she added that the press, as "informers of the public," should cover the candidate; one of the "it depends" respondents said that the press should cover any candidate who played an active part in the event, but did not have to cover a candidate who was merely a spectator. Similarly, about five of the "in most cases" respondents gave explanations that suggested that the press should have covered Agran at such events. Recalculating for such explanations raises the "always" vote for the relevant events to 88 percent.

17. Although these quotes from Chris Black (1994) fall into what I characterize as "national journalistic logic," she was also quite critical of some aspects of national campaign journalism. She described many Washington-based campaign reporters as macho, locker-room "towel snappers," who write

to each other in a code that is not enlightening to the public, and she criticized their tendencies toward cynicism and pack journalism. She expressed more interest in speaking to voters than to party officials, and was more concerned with candidates' messages than most of the national journalists with whom I spoke. Her characterization of Agran was also unusual: "Larry was a serious candidate, but not a credible one"; that is, Agran was serious about his campaign but naive about his chances of having his particular message "catch fire" with New Hampshire voters. Interestingly, the split logic she expressed matched her own characterization of the nature of the *Boston Globe* as a newspaper between local and national: an influential regional newspaper that has major national impact during presidential campaigns because of its status as the closest major newspaper to the New Hampshire primary.

18. Again, students at my university echoed what I heard in casual conversations and correspondence with members of the public. When I gave a lecture summarizing this chapter to about ninety-five students at UNH, ninety of them offered a written reaction. Eighty-five of these, or 94 percent, expressed shock over Agran's campaign experiences and national journalists' explanations of their news judgments. One student wrote: "Things like this happen in communist dictatorships, but in America?" Another wrote: "Let the people decide who is electable." The others were in a similar vein, including descriptions such as awful, shocking, horrible, very wrong, unbelievably unfair, primitive and undemocratic, absurd, sickening, very disturbing, totally outrageous, absolutely horrid, intolerable, censorship, should be illegal, bizarre, makes me extremely angry, scary. Three students gave responses in support of "national journalistic logic." One student's response suggested that there ought to be set criteria for coverage. And one student said he/she was not surprised by what happened to Agran, but thought it was something that needed to be changed.

REFERENCES

Agran nears matching fund mark (1992, May 9). *Washington Post*, 4.

Agran, L. (1991, Aug. 22). The new American Security. An announcement of candidacy for the 1992 Democratic presidential nomination.

Agran, L. (1993, Nov.). Personal interview.

Aldrich, H. (1991, Oct. 16). Will anyone listen to Larry Agran? *Santa Fe Reporter*.

Alter, J. (1992, Feb.). Personal interview.

Baker, R. W. (1992, Mar. 24). Whodunit? How the press killed a candidate. *Village Voice*, 39.

Bennett, D. (1993, Jan.). Personal interview.

Berke, R. L. (1992, Jan. 24). Mayors appear unmoved by the major candidates. *New York Times*, A14.

Berkman, L. (1992, Jan. 20). Agran complains of exclusion. *Los Angeles Times* (Orange County ed.).

Black, C. (1994, Aug.). Personal interview.

Busted candidate (1992, Apr. 2). *Los Angeles Times.*

Clifford, T., and M. Kasindorf (1992, Mar. 22). Top two tangle at Buffalo debate. *Newsday*, 17.

Clinton rating falls in poll (1992, Jan. 27). *New York Times* (AP).

Clinton still making great strides in primary polls (1992, Jan. 1). *Foster's Daily Democrat* (AP).

Decker, C. (1992, Feb. 24). Democrats clash on farming and American Indian affairs. *Los Angeles Times*, 14.

Dennis, E. E. (1992, July). Personal communication.

Doherty, R. (1993, Oct.). Personal interview.

Drehle, D. V. (1992, Mar. 21). Clinton accuses Brown of opposing campaign donation limits 2 years ago. *Washington Post*, 21.

Endicott, W. (1991, Nov. 1). For president: Larry who? *Sacramento Bee.*

Ferguson, D. (1993, Oct.). Personal interview.

Field, T. (1991, Dec. 5). At least give Agran a chance to lose. *Portsmouth Press.*

Florman, C. (1992, Feb.). Personal interview.

Giago, T. (1992, Feb. 18). Vote for Agran in primary. *Lakota Times.*

He's out with the in-crowd (1992, Jan. 11). *Foster's Daily Democrat*, 8.

Hilyard, S. (1991, Dec. 19). Agran's struggle to get noticed. *Concord Monitor*, B1, B10.

How to caucus (1992, Feb. 20). *Casco Bay Weekly.*

Jacobs, A. (1993, Sept.). Personal interview.

Kincade, P. (1993, Oct.). Personal interview.

Kolbert. E. (1993, Mar.). Personal communication.

Lehigh, S. (1992a, Feb. 24). Kerrey and Harkin stand out on local issues, detail. *Boston Globe*, 14.

Lehigh, S. (1992b, Feb. 25). Larry Agran: "Winner" in debate with little chance for the big prize. *Boston Globe.*

McCarthy, C. (1992a, Feb. 1). What's minor about this candidate? *Washington Post*, 23.

McCarthy, C. (1992b, Feb.). Personal interview.

Mann, R. (1993, Nov.). Personal interview.

Merton, A. (1992, Jan. 5). Larry Agran deserves a place in Democratic primary debates. *Boston Sunday Globe* (New Hampshire Weekly section).

Meyrowitz, J. (1985). *No sense of place: The impact of electronic media on social behavior.* New York: Oxford University Press.

Meyrowitz, J. (1992a). The power of television news. *The World & I, 6* (7), 453–73.

Meyrowitz, J. (1992b, Mar.–Apr.). The press rejects a candidate. *Columbia Journalism Review,* 46–48.

Miller, J. (1991, Nov. 29). Agran resents campaign trail tolls. *Union Leader,* 4.

Miller, J. (1993, Nov.). Personal interview.

Nuclear Times's more or less nonpartisan guide to the race for the White House (1991–92, Winter). *Nuclear Times.*

150 in scuffle at auditorium (1992, Apr. 1). *New York Post.*

Parsons, D. (1991, Aug. 23). Larry scenario: Why Agran could be a primary figure. *Los Angeles Times* (Orange County ed.), B1, B12.

Phillips, L. (1992, Jan. 17). N.H. debate format denounced. *USA Today.*

Polls show Clinton ahead of president and the Democrats (1992, Jan. 24) *Union Leader* (AP).

The people aren't making this decision (1992, Jan. 29). *Rapid City Journal.*

Pritchard, C. (1992, Jan. 1). Larry Agran fights label as outsider. *Keene Sentinel.*

Rapsis, J. (1992, Jan. 20). Hundreds protest debate for "exclusionary politics." *Union Leader.*

Rosenbaum, D. E. (1992, Feb. 2). Missing from politics: The blueprints for the future. *New York Times,* E1, E2.

Rosenstiel, T. (1992, Feb.). Personal interview.

Rotch, W. B. (1991a, Sept. 11). Ideas, not names. *Milford Cabinet and Wilton Journal.*

Rotch, W. B. (1991b, Nov. 13). Whose ideas are best? *Milford Cabinet and Wilton Journal.*

Rotch, W. B. (1992a, Jan. 1). N.H. democracy. *Milford Cobinet and Wilton Journal.*

Rotch, W. B. (1992b, Jan. 15). Ideas, a campaign, and a faith in democracy. *Milford Cabinet and Wilton Journal.*

Sanoff, A. (1992, Feb.). Personal interview.

Schanberg, S. H. (1992, Mar. 27). A "minor candidate" worth a listen. *Newsday,* 53.

Schmalz, J. (1992, Mar. 23). Brown, in New York, assails Clinton with a new ferocity. *New York Times,* 1.

Schwartz, M. (1992, Jan. 21). Debate postscript. *Washington Post,* A8.

Smith, C. A. (1992). The Iowa caucuses and Super Tuesday primaries reconsidered: How untenable hypotheses enhance the campaign melodrama. *Presidential Studies Quarterly, 22,* 519–29.

Smith, S. C. (1994). Anyone can grow up to be president! (and other myths of the American presidential election process). *New Political Science, 28–29,* 7–29.

Toner, R. (1991, Sept. 8). Field of maybes is a spirit lifter for Democrats. *New York Times,* 1, 22.

Tuchman, G. (1978). *Making news: A study in the construction of reality.* New York: Free Press.

Unlock the process: People's Party should allow people's candidates a chance (1992, Jan. 9). *Portsmouth Press.*

Welcome to New Hampshire, Larry Agran (1991, Dec. 3). *Atlantic News.*

Wheatley, B. (1992, Feb.). Personal interview.

Willman, D. (1991a, Aug. 22). A long shot, Agran aims to fire away. *Los Angeles Times* (Orange County ed.), B1, B4.

Willman, D. (1991b, Aug. 23) Irvine ex-mayor to seek Democratic presidential nomination. *Los Angeles Times,* 46.

THREE

The Incumbent and His Challengers

The Problem of Adapting to Prevailing Conditions

JIMMIE D. TRENT AND JUDITH S. TRENT

While contemporary presidential campaigns and the subsequent election of one candidate over all others are too complex to suggest that any single element determines outcome, within the vortex of each presidential election cycle there are recurring factors that appear to have much to do with winning and losing. One such constant is that successful candidates either manipulate prevailing conditions by creating the rhetorical agenda (the environment and issues on which the campaign will focus) or they skillfully adapt their campaign communication to meet conditions or issues already in place. But they must do one or the other (or both) to win.

There are elections, of course, in which specific events or conditions are so dominant, so widespread, that candidates can do little other than attempt to adapt. The election of 1992 was one of those elections. Thus, the purpose of this chapter is to examine the ways in which the three major candidates employed or failed to employ the communication strategies typically available to incumbents and challengers as they attempted to adapt to the prevailing conditions. Ultimately, we will argue that one of the challengers, with help from the other, was successful in utilizing prevailing conditions to connect the incumbent president's failures with the dominant or prevailing issues of the campaign. In the interim, we will catalog previously described (Trent and Friedenberg, 1991; Trent and Trent, 1974) communication strategies of the incumbent, challenger, and incumbent/challenger styles as used by each candidate during the general election portion of the 1992 presidential campaign.

PREVAILING CONDITIONS AND THE STRATEGIES
OF THE PRESIDENT

Following the Gulf War in 1991, George Bush enjoyed a public approval rating of 91 percent and was considered to be unbeatable in his upcoming bid for reelection. The confidence of the president and his advisers was shared by many of the most often mentioned potential challengers as Democratic politicians lined up to declare that they would not be seeking the nomination in 1992. If Bush had been able to retain his Gulf hero approval rating, his 1992 campaign strategies might have been those of the typical incumbent. But that was not to be.

Serious problems faced the nation. Many investors all over the country had lost fortunes when savings and loans crashed. More bad news was threatened as reports of major banks being burdened with bad debts appeared frequently. After years of price increases, real estate values were dropping, especially in California. The early prosperity of the Reagan–Bush years had been accompanied by a quadrupling of the national debt to $4 trillion, disappearance of millions of jobs at all levels of industry, and the appearance of families living on the streets of America's major cities. "For those who were working, household incomes were stuck where they were in the earlier 70s!— and then only because the working wife had become an American norm" (Goldman and Mathews, 1992, 23).

These and other problems cut Bush's public support during the primary election as Democratic, independent, and even an articulate Republican challenger delivered daily messages of gloom to television audiences across the country. Still the president displayed no interest in domestic affairs and delayed beginning his campaign for reelection. "By mid-autumn his job approval rating had tumbled nearly 20 points in six weeks, and America's unhappiness with itself was rising toward levels unknown even in the darkest days of Richard Nixon or Jimmy Carter" (DeFrank, 1992d, 58). By the time the president launched his campaign, he had lost the support of the majority of the American public. A *New York Times*/CBS News poll taken June 17–20, 1992, showed that his approval ratings had dropped to what was then believed to be an all-time low of 34 percent, with only 9 percent believing that he had kept all or most of his 1988 campaign promises (Rosenthal and Brinkley, 1992, A1). A week later his approval rating declined another point to 33 percent, with only 28 percent indicating that they intended to vote for the President (Rosenthal, 1992e). A year earlier, the election appeared to be his for the taking. Now, as the general election campaign began, he had lost the presumption that an incumbent usually enjoys.

In addition to declining public approval ratings, the President began the fall campaign facing a condition that soon proved to be as troublesome as his polling numbers. As Reagan's heir, Bush was dependent on conservative support for reelection but he had never been the hero to bedrock conservative Republicans (Rosenthal and Brinkley, 1992). Just three years after his 1988 election to the presidency, Bush was accused of abandoning what conservatives saw as the "Reagan Revolution." In explaining why he was challenging the sitting president of his own party, Pat Buchanan told conservatives that the Reagan Revolution was over because "its inheritor had betrayed 'the most successful political movement of the second half of the 20th century'" with a record that was a "series of surrenders, from higher taxes to racial quotas" (Rogers, 1992, 62).

Although the Buchanan candidacy was relatively short-lived and he never won a primary, the attention he received from the media and the percentage of votes he garnered in the early primary contests made it apparent that the President had some vulnerabilities within his own party. In response, Bush felt it necessary to avoid even the appearance of anything that would further alienate Republican conservatives—all the way from keeping Dan Quayle on the ticket (even though many of his advisers believed the Vice President a handicap [DeFrank, 1992b]), to not considering solutions to problems that would involve raising taxes again or further increasing the national debt, to even appearing to soften his position on social welfare issues such as abortion to avoid once again irritating the Far Right. As a result, beginning with his nomination acceptance speech—an event for which the press built impossibly high expectations by saying it would have to be the "The Speech of His Life" (DeFrank, 1992b)—the sitting president was rhetorically constrained. Even had he had new and cogent views for solving the problems many Americans faced in 1992, he had to recognize that any articulation of them could add to conservative distrust.

The attempt to placate the most conservative Republicans was not left to abandoning centrist positions. The President and his staff also lost control of their own convention by allowing the right-wing ideologues to dominate the platform committee and determine who would speak and when. The result was four nights in which the overwhelming prime-time message broadcast was intolerance and negativism. It was as if America's problems began and ended with "the scarlet sins of liberals, lesbians, gays, Democrats, feminists, Congress, Greens, trial lawyers, single women who had babies, all women who aborted them—and at the head of their advancing columns, Bill and Hillary Clinton" (DeFrank, 1992b, 68).

Another factor that Bush had to face was the candidacy of Ross Perot. Although Perot was not in the race at the time of the Republican convention, the President's staff had already made efforts to combat him. Prior to Perot's July withdrawal, Bush had campaigned in Texas and California, normally Republican strongholds, in order to combat Perot's strength in those areas by attacking his positions on abortion rights and his opposition to Desert Storm (Toner, 1992). When Perot reentered the campaign in October, he was competing most strongly for the conservative voters on whom Bush felt dependent for reelection.

It is within these conditions that the Bush campaign needed to examine the strategies available to an incumbent seeking reelection.

Incumbent Strategies

Bush began the campaign in a vulnerable position. The public believed that the country was in the midst of a recession. Many were feeling personal economic stress and believed that the government should be taking steps to restore jobs and prosperity. Bush's vulnerability resulted from his conviction that the economy was basically healthy and would recover before November. While some of his advisers had urged him to focus on improving the economy following the Desert Storm victory when his public support was strong (Devroy, 1992a), he was listening to White House Chief of Staff John Sununu for domestic policy advice. And Sununu convinced him that action was unnecessary (Devroy, 1992a). Bush's denial that a problem existed left him vulnerable to a public conclusion that he had no plan for improvement and did not care about their problems. This would limit the strategies available to the President.

One avenue that Bush had available for regaining voter support was drawing strength from the prestige and power of the presidential office. Both symbolic and practical strategies that result from position and power are typically available to an incumbent president.

The President made use of each of the traditional symbolic strategies. Early in the campaign he attempted to use "the trappings of the office" to remind voters that they were seeing "the President" as opposed to just another politician. While the challengers were appearing on what Bush called "weird talk shows," the President granted a ninety-minute appearance on "CBS This Morning" in which he "sat among the flower beds and crab apple trees in the majestic Rose Garden, the colonnaded veranda of the Oval Office framing the shot" while taking "questions from 125 slightly bewildered tourists who had been plucked by CBS producers from the White House tour line" (Rosenthal, 1992f, A1). The tourists were impressed but Gary Baer, head of the Family Research Council, a conservative political organization, said that the television appearance seemed to crystallize what he believed was wrong with the Bush campaign. "This is a year when the trappings of the presidency are not enough to cause the President to win the election," Mr. Baer said. "He's got to come up with a more sharply defined program to offer broadly to the American people, and it just didn't strike me that the vision was there today" (Rosenthal, 1992f, A1). The perception that Bush lacked a plan for improving the economy restricted the efficacy of this strategy.

Bush also attempted to use the "legitimacy of the office," assuming the role of the president, the rightful heir to the office, the choice of the people, the one who had the legitimate right to lead; the office gave him that presumption but prevailing conditions were to reduce the effectiveness of this strategy as well. For some moderates, the perception created by the speeches of the Radical Right at the nominating convention was that Bush was not in control of the party. For the most conservative voters, Bush was perceived as undependable and they looked to others for leadership. The end of the cold war had allowed the public to direct attention to domestic policy and away from foreign affairs, the area in which Bush was viewed as presidential. George Bush legitimately viewed himself as The President but the effectiveness of the strategy was reduced by prevailing conditions.

In addition to symbolic strategies, Bush also employed pragmatic strategies in order to use the power of the office. He created pseudoevents, occurrences that differ from real events in that they are performed primarily in the hope that they will be favorably reported or reproduced. For one such event, he flew to Texas to promote a trade agreement with Mexico that he thought would win votes in that pivotal state, even though he realized it might hurt him in other parts of the country (Rosenthal, 1992b). On another occasion, he was prevented from creating a pseudoevent when the major networks refused to show his planned televised press conference by applying an infrequently used standard requiring the "potential for important news" before granting time for a presidential press conference ("Networks Shun Prime-Time Bid," 1992, A8).

Bush's use of another incumbent strategy, making presidential appointments, was limited. His most publicized use of the strategy was the appointment of his respected secretary of state, James Baker, as domestic policy czar in an attempt to restore public confidence in the economy and to emphasize his commitment to the economic well-being of the country. Less noted was his attempt to win the votes of conservative elements of the Republican Party by reminding voters that he had appointed many conservative judges to the federal courts.

Creating special task forces was the only incumbent strategy that Bush did not try to employ. He might have used it with some success, if, for example, he had appointed a blue-ribbon task force to study the economy. But that would have required an admission that something needed to be done, an activist position that prevailing conditions prohibited Bush from taking. He needed the conservative votes.

Bush did make extensive use of a traditional power of incumbents, allocating funds. Government contracts were granted in states where jobs were affected. And after the Florida hurricane, massive federal resources were promised to the disaster areas. "There is going to be one Santa Claus this season," said a GOP official, "and Baker is determined it will be Bush" (Devroy, 1992b, 11). Unfortunately for the President, aid for Florida apparently got tied up in the bureaucracy and many citizens felt betrayed by the time it arrived.

Because the successes of Bush's administration were in foreign policy, the strategy of consulting with world leaders was a natural for focusing voter attention on his strength, legitimacy, competence, and international popularity. It worked that way sometimes but not always. For example, an October meeting on trade policy "gave Mr. Bush a chance to bask in the praise of two colleagues, President Carlos Salinas de Gortary of Mexico and Prime Minister Brian Mulroney of Canada. In public remarks, Mr. Mulroney told Mr. Bush that the trade agreement would have been impossible 'without your compelling vision of the Americas as a hemisphere of prosperity built on cooperation'" (Rosenthal, 1992b, A12). The strategy, however, turned out to be only partially beneficial because Clinton and Perot later made an issue of the agreement when they talked with American workers.

The President's earlier attempts at using the strategy were even less successful. In June, the *New York Times* reported, "with a series of foreign policy events beginning with last week's trip to Panama and Rio de Janeiro, the Bush campaign hoped to highlight his image as a steady commander-in-chief. Last week's trip was less than triumphant, beginning with near tear-gassing of Mr. Bush in Panama" (Toner, 1992, A1).

After a meeting with Russian President Boris Yeltsin, Bush complained about the lack of effect on public opinion: "We had Yeltsin standing here in the Rose Garden, and we entered into a deal to eliminate the biggest and most threatening intercontinental ballistic missiles—the SS-18 of the Soviet Union—and it was almost 'Ho-Hum, What have you done for me recently'" (Rosenthal, 1992e, A10). The Russian threat was just not as salient and believable as it had been in recent years.

In addition to using the fund-granting power of the presidency, Bush used the decision-making powers of the office in a search for votes. He approved the sale of F-15 fighters to Saudi Arabia in time to announce it to defense workers in Missouri (Devroy, 1992b), signed a bill making car jacking a federal crime (Rosenthal, 1992a), announced to farmers a complicated plan for using corn-based ethanol fuel as an antidote for urban smog (Tyson, 1992), vetoed a bill that would regulate cable prices, saying that it benefited special interests rather than the public (Andrews, 1992), and proposed a $2 billion-a-year package of new and retooled training programs that he said could be paid for without new taxes.

In addition to using the powers of the office, the President attempted to change the public perception of his presidency through emphasizing his accomplishments and manipulating perception of domestic affairs.

Incumbents have to run on their records and the strategy of emphasizing accomplishments is important to them. Bush emphasized his foreign and domestic accomplishments. The President took credit for many of the events that happened in the world during his term of office, including the end of the cold war (Rosenthal, 1992c). In discussing his foreign policy accomplishments he said:

> Germany was unified. Central America was transformed through a policy based on free elections and reconciliation. The Soviet Union was dissolved peacefully and groundbreaking arms control agreements were reached. Iraq was defeated after the United States assembled an unprecedented international coalition to prosecute the war, opening the way for peace talks among the Arabs, Palestines, and Israelis. (Devroy, 1992a, A1)

The President listed his accomplishments on the domestic front as "an education program that sets general goals for local schools to reach by the century's end," and the various congressional ideas he had endorsed and believed he had helped shape, such as child care, air pollution, and the rights of the disabled. For conservative voters, he cited his appointment of conservative judges to the federal bench (Rosenthal and Brinkley, 1992).

Domestic policy was not the President's forte. He much preferred working with foreign policy where he could make things happen without congressional approval. As one reporter put it, "The world was Bush's oyster. Mention domestic policy, one pal said, and his eyes would glaze over; his people learned not to schedule meetings on the subject later than, say, 2:30 or 3, when there were always excuses for him to play hooky" (Goldman and Mathews, 1992, 22).

But what Bush claimed as his greatest accomplishment, the ending of the threat of the Soviet Union, was to be his downfall. Without that threat, the importance of foreign policy was diminished in voters' eyes. They wanted a solution to domestic problems and they did not feel the president was interested, that he "neither understood nor cared about their travail" (Goldman and Mathews, 1992, 21). As Sig Rogich, director of Bush's reelection campaign advertising, noted, "We ran away from our strength [in Bush's record as president] because focus groups told us they didn't want to hear anything about international [issues]" (Devlin, 1993, 282).

Instead of presenting an activist domestic program, Bush turned to the strategy of manipulation of important domestic issues. Early in the campaign, he attempted to persuade voters that the economy was not in bad shape and that it would improve. In July, he told a group of agricultural journalists that the economy was doing better than generally recognized and attacked opposition candidates who disputed it: "There is a gap between reality and perception, and part of my job when I do get into the campaign mode is to try to close the gap and be sure that we are judged on reality, not on these erroneous perceptions that are being portrayed by the, in the, [stet] political process. Get it" (Rosenthal, 1992e. A10).

Late in the campaign, with the perceived state of the economy still damaging his chances and appeasement of conservatives preventing proposals for positive actions, Bush attempted to persuade voters that a 2.7 percent increase in the gross national product "undermined . . . Clinton's campaign for change," and he presented the news as evidence to allay voters' doubts about his own stewardship. He said, "Two-point-seven percent is darn good growth and it pulls the rug out from under Mr. Clinton, who's telling everybody how horrible everything is" (Rosenthal, 1992d, A8).

Presidents typically have the option of using the strategy of interpreting or intensifying a foreign policy problem so that it becomes an international crisis. It appeared that Bush had this strategy available also. Foreign policy was the President's strength. He had, after all, "skillfully supported Mikhail Gorbachev in the dissolution of the Soviet Empire and Helmut Kohl in forging German unification." He had pushed the Arabs and Israelis into direct negotiation, advocated freer trade positions, and—perhaps most important for the campaign, if not for history—had "brilliantly stitched together the alliance against Saddam Hussein" (Wines, 1992a, A17).

But his strength was also his weakness. As he had noted with frustration after the Rose Garden meeting with Yeltsin, the public did not seem to care (Rosenthal, 1992e). With the threat of the cold war gone, the public had turned its attention to domestic affairs.

Incumbent/Challenger Strategies

As the campaign drifted toward Election Day, Bush finally caught fire. He abandoned the strategies common to an incumbent, recognized that he did not have the presumption of victory, assumed the role of the challenger, and attacked. According to an aide cited during the last week of October: "The prospect that Mr. Clinton, his opposite on deeply felt issues of military service and economic policy, may actually take away his job has the President both alarmed and angry. . . . He finally looked into the abyss and said 'Whew'" (Wines, 1992b, A11).

On a two-day train trip through the South, Bush began his direct attack with charges that Clinton "could not be trusted with the White House," "had a pattern of deception," "would raise taxes on working men and women," and had "a vast difference in philosophy, in approach to this great country of ours." He compared his record with that of Clinton's as the governor of Arkansas:

I've got to put it in perspective, . . . Arkansas rates 50th in the quality of environmental initiatives, 50th in the percentage of adults with college degrees, 50th in per capita spending on criminal justice, 49th in per capita spending on police protection. And Governor Clinton said the other night, "I want to do for the country what I've done for Arkansas. We cannot let him do that. (Wines, 1992b).

This material also formed the central message of the President's television advertising during the last week of the campaign.

As Bush warmed to the attack, he called vice presidential candidate Gore the "ozone man, a reference to Gore's environmental stands" (Wines, 1992b, A1). And in Detroit, just nine days before the election, he accused Clinton "of being soft on crime" and presented statistics suggesting that violent crime had increased in Arkansas during Clinton's years as governor (Rosenthal, 1992a).

With the President's attack, Clinton began to drop in the public opinion polls. However, by October 26, polls indicated that while Bush was succeeding at lowering Clinton's support, Perot, rather than the President, was benefiting from it. Thus, for a few hours in Denver, Bush switched to a positive approach appropriating "ideas from each of his rivals: . . . Clinton's cultivated image of compassion and reform, and . . . Perot's themes of efficiency and can-do American capitalism" (Rosenthal, 1992c, A1):

The real choice is not between activism and passivity, . . . the real choice is between a liberal activist government that seeks to impose solutions on individuals, families and the private sector, and a conservative activist government that gives individuals, families and business the means to make their own choices through competition and economic opportunity. (Rosenthal, 1992c, A1)

Bush returned to the symbolic strategies of legitimacy and competence:

When you enter that voting booth, ask yourself three common sense questions: Who has the right vision for America's future? Who can get us from here to there? And which character has the character? And who would you trust with your family or with the United States of America in a crisis? (Rosenthal, 1992c, A11)

But the positive approach did not last. By afternoon, the President was in Albuquerque ridiculing Clinton's confusion about the names of military missiles. He emphasized the issues of trust and taxes. "You couldn't trust Clinton's work, Bush argued everywhere, on taxes or anything else; he called it a *pattern*, a habit of deceit, and it seemed at last to be clicking" (DeFrank, 1992c, 93).

Less than a week before the election, with the polls showing Bush and Clinton in a dead heat, Bush had his own trust problem thrust on him when "Special Prosecutor Lawrence Walsh released a revised indictment of former Defense secretary Caspar Weinberger that once again raised questions about what Bush, as Vice President, knew about the arms-for-hostages deal" with Iran (Keen, 1992, 3A). Bush had always denied that he knew about any deal and the indictment called his truthfulness into question. So he dismissed the indictment as a "political ambush" and picked up his attacks on what he called "Slick Willie's" duplicity.

That the sitting president of the United States found it necessary to abandon the traditional strategies of incumbency and move to the dominant mode of the challenger represented another effort to adapt to prevailing conditions.

Adaptation to Prevailing Conditions: Bush

As Bush began his campaign he had both the power and the problems of his presidency. The power available for use consisted of the strategies resulting from occupying the office and the pragmatic strategies available from use of the authority granted to the office. The most serious problems confronting him were the perceived and actual troubles in the nation's economy, his dependence on the shaky support of the right wing of his party, and later the challenge of Perot for conservative support, all of which restricted his flexibility in proposing plans to improve the economy. Somehow, he had to use the strategies of incumbency to persuade voters that, in spite of the problems, he provided the best chance the nation had for regaining prosperity.

Thus, the President employed each of the strategies that resulted from the occupancy of the office (symbolic trappings, legitimacy, and competency), but with varying degrees of success. Their effect on his popularity was minimal or nonexistent. In addition, he used all but one of the pragmatic strategies of incumbency, but they, too, appeared to have little effect on voters' judgments. Pseudoevents were largely ignored by the public or refused publicly by the media. Bush appropriated federal funds for projects in selected geographical areas but the effect seemed to be limited to those regions. His accomplishments were centered in foreign affairs, but with the collapse of the Soviet Union the public's attention was focused on the country's economic woes. Thus, his meetings with world leaders added little to his credibility. Late in the campaign he tried to manipulate perceptions of domestic issues through citing small gains in the economy but it was too little too late and the public no longer believed him.

Tied to what was perceived to be a failing economy, restrained by his conservative supporters, and with incumbent strategies not working, the

President had no recourse except to abandon any "above the battle" posture for the incumbent/challenger attack strategies. In a desperate effort to increase his comparative status by reducing the viability of his opponents, he attacked, using sarcasm, name calling, and accusations in addition to issue attacks. It was the only strategy that worked in terms of raising his standing in public opinion polls.

PREVAILING CONDITIONS AND THE STRATEGIES OF THE CHALLENGER: CLINTON

One of the conditions that faced the Democratic Party challenger, Arkansas Governor Bill Clinton, was that, from the New Hampshire primary onward, it had become clear that the level of involvement desired by the public in 1992 was greater than in previous presidential campaigns. The public mood, "which usually ranges from boredom to mild disdain in election years, was different. . . . It was dead serious" (Klein, 1992, p. 14). A Gallup poll indicated that record numbers of people said they were giving a lot of thought to the election; the ratings of television talk shows rose dramatically when one of the candidates was a guest answering viewers' questions; and everywhere across the nation "the talk was of Ross and George and Bill" (Klein, 1992, p. 14). Although television advertising, opinion polls and pollsters, strategists, and negative campaigning were all part of 1992, they were not the major factor they had been in the 1988 presidential campaign. What had dominated the primaries was voters' insistence that they talk directly with the candidates, let them know their problems, hopes, and fears, and hear candidates' explanations of how they would solve the nation's problems, particularly economic problems. It was, in short, a milieu that required a more personal approach to campaigning, a style that did not appear contrived or manipulated, a milieu that called for interpersonal interaction between ordinary people and the men who sought the presidency, and a milieu that demanded that the candidates stop and listen to voters and actively participate in a dialogue about the nation's problems and voters' feelings of uneasiness and uncertainty.

A second factor within which Clinton had to determine the overall strategy of his challenge was that the administration he sought to overthrow had been effective in attacking previous Democratic candidates during the twelve years Republicans were in power. During those years, two Republican presidents and numerous Republican congressional leaders had been remarkably successful in persuading the electorate that "liberal" was a negative word, that candidates who were liberals were to be feared, and that to be a Democrat was to be a liberal. Both Reagan and Bush, for example, had been able to label their three opponents (President Carter and Democratic nominees Walter Mondale and Michael Dukakis) not only as "tax-and-spend" Democrats but as liberals who were the candidates of fringe groups—people outside the mainstream of traditional American values. Clinton, however, had positioned himself as neither liberal nor a conservative.

Another of the conditions Clinton had to face as the general election campaign began was his status as the first person to run for president who had tried to avoid being drafted during the Vietnam War. The issue surfaced during the New Hampshire primary and never really "faded away," in part because the Governor's failure to remember the exact chronology of his actions during that period added to the so-called character issue and in part because he never had served in the military. The problem was compounded by George Bush's record as a military hero during World War II.

The final prevailing condition to which Clinton had to adapt was the simple fact that by the time the fall campaign was underway, he was not the only challenger. True, he was the candidate of one of the two major parties but he was not the "only game in town." In fact, not only was there a rival challenger, but the rival was attracting media attention and public support by attacking him, and could potentially siphon anti-Bush votes, causing the election to be settled by the House of Representatives.

Other prevailing conditions created opportunities for Clinton instead of restricting him. Bush's prevailing conditions, public frustration with problems in the economy, and conservative limitations on the President's ability to propose a plan to correct problems created opportunities for Clinton. Also, the fact that conservative Republican presidents had controlled the White House for twelve years created a natural situation for a call to change.

Thus, as the Governor of Arkansas adapted the classic communication strategies typically associated with the challenger, he had to do so within confines imposed on his campaign by prevailing conditions.

Challenger Strategies

As Clinton began the fall campaign, he had five tasks necessitated by prevailing conditions. He needed to retain and utilize the personal style he had demonstrated in the primaries, to make contact with people and let them know he cared about their problems. Clinton also needed to eliminate or neutralize the character issue, to persuade the public that he was the candidate who could be trusted to lead the nation out of its problems. Moreover, because previous elections had demonstrated the force of Republican accusations that Democrats are tax-and-spend liberals, he had to retain and emphasize his moderate stance under attack conditions. In addition, the Governor had to limit the number of votes that he would lose to Perot even as he was using the Texan to draw support away from the President. Finally, he had to focus public attention and concern on the perceived failures of Bush's leadership. To meet these goals, he used the traditional challenger strategies.

Public interest in having personal contact with candidates fit well into Clinton's preferred campaign style. Always comfortable talking and listening to people, the Democratic challenger provided opportunities for victims of a troubled economy to personally tell him about their circumstances during the Clinton–Gore bus tours and countless radio and television call-in shows.

The strategy of attacking the record of opponents is used by every challenger. Clinton used it extensively. He attacked Bush on his domestic and foreign policy and attacked the President personally. Although he attacked on many issues, he concentrated on challenging Bush's leadership and concern for people. His attacks focused public attention and concern on the ineffectiveness of Bush's leadership and questioned his desire to solve the nation's problems.

On the domestic front, Clinton charged Bush with a failed economic policy and said the President had offered no plan to improve conditions. "Unlike our competitors, America has no natural economic strategy," he told employees in a manufacturing plant in Oregon. "Instead we have a series of unconnected, piecemeal efforts, and trickle-down economics. Under trickle-down economics, our manufacturing strength has trickled away" ("Clinton Hits Hard on Jobs, Economy" 1992). He told another audience that "if you look at the last 12 years, we now have a chance to assess whether the theory has worked. In 1980, we had the highest wages in the world. Now we are 13th and dropping" ("Excerpts from Clinton Speech to National Guard," 1992). He criticized the administration for failing to do enough to improve education, reduce crime, and support the family values that Republicans claimed to prize, and concluded by saying, "If this administration believed in family values, why do they keep us out of step with the rest of the world?" (Ifill, 1992a)

In September, Clinton's television advertising team began using negative commercials to attack the President. The first one showed "Bush as unconcerned about the economy and . . . earlier footage of him denying that the country was in a recession" (Wines, 1992b, A11).

Foreign policy was supposed to be Bush's strength but both Clinton and Gore attacked administration policies and practices. On Iraq, Clinton said, "President Bush showered government-backed grain credits and high technology on a regime that had used poison gas on its own people. After the war, Mr. Bush encouraged the Iraqi people to revolt against Saddam Hussein but then abandoned them" ("Excerpts from Speech by Clinton on US Roles," 1992). Gore said "if Bush and Quayle are such whizzes [at foreign policy], why is it that Saddam Hussein is thumbing his nose at the entire world?" And Clinton demanded that "Bush explain why he pursued strategies in the Persian Gulf War that left Saddam Hussein in power" ("Clinton Fires Back,"

1992). Clinton also attacked administration trade policy by saying "On Sunday, we learned that when George Bush said that he wanted to be an export superpower, he means exporting factories and jobs—not products and services" ("Clinton Rips Bush for Exporting Jobs," 1992).

Clinton concentrated his personal attacks on Bush's veracity and trustworthiness. After the President's nomination speech, Clinton said he could not be trusted. "We've heard it all before. We've seen it all before. It's 'read-my-lips' time all over again. Except this time we can read the record" ("Clinton: Don't Trust Bush's Lips," 1992).

When Clinton attacked Bush's effectiveness, he strengthened public concern about the President's ability to solve the nation's problems. When he tied the attacks to challenge Bush's truthfulness on taxes and Iran Contra with charges that Bush lacked sensitivity and caring about the economic problems people were facing, he was clearly attempting to create doubts about the character of the President. The President was concentrating attacks on Clinton's character, but Clinton's character attacks related to prevailing conditions while Bush's attacks had their base in events alleged to have occurred years previously.

Clinton also had to retain his image as a moderate while being accused daily of being a typical Democratic Party liberal. He knew that he would be attacked as a "liberal," as had been the presidential candidate of the Democratic Party in each of the three previous elections. Thus he employed three challenger strategies to establish himself as a new kind of Democrat.

The first was taking the offensive on issues. The strategy supported his moderate claims and also helped distinguish his position from the President's. Clinton's use of this strategy started with establishing the central difference between the President and himself. Bush believed that noninterference was the best plan for dealing with the economy, that if the market were allowed to flow without government intervention it would soon recover on its own while Clinton believed an active government role in promoting and sustaining the economy was necessary to compete successfully with other industrialized countries. In explaining the contrast to a public suffering from the recession, Clinton accepted a burden usually placed on the incumbent, that of presenting and defending a plan. Although it was not without risks, no other avenue could have accentuated the difference in the candidates' approaches as well. In a speech before the United States Conference of Mayors in June, Clinton introduced his economic plan: "Putting America First" (Kelly, 1992a).

Later in the campaign, he used the plan as a springboard to defend his moderate position. For example, when speaking to the Urban League, he positioned his economic plan in the philosophical middle and identified it with the league's proposal: "Your plan and my plan—let us be clear—do not involve liberal versus conservative, left versus right, big government versus little government" (Ifill, 1992c, A9). He then sharpened the distinction with an attack: "People try to put on yesterday's broken record that sticks in the same old place in the song. . . . 'Tax-and-spend, tax-and-spend, tax-and-spend.' And then they have their handlers push the arm a little further. It sticks again and goes, 'Liberal, liberal, liberal'" (Ifill, 1992c, A9). Both the attack and taking the offensive position on issues were combined with another typical challenger strategy: appearing to represent the philosophical center of the party.

Clinton had been an early participant in the Democratic Leadership Council, an organization of Democratic officeholders who believed that the Party must take a centrist position if it were ever to regain control of the presidency. Consistent with the views of that organization, Clinton often seemed to be on all sides of every issue. As one columnist summarized his position:

> If a man is known by the company he keeps, Bill Clinton is clearly a left leaning liberal. Also, a right-leaning moderate. In foreign policy he is United Nations multinationalist and an America-first interventionist. . . . Mr. Clinton is, as he likes to say, "pro-business and pro-labor," "for economic growth and for protecting the environment," "for affirmative action but against quotas," for keeping abortion legal and also for "making it as rare as possible." . . . The candidate, his advisors and his supporters all argue that this sort of amorphous talk is a result of an intellectually honest search for answers that avoid the polarization that has come to characterize national debate. (Kelly, 1992, A1)

While assuming the middle and all sides of an issue appears to have been chosen as campaign strategy, there is some evidence that the positions were not adaptations created for the campaign. For example, political scientist Seymour Martin Lipset reported that research which involved examination of tapes of Clinton's speeches given during the last decade revealed that "Clinton was repeatedly reiterating positions that he has taken for years; that tapes of Clinton's speeches of five or ten years ago could have been used in the 1992 campaign. The tone, the ideology were the same." Lipset concluded, "Those who accuse him of pandering or shifting his position on issues in order to get votes today are wrong" ("The Significance of the 1992 Election," 1993, 7).

Clinton also used the challenger strategy of speaking to traditional values as both a defensive and an offensive weapon. He defended against direct attacks from Bush by saying, "I think the implication he has made that somehow Democrats are godless is deeply offensive to me . . . and to a lot of us who cherish our religious convictions and also respect America's tradition of religious diversity" (Nichols, 1992, A5).

Clinton and Gore used their bus tours to, as *Newsweek* reported, "help transform the Democrats into a party representing the most bedrock of American values" (Klein, 1992, 33). The pseudoevent of Bill, Hillary, Al, and Tipper traveling through the small towns of America, stopping wherever they found a crowd, shaking hands and listening to individual accounts of hardship because of the economic downturn, formed a bedrock demonstration of care for traditional American values while satisfying public demand to have contact with the candidate.

The presence of a second challenger in the race posed a different problem. Clinton benefited from having Perot in the campaign when Perot attacked the Reagan/Bush presidencies and emphasized budget deficits. Perot's attacks on Bush reduced support for the President, but Clinton was powerless to do anything but watch when voters turned away from the president and toward Perot. On the other hand, polls did not show Perot as a serious threat in terms of receiving a significant number of electoral votes. Clinton could reasonably assume that many of Perot's votes would come to him at election time if there were a real threat of the President being reelected. However, if he attacked, the Texan's supporters might leave the Governor and turn to the President. Clinton's adjustment to this condition was to attack Bush and avoid alienating Perot supporters.

Adaptation to Prevailing Conditions: Clinton

Clinton continued the personal style of campaigning that he had used during the primary period. During the general election, however, he had the added advantage of a physically attractive, politically moderate vice president on the ticket. The youthful candidates and their wives became the representatives of change as they campaigned together on the media-oriented bus tours.

For those who believed Republican charges against Clinton's character, there was little that could be done beyond the denials and explanations already attempted. The only option left was to neutralize the negative impact on his own candidacy by increasing the President's negatives. The strategy was, in other words, to redirect the issue of character to areas of Bush's vulnerabilities. Accordingly, Clinton began publicly questioning the President's trustworthiness because of his broken pledge not to raise taxes and his denial of knowledge about the Iran Contra scandal. He challenged Bush's values by charging that the President had failed to even recognize the existence of economic problems and did not care that people suffered. In addition to maintaining and emphasizing the problems that already had reduced the President's popularity among voters, the attacks on Bush's character were especially effective because the issues were salient to the public as contrasted with Republican allegations about Clinton's actions years earlier.

Recognizing the success of charges of liberalism against previous Democratic candidates, Clinton countered with the presentation of plans that did not appear to be to the left of center, emphasized his own leadership as a moderate in the philosophical center of the party, and spoke to traditional values. Each of the three strategies was combined with use of the attack strategy. Clinton's moderate offensive positions not only undercut the President's charges of liberalism; they also challenged Bush's leadership as representing the radical conservatives who did not care about people's problems.

The presence of Perot in the race as a second challenger benefited Clinton when Perot attacked Bush on the economy and the deficit. Perot also gave conservatives who would not have voted for Clinton anyway an alternative to Bush. Perot was a potential threat to Clinton but polls indicated that he was not going to win any electoral votes. Also, some voters could be expected to turn to Clinton at election time if they thought their vote would be wasted on Perot. Faced with the possibility that an attack might alienate Perot voters, Clinton chose not to challenge Perot.

PREVAILING CONDITIONS AND THE STRATEGIES
OF THE CHALLENGER: PEROT

Ross Perot reentered the presidential race in October and faced problems that have met all candidates who have not been a nominee of a major political party. No independent candidate has ever come close to winning. The most successful was Theodore Roosevelt, who won six states in the 1912 presidential campaign. In fact, if all the electoral votes cast for all the independent candidates in this century were added together, the total would still be far short of the 270 required for election (Cook, 1992).

Independent candidates start with several obstacles. They suffer from a "can't win syndrome" (Cook, 1992). Typically, independent candidates do not have the resources of the party (human, financial, technological, and organizational) possessed by their opponents and, in addition, the total resources of both the Democratic and Republican parties may be used in opposition.

But Ross Perot was not a typical candidate. No billionaire had ever run for president before. Perot pledged to spend "whatever it takes" and by not accepting public financing, he was free to spend unlimited amounts of his money (Cook, 1992). And he was not without organization. Prior to his withdrawal from the race, he had millions of supporters who had paid $5.00 to join "United We Stand" and had signed petitions to place him on the ballot in all fifty states. In addition, unlike most independent candidates, Perot had not previously been defeated in primary races. In fact, he had never run for an elective office and therefore did not have a political history that could be used against him. His supporters received him not as a politician but as "can do" businessman.

Traditionally, the supporters of independent candidates "have come from the fringes—either the left wing of the GOP, such as Robert LaFollette (1924) and John Anderson (1980), or the Southern-based right wing of the Democratic Party, such as Strom Thurmond (the States Rights nominee) in 1948 . . ." (Cook, 1992, 9). But as John Carlson, a former communications director for the Washington State Republican Party, said, "The people who support Ross Perot are not the type you would usually associate with a third party. . . . He's the first presidential candidate that I've ever seen that is supported by normal people" (Cook, 1992, 9).

If Perot did not have all the problems faced by previous independent candidates, he had two that others have not had. First, he had lost credibility by pulling out of the presidential race in July. Not only had some of his supporters changed their allegiance to one of the other candidates; there was also a lingering undercurrent of distrust among many who would have voted for him before the withdrawal. People reasonably wondered if he would pull out again if the going got tough.

Second, Perot was forced to deal with the problems imposed by the running mate he had selected earlier. During the first Perot campaign, when the major task was getting his name on every state ballot, he selected retired Vice Admiral James Stockdale to be his vice presidential running mate. Perot had intended to replace Stockdale before the fall campaign began. However, when he pulled out of the race in July and did not reenter until October, he had lost the time necessary to replace the vice admiral. Neither well-known nor experienced in politics, Stockdale not only added nothing to Perot's campaign but detracted from it, particularly with his performance in the vice presidential debates.

Thus, as Perot reentered the race, his task was formidable. He had to defeat both an incumbent and a challenger and had to convince voters that his cause was not hopeless, that he could win. His assets were committed supporters, virtually unlimited financial resources, and an image as a successful businessman, someone who would know how to "fix" the nation's troubled economy. And while he used his assets to become a significant candidate, the strategies he chose were those of the traditional challenger.

Although Perot attacked both Clinton and Bush repeatedly, his most prominent attack was his discussion of the deficit, complete with charts that he reportedly made himself. Using his personal wealth to bankroll half-hour nationwide television appearances, Perot systematically explained the amount and seriousness of the growth in the nation's debt during the Reagan/Bush administrations.

Perot was also known for ad homonyms phrased in colorful, memorable terms. He hit Clinton in an infomercial, "Deep Voodoo, Chicken Feathers and the American Dream," saying "Arkansas' poultry industry is no model for job development: chickens keep on clucking and the people keep on plucking after 12 years of Governor Clinton's leadership" (Howlett, 1992, 3A). He accused Bush of "ignoring the nation's deepening debt troubles . . . and not acting to halt the savings and loan crisis while overseeing regulation of the industry as vice president" (Hayes, 1992, A10). He attacked Bush's record on the Persian Gulf war:

> Well, my position is if you don' t like guys like Saddam Hussein—and obviously the President didn't at the end—don't spend 10 years and billions of dollars of American taxpayers' money creating him, which Vice President George Bush did. There's a long, clear record. . . . Vice President and President Bush made Saddam Hussein what he is today. Now I' m going to charge that off to an honest mistake. Then on July 25 they told Ambassador Glaspie to tell him he could take the northern part of Kuwait—now that's a mistake too—and then he took the whole thing. Then they got upset and the rest is history. (Cook, 1992)

Although Perot was often accused of attacking without presenting solutions during the period before he dropped out of the race (February to July), he presented a plan for restoring the nation's economic health after he returned in October. The plan included higher income taxes for the rich, a 50 cent-a-gallon increase in gasoline tax, and holding down increases in Social Security benefits. He placed primary emphasis on the budget deficit and made other programs dependent upon restoration of prosperity. When he, for example, was asked about support for social welfare issues such as day care and temporary leave from the workplace for parents, he allowed that he "favored all those things," but added "we don't have any money right now" (Hayes, 1992, A10).

Perot also took the offensive when he was attacked. In denying that his intent in returning to the race was simply to be a spoiler, he said, "It was already spoiled when I started. We had a $4 trillion debt. We had a $400 billion deficit this year. We've got the most violent, crime-ridden society in the industrialized world, and the worst public schools" (Sack, 1992, A8).

Perot campaigned as a candidate of change, a true Washington outsider who had never held a political office. He was viewed as a T-shirt described him, "I'm just like you only richer." His candidacy undoubtedly hurt Bush but some thought that he hurt Clinton more because he was attracting anti-Bush votes that Clinton needed to win (Cook, 1992). And many did not care about which of the other two candidates Perot's candidacy hurt. As Susan Baer reported in an early analysis, "that the plainspoken, crackerjack businessman is an agent of change is enough for some people. And while other petitioners say they would welcome more specifics on his positions—and expect more—they also say such details take a back seat to issues of character integrity and style" (Baer, 1992, H1).

Perot might have been short on specifics in his plans but he used the strategy of emphasizing optimism for the future to make up for it. He always spoke optimistically when referring to his ability to get things done. "Looking back won't solve any of our problems," Perot said. "Looking forward, working together, we can fix anything. The American people are concerned about a government in gridlock. Our people are good. The American people are good. But they have a government that is a mess" ("Excerpts from Perot's Opening Statement in a Press Conference," 1992, A12).

Adaptations to Prevailing Conditions: Perot

Running as an independent part-time candidate resulted in a set of prevailing conditions unique to Perot. He did not have the support of a major party. His withdrawal and reentry raised questions about his dependability and saddled him with a running mate who had never intended to run for office and who was generally perceived as incapable of fulfilling the duties of the second highest office in the land.

Perot's adaptations were simple and open. When you are a billionaire, you need not be funded by a major party if you are willing to finance your own campaign. He paid for his own advertising, television shows to explain his ideas, and staff as he needed them. His campaign was never short of volunteers. He only needed a party nomination if he stood a chance of winning the election; he did not need it to gain intellectual leadership over millions who were dissatisfied with both political parties, respected and admired his financial success, and gave credence to his ideas and identified with his common man persona. He could work within prevailing conditions without trying to deny them or change them. He gained and maintained the respect of millions of people without changing himself or his ideas. At the end, he was predicting victory from votes coming from a "silent majority" (Howlett, 1992) but he could not overcome the condition that has prevailed for every independent candidate: Independent candidates lose.

CONCLUSIONS

Prevailing conditions had a major effect on the strategies and outcome of the 1992 campaign.

The President began the campaign with the symbolic strategies inherent in the office and thus available to the incumbent as well as the pragmatic strategies traditionally used by incumbents. He also faced a public that perceived an economy in trouble, a low approval rating, a party dominated by a vocal right wing whose votes were needed for election, a billionaire independent challenger who was competing for the same conservative votes, and the nominee of the Democratic Party.

Bush used almost all of the strategies available to incumbents but they were not effective in the conditions that prevailed. Finally, in the last few days before the election, he abandoned the incumbent strategies that were designed to make him look good and switched to the incumbent/challenger strategy of attack. While his strategy met its goal of reducing support for Clinton, it did not build the President's credibility and the shifting conservative voters went to Perot (Miller, 1993).

The Democratic nominee, Bill Clinton, used the strategies typically used by challengers. In addition to attacking the incumbent, he advocated activist programs that promised to meet people's needs, programs that were not available to the President because of his need for conservative support and Perot's competition for those voters. Clinton was forced to overcome the forces of the President's attacks on his character. In challenger fashion, Clinton responded by attacking. He neutralized Bush's attacks by shifting the character issue to portray Bush as uncaring and untrustworthy. And it worked. By election day Clinton's version of the issue, combined with a loss of faith in Bush's ability or willingness to take action to support the economy gave the Governor voter support on the character issue (Miller, 1993). The strategies of the challenger worked for Clinton as he adapted them to the prevailing conditions.

The dominant prevailing condition for independent candidates has always been that they do not win more than a small number of electoral college votes, if they win any at all. And Perot, like his predecessors, did not become president although he was a major factor in determining the outcome of the race. Concentrating on the challenger strategy of attack, Perot raised public awareness of the importance of the national debt. In so doing, he broadened the economic issue to include the ills of the nation along with the woes of individuals suffering from the recession. In addition to burdening the President with an unsolvable problem, Perot identified with the conservatives whose votes Bush needed for victory. And because Perot was not the candidate of a party or a person who had a record in public office, he was free to attack without having to defend. The prevailing conditions prevented Perot from having a chance to win the presidency, but the challenger strategy still made him a powerful force in the campaign.

Bush was damaged by prevailing conditions, conditions that not only prevented the effective use of most of the incumbent strategies but forced him to move to the attack mode of the challenger or incumbent/challenger. His belief that he was in danger of losing the most conservative members of the Republican Party to Perot prevented him from moving toward the philosophical center. In the end, his failure to move to the center cost him a significant number of votes from the moderate members of his party and was unsuccessful in obtaining support from many of the most conservative Republicans (Miller, 1993). The majority of those votes went to Perot, who had championed reduction of the budget deficit while taking more moderate views on social issues (Miller, 1993), but who found no way to overcome the fate of an independent candidate. Clinton won the race by successfully adapting to his prevailing conditions. Using the traditional strategies of the challenger campaign style, he seized the philosophical center and successfully challenged the president on the character issue by convincing voters that he was the stronger leader and the one who cared about their problems (Miller, 1993).

REFERENCES

Andrews, L. (1992, Oct. 4). Bush rejects bill that would limit rates on cable TV. *New York Times*, A1, A17.

Baer, S. (1992, May). The puzzle of Perot. *Cincinnati Enquirer*, H1.

Clinton: Don't trust Bush's lips (1992, Aug. 22). *Cincinnati Enquirer*, A4.

Clinton fires back at GOP on foreign-policy fitness (1992, July 29). *Cincinnati Enquirer*, A5.

Clinton hits hard on jobs, economy (1992, Sept. 9). *Cincinnati Enquirer*, A8.

Clinton rips Bush for exporting jobs (1992, Sept. 30). *Cincinnati Enquirer*, A4.

Cook, R. (1992, June 22–July 5). The road less traveled. *American Caucus, 1*, 9.

DeFrank, T. M. (1992a, Nov.–Dec.). A silver bullet. *Newsweek*, 82–85.

DeFrank, T. M. (1992b, Nov.–Dec.). Rocky road to Houston. *Newsweek*, 65–69.

DeFrank, T. M. (1992c, Nov.–Dec.). To the wire. *Newsweek*, 92–95.

DeFrank, T. M. (1992d, Nov.–Dec.). Unhappy warrior. *Newsweek*, 58–61.

Devlin, L. P. (1993, Nov.–Dec.). Contrasts in presidential campaign commercials of 1992. *American Behavioral Scientist*, 272–90.

Devroy, A. (1992a, Aug. 17). The reluctant activist: Domestically Bush tries to recast himself. *Washington Post*, A1.

Devroy, A. (1992b, Sept. 21–27). The Bush campaign, shake and bakered. *Washington Post*, 11.

Excerpts from Clinton speech to National Guard (1992, Sept. 16). *New York Times*, A15.

Excerpts from Perot's opening statement at a news conference (1992, Oct. 2). *New York Times*, A12.

Excerpts from speech by Clinton on US roles (1992, Oct. 2). *New York Times*, A13.

Goldman, P., and T. Mathews (1992, Nov.–Dec.). America changes the guard. *Newsweek*, 20–23.

Hayes, T. C. (1992, Apr. 27). Wealthy should pay more to trim deficit, Perot says. *New York Times*, A10.

Howlett, D. (1992, Nov. 2). Perot: Counting on "silent majority." *USA Today*, 3A.

Ifill, G. (1992a, July 2). Clinton dodges queries on choice for ticket. *New York Times*, A8.

Ifill, G. (1992b, Oct. 28). Clinton gazing beyond Nov. 3, outlines vision. *New York Times*, A1, A8.

Ifill, G. (1992c, July 28). Clinton resists being labeled a liberal. *New York Times*, A9.

Keen, J. (1992, Nov. 2). BUSH: Angry president revs up attacks. *USA Today*, 3A.

Kelly, (1992a, Sept. 13). Though advisors differ, Clinton's in tune with all. *New York Times*, A1, A16.

Klein, J. (1992, Aug. 17). On the road again. *Newsweek*, 33.

Miller, A. H. (1993, Nov.–Dec.). Economic, character, and social issues in the 1992 presidential election. *American Behavioral Scientist*, 315–27.

Networks shun prime-time bid." (1992, June 4). *The Cincinnati Post*, A8.

Nichols, B. (1992, Aug. 24). Clinton agonized, the challenger counterattacks. *USA Today*, A5.

Rogers, P. (1992, Nov.–Dec.). Assault on the monarchy. *Newsweek*, 62–64.

Rosenthal, A. (1992a, Oct. 26). As polls shift, Bush grabs even small chance of surge. *New York Times*, A14.

Rosenthal, A. (1992b, Oct. 8). Bush seeks a lift from trade pact. *New York Times*, A1, A12.

Rosenthal, A. (1992c, Oct. 27). Bush sounding like his rivals, tones down his attacks, briefly. *New York Times*, A1, A11.

Rosenthal, A. (1992d, Oct. 28). Bush uses latest economic figure to support his assertion of a recovery. *New York Times*, A8.

Rosenthal, A. (1992e, July 1). Taking heat at every turn, Bush shows a boiling point. *New York Times*, A1, A10.

Rosenthal, A. (1992f, July 2). Thorns in a rose garden. *New York Times*, A1.

Rosenthal, A., and J. Brinkley (1992, June 25). Old compass in new world: A president sticks to course. *New York Times*, A1, A12.

Sack, K. (1992, Oct. 6). In debut of his revived campaign Perot is tangled in contradictions. *New York Times*, A8.

The significance of the 1992 election (1993, Mar.). *P.S.: Political Science and Politics, 26*, 7–16.

Toner, R. (1992, June 15). With independent candidate, the race just won't let up. *New York Times*, A1, A10.

Trent, J. S., and R. V. Friedenberg (1991). *Political campaign communication.* Praeger: New York.

Trent, J. S., and J. D. Trent (1974). The rhetoric of the challenger: George Stanley McGovern. *Central States Speech Journal, 25,* 11–18.

Tyson, R. (1992, Oct. 2). Farmers rally 'round Bush ethanol plan. *USA Today,* A4.

Wines, M. (1992a, Nov. 1). Bush calls rival dangerously untested. *New York Times,* A17.

Wines, M. (1992b, Nov. 29). How Bush lost: For want of a strategy, chaos rules. *New York Times,* A1, A11.

FOUR

Looking for "The Vision Thing"

The Rhetoric of Leadership in the 1992 Presidential Election

RONALD F. WENDT AND GAIL T. FAIRHURST

"I'll try to hold my charisma in check."
—George Bush, 1988

"Where there is no vision, the people perish."
—Bill Clinton, 1992

Contemporary political leadership is undergoing an evolution of style. Some leaders are actively seeking to understand the transition while others are ignoring and resisting the trend. The media seems to understand this transition as they continually emphasize how important it is for a leader to have a lucid and pragmatic vision. This strategic leadership style—a method that George Bush flippantly referred to as "the vision thing"—is often targeted by the press as the missing element in an otherwise effective political campaign (Goldman & Mathews, 1992). Just after the 1988 presidential election, *Newsweek* (Goldman, 1988, pp. 88, 110) defined the "V word" as "a set of identifiable goals" and then admitted their surprise at Bush's success given this leader's apparent "want of vision." During the 1992 election year, *Time* magazine repeatedly made mention of the V word, and the June 29 issue featured caricatures of Bush, Clinton, and Perot with a capsulized version of each man's "vision thing." This same issue of *Time* tells of nervous Bush aides who were concerned that their leader was not focused on plans for the future (read, without vision). Media attention to Bush's apparent resistance to the use of vision leadership is perhaps what prompted Bill Clinton (1992) to highlight the vision process ("New Covenant") in his acceptance speech and to frame Bush's "vision thing" statement as a mockery of the practice of "seeing and seeking" future goals.

"The vision thing" has been a topic of concern to organizational and political scientists for some time. Weber (1947) was the first to write of the powerful impact charismatic leaders can have through appeals to ideology. However, the past two decades have seen a resurgence of interest in vision-style leadership. In the political sciences, "vision-style campaigns" have taken hold because of the weakening of political parties and party identification, the breakup of the Democratic New Deal coalition, the rise of the mass media as an instrument of persuasion, and greater numbers of split-ticket voters (Sandman, 1989). In short, the electorate is thinking and acting more independently than they ever have before, making them more receptive to the direct persuasive influence of a vision-style campaign.

In the organizational sciences, beginning in the 1970s interest was rekindled in the role that vision plays in effective leadership. Having a strategic vision was hailed as the key to managing increasingly complex organizations and chaotic environments (Bennis and Nanus, 1985; Nanus, 1992; Westley and Mitzberg, 1989). Based on such influential writers as Weber (1947), Burns (1978), and House (1977), a number of organizational models of charismatic leadership have proliferated. Though they all have visioning as a component, they reveal different types of visionary styles that may be usefully applied to analyze political leaders as much as organizational leaders. Though organizational and political leadership differs in several respects, there are many similarities. There is also precedent for the cross-fertilization of ideas across the two disciplines (e.g., Bass, 1985; Bennis and Nanus, 1985; Conger, 1989; House, Spangler, and Woyke, 1991).

The purpose of this chapter is to use these organizational models of charisma and the debate that has accompanied them to analyze the rhetoric of leadership of the 1992 campaigns. As we have shown, Bush's labeling of "the vision thing" and its aftermath became a campaign issue and produced candidates who tried to pass themselves off as leaders with a vision. In this chapter, we will use these contemporary models of leadership to analyze both the image and the reality of the visionary leadership style of the candidates.

In addition, the framing of ideas, what we term the "management of meaning," is the primary strategy or goal of a successful vision campaign. Having a vision implies that meanings are managed about the future direction of the country. However, to manage meaning about future directions is also to create a set of expectations for behavior or action to follow. The anticipated outcome is successfully managed change once in office. There are some management of change issues, therefore, that are directly related to vision-style campaigns. For example, for an incumbent, a charismatic campaign style cannot be considered in isolation from the extent of managed change as an officeholder. Every new campaign promise or campaign theme is set against the backdrop of goals achieved and the leadership shown in the previous four years. As we will show in the case of George Bush, a relative dearth of managed change can severely constrain a vision-style campaign.

For the challengers, the extent of managed change previous to the campaign, while not insignificant, tends to be less of an influence given that they do not enjoy the same widespread media coverage of their activities as presidents do (except in the case of scandals). For the challenger who gets elected, however, the question regarding managed change is in what ways can a charismatic campaign style prefigure or not prefigure the management of change once in office. How does the vision trumpeted during the campaign get played out once the vision holder is in office? As we will show in the case of Bill Clinton, an effective vision-style campaign does not guarantee the management of change once in office.

MODELS OF LEADERSHIP

The term "charismatic leadership" has emerged as the umbrella term for the various separate but interrelated models of visionary leadership. All of these models owe an intellectual debt to Max Weber (1947) and his initial distinction between two different kinds of charisma: Pure charisma is the result of a leader's exceptional qualities; routinized charisma occurs because of the authority inherent in an office or position. Even though today's political visions are sometimes offered up by "manufactured" charismatics (e.g., charisma based primarily on "photo ops" and staged "media events") rather than what Weber thought of as pure or genuine types, Weber's emphasis on the charismatic mission as one of the bases of organizational and political legitimacy suggests the importance of a vision.

Based on a survey of the literature, Graham (1991) identified four models of charismatic leadership, all of which have visioning as a component: Weberian charismatic authority, personal celebrity charisma, transformational leadership, and servant-leadership. These models can be better understood, however, by first reviewing another model that does not require a vision. This model is known as transactional leadership and is the model against which the transformational, charismatic model has most often been compared. In the paragraphs below, we define transactional leadership followed by the four models of charismatic leadership. Table 4.1 summarizes the four models of charisma.

The *transactional leader* manages by exception; he or she follows the adage, "If it ain't broken, don't fix it" (Bass, 1989). As one who "manages" instead of inspiring or initiating, the transactional manager responds only to the most urgent of problems. Based on a system of contingent reinforcement,

Table 4.1. *Four Models of Charismatic Leadership*

	Weberian charismatic authority	Personal celebrity charisma	Transformational leadership	Servant-leadership
Source of charisma	Divine gift	Personality; social distance	Leader training and skills	Humility; spiritual insight
Situational context	Socioeconomic distress of followers	Low self-esteem of followers	Unilateral (hierarchical) power	Relational (mutual) power
Nature of charismatic gift	Visionary solution to distress	Daring; drama; forceful	Vision as org. strategy; adept at human resource management	Vision and practice of "service"
Response of followers	Recognition of divine gift	Adulation of and ident. w/leader	Heightened motivation; participation; extra effort	Emulation of leader's service orientation
Effects of charisma	Increased wages	Co-depend. relationship w/leader perpetuated	Leader and/or org. goals met; personal development of followers	Autonomy; moral development
Applicability to industry	No	Yes	Yes	Yes
Applicability to government	Yes	Yes	Yes	Yes

Source: Adapted from J. W. Graham (1991). Servant-leadership in organizations: Inspirational and moral. *Leadership Quarterly, 2* (2), 105–19.

the transactional philosophy also tells managers to reward effort and performance and to recognize accomplishments. In addition, while Burns (1978) contends that transactional leadership is a strategy that motivates followers by appealing to their self-interests, and is separate from the transformational, charismatic process, Bass (1985) does not envision the two strategies to be mutually exclusive. Bass (1985) tells us that the situation should determine which strategy (or combination of strategies) to use, and that the transactional manager is especially effective in stable environments.

Weberian charismatic authority depends on a "divine mission" or "gift" and on follower support as primary sources of power. Because followers decide the legitimacy of the leader's inspired visionary program, it is they who grant authority. This "legitimate" authority is different from both inherited, traditional authority, and appointed, rational-legal authority. Supposedly emerging during periods of socioeconomic unrest, charismatic authority derives from a visionary and/or political solution to economic distress (Tucker, 1968, cited in Graham, 1991). Graham uses Weberian charismatic authority as the first of four models of charismatic leadership (see table 4.1).

Graham, borrowing from House's (1977) research of charismatic effects, identifies the second leadership model as *personal celebrity charisma*. Celebrity charisma derives its authority from followers who tend to romanticize leadership—adherents who respond to charismatic celebrities by idolizing and imitating their leaders, often as a result of followers' low self-esteem. House (1977, p. 205) proposes four qualities of this type of charismatic leader, all deriving from the leader's personality: dominance, self-confidence, need for influence, and a strong conviction in the moral righteousness of his or her beliefs. The dysfunction of celebrity charisma is that followers may be less critical and more susceptible to coercive or irresponsible leadership practices.

The third model of charisma proposed by Graham is *transformational leadership*. Transformational leadership, as originally defined by Burns (1978) and elaborated upon by Bass (1985), uses vision, inspiration, intellectual stimulation, and personal attention in persuading followers to transcend their own self-interest for the sake of the organization. In so doing, followers are empowered by the transformational leader to see themselves as agents capable of social change.

What is missing in the transformational model is an emphasis on the moral development of followers. Graham is concerned that individualized consideration and intellectual stimulation of followers, without concern for moral development, "may help tap the creativity of followers for solving organizational problems and serving organizational purposes, but may also discourage critical analysis of the morality of organizational policies and practices" (p. 111). Because of this inattention to moral development in the most current use of the transformational model, Graham revisits the political theories of Burns (1978) to recapture a notion of charismatic leadership that includes ethical decisions based on such "universal" moral principles as liberty, justice, and equality. Graham proposes the model *servant-leadership* as a type of charisma based on humility and a willingness to listen to and act upon the input of followers. Like Burns' "transforming" leaders, servant-leaders must remain sensitive to the needs and interests of all followers, and establish a "moral dialogue" that will guarantee a voice for all stakeholders as well as encourage diversity and dissent.

The servant-leader model of charisma provides an important ethical element lacking in Bass's conceptualization of transformational leadership. Indeed, as Howell and Avolio (1992) suggest, charismatic leadership is a double-edged sword that causes either coercion or empowerment, depending on the ethical inclination of the leader. However, what is missing in the idea of servant-leadership is any explanation of social change processes or a sufficient analysis of those contextual hindrances that make charismatic leadership less than effective.

As Graham's article or most any recent volume on leadership will attest (e.g., Graumann and Moscovici, 1986; Yukl, 1989), there is substantial debate over the components and merits of these models. Based on this debate, two extensions of these models are important to introduce because they are also a basis upon which to judge the presidential candidates.

First, all of these models fail to make explicit a basis of leadership in the *management of meaning*. Smith and Peterson (1988) note that whether it is the symbolic value of what a leader does or does not reward in transactional leadership or the framing and rationales of a vision in the charismatic models, what leaders do is manage meaning. One of the first to write about leadership as management of meaning was Pondy (1978, pp. 94–95):

> the effectiveness of a leader lies in his [sic] ability to make activity meaningful for those in his role set—not to change behavior but to give others a sense of understanding what they are doing and especially to articulate it so they can communicate about the meaning of their behavior. . . . If in addition the leader *can put it into words* then the meaning of what the group is doing becomes a *social* fact. . . . This dual capacity . . . to make sense of things *and* to put them into language meaningful to large numbers of people gives the person who has it enormous leverage.

Pondy's insight is consistent with Pfeffer (1981), who argues that organizations are systems of wholly or partly shared meanings. Some of these meanings relate to what the organization is *for*—goals, values, and ideologies. Other meanings are the means by which the organization believes these purposes should be achieved. Seen in this light, Smith and Peterson argue for a return to Bass's (1985) point that the activities of the charismatic leader and the transactional leader are not just complementary but equally necessary.[1] The charismatic advances a vision and engages in meaning management over the organization's purpose and direction. The transactional leader operates within a more limited and prescribed set of values and engages in meaning management over how those purposes should be achieved. A transactional leader without vision has no direction. A charismatic leader without transactional leadership skills fails in the routine administration of a unit, great vision notwithstanding (Bass, 1985). Further, regardless of *what* leaders manage meaning about, *how* they manage meaning will be judged by their ability to make sense of things, inspire, and provide a meaningful ideological framework on which to base action.

Second, the models of charismatic leadership tend to emphasize leader personality traits or skills and generally fail to consider the leader's ability to implement a vision in a given context. Research on the emergence of charismatic leadership in the U.S. presidency suggests that context is a critical component. House et al. (1991) found that many American presidents developed as charismatic leaders because of crisis situations, the value system surrounding the leader, and the role of the media (see also Boal and Bryson, 1988; Conger and Kanungo, 1988). They concluded that charisma and its contextual features were directly linked to presidential effectiveness.

Research on organizational cultures, however, suggests that it will not be the force of a charismatic leader's personality or an appealing-sounding message that will produce change. Rather, change will occur as a result of a leader's intimate knowledge of the culture and knowing where pressure may be applied to move the organization along in ways consistent with the vision (Schein, 1985). Based on Greiner's (1972) work on organizational change, Smith and Peterson (1988, p. 121) have argued that "Organizational leadership may thus entail not so much the creation of change, but the anticipation of crises and the construction of cultures which are best adapted to handling them."

Lacking, then, in the charismatic models are issues surrounding the ability of leaders to be "change masters" or innovators who successfully adapt to the needs of any situation through the employment of one or more optimum strategies (Kanter, 1983). These are managers of change who can move beyond the inspiration of the vision to the pragmatics of the transformation process. Indeed, this view in not far afield from Weber's (1947) argument on the routinization of charisma. Weber's point was that a charismatic leader must use a bureaucracy though he or she must also keep the resulting formalization processes from reifying into a force that would minimize his or her effectiveness.

As is well known, the routinization of a presidential candidate's charisma is accomplished through a campaign organization. The message and appeal of a candidate are carried through state-by-state grass-roots operations that work local networks to deliver votes and money. Once elected president, however, a candidate often finds charisma difficult to sustain.

The rhetoric of election campaigns is filled with lofty symbols and high ideals, with little attention paid to specific programs (Foss, 1982; Sandman, 1989). Sandman (1989), arguing for the utility of a vision-style campaign, explains that a political vision is often based on such broad and ambiguous themes as "opportunity" and "national security." Foss (1982) contends that the duties of office will usually cause a president to abandon argument by genus (use of ideals, vision) in favor of argument by cause and effect, circumstance, and similitude (pragmatics). Political pressures cause a president to obscure, gloss, or negate a vision established in the campaign as rhetoric becomes much more pragmatic when facing daily problem solving. Thus, a leader who is adept at stimulating change through the management of meaning in campaign rhetoric may not be successful at managing change once in office.

Once in office, many of the instruments of change for a political leader are the same as those for a corporate leader: (1) an insider's knowledge of the system and its subcultures, (2) reactions to crises and critical incidents, (3) management of networks of information and influence, (4) organizational restructuring to streamline bureaucracy, (5) an appreciation for the symbolic (symbols, myths, language), (6) organizational succession, (7) the establishment of trust, (8) the use of consensus to assure buy-in, (9) the use of coalitions, (10) a willingness to compromise, and, of course, (11) a vision that is sufficiently developed in order for followers to see application to their circumstances.

However, because *what* corporate and political leaders do differs in several respects, this necessarily impacts *how* each goes about effecting change. The most obvious differences occur as a result of a political leader's (1) very public campaign in which he or she goes on the record in terms of a proposed vision and political agenda, (2) promotion of legislation and dealings with Congress, (3) attention to a highly diverse set of constituencies and interests, both foreign and domestic, and (4) existence within a fishbowl created by a watchful media (which routinely chronicles discrepancies between campaign promises and behavior once in office). It is not that corporate leaders do not also do some of these things, such as serve multiple constituencies or get reported on by the press, but the level of these activities seems much less comparable. The constraints imposed by what political leaders do will thus affect how they use the instruments of change to accomplish their goals.

In light of this discussion, we now turn to the central issues that concern us. First, to the extent charismatic leadership was demonstrated in 1992 campaign rhetoric or action, what type of charismatic leader did each candidate appear to be? Second, for incumbent George Bush, what role did his history of managed change as president play in the evaluation of his 1992 vision-style campaign? Third, for challenger and winner Bill Clinton, in what ways did his vision-style campaign prefigure (or not prefigure) managed change once he was in office?

THREE CONTEMPORARY CHARISMATICS

While none of the 1992 candidates fit the dominant leadership models perfectly, several politicians displayed a remarkable number of characteristics linked to a particular model.

George Bush: Transactional Leader

Before he was elected in 1988, Bush's acceptance speech at the convention indicated that a president must have a vision ("he must be able to define—and lead—a mission"). He won on the themes of volunteerism, with his "thousand points of light" and "kinder, gentler nation." He pledged economic progress with "no new taxes." He would declare "peace through strength" and the "rule of law" as the other essential elements of his 1988 vision-style campaign (Sandman, 1989).

There is strong evidence that George Bush was primarily a *manager* or transactional leader, and not a leader who was also concerned with transformation. To begin with, Bush's disdain for and lack of a vision is evidenced in his leadership style and his rhetoric. Very much like the corporate manager who manages by exception and responds only in times of great need, Bush often held back and offered little sustained interest in the issues at hand. Bush was criticized for allowing one hundred days in office to slip by without advancing any real agenda.[2] His response to the collapse of the Soviet Union was perceived as lethargic. He ignored the deficit, and seemed to have little or no agenda for domestic affairs. It was ironic that Bush's substantial knowledge of the workings of government, given his past duties, was rarely applied to bring about change. It is ironic, too, that he won a war in the Middle East and did not confront Congress to demand much more than he did.

Bush was referred to as "the managerial president," one who manages and even micromanages. Duffy and Goodgame (1992) described Bush's style of "micromanagement": "The result has been a president who substitutes frenetic movement for lasting action; whose idea of long-range planning is choosing the menu for tomorrow's lunch; who governs by reaction to whatever his staff and events put in front of him. Bush is more than half-serious when he says, paraphrasing Woody Allen, that '90 percent of life is just showing up'" (p. 73).

Consistent with Duffy and Goodgame's observation, Bush often refused to fight for specific programs, claiming to be a pragmatist instead of a philosopher. For example, during one of his later budget negotiations, he simply stopped pushing for anything at all and said irritably: "Let Congress clear it up" (Novak, 1992). And when he was asked about his plans for a second term in office, Bush responded only as a typical middle manager would: "I'll handle whatever comes up" (Klein, 1992). Bush's refusal to take advantage of specific windows of opportunity illustrates his lack of vision, and consequently, an inability to manage change. This reluctance to establish a clear agenda led to a nebulous presidential image. Ted Windt (1992) states that Bush simply failed to define himself. Windt explains that Bush ultimately failed to understand "modern rhetorical presence," that is, that rhetoric functions to give meaning and definition to a presidency. Because of this lack of definition, Bush left it open for the news media (primarily in the form of unflattering visual images like his illness in Japan) to define his presidency.

In the corporate world, "symbolic managers" or "managers of meaning" use heros, stories, rituals, metaphors, and vision to promote change within an organization's culture (Deal and Kennedy, 1982). Bush never seemed to realize the symbolic nature of the presidency. Unlike Reagan and his appreciation for the symbolic, Bush was more likely to react to events than be a catalyst, and rarely took advantage of the opportunities to use symbols. As Hinckley (1990) points out in *The Symbolic Presidency*, Reagan often took advantage of visual and spoken symbolism, and was most influential when he combined rhetoric with visual stimuli. For instance, Reagan, in his inaugural address, made direct reference to the monuments to former presidents, thereby keeping the focus of the speech on the presidency and his identification with past heros and the nation. Bush, on the other hand, never seemed to appreciate the power of symbolic rhetoric or visual symbolism. Hinckley (1990) states that the press was especially critical of Bush's inattention to rhetorical strategies, and cites a *New York Times* editorial of May 25, 1989 that described a Bush speech as "flat and flimsy," calling on Bush to acknowledge "the power of language and bold goals" (p. 142).

Bush's performance as president was the backdrop against which his 1992 vision-style campaign was to be viewed. Bush's 1992 campaign relied heavily on diversionary tactics rather than forthright and specific plans and programs for the future. This had the effect of reinforcing the common perception, established during the Bush presidency, that he neither possessed nor understood visionary leadership. These negative tactics, prominently displayed in his speech to the 1992 Republican National Convention, consisted of: (1) laying claim to multiple (yet somewhat dubious) past accomplishments, (2) overt and subtle attacks on the public and private conduct of his opponent, and (3) laying blame for stagnant legislation on an uncooperative Congress. Bush's first ploy was to insinuate a direct leadership role in such world changes as the unification of Germany, potential peace in the Middle East, peace in El Salvador, the end of communism in Poland, and the breakdown of the Soviet Union ("Our Global Victory"). In effect, Bush (1992) was laying claim to the end of the cold war: "And now the Cold War is over and they [Democrats, Clinton] claim, hey, we were with you all the way" (p. 707). At the same time Bush gives credit to strong leadership from presidents of both parties, he continuously takes credit for world cohesion by referring to himself: "I saw the chance to rid our children's dreams of the nuclear nightmare, and I did. . . . I saw a chance to help, and I did. . . . I seized those opportunities for our kids and our grandkids, and I make no apologies for that" (p. 707).

In this campaign speech, Bush (1992) made direct and covert sugges-tions that Clinton was both inept at leadership and personally corrupt. A few examples of this tactic: "The fact remains that the liberal, McGovern wing of the other party, including my opponent, consistently made the wrong choices" (p. 706). "While I bit the bullet . . . he bit his nails" (p. 707). "Now, sounds to me like his policy can be summed up by a road sign he's probably seen on his bus tour: 'slippery when wet'" (p. 707). "America doesn't need Carter II" (p. 710). Instead of establishing an interpretive framework for clarifying and promoting a plan for the future, Bush's rhetoric of leadership slipped into negative campaigning and overstated accomplishments. In the final portion of his speech, Bush began to outline a somewhat obscure platform, but he regressed into a defensive rather than an offensive posture. By repeatedly laying blame on a partisan Congress, Bush missed a prime opportunity to fully develop his vision campaign: "The gridlock Democratic Congress has said, no" (p. 708). "Let me tell you about a recent battle fought with Congress" (p. 708). "Why are these proposals not in effect today? Only one reason—the gridlock Democratic Congress. . . . I know Americans are tired of the lame game, tired of people in Washington acting like they are candidates of the next episode of American Gladiators. I don't like it, either" (p. 709). In the final analysis, by relying too heavily on negative campaign tactics, Bush failed to establish a clear agenda for change and reinforced views that there would be four more years of too little change.

During the campaign, Bush also failed to recognize and interpret the growing dissatisfaction of the American citizenry correctly. The country was weary of a bad economy as well as ineffective and unfocused leadership, and resentful of money spent on foreign concerns when the social fiber of the country was coming apart. A president without a "vision thing," Bush saw only an ill-defined public need and would lament, "It's vague out there" (Goldman & Mathews, 1992, p. 23).

Bush's strength was his expertise in foreign policy. Yet by campaign time, his foreign policy was compared to "a house built by do-it-yourselfers in the dark" (Goldman & Mathews, 1992, pp. 22–23). In a direct reference to his presidency, *Newsweek*'s analysis also suggested that the reason he failed to get reelected was because inspiration tended to fail him—he "painted by the numbers." Similar to his attitude toward social issues, Bush sometimes waited to address matters of foreign policy until action was demanded of him. Bush (1991, p. 451) referred to the Gulf War as a "job" that had to be done, another fire to be attended to. Similar to his inattention to domestic affairs, Bush's new world order philosophy lacked a specific agenda. Critical of Bush's "procrastination" toward foreign policy, Charles Kegley (1989) states that the former president was somewhat cognizant of missed opportunities for har-mony among the superpowers, particularly in regard to overtures made by

Gorbachev. Kegley quotes Bush: "What I don't want is to have it look like foot-dragging, or sulky refusal to go forward. . . . [But] I would be imprudent if I didn't have our team take a hard look at everything" (p. 726). Kegley inter-prets this "prudence" as a form of indecision and procrastination, a decisional style that in 1988 Larry Speakes described thusly: "With Bush, the popular image may be accurate: That he does not have a strong philosophical base, that he is not decisive, that he is not willing to take stands on the big issues" (quote in Kegley, 1989, p. 726). One term in office and one failed campaign later, the popular image lives on.

Bill Clinton: Transformational Leader and Change Master?

Bill Clinton's 1992 campaign for the presidency shows just how much poli-ticians have come to depend on at least appearing to be transformational leaders in order to gain office. To a limited degree, Clinton accomplished the basics of transformational leadership outlined by Bass (1985); he had a vision that inspired, was intellectually stimulating, and provided consideration for the individual by appearing to reach out to the individual voter.

The transformational strategy of Clinton's acceptance speech at the con-vention revolved around an aggressive metacommunication concerning the inability of Bush to use the visioning process to make change happen. Clinton (1992) told the American public that what "bother[ed]" him most about Bush was the way "he deride[ed] and degrad[ed] the American tradition of seeing and seeking a better future. He mock[ed] it as 'the vision thing'" (p. 644). The candidate then reinforced the urgency of having a clear and prag-matic mission by stating: "Where there is no vision, the people perish" (p. 644). Clinton argued that his "New Covenant" vision would work better to establish a clear and useful program for change than an apparent lack of vision from his opponent. On the surface, the New Covenant vision showed greater utility and addressed many more social problems than did Bush's (1988) vague and underdeveloped Thousand Points/Kinder-Gentler vision.

As Stuckey and Antczak (this volume) indicate, by using clusters of powerful metaphors and constant themes, Clinton was able to present a much clearer definition of his presidency than Bush. Clinton's targeting of domestic issues through the use of images like "community" and themes like "con-nectedness" worked toward establishing a vision of change that seemed focused on traditional values and goals. These elements of Clinton's cam-paign rhetoric appeared to set the stage for social change and a new political regime. However, an effective political vision and transformational leadership capabilities are about much more than the effective use of images and themes. The transformational leader will appeal to and utilize the intellect of his or her audience by replacing sound bites with clear and concise explanations and examples, by going beyond photo-ops to include idea-specific programs, and by driving home themes with concrete examples. Clinton, familiar with corporate empowerment strategies, made a strong argument in his acceptance speech that he was going to (in corporate jargon) "walk the talk." Stating that Bush only "talk[ed] a good game" (in corporate jargon: "talk the talk"), Clinton (1992) went on to specify each point in his vision: health care, streamlining the federal government, crime, the environment, and so on. Of even greater significance was Clinton's willingness to be self-reflective: "But priorities without a clear plan of action are empty words. To turn our rhetoric into reality we have to change the way Government does business, fundamentally. . . . But we Democrats have some changing to do, too. It is time for us to realize that there is not a government program for every problem" (1992, p. 644). He then targeted the solution stemming from his reflection: "we need a new approach to government. . . . A government that is leaner, not meaner, that expands opportunity, not bureaucracy" (p. 644). This is a type of vision rhetoric that utilizes rather than negates an audience; this is a transformational leader attempting to outline a vision that is specific, intelligent, empathic, inspirational, and self-reflective.

Yet how does a vision-style campaign prefigure, or not prefigure the management of change once in office? Clinton's "New Covenant" vision provides some clues as it had a difficult time making the transition from campaign rhetoric to presidential rhetoric. Like most new presidents, Clinton carried his idealistic rhetoric over into the first few months in office, and while the "New Covenant" term was dropped, its successor "change" was even more slippery and obscure. In his inaugural address, Clinton (1993a) spoke of "change" in ambiguous and idealistic terms: "Not change for change's sake, but change to preserve America's ideals—life, liberty, the pursuit of happiness. . . . We have not made change our friend. . . . Together with our friends and allies, we will work to shape change, lest it engulf us" (pp. 258–59). At this point in his presidency, "change" was still an abstract idea. The meaning of the term "change" became more specific when it was explained in terms of "four fundamental components" in Clinton's State of the Union Address (1993b, p. 323). Even then, however, the managed meaning of the term was not complete; the components of change required further definition, not only for an anxious Congress, but also for the press and public. Twelve months after the election, Clinton still spoke of the need to "make change our friend," but a darker tone crept into his rhetoric. At a speech to the University of North Carolina he said, "All around our great country today, I see people resisting change. I see them turning inward and away from change."[3]

What happens to the transformational leader as he suddenly faces the pragmatics of vision implementation within a burdensome government bureaucracy? As the dark tone in Clinton's rhetoric of change to the North Carolina audience indicates, the transition from election campaigning to campaigning for postelection image, policy, and position is a difficult one. A well-developed campaign vision should present an interpretive frame that will serve as a template for initial transformation rhetoric and change strategies (e.g., appointments to office, streamlining bureaucracy, policy setting, resource acquisition). Yet Clinton's early months in office were testimony to the disaster that can befall presidents whose campaign framing strategies do not make a smooth transition into techniques for change facilitation. There was the firestorm over gays in the military, the withdrawals of Kimba Wood and Zoe Baird for attorney general, the disappointment of Judge Stephen Breyer for the Supreme Court before the nomination of Ruth Bader Ginsburg, the withdrawal of Lani Guinier's nomination as assistant attorney general, the $200 haircut, the shakeup of the White House travel office, and the suicide of his close friend and White House counselor, Vince Foster. After Clinton's first six months in office, Maureen Dowd, a writer for the *New York Times,* drew an analogy between Clinton and the cartoon character "Wimpy." Dowd seemed to detect a familiar pattern of first overpromising and then backing down in response to political pressure.[4] Fortunately, NAFTA and budget issues delivered some successes to this young president during his second six months in office, though foreign policy concerns (Bosnia, Somalia, Haiti) and the Whitewater financial involvement also marked that time.

A true transformational leader realizes the interrelationship between meaning and action, and will present a *working* vision—a plan that is easily understood, realistic, and manageable in the sense that it can be packaged, sold, and acted upon. With little Washington experience, however, Clinton could not formulate a working vision, one that could realize the promise of transformational leadership. In what appeared to be a recognition of his lack of insider's knowledge of Washington, Clinton took the usual step of hiring David Gergen, who had served as White House counselor in the three previous Republican administrations.

With or without Gergen's help, if Clinton does not follow up his vision-style campaign with managed change in office he may turn out to be more of a "pseudotransformational" (Bass, 1989) leader and less of a change master. Like the pseudocharismatic, the pseudotransformational leader has trouble turning a vision into reality, but unlike the former, the latter carries a pragmatic mission into office. Once in office, the trappings and nuances of a bureaucratic system, difficult to manage, often prevent or inhibit that most essential duty of office: execution of specific programs.

Two directions seem possible for this president. Clinton, the pseudotransformational leader, will fall back on sound bites, jargon, and token visual symbols, and do little in the way of real governing. Early judgments of his first months in office (with haunting nicknames like "The Great Equivocator," first used by the *Orange County Register*) and some observations regarding his tenure as governor of Arkansas support this direction.[5] Or, Clinton, the transformational leader and change master, will try to provide some of the intellectual stimulation he provided in the campaign as a means of meeting the goals of his dominant vision. He will also use all of his resources to harness government bureaucracy and to promote significant legislation, especially in the expected arenas of the economy and health care. The rhetoric of a transformational leader is certainly present: "I cut the federal bureaucracy by 100,000 positions . . . we are eliminating programs that are no longer needed . . . we are slashing subsidies and cancelling wasteful projects . . . the American people know we must change" (1993b, pp. 324–25). Whichever direction he assumes, the backdrop of his 1996 vision-style campaign is now being constructed.

Ross Perot: Personal Celebrity Charisma and Servant-Leader?

In one sense Perot was a "pure" or "genuine" charismatic in that he supposedly derived his "divine" authority from the will of the people, and his constituency was responding to him in a very emotional manner (Weber, 1947). In another sense, however, Perot was using his "celebrity" as corporate leader to bolster his credibility as political leader. This false or pseudocharisma is planned and manufactured and promoted through the manipulation of news media. Bensman and Givant (1986) tell us that "pseudocharisma" is created by the rational planning and calculation of a warm, sincere, emotional, and inspirational persona, designed to appear spontaneous. In the case of the 1992 election, people were not looking for a "warm" and congenial figure, but one who was strong, experienced, and determined. Because Perot fit this latter description, and because he was well known for his business expertise, his success as entrepreneur, and his massive wealth, Perot might be said to possess a certain status as a charismatic celebrity. On the other hand, he was not able to overcome his image as tyrant and autocrat, nor was he able to exhibit any enjoyment in or knowledge of political negotiation and networking.

The attraction and power of Perot's campaign rhetoric came from his common and earthy figures of speech and his use of real-life stories involving everyday heroes. In order to "fix the mess" that the country was in, Perot (1992, p. 15) said he would finally address the issues that concern the American people, thus bolstering his image as a potential change master. He was also adept at deflecting questions concerning his power. He claimed that "the people" would decide, that he was their "servant": "And now to the American people, I don't belong to anybody but you. You the people own me. If you elect me I go as your servant" (1992, p. 15). And the story of the veteran who loaned Perot his Purple Heart medal as a sort of inspiration helped solidify Perot as a candidate "of the people" (1992, p. 16). Because of his constant identification with the American people and his frequent accessibility during the campaign by way of call-in talk shows and infomercials, Perot's image seemed to be that of a potential servant-leader. Even his expressed moral concern ("I'm not doing this for personal reasons") seemed to be focused on his public. But in the final analysis, Perot offered a style of leadership that was more *pseudoservant* than genuine visionary. He was a candidate "of the people," but he made it clear that change and a political agenda would have to come from the top. Moreover, his vision for the economy, when finally put forth, offered few specifics—something he had criticized other candidates for.

A less autocratic style on the part of Perot might have survived the onslaught of the presidential campaign and fit more closely with the present-day need for a visionary and empowering leader. But are the corporate "change masters," with their unique ability to transform multinationals from static, bureaucratic oligarchies to lean, cost-efficient dynamos, able to cross over into the complex world of political bureaucracy? In Ross Perot's case, evidence suggests not.

Perot's metaphor-saturated rhetoric and his image as a dedicated citizen concerned with the transformation of this country are qualities that helped establish him as a charismatic even in the eyes of a cynical public. However, his autocratic approach to change, as evidenced by his erratic campaign behavior and his corporate track record, made him unwilling to listen and, ultimately, unwilling to respond to those for whom he would serve. Although there are many at IBM, EDS (Electronic Data Systems), and General Motors who will attest to Perot's abilities as a charismatic leader, many of these same people look back on their relationship with Perot as a form of indentured servitude. After the special *Time* (Brack, 1992) issue titled "Nobody's Perfect: The Doubts about Ross Perot" was published, it became public knowledge that Perot was, at times, as much of a tyrant as he was a charismatic. With airtight employment contracts, military-style dress codes, sworn vendettas against competitors, and a less-than-agreeable attitude toward women's issues (at least in the early days), Perot's initial style of charisma left a great deal to be desired. It seems likely that this more authoritarian charismatic image contributed to Perot's failed attempt to integrate an effective business culture with a modern political culture.

But Perot sealed his fate by waiting three months to reenter the campaign. His media blitz ($24 million in two weeks), which revolved around a series of costly infomercials, reinforced his concern for the economy, bolstered his down-home image, and reestablished his credibility among an enthusiastic but dwindling following. But ultimately candidate Perot was unable to merge a business culture with a political culture. A political campaign was not like the businesses he was used to controlling. After dropping out of the race once stories of his paranoia and controlling style began to surface, Perot came to be regarded more as an anachronism than as a visionary leader.

Currently, Perot maintains his image as servant-leader. Perot took a leadership role in the NAFTA debate, saying that he had only the country's best interests in mind. Although he is far from humble, he seems to possess a "spiritual insight" by constantly referencing "God" and the Bible. He also seems focused and obsessed with those alternatives to mainstream government that will help the "common man." Again, this image of servant and protector of the people is campaign rhetoric. This "servant-leader" may have a difficult time staying focused on moral development and enhancement of the common good once faced with the demands of political office.

CONCLUSIONS

The charismatic and transactional models of leadership are useful tools for examining the rhetoric of leadership as presidential candidates attempt to make a transition from the idealism and interpretive strategies of campaign rhetoric to the complex mechanics of adaptation to government bureaucracy and implementation of programs. As we have seen, in his term as president, George Bush proved to be a transactional leader without much real vision. As a result, this tended to negate his claims to vision in the 1992 campaign. Bill Clinton proved to be a transformational leader during the campaign. He had a vision that sounded appealing, he was intellectually stimulating, and he seemed to reach out to the individual voter. His months in office, however, suggest that the vision and charisma of the campaign may not have transferred to the presidency. Finally, Ross Perot's carefully constructed charismatic image was that of the servant-leader. His controlling management style as a corporate leader and erratic behavior during the campaign, however, suggest a somewhat different persona.

We also argued for an extension of the dominant models of charisma that goes beyond questions of managing meaning to questions of managing change. By extending these models, we seek to keep them as dynamic as the social context in which they occur. No one model can fully explain the social dynamics of change, nor the style and aspects of leadership that facilitate such transformation. However, if we are to understand charismatic leadership as a continuous dynamic of social, structural, and ideational transformation, we must begin by analyzing those procedures that streamline bureaucracy and facilitate planned action. The bottom line for government is whether the great bureaucratic machine can be impacted in ways that are not illegal, unethical, too costly, or too impractical. Obviously, certain presidents have had greater success at "greasing the machine" than others.

One might conclude that our Constitution guarantees not only a representative government, but a permanently stagnant political bureaucracy that produces an encumbered form of presidential leadership. This stagnation is, of course, the way our Constitution guards against unlimited power and autocracy. As *The Federalist Papers* remind us, "Ambition must be made to counteract ambition."[6] But inherent in our safeguards is a vision of inert leadership; each president is made slave to the "bureaucratization" of leadership (Ferguson, 1984). Thus, the implementation of a president's vision and the management of change may be destined to be a remote possibility from the picture the candidate paints in the campaign. In commenting on Clinton's apparent "flaccidity" as a president with "no soaring rhetoric, no moral presence, no sense of drama, no sense of fun," Joe Klein of *Newsweek* (1993) noted that even if Clinton retained the charisma that he had as a candidate, progress in implementing his vision and programs would still be unlikely: "it's probable Congress would have withstood a real presidential kamikaze onslaught and—like the toy clown that bounces back smiling no matter how hard you slam it—come out in precisely the same place" (p. 22).

Eisenberg and Goodall (1993) suggest a useful metaphor for envisioning the complexity of organizational communication, an image that seems to capture the essence of political leadership. That image is the tension between *creativity* and *constraint.* A realistic glimpse of the 1992 American presidential campaign lies somewhere between the creativity of the visionaries and the constraints of the bureaucracy they must harness.

NOTES

This essay was originally written for this book. It has also been published in *Communication Quarterly* 42, no. 2, Spring 1994, 180–95.

1. Of course Bass (1985) was writing about his charismatic model of leadership, called transformational leadership, but the same can be said for the other charismatic models as well.

2. Bush was critiqued throughout the popular press both during and after his term as president; for one such example, see the Nov.–Dec. 1992 issue of *Newsweek* (specifically, Goldman and Mathews, 1992).

3. From "Clinton Learns from Early Errors," *Los Angles Times*, Nov. 7, 1993, David Lauter.

4. From "Is 'Slick Willie' Image Now 'Willie the Wimp'?" *New York Times*, June 4, 1993, Maureen Dowd.

5. From "Promise Us Reality," *Cincinnati Enquirer*, Nov. 7, 1993, Dick Armey.

6. From "Checks and Balances," *The Federalist No. 51*, p. 164. In Bailyn (1993).

REFERENCES

ABC News (1992, June 29). *ABC News: Town meeting* [with Ross Perot]. [Television].

Allison, G. T. (1984). Public and private administrative leadership: Are they fundamentally alike in all unimportant respects? In T. J. Sergiovanni and J. F. Corbally, eds., *Leadership and organizational culture: New perspectives on administrative theory and practice.* Chicago: University of Illinois Press, pp. 214–39.

Armey, D. (1993, Nov. 7). Promise us reality. *Cincinnati Enquirer,* D1, D4.

Avolio, B. J., and B. M. Bass. (1988). Transformational leadership, charisma, and beyond. In J. G. Hunt, ed., *Emerging leadership vistas.* Lexington, Mass.: Lexington Books, pp. 29–49.

Bailyn, B., ed. (1993). *Debate on the Constitution.* Vol. 2. New York: Literary Classics of the U.S.

Bass, B. M. (1989). From transactional to transformational leadership: Learning to share the vision. *Organizational Dynamics,* 19–31.

Bass, B. M. (1985). *Leadership and performance beyond expectations.* New York: Free Press.

Bass, B. M. (1981). *Stogdill's handbook of leadership: A survey of theory and research.* New York: Free Press.

Bass, B. M., B. J. Avolio, and L. Goodheim. (1987). Biography and the assessment of transformational leadership at the world class level. *Journal of Management, 13,* 7–19.

Beatty, J. (1992, Feb. 14). Still no "vision thing." *Boston Globe,* 19.

Bennis, W., and B. Nanus. (1985). *Leaders: The strategies for taking charge.* New York: Harper and Row.

Bensman, J., and M. Givant. (1986). Charisma and modernity: The use and abuse of a concept. In R. M. Glassman and W. H. Swatos Jr., eds., *Charisma, history, and social structure.* New York: Greenwood, pp. 27–56.

Boal, K. B., and J. M. Bryson. (1988). Charismatic leadership: A phenomeno-logical and structural approach. In J. G. Hunt, B. R. Baglia, H. P. Dachler, and C. A. Schriesheim, eds., *Emerging leadership vistas.* Lexington, Mass.: Lexington Books, pp. 11–28.

Brack, R. K., Jr. (1992, June 29). Nobody's perfect: The doubts about Ross Perot [Special issue]. *Time.*

Bradley, R. T. (1987). *Charisma and social structure.* New York: Paragon House.

Burns, J. M. (1978). *Leadership.* New York: Harper and Row.

Bush, G. (1988). Acceptance address. *Vital Speeches of the Day, 55,* 1–5.

Bush, G. (1992). A new crusade to reap the rewards of our global victory. *Vital Speeches of the Day, 58* (23), 706–10.

Bush, G. (1991). The possibility of a new world order. *Vital Speeches of the Day, 57,* 450–52.

Campbell, K. K., and K. H. Jamieson. (1990). *Deeds done in words: Presidential rhetoric and the genres of governance.* Chicago: University of Chicago Press.

Clinton, W. (1992). Acceptance address. *Vital Speeches of the Day, 58* (21), 642–45.

Clinton, W. (1993a). American renewal [inaugural address]. *Vital Speeches of the Day, 59* (9), 258–59.

Clinton, W. (1993b). State of the Union 1993. *Vital Speeches of the Day, 59* (11), 322–25.

Conger, J. A. (1989). *The charismatic leader.* San Francisco: Jossey-Bass.

Conger, J. A., and R. Kanungo. (1988). *Charismatic leadership.* San Francisco: Jossey-Bass.

Cooper, N., and S. Monroe. (1988, Nov. 21). Keeping his eyes on the next prize. *Newsweek,* 22.

Deal, T. E., A. A. Kennedy. (1982). *Corporate Cultures: The Rites and Rituals of Corporate Life.* New York: Addison-Wesley.

Dowd, M. (1993, June 4). Is "Slick Willie" image now "Willie the Wimp"? *New York Times.*

Duffy, M., and D. Goodgame. (1992). *Marching in place: The status quo presidency of George Bush.* New York: Simon and Schuster.

Edelman, M. (1988). *Constructing the political spectacle.* Chicago: University of Chicago Press.

Eisenberg, E. M., and H. L. Goodall. (1993). *Organizational communication: Balancing creativity and constraint.* New York: St. Martin's .

Ferguson, K. E. (1984). *The feminist case against bureaucracy.* Philadelphia: Temple University Press.

Foss, S. K. (1982). Abandonment of genus: The evolution of political rhetoric. *Central States Speech Journal, 33,* 367–78.

Gerth, H., and C. W. Mills, eds. (1946). *From Max Weber.* New York: Oxford University Press.

Glassman, R. M., and W. H. Swatos Jr., eds. (1986). *Charisma, history, and social structure.* New York: Greenwood.

Goldman, P. (1988, Nov. 21). Battle of the Republicans. *Newsweek,* 84–110.

Goldman, P., and T. Mathews. (1992, Nov.–Dec.). America changes the guard. *Newsweek,* 20–23.

Graham, J. W. (1991). Servant-leadership in organizations: Inspirational and moral. *Leadership and Quarterly, 2* (2), 105–19.

Graumann, C. F., and S. Moscovici, eds. (1986). *Changing conceptions of leadership.* New York: Springer-Verlag.

Greiner, L. E. (1972). Evolution and revolution as organizations grow. *Harvard Business Review, 50,* 37–46.

Hastedt, G. P., and A. J. Eksterowicz. (1993). Presidential leadership in the post cold war era. *Presidential Studies Quarterly, 23* (3), 445–58.

Hater, J. J., and B. M. Bass. (1988). Supervisors' evaluations and subordinates' perceptions of transformational and transactional leadership. *Journal of Applied Psychology, 73,* 695–702.

Hinckley, B. (1990). *The symbolic presidency.* New York: Routledge.

House, R. J. (1971). A path-goal theory of leadership effectiveness. *Administrative Science Quarterly,* 16, 321–38.

House, R. J. (1977). A 1976 theory of charismatic leadership. In J. G. Hunt and L. L. Larson, eds., *Leadership: The cutting edge.* Carbondale, Ill.: Southern Illinois University Press, pp. 189–207.

House, R. J., W. D. Spangler, and J. Woycke. (1991). Personality and charisma in the U.S. presidency: A psychological theory of leader effectiveness. *Administrative Science Quarterly, 36,* 364–96.

Howell, J. M., and B. J. Avolio. (1992). The ethics of charismatic leadership: Submission or liberation? *Academy of Management Executive, 6,* 43–54.

Hunt, J. G, ed. (1988). *Emerging leadership vistas.* Lexington, Mass.: Lexington Books.

Jackson, J. (1988). Common ground and common sense. *Vital Speeches of the Day, 54,* 649–53.

Kanter, R. M. (1983). *The change masters: Innovation and entrepreneurship in the American corporation.* New York: Simon and Schuster.

Kegley, C. W., Jr. (1989). The Bush administration and the future of American foreign policy: Pragmatism, or procrastination? *Presidential Studies Quarterly, 19* (4), 717–31.

Klein, J. (1992, Aug. 3). Walking small. *Newsweek,* 29.

Klein, J. (1993, May 24). Slow motion. *Newsweek,* 16–19.

Klein, J. (1993, Aug. 2). Clinton's bushed presidency. *Newsweek,* 22.

Kuhnert, K. W., and P. Lewis. (1987). Transactional and transformational leadership: A constructive/developmental analysis. *Academy of Management Review, 12,* 648–57.

Lauter, D. (1993, Nov. 7). Clinton learns from early errors. *Los Angeles Times,* [reprinted in *Cincinnati Enquirer,* A1, A6].

Mommsen, W. J. (1989). *The political and social theory of Max Weber.* Chicago: University of Chicago Press.

Nanus, B. (1992). *Visionary leadership.* San Francisco: Jossey-Bass.

Novak, M. (1992). *Choosing presidents: Symbols of political leadership.* 2nd ed. New Brunswick: Transaction.

Perot, H. R. (1992). Ross Perot reenters presidential campaign. *Vital Speeches of the Day, 59* (1), 15–17.

Pfeffer, J. (1981). Management as symbolic action: The creation and main-tenance of organizational paradigms. In L. L. Cummings and B. M. Staw, eds., *Research in organizational behavior.* Greenwich, Conn.: JAI, 3: 1–52.

Pondy, L. R. (1978). Leadership is a language game. In M. W. McCall Jr. and M. M. Lombardo, eds., *Leadership: Where else can we go?* Durham, N.C.: Duke University Press, pp. 88–99.

Sandman, J. H. (1989). Winning the presidency: The vision and values approach. *Presidential Studies Quarterly, 19* (2), 259–66.

Schein, E. H. (1985). *Organizational culture and leadership: A dynamic view.* San Francisco: Jossey-Bass.

Sergiovanni, T. J., and J. E. Corbally, eds. (1984). *Leadership and organizational culture: New perspectives on administrative theory and practice.* Chicago: University of Illinois Press.

Shamir, B. (1991). The charismatic relationship: Alternative explanations and predictions. *Leadership Quarterly, 2* (2), 81–104.

Smircich, L., and G. Morgan. (1982). Leadership: The management of meaning. *Journal of Applied Behavioral Science, 18,* 257–73.

Smith, R. M., ed. (1988, Nov. 21). How Bush won: The inside story of cam-paign '88 [Special issue]. *Newsweek.*

Smith, R. M., ed. (1992, Nov.–Dec.). How he won: The untold story of Bill Clinton's triumph [Special issue]. *Newsweek.*

Smith, P. B., and M. F. Peterson. (1988). *Leadership, organizations and culture: An event management model.* London: SAGE.

Sowell, T. (1987). *A conflict of visions.* New York: Morrow.

Speaks, L., and R. Pack. (1988). *Speaking out.* New York: Scribner.

Tichy, N. M., and M. A. Devanna. (1990). *The transformational leader.* New York: Wiley.

Tichy, N. M., and D. O. Ulrich. (1984, Fall). The leadership challenge—A call for the transformational leader. *Sloan Management Review,* 59–68.

Tucker, R. C. (1968). The theory of charismatic leadership. *Daedulus, 97,* 731–56.

Weber, M. (1947). *Theory of social and economic organization.* Trans. T. Parsons and A. M. Henderson. New York: Oxford University Press.

Weber, M. (1947). *The theory of social and economic organization: Being Part I of Wirtschaft und Gesellschaft.* London: W. Hodge.

Weber, M. (1968). *Economy and society.* New York: Bedminster Press.

Westley, F., and H. Mintzberg. (1989). Visionary leadership and strategic management. *Strategic Management Journal,* 10, 17–32.

Wildavsky, A. (1993). At once too strong and too weak: President Clinton and the dilemma of egalitarian leadership. *Presidential Studies Quarterly, 23* (3), 437–44.

Willner, A. R. (1984). The spellbinders: *Charismatic political leadership*. New Haven: Yale University Press.

Windt, T. (1992). *Analyzing the 1992 campaign*. Purdue University Public Affairs Video Archives: C-SPAN.

Yukl, G. A. (1989). *Leadership in organizations*. Englewood Cliffs, N.J.: Prentice-Hall.

FIVE

The Battle of Issues and Images

Establishing Interpretive Dominance

MARY E. STUCKEY AND FREDERICK J. ANTCZAK

IDENTIFICATION AS A STRATEGIC CONCERN

Political campaigns are largely, if not entirely, communicative processes (Trent and Friedenberg, 1991), and while candidates for political office are often excoriated for shallowness, duplicity, obfuscation, and preoccupation with the manipulation of surface image to private ends at the expense of the exploration of serious issues for public purposes, something important is communicated in the barrage of words and images that comprise a presidential campaign. Most campaign communication is designed with the goal of building positive images of the candidates, regardless of the ostensible subject (Davis, 1981; Nimmo and Savage, 1976; O'Keefe and Sheinkopf, 1974; Rudd, 1989). Thus, even in its most facile manifestations, campaign communication can be analyzed as symbolic action that assists candidates in developing and maintaining public support for themselves and their policy preferences (Buchanan, 1991; Joslyn, 1990; McKelvey and Ordeshook, 1984).

Candidates do not simply adopt different positions on "the issues"; they also refigure the definitions of the issues themselves, definitions that contain within them guides to appropriate action (Bennett, 1993; Edelman, 1977). The fact that there are poor people, for instance, does not necessarily constitute a demand for political action. But the perception that poverty is the culpable result of individual or systemic failure does, by locating responsibility, demand certain governmental action or inaction. Every candidate adopts a discourse that carries within it certain claims to truth, claims about the nature

117

of the politically relevant world (Edelman, 1988). Campaign communication involves the contest between these competing discourses. The prize in a presidential election is establishment of interpretive dominance. The victor is positioned to set the terms of debate for the next four years. This interpretive dominance is attained through the presentation of candidate image as representative of the electorate (Hellweg, 1979; Kendall and Yum, 1984). Because all language is figurative, all campaign communication, even the most apparently vapid, reveals something about these contested discourses.

Kenneth Burke remains one of the most insightful scholars of the figurative nature of language. For Burke, "even if a given terminology is a reflection of reality, by its very nature as a terminology it must be a *selection* of reality; and to this extent it must also serve as a deflection of reality" (1966, p. 45). No language can simply represent or directly convey reality. All language use is tropic, that is, any use of language involves a choice about how to figure language—how to shape, and thus in one way or another, selectively define reality. Because campaigns are processes through which one candidate's selective definition of reality comes to dominate that of others, campaign communication can be usefully categorized and analyzed within the framework of Burke's "master tropes," each of which ask us to see one reality in terms of another: metaphor (perspective), metonymy (reduction), synedoche (representation), and irony (dialectic). The tropic structure allows us to focus attention on the ways in which candidates seek to dominate and control the processes of defining issues and images in a national campaign to create the appearance of identification with, and thus representation of, the electorate.

A BURKEAN APPROACH TO IDENTIFICATION

Identification, for Burke, is a process of creating an ideologically based unity with an audience (1969). This is precisely the sort of unity that candidates seek to create with the voting public, because by establishing unity candidates also establish the dominance of their interpretation of the political world. For Burke, ideological invocation is more powerful than explicit persuasion, for meaning is derived from the interaction among speaker, message, and audience. Grammatical and lexical forms of persuasion contribute to this identification:

> At least, we know that many purely formal patterns can readily awaken an attitude of collaborative expectancy in us. For instance, imagine a passage built about a set of oppositions (*we* do *this*, but *they* on the other hand do *that*; *we* stay *here*, but *they* go *there*; *we* look *up*, but *they* look *down*, etc.). Once you grasp the trend of the form, it invites participation regardless of the subject matter. Formally, you

will find yourself swinging along with the succession of antitheses, even though you may not agree with the proposition that is being presented in this form. (1969, p. 58)

Burke did not argue that poor propositions could be made irresistible by placing them within a certain rhetorical form, but simply that the form of an argument inescapably affects its persuasiveness because of the appeal the form itself carries:

> Of course, the more violent your original resistance to the proposition, the weaker will be your degree of "surrender" by "collaborating" with the form. But in cases where a decision is still to be reached, a yielding to the form prepares for assent to the matter identified with it. Thus, you are drawn to the form, not in your capacity as a partisan, but because of some "universal" appeal in it. (1969, p. 58)

Candidates tie symbolic content to a grammatical form in order to achieve the sense of identity—or in Burke's word, "consubstantiality"—with the electorate. The electorate assists in the creation of this sense of representation as identification by participating in and collaborating with the arguments as presented by candidates.

> In any interaction, including the rhetorical interactions between speakers and democratic audiences, human substance may be shared. The physical and symbolic differences that are the occasions of communication must be located and bridged if speaker and audience are to become "consubstantial," to share such substance. But when they do, insofar as they do, they are identical, identified. (Antczak, 1985, p. 11)

For Burke, those things that appear furthest apart are also those that are most similar; apparent similarities can mask great differences. To be a leader, one must be of the led and yet also other. If leaders are too much "the led," they lose their claim to superiority and thus their claim to leadership; if they are too much "the other," they lose their claim to identity, and again their leadership. Candidates seeking to validate their claims to leadership must walk a constantly shifting line between identification and otherness.

This line becomes somewhat easier to locate when one realizes that "from the standpoint of rhetoric, the implanting of an ultimate hierarchy upon social forms is the important thing" (1969, p. 191). This hierarchy is ideological in nature: "the hierarchic ordering of the subsocial realms could be considered as an 'ideological reflex' or extension of the persuasive principle experienced in the social realm" (p. 191). Thus, within every discourse, there is a hierarchy of terms, representative of an implied social order. Candidates as rhetors can maintain both identity and separation by refiguration of the hierarchy implicit in their discourse. These refigurings can best be understood by examining the candidate's public speech through the lens provided by Burke's master tropes.

BURKE'S MASTER TROPES
AND THE 1992 GENERAL ELECTION
METAPHOR

The key to understanding metaphor (or perspective) is also the key to understanding the most fundamental goal of campaign communication: establishing the authority of the candidate's perspective, the foundation of interpretive dominance. For Burke, metaphor refers to the process of "seeing something in terms of something else . . . the thisness of a that or the thatness of a this" (1945, p. 503). As perspective, metaphor functions to see one character in terms of another. The task of all campaign communication must be to focus the potential voters' attention on one candidate in the terms preferred by the other.

To understand Bill Clinton in terms of George Bush, for instance, is to see Clinton as a youthful, unpatriotic, inexperienced, rash, and fundamentally untrustworthy character. Throughout the campaign, Bush tried to undermine the status of his opponent, making comments like, "My feisty little friend from Texas, Ross Perot, had one thing right. He said the grocery store is no preparation for Walmart. Well, I think the man's on to something" (1992g). This comment, which Bush repeated often, had two advantages. First, Bush used Perot as a surrogate, allowing him to attack Clinton while avoiding the appearance of inappropriate hostility. Second, Bush simultaneously demeaned Perot, relegating him to the status of a "little friend," however feisty. By referring to Perot thus "affectionately," Bush again minimized the hostility of his attack, thus reducing the possibility of further alienating Perot's supporters. If Bush's definitions of his opponents become dominant, then the electorate is faced with three "choices": a grocery clerk, a diminutive Texan who cannot be taken seriously, or the incumbent president.

To understand Bush in terms of Clinton, however, is to arrive at a very different perspective on the campaign; character as well as experience are defined differently. Seen through what Burke would call Clinton's "terministic screen," Clinton may not have served his country in a war like World War II but, like his contemporaries, Clinton had to face moral choices about military service in a war that bears more parallels to the conflicts this nation is likely to face in the future. Clinton regarded Bush as unlike most Americans in that he had an uncle who could give him hundreds of thousands of dollars to get a start in business, while Clinton has risen on his own merits from a much more modest, more sharable starting point, the metaphor of "a place called Hope." Clinton understands what "family values" must mean in a time when women may have careers and accomplishments of their own, a time when in most families both parents must work. Unlike Bush, therefore, Clinton is a person of our times and circumstances. Speaking at Notre Dame, he said:

> If we truly believe, as almost everyone says, no matter what they believe on certain issues, that children are God's most precious creation, then surely we owe every child born in the United States the opportunity to make the most of his or her God-given potential. I want an America that offers every child a healthy start in life, decent schooling, a chance to go to college or job training worthy of the name, not only because that's essential for our common economic success, but because providing opportunities is how we fulfill our obligations to each other and the moral principles we honor. (1992i)

Clinton went out of his way to convey his caring and his understanding. During the presidential debates, for instance, Clinton moved (or, when restricted by a podium, leaned) toward the audience, toward the cameras. He often held his hand out, palm raised, in a gesture that combined confidence with supplication. When asked questions by citizens, he often nodded his head, never interrupted the speaker, waited courteously to hear the complete question, and often remembered and used their names. He avoided the appearance of giving "canned" presentations and was at his best when he was responding "naturally" to "real" people, and when he was speaking for those people to a larger polity:

> All of you, in different ways, have brought me here today to step beyond a life and a job that I love, to make a commitment to a larger cause. . . . I refuse to stand by and let our children become part of the first generation to do worse than their parents. I don't want my child or your child to be part of a country that's coming apart instead of coming together. (1991a)

In Clinton's rhetoric, George Bush and the Republicans were responsible for the ills that afflicted America. "Families are coming apart, kids are dropping out of school, drugs and crime dominate our streets. And our leaders here in Washington are doing nothing to turn America around" (1991b). Clinton, because he understood the problem and because he cared about offering solutions, was dedicated to curing those ills. "As I've traveled around this country, I've seen too much pain on people's faces, too much fear in people's eyes" (1991c). That pain and that fear were occasioned by the economic policies of the Reagan/Bush administrations, which were established as the defining issue of the 1992 general election.

Moreover, for Clinton, Bush was the product of a past age, and consequently, did not understand the demands of the present; his very virtues betrayed his shortcomings. Bush's emphasis on the metaphor of a nebulous "new world order" was less an evidence of the president's skill in foreign policy than the prime indicator of Bush's inability and unwillingness to recognize, respond to, or do anything but distract from the genuine domestic needs of the electorate. Clinton said, "And if those questions are hard for us, with all the privileges that God has given us, think about how much tougher they are for most families who are working harder for less money these days, and how devastating they can be for those families confronted with layoffs, illnesses, alcohol and drug problems, or a violent neighborhood" (1992a). Clinton was able, in a way not available to Bush or Perot, to make connections between classes, between races, to call on the commonality of experience, because his experience spanned so much. He was thus able to forge identification with the audience, and to ask them to forge identification with one another, and with other audiences previously foreign to them.

To understand either of the major party candidates in terms of Perot is to deemphasize these differences of character and experience, and to emphasize in their stead the common connection to the mainstream political process. Both Bush and Clinton were, for Perot, personifications of "politics-as-usual," while Perot represented the uncommon common man who "truly" speaks for the legitimate interests of The People. When Bush emphasized his experience during the second presidential debate, for instance, Perot responded, "I don't have any experience in running up a $4 trillion debt" (Apple, 1992). Throughout the campaign, Perot offered himself as a candidate who will "do it, not just talk about it," a candidate therefore different from the other candidates (Sack, 1992). And while Perot's performance at General Motors—an institution more like the federal government than his more successful enterprises—gave some reasons to doubt his "under-the-hood" credentials, neither of the other candidates had a vocabulary in which Perot's failures could be brought to bear in a way relevant to the campaign.

Metaphors provide context for the campaign and thus extend further and cover more than the individual character and experience of the candidates. Clinton's metaphors of community, stressed throughout the campaign, competed with Bush's efforts to echo Reagan on economic individualism. Where Clinton offered to expand programs, Bush said, "Make no mistake: political and economic freedom are linked; they are inseparable. And just as people have a God-given right to choose who will govern them, they also must be free to make their own economic choices. When we lift barriers to economic freedom within and among our countries, we unleash powerful forces of growth and creativity" (1992c). But in the perception of at least some people, barriers to choice remained. This appeal would have been more effective if more voters held the image that they had satisfactory access to real economic choices.

Perot's metaphors proferred generalized, often confused, protests against both Clinton and Bush, and the national parties that they would bring to, or keep in, power.

> We used to have the world's greatest economic engine. . . . We let it slip away and with it went millions of jobs and taxpayers. Let's take a little time to figure out what's happened to the engine. Let's raise the hood and go to work. Let's diagnose the problem. I can tell you before we look at the engine, an engine tune-up ain't going to fix it. We're going to have to do a major overhaul. (Sack, 1992)

Metaphors form the basis of a candidate's interpretation of the politically relevant world, for they provide the vocabulary through which that world will be interpreted and understood. They help determine which issues are seen as relevant, and how those issues will be interpreted in light of the images the candidates try to project. Once the defining metaphors of a campaign are laid out, the context is defined and the competing discourses of the candidates take shape.

METONYMY

Metonymy, which Burke also understands as reduction, functions to incorporate some incorporeal or intangible state in terms of the corporeal or tangible. Metonymy functions to render these big and complex "truths" more accessible. The Reagan welfare mother buying vodka with food stamps anecdote is one example of metonymy; in this small vignette, Reagan captured an enormously complicated web of conservative beliefs about the welfare system. Reagan excelled at the art of reduction—the entire welfare system into the person of one welfare mother—to communicate his policy preferences.

George Bush lacked this skill; thus he was unable to resist when such reductions were applied, ever more frequently, to him. For example, Bush's inability to identify with the average American was crystallized in his statement that "I'm not prepared to say that we are in a recession" (1992a). By stressing themes of optimism and reassurance that the country was on the right path, Bush attempted to force his definition of the American experience on an electorate whose daily lives were evidence against that definition. In neglecting to respond to that evidence, Bush undercut his own interpretive status and his image as the only candidate worthy of the people's trust.

While Perot brandished cardboard charts and Clinton boarded a bus, Bush remained aloof and isolated behind his presidential podium, seemingly unable to comprehend the national mood. His public speech frequently fragmented, and eventually became inchoate:

> Let me tell you another one, and this one concludes it. Governor Clinton and Senator Gore, the Ozone Man, is [sic] going around the world—[laughter]—you listen to some—hey, this guy is strange. They've got Gore muzzled back now. You have no timber workers, only a bunch of owls, if you listen to him. You'd have no farmers, only a great big wet hole out there somewhere if you listen to him. But here's the point: They differ. They differ. They want bigger Government. He talks about growing Government. I want to grow the private sector. I want to grow jobs in the private sector. (1992h)

The image of fragmentation and lack of vision that plagued Bush throughout his presidency became symbolic of his campaign: The "vision thing" became shorthand for all of Bush's political problems—metonymy with a vengeance.

This was particularly destructive to Bush's efforts to establish interpretive dominance in light of the Clinton campaign. Clinton's speeches were full of plans and proposals, three-part answers, and clear statements of purpose. The clearest theme running through the Clinton campaign rhetoric is that of "connectedness." Foreign and domestic policy are connected to one another (1991c, 1991d), today's problems are connected to the difficulties faced in the past (1992b, 1992c), and all Americans are connected by their faith in the American dream (1992a, 1992e). Most of his speeches contained overt appeals to community and a rejection of the "politics of hate and divisiveness" (1991a, 1991b, 1992d).

As one who lived the American Dream, Clinton was able to present his life as a parable for the nations and to implicitly argue that, by electing him, Americans would be able to restore the American dream that they were in danger of losing:

> For me, the American Dream is not a slogan. It has been a way of life. I was born in 1946, as America was entering the greatest economic boom the world has ever seen. I grew up in a state where almost half the people lived below the poverty line. My mother was widowed three months before I was born. I was raised by my grand-parents until I was four. . . . We didn't have much money. But growing up, I and my generation always knew that if we worked hard and played by the rules, we'd be rewarded—and I have been, beyond my wildest dreams. Millions of young people growing up in this country today can't count on that dream. They look around and see that their hard work may not be rewarded. Most people are working harder for less these days, as they have been for well over a

decade. The American Dream is slipping away along with the loss of our economic leadership. (1992a)

In thus presenting his life as the American Dream, Clinton could also embody the solution to the threat of its loss. This represented a claim to competence potentially far more powerful than, say, experience in foreign policy or personal friendship with foreign leaders. The ability to read a map is, in uncertain circumstances, more important than experience behind the wheel of a car that is going in the wrong direction.

For his part, Perot relied on a series of "infomercials" to make his point, substantively as well as symbolically, that he was fighting the people's battle to revitalize a moribund political process. His deliberately amateurish poses, his folksy turns of speech, and his insistent focus on the economy supported him in his claim to be Champion-of-the-People.

All three candidates sought to present themselves as the part most representative of the whole, as that whole was defined through their use of metaphor. Bush and Clinton engaged in a war of dueling biographies, each trying to interpret his life and that of their opponent in ways that would further their claim to having lived the most symbolically representative life. Perot used a more restricted metonymy-as-biography, focusing on the key element of past complicity in the political process he was interested in changing.

SYNECDOCHE

Synecdoche is similar to and overlaps metonymy. The issue surrounding synecdoche is "which part should represent the whole?" One of the main tasks of political candidates is to present themselves as the part that most accurately reflects the whole, to encapsulate the polity in their being, and to represent the average American as identical to the possibilities for all of the people.

Bush attempted to define and thus dismiss his opponent by tying him to Michael Dukakis and to the Democratically run and scandal-ridden national Congress, attempting to underline his belief that Clinton was a part ill-suited to represent the whole:

Remember Michael Dukakis, the tank driver? [Laughter] Well, Bill Clinton nominated him for president 4 years ago. This year, according to an article in the *New York Times*, 39 percent of Governor Clinton's economic proposals are virtually identical to the ideas Governor Dukakis was pushing: higher taxes, more spending, a bigger deficit. . . . Bill Clinton and his friends in Congress would let the lion of inflation out of its cage. I say, let's lock it away; keep it away from your bank account, keep your savings sacrosanct, not to be wiped out by inflation. (1992h)

Bush worked hard to establish the dominance of these definitions, especially those regarding Clinton, his main opponent. He invoked his definition of Clinton in the latter days of the campaign and in a variety of contexts, frequently in comparative terms. Unlike Bush, Clinton did not serve his country in war; unlike Bush, Clinton did not build a business; unlike Bush, Clinton did not have a commitment to "family values"; for example, Bush said:

> When you get down to it, leadership is about trust. Trust runs both ways. You need a leader who you can trust, but you also need a leader who trusts in the American people, trusts you and not the Government to make the important decisions about your lives. . . . Let me tell you about how I learned about competing in the world. I'm a Texan, moved there in 1948, built a business there, raised my family there. (1992d)

Bush's claim to representation is derived from his life experience as having lived through the growth of the United States into a superpower and its eventual status as the only remaining superpower: "The cold war has ended. What a miraculous year it's been. We stand on the verge of a new age of competition. Our ideals triumphed in the cold war, and the new wave of democracy represents nothing less than the political restructuring of the entire world. That was a tough fight, a long fight, but it was worth it" (1992a). Implicit in this definition of the political world is the observation that it was a fight in which George Bush participated and Bill Clinton did not. Lacking that firsthand experience in and knowledge of American triumphs, Clinton lacked the credentials to lead the nation in its moment of triumph:

> From the fall of the Berlin Wall to the last gasp of imperial communism, from the four decades of the cold war to the 40 days of Desert Storm, America has led the way. We won the cold war— history will show this—we won the cold war because we Americans never shirked responsibility. . . . That's why today, as the cold war ends, America stands alone as the undisputed leader of the world. . . . No one said it was easy. Leadership demands character and experience. (1992b)

Bush united character and experience as equivalents, as significators of one another. He argued that his character was the total of his experiences—as a fighter pilot in World War II, a dedicated family man, a prosperous businessman, and a public servant. Clinton's character, on the other hand, became the total of his experience—as defined by Bush—a draft dodger, womanizer, governor of a poor state, and bystander during the great conflicts of the age:

Just pause for a moment to reflect on what we've done. Germany is united, and a slab of the Berlin wall sits right outside this Astrodome. Arabs and Israelis now sit face to face and talk peace, and every hostage held in Lebanon is free. The conflict in El Salvador is over, and free elections brought democracy to Nicaragua. Black and white South Africans cheered each other at the Olympics. The Soviet Union can only be found in history books. The captive nations of Eastern Europe and the Baltics are captive no more. And today on the rural streets of Poland, merchants sell cans of air labeled "the last breath of communism." If I had stood before you four years ago and described this as the world we would help to build, you would have said, "George Bush, you must be smoking something, and you must have inhaled." (1992e)

Rather than trying to establish himself as representative of the nation, Bush chose to undermine Clinton's claim to representation. In so doing, Bush may well have undermined trust in his opponent, but he also failed to erase doubts concerning himself. Endlessly reminding voters of his success at leading a multinational coalition in Kuwait did little to inspire confidence in his ability to lead a recalcitrant Congress in the United States. In the foreign policy realm, Bush could be the skillful diplomat, the principled leader, the archetypical moral American. But in the economic realm, where Americans felt and were made to feel more deeply located in 1992, he was a man who was battered in the early going by Pat Buchanan for his unprincipled reversal of his "read my lips; no new taxes" pledge. Worse, he was the man who did not understand the recession, and who, devastatingly, was amazed at the sight of a checkout machine commonly used in grocery stores. In the frame of domestic politics, Bush thus came to represent the people who "just didn't get it," not The People themselves.

As such, Bush became an easy target for Ross Perot. For Perot, as for many voters in 1992, the problem was the process, and George Bush seemed, after so many years and modes of involvement, to represent that process. By failing to establish himself as the part most representative of the whole, Bush lost control of the definitional process. His leadership was consequently defined and interpreted by others.

Clinton was not without potential problems in this area, however. While he was the man who jogged to McDonald's, he was also a "draft dodger" who had marital difficulties, who may or may not have flirted with drugs in the 1960s, and who, as a southerner and graduate of Yale, was certainly outside of the American mainstream of experience. This complexity, however, while somewhat troublesome, was also useful to Clinton. It was exceptionally difficult for his opponents to label him neatly and thus dismissively. A "good ol' boy" whose wife made more money than he did? A graduate of Yale in Arkansas? Clinton possessed a variety of experiences that he could use as a plea to inclusion. He could argue convincingly for the complexity of American experience, for he embodied much of that complexity.

All candidates claim that they are the part that best represents the whole. For Bush, that claim rested upon his superior claim to the people's trust. His claim was undermined as his campaign came to be defined in terms of what he was not, rather than what he was. Clinton, by contrast, was able to offer an appeal of positive representation, an ability to unify and embody a complex polity. It was to prove the more persuasive image.

IRONY

There are few critical concepts as contested as the definition of irony. But Burke's notion does offer what amounts to a special advantage for the study of political campaigns: insight into what happens when competing issues and images cross, collide, and begin to interact, and how to study that interaction as a single persuasive event.

Burke defines irony, or dialectic, as the interaction of mutually related perspectives. While there is always one character (candidate) who dominates, other characters function as necessary modifiers of and foils for that character, who is understood in connection and by comparison rather than as an isolated individual. In the *Grammar of Motives*, Burke notes, "[I]rony arises when one tries, by the interaction of terms upon one another, to produce a development which uses all the terms" (1945). From the overall point of view, none of these "subperspectives" can be thought of as completely right or wrong in themselves. They are instead all positions affecting one another to produce the total movement or development.

Here Burke's notion of irony has special utility for the critic trying to make something intelligible out of the cacophony of campaigns. The problem is that campaigns are full of absolute claims—claims about representativeness, reductions of issues and images, attempts to provide the single, preemptive perspective through which all the figurations of a campaign are to be understood. What Burke provides is the analytical vocabulary in which critics may study what campaign tyros know in their experience: Any campaign must remain fragmentary until it produces a kind of development in which its terms can interact on one another, a way of seeing "this-in-terms-of-that."

We reach certain conclusions about how Clinton's claim to "feel your pain" relates to Bush's surprise at the supermarket checkout scanner; how Bush's experience and claims to expertise in foreign policy relate to the foreign and domestic issues Clinton put forward as newly important and requiring different leadership; how Bush and Clinton and Perot promised to be agents of change, and how the change each of them respectively promised squared with the need for change—and for its dialectical pair, continuity—that each of us feels. Irony is Burke's name for the process by which the terms and figures of campaign rhetoric come to affect one another, the process by which each comes to have not the meaning asserted by its proponent, but the meaning arrived at in an orderly development that results in "the observer who considers the whole from the standpoint of the participation of all the terms rather than from the standpoint of any one participant" (1945, p. 531).

Bush's World War II service record gained its force not simply in contrast to Clinton's lack of military service, however much Bush proponents might have wished it, but also in contact with Bush's own claims about the fall of communism, the consequent relevance of cold war bipolar visions of the international scene, the perceived capacities and limits of the United States to address issues on a variety of fronts (e.g., the commitment of troops to Somalia; the lack of a similarly firm commitment vis-à-vis Bosnia), the urgency of other priorities stressed by the other candidates, the potential importance of traits manifested by the other candidates, and so on. The "tax-and-spend liberal" charge against Clinton gained its particular force in relation to charges of governmental gridlock, concerns about the size of the deficit run up during the terms of Republican presidents, the perceived fairness in the distribution of the tax burden, Clinton's degree of apparent independence from "special interests" within the part (a concern that, like many others pertinent to this self-proclaimed "new kind of Democrat" itself, draws some of its salience from previous campaigns), Dukakis's plaintive relation to Jesse Jackson seen in terms of Clinton's rebuke of Sister Souljah, and the relevance of old slogans to proclaimed new realities with which politics must deal. Paradoxically, Clinton's disparaging nickname "Slick Willie," labeling him as a man capable of adroit manipulation, may have lent credence to Clinton's claim that he was well able to negotiate through and manage, if not resolve, these difficult new political realities.

Perot, of course, promised in his turn not to manage these tensions but to eliminate them. His preference for results rather than procedures and ends rather than means, while fundamentally unconsultative and even anti-democratic, contained a certain broad appeal in the context of gridlock and the generalized frustration with "politics-as-usual": Whatever Perot was, he was not the usual breed of power-seeking politico. He was the wildcard of the campaign—nonpolitical and unpredictable, a voice of protest if not the voice of reason. Perot defied categorization in the same way he defied the system, unbalancing them even as he often appeared unbalanced himself.

Burke identifies this dialectical irony as a form of humility: No one character can really be superior in that he or she needs the other characters as necessary modifiers (1945, p. 512). But when one campaign supplies the other too readily with the modifiers it seeks, that campaign undermines itself. Opponents of Perot cited his relative instability and nonconsultativeness, impressions given depth by his sudden withdrawal and reentry.

Opponents of Bush sought to describe him as out of touch in several important ways. He was out of touch with what might be regarded as common experience: Aside from his dalliance with the supermarket scanner, the president was seen playing golf and powerboating in the middle of what he himself proclaimed a crisis vis-à-vis Iraq. But they also accused him of being out of touch with his own themes: Besides his own reelection, they charged, Bush had no coherent sense of what he believed in, no coherent sense of himself. One of Bush's most influential responses was a speech in Michigan, late in the campaign as the Clinton margin seemed to be narrowing, which staggered from charges about "Captain Ozone" to invocation of the Beat Generation's outdated expression "crazy, man, crazy" that were as inappropriate in tone to the seriousness of the issues he claimed to care about as they seemed hopeless, almost lonely anachronisms.

But opponents of Clinton who criticized him as not tough enough to be president found their charges confronting a Clinton tough enough to make it through a series of extraordinarily brutal primaries. Those who accused him of being an old kind of Democrat (as did Paul Tsongas, labeling Clinton "pander bear") found their charges confronting his appeal to the business community and Reagan Democrats, to the West, and even to the South. And when President Bush sought to score points against Clinton by accusing him of having spent too much of his life in public service, he found the charge complicated by his own history and vitiated by Bush's selecting and maintaining Dan Quayle as vice president, since a life spent largely in political office had not been enough by itself to disqualify either man from the presidential ticket.

Clinton, by virtue of his own various personal experience, could encompass the various experiences of the nation and establish the dominance of his vision for and of that nation. He was not reducible to neat epigrams or dismissive phrases. Clinton managed always to be more complex than the definitions others offered of him; that elusiveness played to the advantage of his own definitions.

Like Clinton, Perot resisted easy categorization, although his erratic behavior contributed to a perception that his was at least a less stable, perhaps a less dependable complexity. George Bush, on the other hand, never found a language in which to describe the political context in a way satisfying to him and plausible for the electorate. Lacking an effective language, he lost control of the definitional process; his discourse was defined, disastrously for the president, by his opponents.

CONCLUSIONS

Burke dedicates *A Grammar of Motives* "ad bellum purificandum" (1945, p. i). We do not tend to think of war as the sort of thing that admits of purification. But in fact the very system of campaigns and elections, rather than deciding things by *force majeur*, is already a step toward that purification. We do tend to locate what is most worth attention in the electoral contests themselves, to understand them much more narrowly than Burke enables us to do, and to read them in terms of persuasion. In this way criticism is simplified, but the "war" we study is not in Burke's sense purified. Burke would suggest that where winners and losers can be definitively distinguished, we generate the false sense that war can not only be purified, but won. In point of fact, such results can be ephemeral: Has there ever been any elected official who did not disappoint at least some of his or her supporters, who did not prove to be someone else other than his or her campaign image after election? Indeed, how many elections are conducted over the issues that prove to be most central during the term of office? But the prospect of determinate outcomes in the electoral wars may distract us from more important contests, contests for interpretive dominance among sets of issues and images.

The intent of this analysis has not been to claim that electoral outcomes are unimportant for the student of campaign communication, but rather to show how they can be less importantly definitive of political conflicts than the contests over the terms of ongoing debate. These contests are never finally resolved, even following an election. But it is during an election campaign that we "come to terms," as it were, with most of these contests and make them explicit; and it is in the wake of these campaigns, if only temporarily, that one discourse becomes largely dominant. That domination can be an immensely influential outcome of the campaign and election process. For instance, following Ronald Reagan's victory in 1980, Democrats were faced with having to shake the label of being Far Left liberals whose proposals amounted to a policy of "tax and spend" and who were therefore presumptively out of touch with what was now to be regarded as mainstream America. Democrats spent their time struggling against these labels—in different ways, with varying degrees of success—for the better part of the decade. But by 1992 Republicans emerged from the many-sided interplay of political terms as "just not getting it" and Democrats, in the person of Bill Clinton, could again be seen as more representative of the average American, at least in his or her most current construction. In these terms Democrats could now seem, however temporarily, more inviting for identification.

A critical approach to political communication springing from Burke's master tropes also holds promise for areas of scholarship that lie at least partly beyond the boundaries of this study. For example, the terms in which candidates may become more appealing for identification frame not only campaigns, but the scene and substance of subsequent governance—the legislative and executive possibilities made more or less accessible by their outcomes. These might include at least the following: the particular situations that seem to require action more and less urgently; the options taken to be worthy and unworthy of serious discussion; the considerations of timeliness that come to constrict or distend the progress of that discussion; the particular proposals that reach, and fail to reach, the threshold of formal decision; the selection among the outcomes of those decisions that are seen as important, in its relevance to the situation addressed and its degree of subsequently perceived success or failure; and the ways in which those decisions and outcomes open and close possibilities of identification for future campaigns, which in the contemporary political calendar are always just around the corner. In *A Grammar of Motives* Burke provides students of campaign communication a critical vocabulary in which such evolving and ramifying identifications may be examined and understood.

But even for studies that restrict their attention to campaigns, Burke provides not only an approach but a rationale for viewing electoral contests in a way arguably more appropriate for our mass (and massively) mediated politics: all the elements of each individual campaign; all the rival campaigns together; the political, material, and popular culture surrounding, feeding, and feeding back on the campaigns; the media coverage; the attempted and successful manipulations of and spins on that coverage; every intended and stray factor influencing the direction and weight and force of communication, all as an interdependent whole. We contend that examining campaigns in terms of identification in this way may provide a more comprehensive and coherent alternative to existing approaches of examining campaigns in terms of persuasion.

What we have shown in this chapter is more modest, if not less essential. By examining language use as symbolic action aimed at identification, communication scholars may make clearer how candidates' images get their meaning for a given campaign; how the complex issues of public life may be reduced to shapes that are accessible and that may communicate policy preferences; how claims of representativeness may be constructed, and how they compete; and how campaign communications—strategic or unintentional, from the campaigners themselves or from other sources—affect one another to produce a development of meanings in which campaign issues and images gain their specific powers of identification and may establish interpretive dominance.

NOTE

This essay was originally written for this book. It has also been published in *Communication Quarterly*, 42, No. 2 (Spring 1994), 120–132.

REFERENCES

Antczak. Frederick J. (1985). *Thought and character: The rhetoric of democratic education*. Ames, Iowa: Iowa State University Press.

Apple, R. W. (1992, Oct. 12). Perot is colorful. *New York Times*, A1.

Bennett. W. Lance (1993). Constructing publics and their opinions. *Political Communication, 10*(2), 101–20.

Buchanan, Bruce (1991). *Electing a president: The Markle Commission research on campaign '88*. Austin, Tex.: University of Texas Press.

Burke, Kenneth (1945). *A grammar of motives*. Berkeley: University of California Press.

Burke, Kenneth (1966). *Language as symbolic action*. Berkeley: University of California Press.

Burke, Kenneth (1969). *A rhetoric of motives*. Berkeley: University of California Press.

Bush, George (1992a, Jan. 13). Remarks to the American Farm Bureau. *Weekly Compilation of Presidential Documents* [hereinafter *Weekly Compilation*]. Washington, D.C.: Office of the Federal Register, National Archives, and Records Administration.

Bush, George (1992b, Feb. 24). Remarks at the Bush-Quayle campaign kick-off in Bethesda, Md. *Weekly Compilation*.

Bush, George (1992c, Apr. 23). Remarks to the Forum of the Americas. *Weekly Compilation*.

Bush, George (1992d, Aug. 3). Remarks to Shaw Industries employees in Dalton, Ga. *Weekly Compilation*.

Bush, George (1992e, Aug. 20). Remarks accepting the presidential nomination at the Republican National Convention. *Weekly Compilation*.

Bush, George (1992f, Oct. 3). Remarks to the community in Clearwater, Fla. *Weekly Compilation*.

Bush, George (1992g, Oct. 20). Remarks to the community in Cornelia, Ga. *Weekly Compilation*.

Bush, George (1992h, Oct. 20). Remarks to the community in Spartanburg, S.C. *Weekly Compilation*.

Clinton, Bill (1991a, Oct. 3). Announcement speech. Little Rock, Ark. [All of the Clinton speeches were obtained from the Democratic National Committee.]

Clinton, Bill (1991b, Oct. 23). The new covenant-Rebuilding America. Georgetown University.

Clinton, Bill (1991c, Nov. 20). A new covenant for economic change. Georgetown University.

Clinton, Bill (1991d, Dec. 12). A new covenant for America's security. Georgetown University.

Clinton, Bill (1992a, Apr. 16). Economic address. Wharton School of Business, Philadelphia.

Clinton, Bill (1992b, May 2). Democratic Leadership Council Convention. New Orleans.

Clinton, Bill (1992c. May 14). They are all our children. Los Angeles.

Clinton, Bill (1992d, May 18). Let us rise to the challenge. Los Angeles.

Clinton, Bill (1992e, May 21). Family values address. Cleveland City Club.

Clinton, Bill (1992f, Sept. 11). The values of America: Remarks by Governor Bill Clinton at the University of Notre Dame.

Davis, Dwight (1981). Issue information and connotation in candidate imagery: Evidence from a laboratory experiment. *International Political Science Review, 2,* 461–79.

Edelman, Murray (1977). *Political language: Words that succeed and policies that fail.* San Diego: Academic Press.

Edelman, Murray (1988). *Constructing the political spectacle.* Chicago: University of Chicago Press.

Joslyn, Richard A. (1990). Election campaigns as occasions for civic education. In David L. Swanson and Dan Nimmon, eds., *New directions in political communication: A resource book.* Newbury Park: Sage, pp. 86–122.

Hellweg, Susan (1979). An examination of voter conceptualization of the ideal political candidate. *Southern Speech Communication Journal, 44,* 373–85.

Kendall, Kathleen E., and June Ock Yum (1984). Persuading the blue-collar voter: Issues, images, and homophily. In R. N. Bostrom, ed., *Communication yearbook.* Beverly Hills: Sage, 8:707–22.

McKelvey, Richard D., and Peter C. Ordeshook (1984). Rational expectations in elections. *Public Choice, 44,* 61–102.

Nimmo, Dan, and Robert L. Savage (1976). *Candidates and their images.* Santa Monica: Goodyear.

O'Keefe, M. Timothy, and Kenneth G. Sheinkopf (1974). The voter decides: Candidate image or campaign issue? *Journal of Broadcasting, 18,* 402–12.

Rudd, Robert (1989). Effects of issue specificity, ambiguity, on evaluations of candidate image. *Journalism Quarterly, 66,* 675–82.

Sack, Kevin (1992, Oct. 7). Perot, in TV talk, dissects economy. *New York Times.*

Trent, Judith S., and Robert V. Friedenberg (1991). *Political campaign communication: Principles and practices.* 2nd ed. New York: Praeger.

SIX

The Debate Challenge

Candidate Strategies in the New Media Age

Diana Owen

Jack Germond and Jules Witcover open their account of the 1992 presidential contest, *Mad as Hell,* by describing what they consider to be the turning point in the campaign. The event was the second presidential debate. Candidates George Bush, Bill Clinton, and Ross Perot answered questions from audience members instead of from the usual panel of journalists. The precise incident was sparked by an exchange with a twenty-five-year-old single mother.

Marisa Hall posed the following question to the candidates: "How has the national debt personally affected each of your lives? And if it hasn't, how can you honestly find a cure for the economic problems of the common people if you have no experience in what's ailing them?"

Perot, responding first, stated that the national debt had caused him to put his private life and businesses on hold and to get involved in the political process.

Bush, following Perot, seemed confused by the question. After meandering around the issue for several minutes, he retorted, "Are you suggesting that if somebody has means, the national debt doesn't affect them? . . . I'm not sure I get—help me with the question and I'll try to answer it."

Clinton quickly seized the moment. In order to show solidarity with Ms. Hall, he stepped away from the stool he was leaning against and walked toward her. He talked about the people he knew personally who had lost their jobs, their livelihoods, their health insurance. The solution was to invest in education, to create jobs, and to control health care costs.

As Clinton was speaking, the television camera panned to Bush, who was looking at his watch (Germond and Witcover, 1993).

Given what debates have become in the presidential electoral arena, it is not unreasonable for Germond and Witcover to use these few short minutes of television drama to sum up the entire 1992 campaign. This exchange captured what the election meant for millions of people who tuned into the debates or heard about them later. Ross Perot was good theater. George Bush "didn't get it." And Bill Clinton could connect with the people.

Televised debates are now institutions of the American electoral process. Although there was a sixteen-year hiatus after the "Great Debate" between Kennedy and Nixon, debates have been held in every election since 1976. Presidential campaign debates have proliferated during primaries, and the "main events" staged during the general election are much anticipated by the press and the public.

With each passing electoral contest, debates have gained in importance. The media have accorded debates a central role in their election coverage, coming as they do at a crucial point late in the campaign. As we shall see, debate reporting has come to constitute its own category of election news characterized by its own style of coverage. The press plugs the event like a boxing match, hyping the bout, handicapping the contestants, and booking odds on the outcome.

Until recently, few voters made electoral decisions based on candidates' debate performances (see Ranney, 1979; Kraus, 1980). Debates reinforced viewers' feelings about candidates, but rarely changed their opinions (Trent and Friedenberg, 1991). Increasingly, however, voters rely on debates when evaluating candidates and even when making their vote choices. More voters are undecided late in the campaign and look to debates as the one opportunity they will have to compare the candidates directly (Rouner and Perloff, 1988; Gersh, 1993).

Finally, serious presidential contenders face extreme pressure to debate. It is nearly impossible in the current political environment for candidates to consider opting out. Incumbent presidents cannot pursue a "Rose Garden strategy" when it comes to debates without creating a public perception that they have something to hide—a lesson Jimmy Carter learned in 1980. Nonincumbents also cannot afford to appear cowardly or evasive by avoiding debates. Thus, debates pose a complicated tactical challenge for candidates.

This chapter will explore presidential campaign debates as a strategic communication form used by candidates. The following questions will be addressed: Why have debates become such an integral part of presidential election campaigns? What strategies have candidates developed for managing campaign debates in the mass media age? Finally, how have candidates adapted their debate strategies to meet the challenges of a changing campaign media environment?

In addressing these issues, we will examine the ways in which the context within which debates take place is shaped by the medium of television, the press, and the public. We also will focus on the tactics employed by candidates during four phases of the debate process. These include: (1) the negotiation phase (or the debate over the debates); (2) the preparation phase; (3) the debates themselves; and (4) the postdebate phase. Finally, we will speculate about the future of presidential debates and the consequences debates hold for our democratic polity.

PRESIDENTIAL DEBATES IN THE MASS MEDIA AGE

Debates, as they have become institutionalized in American presidential campaigns, are a product of elections in the television age. As such, the rules governing debate strategies reflect the more general practices followed by candidates in the era of the mass media election. Examining debates reveals the ways in which characteristics of campaigns themselves are both changing and remaining the same over time (Jamieson and Birdsell, 1988).

A rough, yet rather stable, set of television-oriented "news management" conventions has evolved. As we shall discuss shortly, these conventions emanated from a struggle between candidates and the press to gain the upper hand in controlling the flow of election information. As these two actors fought it out, the public's role in the process became increasingly marginalized until 1992.

In the 1950s and early 1960s journalists and candidates underwent a period of adjustment to television's entry into the campaign arena. Reporters needed to adapt the style and content of electoral coverage in order to meet the challenges of the television format compared to that of print and radio. Presidential aspirants likewise needed to modify their strategies. This period of adjustment gave way to a tug of war between candidates and the press for control of the airwaves, and by the 1980s it appeared as though the press had won (Patterson, 1993).

During the 1992 presidential campaign, however, the genesis of change in this dynamic was evident. Candidates and the mass public began to assert themselves more aggressively into the media game. While candidates generally followed established patterns of debate strategy, breaks with conventions of "media management" that transpired during this campaign had an impact on the presidential and vice presidential debates,

Thus, our discussion will focus on the evolution of the rules of the game that were established for debates in the era of the mass media election. In so doing, we will address the changes that came about during the 1992 contest.

This analysis will set the stage for some concluding thoughts about the roles of candidates, the press, and the public in debates held in the current media election environment.

The Rules of the Mass Media Election Game

When television began to assume its dominant role in the electoral process around 1960, a set of rules for running campaigns was established. Candidates were forced to adjust their electioneering techniques to meet the presentational demands of the medium. They tailored their appeals to accommodate television's visual dynamics, as well as its spatial and temporal boundaries. They also modified their personal styles to convey a sense of pseudointimacy that the medium fosters. Television thus transformed the public's relationship to politics because of its unique way of portraying the political world (Ranney, 1983; Hart, 1994).

Television's appearance on the election scene also prompted changes in the relationship between candidates and journalists. Campaign organizations realized that they could exercise some control over coverage of their candidates if they adapted "news management strategies" that conformed to the norms of press reporting. Campaigns adjusted their schedules to accommodate journalists' deadlines. They created "news" for the press to cover by staging pseudoevents with enough requisite drama and hoopla to make good copy and to provide eyecatching visuals.

After about a decade, this "news management" strategy caused candidates to lose ground to journalists in the struggle for control over the campaign agenda. Patterson argues that in the 1960s candidates were the focus of campaigns. Presidential aspirants spoke for themselves, personally relating their positions on issues and their assessments of political events. By the 1970s, however, campaigns had become "journalist centered." The press overwhelming came to speak for candidates. Journalists emerged as media stars whose performances sometimes overshadowed those of the candidates.

Debates offer a case in point. Serving as moderators and questioners in debates, journalists control what specific issues the candidates will address. As postdebate analysts, the press decides what is newsworthy about the candidates' performances and what is not. Candidates at times seem almost tangential to the process.

Empirical evidence to support these trends is compelling. Patterson discovered that presidential contenders were depicted speaking their own words 84 percent of the time in 1968, and the average sound bite for a candidate was forty-two seconds in length. Twenty years later, for every one minute a candidate spoke, a journalist spoke for six minutes. The average sound bite had shrunk to ten seconds (Patterson, 1993, p. 73).

While candidates saw their role in the process contract, voters were all but left out of the mass media election. As politics increasingly was conducted via television, citizens became observers rather than active participants. While many followed campaigns on television, few actually took part in ways other than voting.

The Special Status of Debates in Elections

In an election process in which citizens are regularly bombarded with banal media messages, debates are granted a special status in the hierarchy of campaign communication forms. The public accords greater credence to debates than to news coverage and candidate advertising (Owen, 1991). Voters believe that presidential debates are important (Lichtenstein, 1982). Thus, as we shall see shortly, debates pose a special set of strategic problems for candidates.

There is a long and distinguished history of candidate debate in the United States that precedes the television age. Candidates would engage in lengthy, substantive public orations, the text of which was circulated in newspapers. On the foundation of this type of discourse, debates earned a reputation for furthering democratic ideals (Jamieson and Birdsell, 1988; Kraus, 1988). Debates also are surrounded by the aura of "history in the making" to which the public desires to bear witness (Meadow, 1983).

The unique format of debates contributes to their appeal as well. Debates physically bring candidates together in the same forum. The audience has the opportunity to make direct comparisons between the candidates performing on what is perceived to be a level playing field. This conforms to the public's expectations of fair play (Lengle and Lambert, 1994), which is not always evident in other aspects of campaigns.

Debates attract a wide viewing audience. Since the 1960 Kennedy–Nixon debate, candidates can count on anywhere between 60 percent and 90 percent of the population tuning in to at least part of a debate (see Payne et al., 1989). Debates have suffered from a decline in audience share as measured by Neilson ratings over time (Lengle and Lambert, 1994). Still, over 88 million people viewed the third presidential debate in 1992 (Como, 1992). In fact, more people watched the debates than the World Series (Germond and Witcover, 1993). The number of people exposed to information about the debates is even more impressive when post debate analyses are taken into account (Chaffee and Dennis, 1979; Sears and Chaffee, 1979; Robinson, 1980; Lemert et al., 1988).

Thus, debates offer presidential contenders the opportunity to reach a wide and diverse cross-section of the American electorate. Even people who are not attentive to campaigns face social pressures to watch debates, which have assumed qualities of a sporting event. The audience is largely an active one, as the viewers have made a conscious effort to tune in, to pay attention, and to root for their favorite candidate.

ESTABLISHING THE CONTEXT FOR DEBATES: THE PRESS AND THE PUBLIC

Candidates' strategies for managing debates are conditioned by their beliefs about the press's and public's expectations, demands, and use of debates. Therefore, it is beneficial to briefly explore how the press and the public shape the environment within which debates take place before addressing candidates' debate tactics.

Debates and the Press

The press's coverage of debates fits established norms of campaign reporting. Diamond and Friery (1987) note with some surprise that the same model of press coverage that held during the 1960 presidential debates pertains to subsequent events. In many respects, debates have become another component of the "horse race" and image-based coverage that dominates during elections. Yet debates stand out in that they are covered like special events that provide a break in the monotony of a long campaign season. Strategically, debates provide the media with an opportunity to reinvigorate interest in their coverage of the campaign among an audience whose patience with the process is wearing thin.

Journalists deem debates highly newsworthy. They hype debates as they would the championship series of a sporting event—as the most important event of the campaign. The media prep the public for the debates. They play a major role in setting the debate agenda by highlighting particular issues (and nonissues, such as how the candidates look) which the public will hone in on. The media also set citizens' expectations about candidates' performances. In 1992, for example, the pressure was on George Bush to score a knockout in the third debate after his less than stellar appearances in the previous two. Bill Clinton needed to do nothing more than hold his own after scoring big points in the second match.

Journalists, particularly those working for the mainstream media, operate under the assumption that the public is easily bored with too much substantive information. Thus, many news organizations adopt a strategy for sustaining the debates as hot topics in the public's eyes providing as little information as possible in the sexiest packages (Martel, 1983). The press compensates candidates who make their job easy by providing good sound bites with good coverage. Reagan, for example, was able to lay to rest the age issue in 1984 by stating, "I am not going to exploit, for political purposes, my opponent's youth and inexperience."

Journalists also reward candidates who play it safe. The only thing better for press copy than a carefully scripted sound bite worked into an answer is a slipup. As the introduction to this chapter illustrates, a single gaffe can come to symbolize a candidate's entire debate performance. George Bush had as much difficulty overcoming the perception that he "didn't get it," as Gerald Ford had recuperating from his misstatement that Eastern Europe was free of Soviet domination (Swerdlow, 1987).

Debates have become an integral ingredient of "horse race" coverage, as the press fixates on polling. Some observers go as far as to say that debate coverage has become "poll driven" (Gersh, 1993). The "horse race" element of debate coverage has two distinct components. The media focus heavily on the candidates' standings in the polls prior to and following a debate. They examine changes in momentum that may result from a candidate performing well or poorly from one debate to the next.

In addition, the media are obsessed with declaring "winners" and "losers" in debates. Spot public opinion polls conducted immediately following debates are used to determine victory and defeat. Unfortunately, all too often careful analysis falls by the wayside in the rush to make news. Postdebate polls in 1992, for example, varied significantly for all three debates (*Star Tribune*, 1992; Hines, 1992). Early polls following the third debate indicated that Clinton had won, while subsequent surveys gave the nod to Bush (Ely, 1992).[1]

"Horse race" coverage of debates is in and of itself a tactical device that candidates must take into consideration. However, the media focus an ever larger proportion of their attention on candidates' debate strategies. Lemert et al. (1988) conducted an extensive content analysis of television news coverage of debates. Their study revealed that in 1976, 12.7 percent of coverage was devoted to candidate strategies. By 1988 this figure had climbed to 25.9 percent.

Debates and the Public

The media and candidates commit so much time and energy to debates because they perceive that debates are meaningful to the public. There is evidence that these perceptions are on target, especially with regard to more recent contests. Voters admit that debates are important to them. In 1992 more than one-half of voters claimed that debates were one of the best ways of gaining information about candidates. One-third felt that debates helped them decide whom to vote for (Gersh, 1993).

The effects of debates and the accompanying media hype on the public's perceptions of candidates and their voting behavior are difficult to measure.

Scholarly research has demonstrated that debates augment people's knowledge about candidates' qualities and positions on issues and that they increase the saliency of elections to voters (see Miller and MacKuen, 1979, 1980; Chaffee and Dennis, 1979; Swanson and Swanson, 1978; Graber, 1984; Lemert et al., 1988). One of the most consistent findings is that debates reinforce voters' decisions. Many voters selectively process candidates' debate performances. Viewers interpret candidates' statements in a way that is consistent with their own preconceptions of what the candidates stand for (Trent and Friedenberg, 1991). Some contrary findings indicate, however, that since debates come so late in the campaign, learning is minimized because the information presented is redundant (Sears and Chaffee, 1979; Graber and Kim, 1978).

There is limited evidence that debates actually influence some people's voting decisions, especially those who are undecided at the time the debates take place. Voters most likely to be swayed by debates and the surrounding media blitz are people who possess less political interest and knowledge, and who are not very secure about their political decisions (Bishop, Oldendick, and Tuchfarber, 1978; Newton et al., 1987; Rouner and Perloff, 1988).

A candidate's superior performance in debates can work to her or his advantage, although it may be far from enough to change the course of an election. A study of the 1984 contest found that Walter Mondale, whose debate performances were considered a high point in his bid for the presidency, gained three out of four votes among people who relied upon debates to make their decision. However, less than one-tenth of the electorate used debates for this purpose (Pomper as cited in Diamond and Friery, 1987).

In a close election even relatively minor shifts can alter the outcome. Debates' potential to have this effect has grown in recent years. Fewer people are making up their minds early in campaigns, and they are looking to debates to break the deadlock. Anecdotal evidence suggests that this was the case for a significant number of voters in 1992, who told reporters that the debates influenced their vote choice (Como, 1992)

CANDIDATES AND THE CHALLENGE OF DEBATES

In spite of the mixed findings regarding the actual impact of debates on public perceptions of candidates and vote choice, both presidential contenders and the press behave as if these events can and do make a big difference in the election. From the moment the issue of debates is raised during the campaign, the media track the candidates' every move. Thus, candidates must be extremely careful in managing even the minor details surrounding debates. Given the saturation of press coverage about debates, tactical errors can cost campaigns momentum just when a last burst of energy is needed to assure a strong finish.

It should be noted that candidates have a single goal in mind when they decide to engage in debates: victory. As Kraus states, "The first fact is that the candidates are not interested in educating the public or in arriving at truth, but in *winning* the elections. The second is that the candidates want to, and ultimately do, *control* most of what they do in campaigns. . . . The rationale is simple: More control over events increases the probabilities of impressing the electorate, gaining advantages over the opponent, and winning the election" (Kraus, 1988, p. 30).

The Issue of Sponsorship

Since 1960 control over the formal aspects of the debate process has been an area of contention, and it is far from being resolved today. Some organizational entity is needed to oversee negotiations with the candidates and to run and raise funds for the debates themselves. There have been a series of different sponsors since the first televised event. The three major television networks—ABC, CBS, and NBC—sponsored the "Great Debate" between Kennedy and Nixon. Network sponsorship was highly criticized as representing a conflict of interest, and the torch was passed to the League of Women Voters. The league sponsored presidential debates in 1976, 1980, and 1984, and initiated the tradition of vice presidential debates, holding them in 1976 and 1984.

While the league is nonpartisan and does not have a vested interest in debates other than as a means of promoting democratic values and education, it lacks the clout to assert authority over the process, especially when negotiations are deadlocked. Thus, the bipartisan Commission on Presidential Debates was formed in 1987 in an attempt by the two major parties to institutionalize debates and to establish some continuity in the guidelines governing the process while maintaining flexibility (Burchfield, 1993). The commission sponsored the 1988 and 1992 debates.

Candidates have benefited strategically from the proliferation of debate sponsors because few formal rules have been established, allowing them the opportunity to bargain for debates that suit their personal styles. Thus, debate sponsors act primarily as facilitators of candidates' desires rather than as powerful arbitrators of debates (Hellweg et al., 1992). Some partisan operatives feel that the Commission on Presidential Debates asserted itself too heavily into the process in 1992, and the sponsorship debate looms large as we gear up for the 1996 contest.

Although the commission is at present the most obvious alternative, it is in fact only one of several potential debate sponsors. In 1992 the commission submitted a plan for debates to the candidates that was immediately accepted by Bill Clinton. The Bush campaign considered this to be only a proposal and not a mandate, and did not respond in kind. This left the impression with the press and the public that the president did not want to debate. The Clinton campaign reaped the benefits of this tactical miscalculation (Burchfield, 1993).

The role of the sponsor comes into play during the first three phases of the debate process, although it is most evident during the negotiation phase. We turn now to explore how candidate strategies are operationalized during each phase.

Phase I: The Negotiation Phase

The negotiation phase—the debate over the debates—has become ritualized in presidential election campaigns. Protracted conferences are held among candidates, their campaign committees and representatives, and the sponsor of the debates. The press is often present at these meetings (Kraus, 1988), and if not, information is leaked to them (Martel, 1983).

The debate over the debates is largely a product of press norms. As *Newsweek* correspondent Jonathan Alter remarks, "The press needs the debate over the debates the way a bear needs honey. It's just another story that a very hungry institution with an insatiable appetite for campaign news must have. So, if there isn't a good debate over the debates in the run-up, the press will essentially create one" (Gersh, 1993, p. 40).

The media-fueled debate over the debates generates a strategic problem for candidates from the outset. Coverage plays up the conflicts, bickering, and positioning of candidates, rather than more positive messages about their qualifications and viewpoints. Coming late in the campaign as it does, the public is more attentive to election communication as it anticipates casting the vote. Mudslinging tires voters and turns them off, especially when nastiness is pervasive throughout the campaign as it has been in recent years. If attack strategies pervade debate coverage, candidates run the risk of alienating voters before they decide to tune in, as they come to expect more of the same during the debates themselves.

Candidates can either establish debates as an advantage or a liability during the negotiation stage. The decisions they make will determine the form and content of debates. Once the candidates agree to debate, the timing, location, format, topics to be covered, and who will serve as questioners and moderators become important matters of strategy. How candidates manage the negotiations can influence their ability to exercise control over the outcome.

Ostensibly, candidates must decide whether they want to take part in debates. In earlier days, it was possible for an incumbent to avoid debating a challenger. Today, all major party candidates face severe political penalties for not debating. Both the press and the public view candidates who will not participate as evasive and fearful of confronting their opponents.

In spite of these factors, candidates still go through the "decision to debate" ritual. The timing of the announcement of this decision is an important tactical matter. As we have seen with Bush in 1992, even if a candidate plans to debate, the slightest perception of hesitancy can cost him or her. Challengers and candidates behind in the polls find it in their best interest to call for debates first in order to force the opposing candidate to respond defensively.

Once it has been established that debates will be held, major party candidates also must decide if they want to include other presidential aspirants. Typically, the inclusion of a third party candidate in the presidential debates has been a source of controversy. The candidates' inability to reach an agreement about whether George Wallace should be included prevented debates from being held in 1968. Eugene McCarthy was excluded from all debates in 1976. Incumbent president Jimmy Carter refused to participate in a debate that included John Anderson in 1980, although Ronald Reagan took part (Swerdlow, 1987).

The situation was different in 1992. Although Ross Perot did not formally take part in debate negotiations, neither major party candidate would consider excluding him from the debates. George Bush and Bill Clinton did not want to alienate Perot's supporters who might potentially jump ship on Election Day. During the debates themselves, both candidates made obvious attempts to court Perot voters.

The scheduling of debates is also a major consideration. Each side tries to determine how much time they need to prepare and at what point in the campaign the debates will help them most. If more than one debate is to be held, as is the norm, the amount of time between events becomes an issue. In 1992 Harry Thomasson, Clinton's media adviser and a Hollywood producer, suggested that the debates be scheduled in close succession—four debates in eight days—like a television miniseries in order to build viewership (Burchfield, 1993). The plan was implemented and it worked. Viewership and interest in the debate process mounted with each successive debate.

Negotiating the debate format has become a tactical communication strategy (Germond and Witcover, 1993), although the press makes more out of these mediations than is warranted. With the exception of a single debate in 1992, the format of general election campaign debates has varied little since 1960, although a wide variety of formats has been used in the primaries. American-style debates are not really debates, but glorified press conferences. Most politicians are comfortable with a format that includes some combination of a moderator and a panel of journalists who serve as questioners because they are used to question-and-answer sessions. What they seek to avoid is a format that encourages direct confrontation, as this introduces a great deal of uncertainty into the process. Vice presidential debates have become the forum for heated exchanges that satiate the media's hunger for conflict.

Both candidates and the media see the need to employ a format that keeps the public's attention. Presidential aspirants and the press assume that average citizens have short attention spans, and that voters go into the debates looking for the candidates to clash, and not necessarily to learn about the issues. Thus, formats that move things along and set up the debate like a sporting event are favored.

This mind-set is responsible for the experiment with a town hall format tried during the second debate in 1992. Citizens from the audience posed questions to the candidates with a journalist moderating the proceedings. Town hall-style debates have been used regularly during primary campaigns, but never during the general election.

The decision to use a town hall format in 1992 was not problematic. Clinton proposed it, and Bush accepted. Both campaigns realized that there was extensive public support for such a format given the popularity of call-in shows and televised town meetings during the campaign (Burchfield, 1993).

The Clinton campaign took a gamble when it proposed the town hall meeting, and it paid off. Clinton had used this format frequently during his bid for the presidency, and it fit his informal personal style. His campaign also believed that the public would give him an easier time than the press. Throughout the election, Clinton had been plagued by questions about his character. His handlers believed that the citizen questioners would go lighter on issues of personal misconduct than would journalists, and that the public would hit hard on issues of the economy, unemployment, and health care, which were sore points with Bush. Clinton's guess was correct, as the citizen questioners went so far as to chide the candidates for spending too much of their time on mudslinging (Germond and Witcover 1992).

Once the debate format is established, other logistical considerations need to be worked out, including the location of the debate. The selection of the moderator and questioners becomes especially important. Because their goal is to generate controversy in an effort to keep the debate audience satiated, journalists have an incentive to goad candidates into combat. Candidates do their best to choose questioners who will keep bloodshed to a minimum, but this is often difficult. Debates have been known to devolve into contests between candidates and panelists (Hellweg et al., 1992).

Phase II: The Preparation Phase

Once negotiations have been settled, candidates must set the stage for the events themselves. Several tactical measures are employed at this time. First, candidates must prepare for the debates. They also compete with the media to control the debate agenda and to set the public's expectations about their performance. Finally, campaign organizations attempt to set in motion a coherent media strategy, where their other campaign media compliment the messages they plan to get across in the debates.

The bottom line about debates is that they are not spontaneous events where the public gets to see the candidates battle it out face-to-face, even when a town meeting format is used. They are carefully scripted, made-for-TV dramas. In preparation, candidates are grilled by members of their campaign team and engage in mock debates. They pore over massive briefing books and try to anticipate questions and the opponents' responses. Most important, candidates commit to memory a stockpile of sound bites to be inserted at the appropriate moment during the confrontation. It was not just quickness on his feet that allowed Lloyd Bentsen to provide the tag line of the 1988 vice presidential debates, replying to Dan Quayle, "Senator, I served with Jack Kennedy. I knew Jack Kennedy. Jack Kennedy was a friend of mine. Senator, you're no Jack Kennedy." It was a superior ability to learn his lines.

In their battle to beat the press at its own game, candidates work hard to alert the public to the goals they hope to achieve via the debates. They accomplish this by leaking their strategies in order to set the context for the postdebate interpretations by both pundits and the public. Campaigns also launch an all-out coordinated media strategy, where they run ads and stage pseudoevents that outline the themes that the candidates wish to emphasize during the debates. Candidates tend to go on the attack at this point, raising objections to their opponents that they hope will be on the voters' minds as they watch the debates.

This can be risky business if the candidates' performances fail to live up to expectations or to accomplish the objectives that they have set for themselves. The press then chronicles these failures as part of the postdebate fallout. Again, we can use the 1992 presidential contest to illustrate this point. Bush's primary goal, especially by the time of the third debate, was to emphasize the issue of Clinton's character. Poll results revealed that the public felt somewhat uncomfortable with Clinton's personal qualities and his past. The Bush campaign mounted a full-scale assault, airing ads that accused Clinton of transgressions, such as draft evasion during the Vietnam War. Bush himself emphasized these points in speeches (Shogan, 1992). Bush claimed that this was not mudslinging, but a matter of Clinton's integrity, which is integral to one's ability to govern (Wiessler and Regeley, 1992). While Bush was generally considered to have performed well in the third debate, postdebate analyses focused on how the economy and other substantive issues resonated louder with the public than the character issue. Bush was portrayed as hitting below the belt, while Clinton took the high ground.

Please III: The Debates Themselves

Television has rendered it important for candidates to adapt image management skills to meet the demands of the debate format. There are a variety of factors of which the candidates must be cognizant when they are on stage other than debating itself. They must be aware of how they look, how they act, and how well they are connecting with the audience. These factors, in addition to any rousing sound bites or gaffes, will be more central to media coverage of the event than debating points or the substantive content of their speech.

Much has been made of the contention that Nixon's haggard appearance during the 1960 debate contributed to television viewers' perceptions that he had lost. Thus, how the candidates look and behave on camera has been a major compulsion of the press. Seemingly minor physical issues, such as whether candidates sit or stand during the debate, can convey impressions about the contenders. In 1976 Carter argued vehemently that a stool be provided so that he could sit during the debates. He used the stool to convey his informal style, while Ford remained standing throughout the events (Martel, 1983). In 1984 Dukakis requested that he be allowed to stand on a wooden box behind his lectern so that he would not appear diminutive compared to Bush.

This matter cannot be underscored enough by the example of George Bush glancing at his watch on camera during the second debate in 1992. This simple gesture sparked a multiplicity of interpretations by the media, and therefore, was accorded far more significance by the public than it deserved. The glance was proof that Bush was bored, that he was merely going through the motions of the debate and could not wait to get it over with, that he did not care about the people. Even deeper, it symbolized that time was running out on his candidacy and that his days in the White House were numbered. The press did not even entertain the idea that perhaps the president just wanted to know what time it was.

Candidates' debating strategies depend heavily upon where they stand in the polls and how they have fared in any previous debate encounters. Candidates who are ahead in the campaign and who have dealt a blow to their opponent in prior matches will play it safe in debates. If they succeed in simply treading water it is enough to declare a pyrrhic victory, even if the post-debate polls put them in second place. Thus, leading candidates can afford to be somewhat ambiguous in their answers and work to avoid confrontation. Trailing candidates must pursue a more aggressive strategy. Underdogs attempt to highlight the superiority of their views over those of the opposing candidate and to draw him or her into the fray.

In order to take control over the debates, candidates employ several tactics. They should establish a consistent theme that they will emphasize throughout the debate. They also need to coopt the issues and define them in their own terms. This frequently means that candidates must recontextualize questions in order have them conform to their agenda. Finally, candidates should introduce buzz words and define them in a way that resonates with the public. For example, Bush used the term "trickle down government" as a put-down of the Democrats' policies regarding the bureaucracy (Gersh, 1993).

Phase IV: The Postdebate Fallout Phase

Because debates are a product of television, some observers argue that TV "spin" has become more important than the actual debates (*Star Tribune,* 1992). As we have noted, the public's immediate postdebate reactions are often fleeting. Therefore, the persistent media commentary following the events themselves can define public opinions about and perceptions of candidates' debate performances.

Conventionally, the most central components of the postdebate phase of campaigns have included campaign organizations' efforts to place the best possible "spin" on their candidates' performances, and the press's declaration of winners and losers based upon poll results. In 1992 all of these things happened, but candidate-generated "spin" took a back seat to press polling.

The postdebate fallout phase differed in 1992 for several reasons. First, technological advances worked to speed up and systematize the process. Instant polls made it possible for the press to declare winners and losers on the spot. ABC, for example, had poll results within fifteen minutes after the debate and the results of focus group interviews with undecided voters within ninety minutes (*Star Tribune,* 1992). Flash polls made it possible for the press to get to the heart of its most important debate story—declaring the winner and loser—almost immediately. Thus, they were less dependent upon "spin doctors" arguing that their candidate won to fill time after the debate.

It is too early to declare that "'Spin' is dead," as did *Newsweek*'s Jonathan Alter (Gersh, 1993, p. 40). While campaign-induced "spin" was less the focus of news reports, it was still very much in evidence. "Spin" also became more "high tech" during this campaign. Computer technology was used to generate more systematic postdebate "spin." Beginning with the first event, the Bush campaign set up a computer system to analyze the content of the debate. Based on the results of this analysis, "spin doctors" were assigned specific components of the content to emphasize with the media. The formula worked effectively, and the Clinton campaign also adopted it for subsequent debates.[2]

In addition to technology's contribution to the process, the inclusion of a third party candidate in the debate changed the postevent dynamic. During the first debate, especially, Perot drew attention away from the two other candidates as his candid style caught the major party representatives off guard and generated press stories. More important, his presence made declaring a winner a more complicated process. Coming in third was a daunting prospect for Bush and Clinton. However, coming in second was not considered a loss for Clinton in the third debate (*Star Tribune*, 1992).

THE YEAR 1992: THE GENESIS OF CHANGE

Campaign practices change incrementally from election to election. The debates in 1992, with the significant exception of the town hall format, resembled their 1960s' counterpart in form. There are substantial indications, however, that 1992 marked a turning point in the conduct of presidential campaigns in the mass media age. Candidates still engaged in "news management" strategies. At the same time, they made an effort to regain some of the control over the process that had been surrendered to the mainstream press by reaching out to the public via popular media channels, thus establishing a new "infotainment media" strategy. Ross Perot initiated this strategy by declaring on CNN's "Larry King Live" his willingness to run for president if drafted by the American people. Other candidates followed suit with appearances on MTV and television and radio talk shows, as well as by seeking coverage in personality and entertainment magazines. Clinton received much publicity for his ability to command cover stories on both *People* magazine and *Rolling Stone* during the campaign.

There were other manifestations of the new "media populism" as well. Members of the mass public were encouraged to participate in the process via talk forums. Average citizens assumed the roles of reporter and analyst. They posed questions to candidates during televised national town meetings. They deliberated the pros and cons of candidates' personalities and issue positions on television and radio. After a long period of stagnation, politics was enlivened as candidates reached out to voters on their own terms and citizens responded.

This moderate state of upheaval in the rules of the mass media election game was reflected in the way the debates played themselves out in 1992. The effects of media populism were exhibited in a newfound voter stridency, as the public made it clear that it would not tolerate debates as usual. Citizens' expectations about what should transpire during debates changed sharply because of the role "infotainment media" had come to play in the campaign. In the past, debates represented the best chance for voters to observe candidates "live" and unedited (Lemert et al., 1988). In 1992 voters had many opportunities to view candidates outside of the mainstream media's filtering lens. In past debates, the public was relegated to the role of bystander or cheerleader. In 1992 voters became integral to the debate script.

As a result, all phases of the process were more chaotic and frenetic than usual, and changes did take place. Perhaps the best illustration of this point is the fact that the three presidential debates and one vice presidential debate employed four different formats. The first debate, conforming to precedent, employed a panel of journalists. The innovative town hall format was implemented during the second debate. For the final presidential debate, three reporters split their time with a moderator. A single moderator oversaw the vice presidential debates, allowing candidates Al Gore, Dan Quayle, and James Stockdale considerable time to interact directly with one another.

While political practitioners, observers, and journalists are divided about which format worked best (see Germond and Witcover, 1992, 1993), citizens were clear in their preference for the town hall format. A Times Mirror Center poll conducted at the end of October 1992 revealed that 46 percent of the public preferred that candidates be questioned by voters, compared to 28 percent who endorsed the single moderator format with no other questioners and 14 percent who favored a panel of reporters. Five percent stated that it made no difference, and 7 percent did not know.[3]

ABC News' Carole Simpson, who moderated the town hall meeting, found widespread anecdotal evidence to support voters' preference for the format. Some even told her that the debate influenced their vote. She offers an explanation for the audience's reaction, which she links to the proliferation of talk politics during the campaign. "I think voters who are used to the overabundance of talk shows want to see those people reacting with others like them. I think they want that connectedness" (Gersh, 1993, p. 40).

Bringing voters more directly into the process paid off strategically for the press and for the candidate who could manage the town hall format best—Bill Clinton. Usually excitement dwindles after the first debate and viewership falls off. The opposite occurred in 1992, as over a half a million new audience members tuned in to each subsequent debate (Ely, 1992). Since the town hall format was a novelty, it received far more attention than the other more conventional debates. Thus, Clinton was able to generate substantial political capital because he could showcase his relational style in the most highly publicized and popular of the debates. As the introduction to this chapter illustrates, Clinton used gestures, such as stepping closer to the audience, and rhetorical devices, such as speaking to the voters as if they were personal friends, to establish a bond with the public.

THE FUTURE OF DEBATES

As the foregoing analysis portends, the fact that presidential debates are going to continue to occur is unarguable. What remains up in the air is the form and content these debates will have in the era of media populism, as well as how candidates will handle them. Despite the efforts of an array of commissions, political parties, and Congress to formalize the debate process and to establish formal rules of conduct, it appears as though during each election candidates will face anew the challenge of debate negotiation, preparation, and media fallout.

However, it is doubtful that presidential contenders would want it any other way. Flexibility in the process works in the candidates' best interest, as they are able to settle on formats that highlight their personal styles and conform to changing media and public expectations about how debates should be conducted.

The 1992 campaign provides a lesson to candidates running in the near future. Citizens were given a role in the debates, and it is clear that they will not tolerate being left out of the process. Bill Clinton capitalized on these sentiments in his closing statement of the final presidential debate. He stated that the citizen questioners used in the second debate had gone "a long way toward reclaiming this election for the American people and taking the country back" (Germond and Witcover, 1992, p. 2448).

MEDIA POPULISM, DEBATES, AND DEMOCRACY

As Clinton's statement indicates, the small steps toward change that were initiated in 1992 clearly have larger implications for the future of our democratic polity. At this point in time, it appears as though the new media populism holds the potential for greater democratization of the electoral process. A higher value was placed on citizen input by political and mass media elites than in the recent past. As average citizens became part of the media campaign itself, the public's interest in politics escalated. People followed the election more closely, learned more about the candidates and politics generally, and participated more in the election. One indication of this phenomenon is the increase in voter turnout in 1992 after decades of decline.

There is also evidence that the quality of political discourse improved. Contrary to popular belief, citizens were more interested in issues than in tabloid-style attacks on candidates' characters, as our discussion of the third presidential debate illustrates. In addition, citizen participation diminished the role of the journalist as the intermediary between the politician and the voter. Press stars were frequently overshadowed by average voters, such as Marisa Hall, whose real concerns resonated sincerely with the public.

As a result, political discourse became more of an interactive process among candidates, the press, and the public. Instead of candidates and journalists telling the public about the campaign, voters *engaged in a dialogue* with them, hashing out issues in a wide array of public forums.

Media populism raises specific issues regarding debates. What do debates offer in the age of "infotainment politics" when much of voters' demands to see and interact with the candidates up close and personal is met through other forums? There is an interesting irony surrounding debates that helps perpetuate their singular role in elections. The public maintains a view of debates as the bastion of democratic ideals in the midst of an unsettling mass media campaign even though reality does little to reinforce this perspective. Debates draw large and eager audiences but rarely fail to disappoint. Having weathered a long campaign bombarded by often acrid and conflicting media messages, the public looks forward to debates as having the potential to offer something different and more meaningful. Given this dynamic, debates can be counted on as a court of last resort, offering candidates one final chance to influence the jury.

NOTES

1. In addition to the fact that hastily conducted public opinion polls may be inaccurate, studies have shown that citizens' assessments of candidates based on their debate performances are highly volatile. Viewer's opinions about candidates established in the period immediately following debates generally dissipate after a few days (Lang and Lang, 1978; Miller and MacKuen, 1979).

2. Personal interview with Rich Bond, former chairman of the Republican National Committee, June 1, 1994.

3. The survey was conducted October 20–22, 1992, and consisted of telephone interviews with a national sample of 1,153 registered voters. The sampling error is plus or minus three percentage points.

REFERENCES

Bishop, George F., and Robert W. Oldendick, and Alfred J. Tuchfarber (1978). Debate-watching and the acquisition of political knowledge. *Journal of Communication*, 99–113.

Burchfield, Bobby R. (1993, May 4). The role of the Commission on Presidential Debates: Looking to the future with an eye on the past. Presentation to the Commission on Presidential Debates.

Chaffee, Steven E., and Jack Dennis (1979). Presidential debates: An empirical assessment. In Austin Ranney, ed., *The past and future of presidential debates*. Washington, D.C.: American Enterprise Institute, pp. 75–106.

Como, James (1992, Nov. 16). Debates and showbiz: 1992 presidential and vice presidential campaign debates. *National Review*.

Diamond, Edwin, and Kathleen Friery (1987). Media coverage of presidential debates. In Joel L. Swordlow, ed., *Presidential debates: 1988 and beyond*. Washington, D.C.: Congressional Quarterly, pp. 43–51.

Ely, Jane (1992, Oct. 21). Everybody is ready to see election over. *Houston Chronicle*, A24.

Germond, Jack W., and Jules Witcover (1992). A little scolding can go a long way. *National Journal*, 24(43), 2448.

Germond, Jack W., and Jules Witcover (1993). *Mad as hell: Revolt at the ballot box, 1992.* New York: Time Warner Books.

Gersh, Debra (1993, Apr. 24). Improving presidential debates. *Editor and Publisher*, 40.

Graber, Doris (1984). *Processing the news: How people tame the information tide.* New York: Longman.

Graber, Doris, and Young Yun Kim (1978). Why John Q Voter did not learn much from the 1976 presidential debates. In Brent D. Rubin, ed., *Communication yearbook 2.* New Brunswick, N.J.: Transaction Books, pp. 407–21.

Hart, Roderick P. (1994). *Seducing America: How television charms the modern voter.* New York: Oxford University Press.

Hellweg, Susan A., Michael Pfau, and Steven R. Brydon (1992). *Televised presidential debates: Advocacy in contemporary America.* New York: Praeger.

Hines, Craig (1992, Oct. 11). Campaign '92: TV debates crucial to Bush re-election bid. *Houston Chronicle*, A1.

Jamieson, Kathleen Hall, and David S. Birdsell (1988). *Presidential debates: The challenge of creating an informed electorate.* New York: Oxford University Press.

Kraus, Sidney (1988). *Televised presidential debates and public policy.* Hillsdale, N.J.: Erlbaum.

Kraus, Sidney, ed. (1980). *The great debates.* Bloomington, Ind.: Indiana University Press.

Lang, Gladys Engel, and Kurt Lang (1978). Immediate and delayed responses to a Carter–Ford debate: Assessing public opinion. *Public Opinion Quarterly*, 322–41.

Lemert, James B., William R. Elliott, James M. Bernstein, William L. Rosenberg, and Karl J. Nestvold (1988). *News verdicts, the debates, and presidential campaigns.* New York: Praeger.

Lengle, James I., and Dianne C. Lambert (1994). No—presidential debates should not be required. In Gary L. Rose, ed., *Controversial issues in presidential selection,* 2nd ed. Albany, N.Y.: State University of New York Press, 187–98.

Lichtenstein, Allen (1982). Differences in impact between local and national televised political candidates' debates. *Western Journal of Speech Communication* 291–98.

Martel, Myles (1983). *Political campaign debates: Images, strategies, and tactics.* New York: Longman.

Meadow, Robert G. (1983). Televised campaign debates as whistle-stop speeches. In William C. Adams, ed., *Television coverage of the 1980 presidential campaign.* Norwood, N.J.: Ablex, pp. 89–101.

Miller, Arthur H., and Michael MacKuen (1979). Learning about the candidates: The 1976 presidential debates. *Public Opinion Quarterly*, 326–46.

Miller, Arthur H., and Michael MacKuen (1980). Informing the Electorate: A national study. In Sidney Kraus, ed., *The great debates*. Bloomington, Ind.: Indiana University Press, pp. 269–97.

Newton, James S., Roger D. Masters, Gregory J. McHugo, and Denis G. Sullivan (1987). Making up our minds: The effects of network coverage on viewer impressions of leaders. *Polity*, 226–46.

Owen, Diana (1991). *Media messages in American presidential elections*. Westport, Conn.: Greenwood.

Patterson, Thomas E. (1993). *Out of order*. New York: Alfred A. Knopf.

Payne, J. Gregory, James L. Golden, John Marlier, and Scott C. Ratzan (1989). Perceptions of the 1988 presidential and vice-presidential debates. *American Behavioral Scientist, 32*(4), 425–35.

Ranney, Austin (1983). *Channels of Power*. New York: Basic Books.

Ranney, Austin (1979). *The past and future of presidential debates*. Washington, D.C.: American Enterprise Institute.

Robinson, John P. (1980). The polls. In Sidney Kraus, ed., *The great debates*. Bloomington, Ind.: Indiana University Press, pp. 262–68.

Rouner, Donna, and Richard M. Perloff (1988). Selective perception of outcome of first 1984 presidential debate. *Journalism Quarterly*, 141–47, 240.

Sears, David O., and Steven H. Chaffee (1979). Uses and effects of the 1976 debates: An overview of empirical studies. In Sidney Kraus, ed., *The great debates*. Bloomington, Ind.: Indiana University Press, pp. 223–61.

Shogan, Robert. (1992, Oct. 19). It's high noon as Bush loads up for debate. *Los Angeles Times*, A1.

Star Tribune (1992, Oct. 13). The new debate: Did Perot or Clinton win? *Star Tribune*, A1.

Swanson, Linda L., and David L. Swanson (1978). The agenda-setting function of the first Ford–Carter debate. *Communication Monographs, 45*, 347–53.

Swerdlow, Joel L., ed. (1987). *Presidential debates: 1988 and beyond*. Washington, D.C.: Congressional Quarterly.

Trent, Judith S., and Robert V. Friedenberg (1991). *Political campaign communication*. New York: Praeger.

Wiessler, Judy, and Cindy Regeley (1992, Oct. 19). Campaign '92: Debate viewed as last chance for president. *Houston Chronicle*, A1.

SEVEN

The Question of a Return
to Basic American Values

"My Mother and Winston Churchill"
in the Heroic Narratives of Ross Perot's Infomercials

MONTAGUE KERN

On November 5, 1993, as part of its stepped up effort to save the North American Free Trade Agreement (NAFTA) from defeat in Congress, the Clinton administration challenged Ross Perot to a debate. Perot, who had crusaded against NAFTA since his independent presidential campaign ended in his achieving the highest vote tally ever for a third party candidate a year before, called the administration "desperate" and accepted the offer. He had spent the day lobbying Capitol Hill, where he called NAFTA "another stupid agreement rammed through by special interests" and declared it "dead on arrival" among ordinary citizens (Kamen and Balz, 1993). A debate with Vice President Al Gore would follow.

Once again, Ross Perot was involved in a dramatic conflict. He claimed to represent "ordinary citizens" in their heroic battle with "special interests" whose cause was being championed by the newly elected president of the United States. The policy tradeoffs in terms of costs and benefits of the agreement were unclear in the front-page news story, but Perot's ability to challenge a president was not.

Perot's political commercials in the 1992 presidential election con- tributed to his rise in public consciousness and support. He laid the deficit and the North American Free Trade Agreement at the door of "corrupt politicians" in thirty-minute "infomercials" in which the principal visuals were

157

himself and the charts and graphs that described the deficit problem. He had a gift for memorable phrases. His characterization of NAFTA as producing "a giant sucking sound" of American jobs going south became one of the classic images of the 1992 campaign. He also represented himself as an individual who, unlike the "corrupt" politicians running America, never did anything for himself alone. He, unlike them, was a civic-minded individual who sacrificed for the common good.

In the 1993 NAFTA debate, under painful questioning from the vice president that he had been able to avoid during much of the 1992 presidential election campaign, Ross Perot's civic-minded persona began to crumble as Gore pointed to cases that challenged the "sacrifice all for others" argument. One was the fact that the Perot family benefited financially from U.S.-Mexican trade through a family-owned "tariff free" airport in Austin, Texas, while, in opposing NAFTA, he sought to deny such commercial benefits to the nation as a whole. Such information about the Perot family's financial dealings, which was not available to the American television audience during the 1992 general election campaign, ran counter to the central premise of his third party candidacy: that he was a latter-day Cincinnatus.

Civic-minded self-sacrifice was indeed Perot's central claim, expressed in dramatic narratives that featured him as a central, albeit reluctant hero. Such narratives first reached the mass American audience in a best-selling book, Ken Follett's *On Wings of Eagles* (1983), which was commissioned by the billionaire, unbeknownst to the reader of the thrilling tale of Perot's successful rescue of Electronic Digital Systems (his company's) hostages in Tehran, at a time when the administration of President Jimmy Carter was so visibly unable to achieve the same objective. Such stories were retold on the talk shows during the primary season and early summer months of the 1992 presidential election campaign, and then refined and elaborated in a massive fall 1992 political advertising blitz. Service in the common good, rather than self-interested individualism, was, Perot argued, central to his character.

Such an appeal is as old as America itself. As anthropologist Robert Bellah has argued in a trenchant commentary on American political culture, civic-minded expressions of willingness to stand on principle and work for the common good have been intrinsic to important struggles in American history. They have been central to the appeal of religious reformers from the time of early Puritans such as John Winthrop through the nineteenth-century leaders who struggled to realize the ancient hope of a just and compassionate society. They have been central to the struggles of republican reformers since Thomas Jefferson who have sought to build a nation according to principles of citizenship and participation. And they have been central to traditions of Manifest Destiny and national glory, which have long also played a major role in American national life (Bellah, 1985).

In dynamic tension with such values, however, is American individualism, which in its more utilitarian and business-oriented form, is as old as Benjamin Franklin's advice that hard work and sacrifice, combined with a positive mental attitude, will pay off for the individual. His maxim, "Early to bed, early to rise, will make a man healthy, wealthy and wise," hallowed in American tradition, is a central component of the American Dream. It underlies the Horatio Alger rags to riches stories on which the hope of American citizens in a nation founded on egalitarian principles are expressed. Personal effort, undertaking one's "personal best," is key to successful fulfillment of the American Dream. Such hopes, unfortunately, by the time of the Perot candidacy in 1992, were problematic for an increasing number of disaffected Americans (Luttwak, 1993).

Still, the premise of American communitarianism is that Americans are an optimistic people with a profound belief in a good society. And Perot made just this argument, telling stories about the goodness of Americans on all levels, in his own family and in his educational, community, and business lives. Such stories illustrated his own goodness as well. He is indeed the central, heroic figure in the stories, which comprise a series of dramatic narratives, each intended to break down the distance between himself and the ordinary citizen.

Understanding Perot's advertising appeal thus requires an analysis of his narrative approach to argumentation. Walter R. Fisher defines "narration" as "symbolic actions—words and/or deeds—that have sequences and meaning for those who live, create, or interpret them." Through narratives, the story-teller invites the listener to act in accord with the "reality" embraced in the story. According to Fisher, "narrative rationality differs from prior logics in several . . . fundamental ways. . . . It is not the individual form of argument that is ultimately persuasive in discourse. That is important, but values are more persuasive."[1] Narratives are stories through which both individual and collective identities emerge.

Formal narratives usually follow a structure. This includes first, a setting, scene, or context, an arena within which action occurs. Characters are introduced and their actions are described in relation to events that occur through time. A significant conflict is explicated, along with its resolution (Mischler, 1986). Finally, a point is usually made through which identity emerges. This point may well be a statement of basic belief concerning what is believed to be true about the world, or a statement of values concerning how life should be lived.

Questions of narrative and values have rarely been addressed in political advertising research (Louden, 1990: Morreale, 1991). It is therefore particularly fitting that we do so here, as we consider the third party candidacy of an individual who is best known for the fact that he successfully brought important national issues such as the deficit to the public consciousness, which President Bill Clinton was subsequently required to address. Less well known is the fact that Perot built the character side of his third party candidacy on an ideal of civic virtue which, he argued, is best expressed in American family life. Others made claim to the "family values" issue in grand and competing displays at their national Republican and Democratic conventions (Andersen, 1993). It was, however, a hallmark of the Perot campaign. I "threw that ball into the ballpark," he said when asked about the question of family values on the June 11, 1992 "Today" show during the height of his popularity. Asked "Who are your heroes?" by hostess Katie Couric, Perot responded promptly, "My mother and Winston Churchill." He proceeded to balance the values of a woman who lived near the railroad tracks and believed it was important to help those poorer than herself against the wartime leader who said, "Never, never, never say never."

Through a campaign that utilized a strategy of avoiding the press, and using political advertising, appearances on talk shows, and participation in political debates, Ross Perot's fortunes soared in October 1992, as he reentered the presidential election campaign amidst considerable elite and popular suspicion concerning his reason for having left the campaign in the summer (potential Republican sabotaging of his daughter's wedding). He rose in the polls to garner a record third party candidate vote of close to one-fifth of the presidential vote, which offered confirming evidence of the independence from partisanship of many American voters (Wattenberg, 1994). Positive voter reactions to Perot's general election debate and talk show performances have been examined, and the view developed that they helped offset adverse reactions to skeptical general election press coverage (Zaller, 1993).

A full assessment of the nature and value for voters of the 1992 political advertising, in relation to other messages, is made elsewhere in a large-scale study of media, candidates, and voters in four states (Just et al., 1996, forthcoming). Here it is important to note that voters took notice of Perot's political ads, and compared them favorably with those of other candidates. A CBS–*New York Times* poll found that "Voters who saw television ads said they paid the most attention to Perot's. They rated his as the most truthful and said the ads made them most likely to vote for Perot" (Frankovic, 1993, pp. 127–28). Times-Mirror polling found Perot's ads "the most informative" by far, with 55 percent of those who saw ads reporting this view as compared with 20 percent for Clinton and 8 percent for Bush (Schneider, 1992, p. 2814). Voters who saw greater numbers of Perot's political ads were, according to one study, in the mid- to upper range of political attentiveness (Zaller, 1993). For them, the informational aspect of his ads was important, symbolized by his use of charts and graphs in some of his thirty-minute infomercials. Much more than information about issues was conveyed in Perot's advertising, however. We will briefly examine Perot's ads in the 1992 election context, and probe the nature of his 1992 political advertising and its strategic use in relation to that of other candidates.

PEROT'S ADS IN THE 1992 ELECTION CONTEXT

Voters' concern with the economy drove the 1992 electoral communication process. This was unlike 1988, when in the absence of such overarching concerns the candidates had more freedom to shape and structure messages, linking character with issues such as patriotism and crime. Survey research undertaken in four states during the general election determined that the most successful advertising campaign in the 1992 election was the negative Republican primary campaign of Patrick Buchanan, which focused blame according to voters' economic concerns, linking or "dovetailing" the allegedly weak character of his opponent with the tax issue (a wimp, who broke his promises).[2] On the positive side, Bill Clinton's advertising dovetailed his concern for health care with scenes of the candidate in emotionally charged situations, and so contributed to voter impressions of a caring candidate. This impression remained important for Clinton throughout the rest of the election as voter assessments turned from scandal to concern about trust and finding a candidate with better answers to the problems of the economy (West, 1993; West, Kern, and Alger, 1992). In the general election, a lesser role for political advertising was found.[3] Exposure to their advertising nevertheless affected voter assessment of Bill Clinton and Ross Perot. In the case of Perot, the same four-site survey determined that there was a statistically significant relationship between viewing Perot's advertising and the belief that he "cared" about voters, and could best handle the economy (West, 1993; Alger, Kern, and West, 1993; Kern, West, and Alger, 1993). It is important, however, not to overstate media "effects," as, more broadly, voters bring their own affects, values, experiences, and issue concerns to the process of constructing impressions of candidates as they connect with mediated information (Neumann, Just, and Crigler, 1992; Kern and Just, 1994). Indeed, most studies have shown that Perot had great appeal among persons concerned about issues—the federal budget deficit, foreign competition, and political corruption (Zaller, 1993).

Still Perot captured attention through the mass media. Success for his advertising in gaining voter attention related to its connection with varied media formats and its billing as an informational campaign. Perot developed a "news"-based question-and-answer format in his biographical commercials. This built on the credibility of news and contributed to his success in developing a campaign that related to voter concerns about past candidate "manipulation" using political advertising. The image was also of the "unprofessional" candidate or "noncandidate" candidate. The effort was important in the context of a climate of voter concern about candidate manipulation. This aspect of Perot's effort involved the following:

- Perot started airing his first fall ads at about the time of the first presidential debate, in early October, and in fact advertised a thirty-minute infomercial during the debates. The debates were a broadly popular source of voter information, and the public responded positively to Perot's debate performance.[4] Thus the commercials were associated with a popular format that was perceived as positive for democracy, not as "manipulative."
- Perot picked up the "interactive" idea, which was emerging as a major new thrust of candidate and voter concern in the general election, within the format of his commercials. Thus he might note in one infomercial, for example, that he had changed his charts and graphs and his pointer in response to voters' expressed concern about them.
- Perot ran his advertising campaign as the "unprofessional campaign" at a time of public concern about the negativity and manipulative quality of professional political campaigns. His highly publicized fight with his campaign professionals, who resigned from his campaign in the summer, lent credibility to this idea. So did his format, which featured talking heads and "scrolling words" rather than moving pictures.
- Perot developed a question-and-answer interview format for his advertising commonly used in news programming. Thus, two of the three thirty-minute biographical commercials he developed featured Perot responding to questions put to him by a man who appeared to be a reporter.
- Perot used two of the "new" interactive formats, one in relation to the morning talk show extended interviews and the other an answering machine message advertised through the 1-800 number included in his ads, to tell callers not only the location of his nearest office, but where Ken Follett's commissioned best-selling book, *On Wings of Eagles*, could be purchased.

Some important questions to consider are whether Perot in fact used the expanded format of his ads to change the pattern of candidate avoidance of explicit policy discourse in political commercials. Did he give voters greater insight into how he would handle policy issues once in office? In the spring Perot took the lead in raising the issue of the deficit to the level of an important voter concern through his extensive discussions on the talk shows (Zaller, 1993). In the fall commercials did he move beyond this to offer positive solutions for how to deal with it? Or did Perot's fall advertising instead represent a continuation of his past pattern of sounding an alarm, assigning blame for past performance, and simply calling for new leadership to deal with the problem? Was his closing argument, in short, largely comparable to that of challenger politicians in the 1980s, who relied primarily on thirty-second spots charging that the incumbent is so linked with failed political institutions and morally questionable behavior that he or she no longer represents voter concerns? (Kern, 1989).

Overall, Perot's fall advertising, while explaining complicated issues such as the deficit by means of charts and graphs in thirty-minute infomercials, offered some answers to the concerns he raised. Perot offered a solution to the deficit dilemma in the second of his half-hour infomercials. While suggesting "shared sacrifice" he recommended cutting federal entitlement programs, as well as imposing a gas tax. Nowhere else in all his commercials, however, was the plan mentioned in this ad elaborated. In the thirty-second spots that he ran for thirty-two days on radio and television, these controversial policy solutions were never mentioned. Instead, his ads focused in serious tones on the reiteration of problems: the deficit, the corruption of politicians, the need to direct attention to the economy and jobs. Affect-laden visual symbols, such as children or a Purple Heart or a ticking clock, served as the background for Perot's favored "scroll-like" commercials. In dovetailing fashion, the Texas businessman without prior government experience, who adhered to no known party or political ideology but who had balanced a budget, was offered as the solution to major national problems, trade, jobs, the deficit.

While launching a strong critique of government and politics as usual, however, Perot's thirty-second commercials stylistically contrasted with Clinton's and Bush's ads, which were attack ads directed at individual candidates. In Clinton's case, the attack continued the Buchanan pattern of linking performance on the economy with character (weak leadership, breaking promises). In Bush's case the focus was on trust issues, without the positive advertising mix included in the Clinton advertising campaign. Perot's ads more clearly targeted the candidate's own issues—including government corruption. Voters considered them to be a breath of fresh air in a negative political advertising environment (Alger, Kern, and West, 1993).

Yet would Perot use his advertising to clarify his key credential for leadership, which was the fact that he was a billionaire businessman who had never held public or elected office? He was a billionaire who—ironically, in view of his critique of bloated government—had built a business based on government contracts. His major credential was that he could handle a balance sheet and therefore could balance the federal budget. Here, we examine the possibility that instead of arguing this key credential on its merits, he used narrative logic to link his candidacy with the communitarian ideal of America as a "blessed" community.

STORIES INVOLVING SACRIFICE

Central characters in stories may be heroes, villains, or ordinary people. Stories involving heroes who engage in action in a number of different social contexts (as well as cosmic ones, involving supernatural forces) usually include a civic or communitarian motivation on the part of the central actor; there is also a beneficiary (family, community, nation, world) in whose behalf a sacrifice (of time, money, life) is made. The central actor, or hero, undertakes action on behalf of the beneficiary, not himself or herself. In so doing, he or she redeems the whole community.

Hero stories are central to religious (the Torah, Bible) and secular (*Star Wars*) cultures. Such stories undergird the concept of the nation itself, as in their telling and retelling national identity emerges around basic values. These frequently involve heroes who emerge in a war or crisis context (Paul Revere, George Washington, Abraham Lincoln, etc.) when issues of basic safety and protection are at stake, and political learning can thus be expected to be most acute (Boulding, 1958). Candidates frequently associate themselves with such heroes in forms of narrative argumentation that transcend logic and frequently rely heavily on symbols that have taken on affective or emotional value (Elder and Cobb, 1983).

Such stories feature individual protagonists, or in some cases heroes, involved in five levels of conflict: conflict with themselves, conflict between people, conflict with the unknown (or God), conflict with nature, or conflict with social or political institutions (McCartney, 1987). On the highest dramatic level, the hero is battling the unknown and is willing to risk or sacrifice his or her life for others.

In the most influential presidential-level political advertising campaign of the 1980s, that of Ronald Reagan in 1984, a mythic narrative was told in the convention film, *Presidency*, of the president's personal rebirth and renewal following an assassination attempt. The president undertakes such heroic action and sacrifices even to the extent of being shot, thereby experiencing renewal on a higher level ("My life is no longer my own") and redeeming the country in the process. Following a visual recreation of the assassination attempt, triumphant music signals the president's transition into mythic time, as he goes out into the world and visits the graves of American war heroes who died at Normandy Beach (*Presidency*, Republican National Committee, 1984; Morreale, 1991).

Might Perot have participated in this form of argumentation, which involves a hero and stories of personal sacrifice? To find out, we examined the three long Perot biographical infomercials aired in October, in which he offers his credentials for the presidency. A coding sheet was developed, drawn from an analysis of narrative discourse in news stories (McCartney, 1987). Use of this coding sheet made it possible to determine whether, and in what measure, narratives occurred in the discourse and the types of narratives that were told. The unit of analysis was individual stories that occurred in the discourse. Noted were the narrator, the central character, whether or not he or she sacrifices on behalf of a beneficiary, the conflict that emerges as the story plot thickens, whether the conflict is an internal one (the character in conflict with himself or herself) or one that involves a social actor or a higher power, the context within which the action occurs, and the point or moral of the story. This latter always turned out to be a value statement or a standard for individual or group action.

From this analysis it is clear that Ross Perot is not engaged in internal conflict or self-analysis. He is, however, engaged in heroic conflict on all social levels, beginning with the family, where he learns the lessons that he then applies in all other contexts, including, finally, his confrontation with a higher power in a life-and-death experience, as he flies to Tehran to personally assist a hostage rescue mission alongside other valiant American heroes.

The basic form of the biographical infomercials is that of narratives told by individuals, including Perot and members of his family, who tell stories in response to softball questions posed by an "interviewer." The use of family members to tell stories that he presumably will not tell about himself illustrates the fact that Perot is a reluctant or modest hero. Photo album-like visuals accompany family stories, and televised news clips illustrate the retelling of Perot's heroic actions abroad.

There were twenty-five narratives in the three infomercials. These can be divided into four major conflict situations that occur in a variety of interlocking social contexts. Interestingly, self-sacrifice is a central motif in all of the stories, illustrating the view that goodness is learned in the home, radiates out into broader social, business, and national arenas, and finally, in snowballing fashion, returns as its own reward into family life. Three basic conflict categories emerge, all of which involve self-sacrifice. The largest of these categories, sacrifice for a value, is first learned at home. It is then applied in the business world, as a number of stories are told focusing primarily on values in this context. Two other major categories of stories emerge: those that involve sacrifice in family and community settings, and those that involve sacrifice on behalf of the nation.

From this some basic principles emerge. Through narratives, we see a central actor moving in all social contexts, confronting challenges, and indeed sometimes overwhelming odds, yet emerging as a success. Who benefits from this success? Perot admittedly. But more significantly, in the greater number of stories, others are the primary beneficiaries, as Perot treats people in all walks of life just as he would treat his own family.

The voter is invited to believe in Perot because these stories illustrate the values of integrity and standing on principle, which are key requirements of leadership. Such values are learned at home, in a context most viewers can understand. In the "good society" Perot describes the home environment is one that involves sacrifice to empower others; from such environments true leaders may be expected to emerge. Coincidentally, the home environments described here are familiar to the home video audience. This fact has not escaped the attention of political communicators, who frequently engage in "intimate," family-related discourse, driven by the requirements of their primary medium of political expression, commercial television, which is highly personal and rife with family dramas (Jamieson, 1988; Kern, 1989).

In telling dramatic stories, featuring Perot moving out from the family context into the wider world, Perot's advertising is thus extending and revising familiar formats. The implicit deal he offers voters, however, is unique in its integration and multiplication of contexts: What I did for my family, community, company, nation—I will do for you.

STORIES OF SACRIFICE FOR A VALUE

Perot plays the central role in a variety of stories that illustrate the value of sacrifice on behalf of a value. Stories in this category are ones that he largely tells about himself. The argumentation is character-based and consistent, as principles he learned in his family inform his behavior first in his personal educational and community contexts, then in his business life, and finally, in his willingness to sacrifice on behalf of the national good. From these stories the concept of the business as family emerges. Given the uniqueness of this appeal and the fact that it generated such voter interest in a third party candidate, it is worthwhile examining these stories in some detail.

Business Contexts

We turn first to an analysis of stories with business contexts, because this is the primary case that Perot has to make to the American people.

Perot's father coaches his son to become a good businessman. Perot is a leader in training as, even in childhood, he sacrifices his free time. Every afternoon, he must buy and sell cattle and horses. This is because he was not allowed to take a horse home. He benefits, however, both through the companionship of his father (his "best friend"), with whom he was able to ride horses each afternoon, and through learning that you enter business to win, to make a profit. To do this, you must buy and sell the same day. In this story, the only one that focuses specifically on bottom-line values, Perot illustrates one value, learned at his father's knee: *Enter business to win, to make a profit.* Without sacrifice, however, success may not come (Biography I).

In another story, which illustrates the benefits of hard work and principles learned at home, Perot, working for IBM, discovered that most people worked for half a day. "I worked for the whole day, every day." As a result, he set a sales record and was one of the top salesmen. *All who work hard will benefit.* In this story, however, another value is revealed—*the basic integrity that underlies success* (Biography I).

Another story illustrates the value of standing on principle. Perot stands up for his rights in relation to the newspaper agency for which he worked as a boy. His boss tried to decrease Perot's payment because of his success. He was given a difficult route, but did well with it. His boss decided to decrease his rate. He went to the agency head and told his story. He was allowed to keep his previous, more favorable rate. Although only thirteen, he was brave enough to directly confront authority. *Not only Perot, but all people benefit when one individual stands up for principle* (Biography I).

In another story Perot was confronted at EDS with the dilemma of whether to select employees according to socially generated criteria, such as affirmative action. He decided against this despite its popularity. In so doing he again applied the egalitarian values learned in his home (Biography II).

At EDS as well, the question emerged whether Perot and his family should get more medical benefits than his employees. The dilemma was resolved: Everyone in the company should have the same medical care, the same doctor and benefits, as his own family. This principle emerged in 1994 in Bill Clinton's health care policy. It originated with Ross Perot. In this story, as in his explanation for opposing socially generated hiring practices, a value emerges: *A business is like a family* (Biography II).

A logical extension of this approach is that rich families are not primarily concerned about the bottom line. This, at any rate, is the picture of the Perot family that emerges. The money that his family makes beyond what they need to meet their needs is given away in a narrative illustrating how family love extends into community service. Thus, Perot suggests that his wife, like his parents, has been a positive influence on him in the area of community service. As soon as he and his wife had more money than they needed for their personal use, they began to undertake charitable activities. They established a school for the handicapped. His children, following this example, established a hospital in honor of their mother. They "hope every child born in the hospital has a mother like ours." The value? *Money does not buy happiness; happiness comes from good works* (Biography II).

In four other business-related stories Perot illustrates how he will sacrifice himself, even to the point of risking his own life, for his employees. This is because family values apply in the business world. The sacrifices one would make for one's own family should be applied in a business context.

In one story, it is clear that all individuals who work for his firm, EDS, are like a big family. Perot is aroused one morning at 2:00 A.M. by a request to rescue some employees who have been taken hostage by the government of Iran. He calls an old associate, who can handle commando-style operations, for help. The friend ceases his mourning for his deceased wife to undertake the action despite the risk not only to himself but to his family. In another story, other commando team members similarly leave their wives, children, and mortgages to join the effort (Biography II).

The plot thickens as Perot relates how his mother, who is seriously ill with cancer, confronts the possible loss of her son as he goes to Iran toward the close of the rescue operation. She says he should go, despite the personal risk. Indeed, she cheers him on, saying that despite her personal illness, she will go to the airport to welcome him and the hostages back home after the mission has proved to be successful (Biography II).

Finally, Perot relates how he secretly visits the hostages in prison and tells them of his plan to rescue them. This visit to Tehran involves great personal risk, as he would, at that point, "make the best hostage." His picture is plastered all over the Tehran airport. It is his "luck," however, to survive, and fly to Turkey to back up the rescue team (Biography II). All of these stories, and more, are recounted in *On the Wings of Eagles*. A compelling value emerges as the full extent of Perot's willingness to sacrifice on behalf of others is revealed: *A chief executive officer of a company should risk all, even his life, for his employees.*

Perot's stories of sacrifice on behalf of basic American values in business contexts illustrate the value of community. Only one of the stories deals with the bottom line. Above all, he seeks to ground his discourse in the related ideals of personal integrity and a positive, family-oriented basis for social interaction, even in a business environment.

The Educational Context

Similar values are illustrated in Perot's story of "the first time anyone listened to me." He risked standing on principle, as student council president at Texarkana Junior College, a small college that was seeking to expand. The board announced that new facilities would be built one block away from the college in an area with limited space. Students and many of the faculty thought the proposed plan was inadequate to meet future needs, and that the college should relocate instead. Despite the fact that students should be seen and not heard, Perot, whose parents taught him to stand on principle, went to talk to the administration. "I stood there and got my head torn off. It didn't matter." Today the college is on a larger site, a part of the University of Texas system, and a "great resource" in that part of the country (Biography I).

Conflicts with Special Interests

In a category of narrative clearly designed to illustrate how he will stand up to the special interests that he says are at the root of all of America's problems, Perot tells of his own personal confrontations with special interests in a story that also illustrates the value of standing on principle.

As a student at the Naval Academy Perot was class president and chairman of the honor committee. One student at the academy who was from a prominent family did something improper. The honor committee decided to dismiss him, but because of his family, the administration did not follow through on the recommendation. Perot was angry, and resigned from both of his posts. School officials, backing down, called him and said they would expel the transgressing student from the academy. The value? *Society benefits when an individual challenges special interests* (Biography I).

STORIES OF SELF-SACRIFICE
FOR FAMILY AND COMMUNITY

In another major category of stories, Perot illuminates the basic nature of family interaction: mutual caring. Using narratives, he illustrates how good and caring people thus emerge in family settings, and how the good deeds of those who emerge in such a caring family environment radiate out into the community, benefiting all. A circle is described, as Perot and his children use narratives to illustrate how values learned within the Perot family inform their family and community lives. Egalitarian principles learned at home are applied in the community at large. Finally, goodness has its own reward, as those who believe in egalitarian principles and care for others on this basis, in turn receive benefits.

In one story Perot tells in his October advertising, he describes how his mother taught him to be kind to people, and that poor people are like everyone else but just down on their luck. She always fed homeless people, even when the family was poor. One day a person said to the family, "Do you know why so many homeless people come to this house?" The person pointed to a mark that was by the house. Perot asked his mother whether she wanted him to get rid of the mark, in order to keep poor people away from the house. "No," she said, "poor people are just like us. They're just out of luck."

Perot's mother had an ideal, helping homeless people, and the family sacrificed because of this ideal, even though sometimes the Perot family did not have enough to eat. The value behind this sacrifice? *Help others, even homeless people, because all are equal* (Biography I).

When his father had a kidney operation, young Ross could not service his paper route customers for several days. Other students did not want to do so, because the route was too rough. He went to his customers and said he could not deliver the paper on time. Perot makes it clear that the customers were poor. But they did not cut their payments to him, although he delivered the paper late. When he launched his 1992 presidential election campaign, one of them called to offer support, and the famous Ross Perot and his former customer spoke like long lost friends. Value? *People are good and will help each other out, irregardless of social status* (Biography I).

Perot's parents emerge as heroes as Perot describes how they sacrificed to make their children happy. One day he came home to find his mother in tears. "Why are you crying?" he asked. The family was poor, and Perot's father had to sell his horse to buy Christmas gifts for his children. The children benefit from his sacrifice. Perot says he was "born rich" because his parents tried to do everything for him (Biography I).

Family members report that Perot emerges in his turn as a hero, as he sacrifices for his children. His daughter, Carol, for example, reports on her request to take in a stray cat. He did not want to do this, Carol reports, but he did it for her. The beneficiaries? His daughter and the ideal of animal protection (Carol, Family Biography).

Perot sacrifices his time, effort, and money on behalf of the city of New York. One Christmas, his daughter, Susan, presents him with a dilemma, the fact that the police horses in New York are too old. Perot purchases new horses for them as her Christmas present. "I felt like a queen," Susan said of her subsequent invitation to spend a day with the New York City Police (Susan, Family Biography).

Perot sacrifices his time and effort on behalf of a neighbor who had a car accident, according to a daughter who was thereby made proud (Family Biography). The value of these stories? *Self-sacrifice for the community benefits family* as good works are their own reward.

On a more daring level, appropriate to the male members of the family, his son, a pilot and businessman who later joins his father's firm, reports that he risked his life to reclaim a flight record previously held by the United States. He explains his father's anxiety about the trip. In the end Perot overcomes his doubts, and encourages his children to be their best. The beneficiaries? His family, as well as the country, which retakes the trophy (Family Biography).

STORIES OF SACRIFICE FOR COUNTRY

The hero emerges early in Perot's national self-sacrifice stories. Even as a young man, he answered a higher calling.

An internal dilemma emerged for Perot while he was still at the Naval Academy. He had met and fallen in love with a very popular young woman.

He was in competition with a number of medical students for the hand of his popular future wife. Everybody who saw her fell in love with her. He worked for the navy, however, and was called to duty in Korea. He decided to go, and went out on all the missions on an aircraft carrier. He benefited in the long run, however, as he both won the fair lady's hand and met an official from IBM on deck who offered him his first civilian job (Biography I). The value that emerges? *Sacrifice for principle benefits not only the community but, ultimately, the individual as well.*

Perot's major public link with national policy is his effort to rescue Americans missing in action in Vietnam. Interestingly, the stories are quite similar to the stories that he and his family tell of his effort to rescue the EDS hostages in Iran. The moral? *Business and national interests are one.*

A number of stories relate to his efforts on behalf of American hostages in Southeast Asia:

- A dilemma emerges during the Vietnam War. Hostage wives seek Perot's help because the government is clearly not doing its job. Should he sacrifice his Christmas vacation to go with POW wives to Paris to ask for information about their husbands (and alone, later, to go with business associates to Laos for the same purpose)? He decides to do so. Who benefits? POWs and their relatives and, by extension, all Americans willing to serve their country (Biographies I and II).

- A family member reaffirms the sacrifice involved in this effort, as Perot expends his time, money, and effort trying to find American soldiers that he believes are still alive (Biography I).

- At the request of hostage family members, Perot confronts the Central Intelligence Agency after determining that 350 American prisoners are held in Laos. The CIA refuses to take action, arguing that if a rescue were attempted the prisoners would be killed. If elected to the presidency, he will never leave a prisoner behind (Biography II).

- After he has successfully been instrumental in bringing Americans missing in action back to the United States, the prisoners call Perot to thank him for his effort. He says others should be thanked instead. A parade is held in San Francisco. In a clear gesture of self-sacrifice, Perot implies that he himself watches the parade from the sidelines. The value: *Acknowledge others' contributions, not your own—the true hero is modest* (Biography II).

CONCLUSIONS

From this analysis it is clear that civic-minded self-sacrifice is the core of Perot's discourse. In Perot's own stories he talks about ordinary people and their lives. He tries not to appear to make himself the hero (this is for others to do). His many sacrifices are described, however, in great detail in a narrative fashion from which morals are drawn about civic virtue. Through the telling of such stories, Perot's campaign attempts to capture the American values of standing on principle and community-minded public service. These have informed discourse at major turning points in American history, as Robert Bellah has noted, from the time of the founding of the nation. Such a turning point occurred in 1992, as Americans grappled with who they were as a people and whether the political system could work on behalf of the nation as a whole.

Yet at the same time Perot himself, as a businessperson, represents a Horatio Alger-like story. His life represents a rags to riches story, and he is clear about the value of the bottom line in business dealings. From his depiction of his life, however, we see little hint of individualistic selfishness. Instead, we are treated to a cornucopia of family values, which can be readily understood by voters in all demographic categories, operating in all social contexts. Thus distinctions of education and class are broken down. The desire for mutual empowerment that is found in families is illustrated throughout society in the Perot version of reality.

Indeed, all Americans are equal. There is no difference between poor and rich, black and white. Narratives that illustrate such basic American values were the heart of the Perot campaign. Through such narratives, answers to central policy concerns are avoided. Despite its billing as oriented toward "the issues," we do not find heavy weighing of policy alternatives, either in the short spot ads that were most memorable to voters over a thirty-two-day period or in the longer biographical ads that present the candidate's credentials for public office. Further, and perhaps even more tellingly, at no point in any of the biographical ads did Perot invite business associates or leaders to describe how he balances a budget or makes economic choices. Thus Perot's key credentials claim—that he knows how to make significant economic choices—is nowhere backed up with real information about his business choices despite numerous personal narratives. Instead, issues relating to such credentials are lost in a wash of intimate and personal stories.

In reducing all social, economic, and national contexts to that of the family, Perot is expressing a communitarianism that would be unfamiliar to civic activists like Puritan father John Winthrop or to founding father Thomas Jefferson who theorized more broadly about the common good. Perot is, however, sounding a trumpet call that is not unknown to Americans who obtain their information from television. In the 1980s intimate communication, including family-related discourse, became prominent, driven by the primary format of political expression, television, which is rife with family dramas. In telling dramatic stories, featuring himself, moving out from his family into the wider world, Perot's advertising is extending and revising familiar formats.

Continuing a tradition of advertising from the 1980s, he "dovetails" character and issue traits, arguing that his experience as a businessman makes him capable of handling public policy on behalf of the public as no politician could. And in exemplifying business values he does so in a fashion that abnegates any hint of greed, suggesting that not only business but the nation as a whole should be run as a family. Underlying his messages is a desire for order: Americans missing in action should be gotten back where they belong. Political, business, and family affairs should be conducted in an ethical and orderly fashion.

In a time of great economic uncertainty that led to a desire for political change, Ross Perot rose as a third party candidate with an appeal that transcended partisanship and ideology. His presidential campaign drew on traditions of past political advertising campaigns, but altered them to conform to the richer, more interactive information environment of the fall 1992 general election, which included more popular participation and issues discussion in news and extended interview formats. It is important to remember that, like all third party candidates, Perot's candidacy was driven by voters' issue concerns: about the economy, the deficit, and political candidates. Still, understanding Perot's advertising campaign requires attention to much more than his elaboration of issues.

It is therefore incumbent upon scholars to probe more deeply into Perot's campaign expression, which was built not only on charts and graphs, but on narratives and the communitarian values they illustrate. At the heart of Perot's information campaign was the rhetoric of family values, never argued logically. Instead, sacrifice stories undergirded his effort. They were beamed wholesale to Americans, many of whom desperately sought a leader who came from "outside" a system they perceived to be flawed by utilitarian, self-serving politicians. The legacy of Perot's candidacy is being felt by the 1992 victor, who must live with the perception that he received only 43 percent of the vote. It was also felt in the 1994 election campaign, as the successful Republicans appealed to Perot's voters, and with the assistance of his pollster, Frank Luntz, couched their "Contract with America" in Perot's language, the language of interlocking values such as responsibility, on family, business and national levels.

In the final analysis, what did Ross Perot, the son of a horse trader, have to offer the American voter? Not only a promise on the issues. But a promise that emerges through bottom-line narrative logic: What I did for my family, my community, my company, my country, I will do for you.

NOTES

Support for this research was provided by the National Science Foundation (SES-9122729), the MacArthur Foundation, the Ford Foundation, the

Twentieth Century Fund, the Joyce Foundation and the Carnegie Foundation. Generous help also was provided by the Joan Shorenstein Barone Center on the Press, Politics and Public Policy at Harvard University.

1. Walter R. Fisher, *Human Communication as Narration: Toward a Philosophy of Reason, Value and Action* (Columbia, S.C.: University of South Carolina Press, 1989), pp. 58 and 48.

2. "Dovetailing" is a process of developing a message in which character and issue reenforce each other. This may be expressed visually, as through the airing of a visual of an overweight Tip O'Neill, former House Democratic leader, representing "bloated" federal government. Ross Perot is attempting to "dovetail" the character claim, "I am a good businessman," with the argument, "I am therefore uniquely able to tackle the federal deficit issue."

3. The diminished role is not surprising for three reasons:

(a) The first reason relates to the difference between primaries and general elections. In the primaries, the party label is not such a factor because of the intraparty nature of the contests, because the candidates are focusing on individual states, and because the public is being newly exposed to most of the candidates.

(b) A second reason for the diminished but still significant political advertising impact relates to the increased importance for voters of other sources of information in 1992 as compared with 1988. Responding to expressions of voter concern about the campaign process and their information environment, candidates and news media alike developed alternative forms of communication in the fall of 1992 that differed from those generally available to voters in the 1988 general election and the 1992 primary season. "Interactive" debates, extended interview talk shows, and network and local news broadcasts all played new and different roles for voters in the fall general election campaign. Candidates, voters, and media repeatedly interacted with each other, converging and diverging over the course of the election in a continuing process of constructing campaign meaning and messages (Just et al., 1996, forthcoming).

(c) The third reason may well relate to the fact that advertising can only be relevant for voters in a positive sense to the degree that it addresses their current issue concerns. In the case of one candidate, George Bush, his advertising campaign became hostage to his own issue priorities, which were no longer those of the voters: foreign policy, success in "winning" the cold war, America acquitting itself well in the Persian Gulf War, and reestablishing global faith in American commitments (Kaplan, 1992).

4. Kathleen Frankovic of CBS News polling argues that the debates were decisive in the strong showing of Ross Perot. According to the CBS News exit polls, 60 percent of the public believed the debates were among the factors that helped them decide how to vote, as compared with 45 percent for

"performance on talk shows" and figures in the twenties for paid candidate political advertising.

The poll evidence for the debate impact on Perot's image is greatest in relation to the first debate, as CBS asked the question on the night of the debate and two days later: "In general, how did Sunday night's debate affect your opinion of [candidate X]? Did it make you think better of him, worse of him, or didn't it affect your opinion?" They found: 16 percent that night/14 percent two days later thought better of Bush; 35 percent/31 percent thought better of Clinton; but an astounding 61 percent/57 percent thought better of Perot (Frankovic, 1993). During this first debate Perot advertised his first thirty-minute infomercial. It was aired the following week, amid stories about his strong debate performance. It gained a wide audience, beating out the major prime-time entertainment programs offered on the competing networks. Perot's shorter fifteen- and thirty-second radio and television ads began to air shortly before the first debate, at Perot's race reentry on Oct. 1.

REFERENCES

Alger, Dean, Montague Kern, and Darrell West (1993). Political advertising, the information environment and the voter in the 1992 presidential election. Paper prepared for the annual meeting of the International Communication Association, May 27–31. Washington, D.C.

Andersen, Kenneth E. (1993, Nov.). The role of ethical/value issues in campaigns: A long-term view of "family values." *American Behavioral Scientist, 37* (2), 302–307.

Bellah, Robert A. (1985). *The Good Society.* NY: Alfred A. Knopf.

Biography I (*A Conversation with Ross Perot, Part I*).

Biography II (*A Conversation with Ross Perot, Part II*).

Boulding, Kenneth (1958). National images and international systems. *Journal of Conflict Resolution, 3*(2), 120–131.

Devlin, L. Patrick (1986). An analysis of presidential television commercials, 1952–1984. In Lynda Lee Kaid, Dan Nimmo, and Keith R. Sanders, eds., *New perspectives on political advertising.* Carbondale, Ill.: Southern Illinois University Press, pp. 21–52.

Elder, Charles E., and Roger W. Cobb (1983). *The political use of symbols.* New York: Longman.

Family Biography. Ross Perot's family describes the candidate.

Fisher, Waiter R. (1989). *Human communication as narration: Toward a philosophy of reason, value and action.* Columbia, S.C.: University of South Carolina Press.

Follett, Ken (1983). *On Wings of Eagles.* New York: Signet.

Frankovic, Kathleen A. (1993). Public opinion in the 1992 campaign. In Gerald M. Pomper, ed., *The election of 1992.* Chatham, N.J.: Chatham House, pp. 110–131.

Gronbeck, Bruce E. (1984). Functional and dramaturgical themes of presidential campaigning. *Presidential Studies Quarterly, 14,* 486–511.

Jamieson, Kathleen Hall (1988). *Eloquence in an electronic age: The transformation of political speechmaking.* New York: Oxford University Press.

Jamieson, Kathleen Hall (1992). *Dirty politics.* New York: Oxford University Press.

Just, Marion, Ann Crigler, Dean Alger, Timothy Cook, Montague Kern, and Darrell West (1996, forthcoming). *Crosstalk: Citizens, Candidates and Media in a Presidential Election.* Chicago: University of Chicago Press.

Kamen, Al, and Dan Balz (1993, Nov. 5). Administration challenges Perot to debate trade pact: NAFTA critic accepts offer to face Gore. *Washington Post,* 1.

Kaplan, Harold (1992, Dec. 12). Annenberg School Election Debriefing, Philadelphia, Pa.

Kelley, Michael (1992, May 26). Perot stresses homey image, but the image is no accident. *New York Times,* 1.

Kendall, Kathleen E. (1993, Nov.). Public speaking in the presidential primary through media eyes. *American Behavioral Scientist, 37*(2), 240–51.

Kern, Montague (1989). *30-second politics: Political advertising in the 80s.* Westport, Conn.: Praeger-Greenwood.

Kern, Montague (1993). The advertising driven "new" mass media election and the rhetoric of policy issues: The 1990 Gantt–Helms senate race. In Robert J. Spitzer, ed., *Media and public policy.* Westport, Conn.: Praeger-Greenwood, pp. 133–150.

Kern, Montague, and Marion Just (1994). *Voter construction of campaign images in response to televised news and political advertising.* Cambridge, Mass.: The Joan Shorenstein Barone Center on the Press, Politics and Public Policy, The John F. Kennedy School of Government, Harvard University.

Kern, Montague, Darrell West, and Dean Alger (1993). Political advertising, ad watches and news in the 1992 election. Paper prepared for the annual meeting of the American Political Science Association, Washington, D.C.

Louden, Alan. (1990, June). Transformation of issue to image and presence: Eliciting character evaluations in negative spot advertising. Paper prepared for the annual meeting of the International Communication Association, Dublin, Ireland.

Louden, Alan. (1991, May). *A narrative approach to the examination of political advertising: Perspectives on the 1990 Gantt–Helms senate campaign.* Paper delivered at the annual meeting of the International Communication Association, Chicago, Ill.

Luttwak, Edward N. (1993). *The endangered American dream: How to stop the United States from becoming a third world country and how to win the geo-economic struggle for industrial supremacy.* New York: Simon and Schuster.

McCartney, Hunter P. (1987, Spring). Applying fiction conflict situations to analysis of news stories. *Journalism Quarterly, 64*(1), 163–70.

Mischler, Elliot G. (1986). *Research interviewing: Context and narrative.* Cambridge, Mass.: Harvard University Press.

Morreale, Joanne (1991). *A new beginning: A textual frame analysis of the political campaign film.* Albany, N.Y.: State University of New York Press.

Mumby, Dennis K. (1993). *Narrative and social control: Critical perspectives.* Newbury Park, Calif.: Sage.

Neumann, Russell, Marion Just and Ann Crigler (1992). *Common Knowledge.* Chicago, Ill.: The University of Chicago Press.

Pfau, Michael, and Henry Kenski (1990). *Attack politics.* Westport, Conn.: Praeger-Greenwood.

Presidency (1984). Republican National Committee.

Rosenthal, Andrew (1992, May 22). The politics of morality. *New York Times,* 19.

Schneider, William (1992, Dec. 5). When issues, not personalities, rule. *National Journal.*

Wattenberg, Martin P. (1994). *The decline of American political parties, 1952–1992.* Cambridge, Mass.: Harvard University Press.

West, Darrell (1993). *Air wars.* Washington, D.C.: Congressional Quarterly Press.

West, Darrell, Montague Kern, and Dean Alger (1992). Political advertising and ad watches in the 1992 presidential nominating campaign. Paper prepared for the annual meeting of the American Political Science Association, Chicago, Ill., Sept. 1–5.

Zaller, John (1993). The rise and fall of candidate Perot. Paper prepared for the annual meeting of the American Political Science Association, Washington, D.C.

EIGHT

Political Advertising

Strategies for Influence

MARILYN S. ROBERTS

OVERVIEW

The 1992 presidential campaign left both professional journalists and the academy of interdisciplinary scholars who study these elections with a plethora of explanations as to its meaning. The campaign of 1992 mirrored the protean changes in new technologies, more personalized and precisely targeted candidate appearances on talk shows, on local newscasts via satellite feeds, multisite electronic town halls, and electronic mail. One might argue that the expansion of these newly discovered nonpaid forms of political communication channels to "get the candidates' messages out" might reduce the campaigns' dependency on paid political advertising. However, there appears to be no reprieve from the magnitude of paid advertising messages. Devlin (1993) reports a record $133 million combined spending by the campaigns of George Bush, Bill Clinton, and their respective political parties, and by Ross Perot. The vast majority of the millions of dollars was used to purchase commercial airtime. This record level of spending indicates that candidates believe political advertising works and influences voters' thinking and ultimately their candidate choice. A question of real importance is how voters used political advertising messages in 1992 to influence their thinking about the candidates.

THE PURPOSE OF THE CHAPTER

This chapter seeks to examine the responses of voters who were exposed to one of the most pervasive and costly forms of political communication in

179

1992: presidential campaign commercials. The record $133 million spent collectively by the three major presidential candidates and the two major political parties was used to define themselves, each other, and their agendas for change. With all of the exposure to presidential campaign messages, how much influence did these hundreds of thousands of gross impressions really have on voters' thoughts about the campaign?

To examine the impact of the presidential campaign commercials in 1992, the author asked three exploratory research questions. First, in a post-election unaided recall survey, what type of campaign information from presidential advertisements do respondents report influenced their thinking about the campaign? Second, how is the reported influence of political advertising associated with the respondents' direction of favorability or unfavorability toward the three 1992 presidential candidates? Third, what does the type of advertising information reported by respondents imply about the previous research findings in political advertising?

The chapter begins by reporting prior research on the impact of negative, emotional, and visual factors used in campaign commercials, and how voters choose among candidate images, and semantically process campaign commercials. It then outlines the methodology used to examine the unaided recall responses regarding the influence of the presidential campaign commercials and their direction of influence, before presenting the results of the study.

WHAT WE KNOW ABOUT MESSAGE EFFECTS

Negative Messages

Roberts (1991) states that the only difference in the symbols used in positive and negative campaign commercials is in their intent—either to inflate or to deflate the bond of trust between the candidate and the voter. All political advertising, regardless of the direction of intent, is crafted to manipulate societal myths, icons, public and private symbols by visual and aural editing techniques to form "the message." Yet a growing body of literature distinguishes between the message effects of positive and negative appeals and their intended, and sometimes, unintended effect.

Negative messages, when properly produced, impact negatively on the intended target of the message: the opponent (Boydston and Kaid, 1983; Kaid and Boydston, 1987; Merritt, 1984, and Weigold and Sheer, 1993). Conversely, negative messages may create a backlash of unintended effects by impacting voter attitudes more negatively on the sponsor of the attack than on the attacked (Hill, 1989; Faber, Tims, and Schmitt, 1993). Johnson-Cartee and Copeland (1991) show that the type of attack determines the potential backlash effect of a negative advertisement. Direct attacks have the greatest potential for backlash, followed by the direct comparison. The implied comparison is found to be the least likely to create a backlash, because the format encourages viewers to generate their own arguments. Johnson-Cartee and Copeland (1991) also suggest that voters are more tolerant of attack advertising that is based on issues than on vicious personal attacks, which are highly susceptible to backlash. Roddy and Garramone's (1988) findings concur that negative advertising based on issues produced significantly more positive evaluations of the ad's sponsor. Their work also indicates that voters who view negative issue advertising are significantly less likely to vote for the opponent than voters who see negative image attack ads.

Faber, Tims, and Schmitt (1993) indicate that backlash effects are more likely among partisans of the target candidate. Their findings also suggest that independents are somewhat more likely to report backlash effects than intended effects. They show that voter attributes such as partisanship, the level of involvement, and the level of alternative information sources impact political decision making. The researchers' findings suggest that the level of political involvement positively influences the degree of impact that negative political ads exert. It is noteworthy that the findings of Faber, Tims, and Schmitt run counter to previous studies, which showed that passive, low-involvement voters were more positively influenced by negative ads. Faber, Tims, and Schmitt "found that when voting preference is the dependent variable, people who are more involved and interested are most influenced by negative ads" (p. 74).

Emotionality and Visual Imagery

The degree of emotionality and visual imagery used in political advertising messages also relates to a political advertisement's effectiveness. The works of Lang (1991) and Shapiro and Rieger (1989) appear to suggest that emotional political advertisements are better recalled than nonemotional appeals. Lang and Lanfear (1990) suggest that negative emotional appeals are better recalled than positive political advertisements. Lang and Lanfear also demonstrate that ads do not require large production budgets to be memorable. However, visual complexity such as cuts, edits, and dollies, can make an advertisement more interesting and likely to gain the viewers' attention. Advertisements that move quickly from frame to frame may result in a high level of viewer attention, but they simultaneously encourage a lower level of recall of the content. One solution to this dilemma of maximizing memory while gaining attention is recommended by Lang and Lanfear (1990). They suggest that important information be presented both visually and verbally in the advertisement.

Kaid and Davidson (1986) define how the candidates choose to present themselves to voters through their political advertising as "videostyle." The researchers' findings suggest that verbal and nonverbal messages and production techniques differ depending on whether one is the incumbent candidate or the challenger. Based on interviews with political advertising producers, the study concludes that these professionals are concerned ultimately about reaching the voter emotionally. Kern (1989) concurs that the relevant metaphor for today's mass media campaign is the commercial message, that of "touching someone" (p. 207). Kern illustrates her point by using a conversation about the 1986 campaign elections with Democratic consultant Frank Greer in which he states:

> We're real strong on message and language and we're real strong on issues. People make decisions also on how they feel about a candidate, however. The one thing music does, the way it's used in commercial advertising, the way it's used in movies, the way it's used everywhere, it creates a feeling about a candidate. I think you need to do that, as well as communicate a message about issues. . . . Visuals do that as well. (p. 40)

Kern offers two concepts in understanding the theories of affect used in advertising. One concept is referential advertising, based on works of critical semiotic theorist Judith Williamson. Kern argues that the basic premise of advertising is that of "transferring meaning from one affect-laden symbol, such as a child, place, or object, to a product." The second concept, referred to as "the wheel of emotions," focuses on how people organize their feelings and how advertising can best tap into them. The concept, developed by Stuart J. Agres, research director for the advertising firm of Lowe-Marschalk, combines the "get 'em sick, then get 'em well" idea that underlies conventional theories about how ads organize emotions. With the simple referential idea of using symbols and sounds that already have meaning, whether cognitive or affective, in political advertising, voters' emotions can be effectively tapped.

More recently, the work of Burns, Biswas, and Babin (1993) suggests that visual imagery effectively shapes impressions. Although not dealing specifically with political advertising, the researchers' findings indicate that visual imagery is a mediating factor of advertising effects. Their work concludes that visual imagery vividness has the potential to explain consumers' mental reactions to certain advertising strategies, including attitudinal and intentional consequences.

Choosing among Candidate Images

Walter Lippmann (1922) wrote, "The only feeling that anyone can have about an event he[she] does not experience is the feeling aroused by his[her] mental image of that event." The word "image" has been defined and applied to candidates in various ways. Krock (1960) refers to candidate image as an "acquired personality." Hahn and Gonchar (1972) define candidate image as "the interaction of his [her] personality and orientation to the world with ours." Nimmo and Savage (1976) and Bowes and Strentz (1978) define candidate image as "perceived attributes." Graber (1972) examines presidential images and the mass media's contribution to the formation of candidate images. She states:

> the mass media are significant in furnishing raw material for the formation of political images. Most people do not invent political images out of thin air. Rather, they combine current political data supplied by the mass media with existing knowledge and attitudes and then weave these into a plausible and pleasing GESTALT. (pp. 50–51)

Similarly, Garramone (1986) defines candidate image as "the sum of the perceived personal and professional characteristics of the candidate." She suggests that advertisements drawing attention to different characteristics of a message may influence the way voters process the information. Garramone argues that image commercials often emphasize visual content. She notes that issue commercials tend to use the candidate on camera, while image advertisements tend to tell the viewer about the candidate's personality qualities.

Patterson and McClure's (1976) research suggests that voters find it easier to learn about candidate images than about candidate issues. When describing Jimmy Carter and Gerald Ford, the respondents in the study refer to the candidates' images three to four times more often than to the candidates' stand on issues. Weaver et al. (1981) examine the 1976 presidential campaign. The study tests the agenda-setting hypothesis of mass media in a year-long, three-site investigation. The results produce strong evidence of the vital role that the mass media play in shaping candidates' images. The researchers report the following: "These findings support the idea that media agenda-setting (at least newspaper agenda-setting) extends to candidate images as well as to issues and that media emphasis or deemphasis of certain image attributes contribute to voter evaluations of candidate" (p. 192).

Another illustration of how voters use media information to form candidate images is seen in the work of Jamieson (1992). Jamieson refers metaphorically to voters as "pack rats," taking bits and pieces of political information and storing them in a single place to form the overall impression of the candidate. She argues that information becomes blurred over the course of the campaign. "Lost in storage is a clear recall of where this or that 'fact' obtained from news mixes with that from ads," she writes (p. 17). Jamieson further argues that the construction of candidate images does not occur by chance. Political consultants purposefully orchestrate pseudoevents to manipulate the visuals that appear on the nightly news about the campaign and have direct control over the images of their candidate in candidate-sponsored advertising.

Positioning a candidate and creating an electable image requires continual monitoring of public opinion polls and a keen understanding of the voter segments required to be successful during the various phases of the campaign. Newman (1994) discusses the 1992 presidential candidates' strategies for establishing their images. He concludes that "Clinton was successful in building an image of change that was consistently reinforced throughout the various phases of the campaign. His image was supported with views on the economy and social welfare that differentiated him from his competitors throughout the political campaign." Newman attributes Bush's downfall to the "disparity between the image he had created in his own mind and the one that translated into the minds of voters." Thus, Bush saw himself as a world leader, not the leader of America's domestic renewal and change. Newman's reflections on Perot's image are that "Perot's offer to be the servant of the people was clearly an attractive position but not potent enough to win the election for him" (p. 101).

The work of Roberts, Anderson, and McCombs (1994) indicates the potent predictive power of candidate images. The researchers' findings provide empirical support for the assertion that voters create a gestalt (Graber, 1972) or "pack rat" (Jamieson, 1992) image of candidates. In examining the 1990 Texas gubernatorial campaign, they found that candidate image appears to be an extremely strong predictor of the sample panel respondents' reported actual vote for governor.

Semantic Processing of Advertisements

Biocca (1991a) raises the question, "Are there blueprints to the structure of an ad?" The meaning voters associate with a presidential campaign is not there by chance. Biocca states that "we can safely postulate that a relationship exists between the structure of the political ad and the psychological processes of the viewer" (p. 11). Biocca (1991b) examines the semantic processing of televised political ads. He states:

> Viewed in cognitive terms, the struggle over the candidate's image is the struggle over the semantic processing of political commercials by voters. In the mind of the viewer the imagery of the political commercial is represented by networks of semantic nodes and markers radiating from a central concept, the candidate. (p. 27)

Biocca (1991a) advocates the decomposition of a political ad into words, images, and sounds. By doing so, researchers can examine the ad for "units" of meaning. He cautions that discussions of political ads can "too easily succumb to statements about how the ad 'carries' meaning." It is more useful to perceive an ad as *evoking meaning* that already resides in the viewer. As to an ad's effect on voters, Biocca states:

> The ad activates a pattern of semantic processing in the viewer that will change upon repeated viewing of the ad. . . . It follows that an ad only "creates" meaning by forging new associations (new configurations) of sememes in the mind of the view. . . . The expression unit—a word on this page, for example—can be publicly circulated and experienced by others. That is the whole point of advertising. It is this public circulation of signs and codes and the social construction that make communication codes so profoundly political. In elections the sign is used in the narrowly political sense to suggest legitimacy, mobilize voters around the sign ("symbol"), and alter the meaning of opponents (pp. 22–23)

To understand the effectiveness of a specific ad to activate a pattern of semantic processing within the viewer, Biocca (1991c) argues that one must understand the function of semantic framing, which he refers to as the "Mondrian approach." "Semantic framing using juxtaposition operates by a very simple principle: put any two images, codes, or discourses side by side and they will semantically interact" (p. 75). The ad's Mondrian-like quality forms a collage of images that activates semantic processing by the viewer. Since presidential commercials are constructed by political consultants working for a specific candidate, the notion of constructing a collage of images that enhance a candidate's positive perception, while simultaneously attempting to dissuade viewers from forming a positive perception of the opponent, via negative semantic framing, is quite plausible.

Garramone (1986) examines the influence of political commercials by applying the transactional model of mass communication effects as set forth in McLeod and Becker (1981). The transactional model postulates that media effects can be better understood by combining specific knowledge about the message characteristics, audience orientations, and contingent conditions that enhance and/or constrain the formation of candidate images. Garramone and Biocca both ground their ideas about semantic processing in the works of Rumelhart and Ortony (1977) and Rumelhart (1980, 1983) on the concept of schema. Schemata are defined as cognitive representations of generic concepts. Thus, schemata constitute all of the candidate attributes, party expectations and the relationship among all the accumulated valence and salience of mediated knowledge and personal affect in the mind of the viewer.

In order to gain new insights into how presidential campaign commercials affect voters' cognitive processing, we must first collapse the commercial into a series of semantic frames. Biocca (1991b) defines a semantic frame as "a textual or message strategy for the activation of desired schema in the mind of the viewer" (p. 38). Framing organizes information and inferences about verbal, visual, and aural information. An individual commercial contains many frames. Thus, the same commercial may stimulate varying levels of support, distortion, and oppositional decodings of meaning. Biocca (1991b) concludes:

> Based on some knowledge of the average code competence of various audiences or the universe of schema likely to be activated, an analyst may be able to model (a) the various "meanings" of the message paths of semantic activation for different audiences, and (b) the changing meaning of a message over the course of various exposures. (p. 82)

Therefore, if watching presidential campaign commercials creates meaning, that meaning and its direction of influence may be retrievable from some voters. Since a commercial is made of many frames, particular frames are more memorable than others. Lippmann's (1922) thoughts about the effect on feelings aroused by the mental images in our minds hold just as true for political advertisements as they do for news. A growing body of public opinion literature currently applies the concepts of schema and framing to news coverage. Goffman (1974), Tuchman (1978), Lau and Sears (1986), Graber (1988), Iyengar (1991), Neuman, Just, and Crigler (1992), and Pan and Kosicki (1993) are examples of work in this area. Therefore, the information that respondents recall from campaign commercials as having influenced their thoughts about a campaign should also be considered potent and scrutinized through the concept of schema.

METHODOLOGY

The purpose of this chapter is to examine the responses of voters who were asked to recall information about the influence of presidential campaign commercials. A post-presidential election telephone survey was conducted in Franklin County, Ohio, using a stratified cluster sample of 931 registered voters. The interviews were conducted from the day after the election through January, 1993. The response rate was 52 percent. The present study was part of a larger national election project.1 Respondents were asked the open-ended question, "Which television ad most influenced your thinking about the campaign?" No prompting was given to aid the recall of the 1992 presidential campaign commercials. If the respondent provided an unaided response to the question, two additional questions were then asked in order to indicate the direction of influence of the recalled advertisement. The first question was, "Did the ad make you feel more favorable toward Bush, Clinton, Perot, or none of the candidates?" Following this response, the second question was asked: "Did the ad make you feel less favorable toward Bush, Clinton, Perot, or none of the candidates?" The respondents were also asked to provide the standard demographic information, as well as media usage and voting behavior information.

RESULTS

Description of the Respondents

Of the total 931 respondents in the larger study sample, approximately one-fourth (24%) were able to provide an unaided response to the question, "Which television ad most influenced your thinking about the campaign?" Thus, only these respondents (N=226) form the data set for analysis in the current study. Of the 226 respondents, 40 percent were male and 60 percent were female. In educational level, approximately one-fourth (N=54) had less education than or equal to a high school diploma, while 29 percent (N=66) had either vocational or technical training or some college. Slightly more than one-fourth of the respondents (N=61) had received a bachelor's degree, while approximately 20 percent (N=45) had done postgraduate work or completed graduate or professional degrees.

The breakdown of the respondents by age indicated that 20 percent (N=45) of the sample were 30 years of age or less. Slightly less than one-third (31%) were between the ages of 31 and 40. One-fourth (N=56) were between 41 and 50 years old, while less than one-fourth of the sample (N=53) was over 50 years of age. In household yearly income levels, one-fourth of the respondents (N=42) had household earnings of less than $25,000 per year, while the majority (74%) had yearly household incomes of $25,000 or greater.

In the media usage questions, respondents were asked how much attention was paid to campaign news on television. Approximately 44 percent (N=100) reported that they paid "a lot" of attention, while more than one-third (N=79) paid "some" attention to campaign news on television. Fifteen percent (N=34) of the respondents stated that they paid "a little" attention, while only 13 (6%) respondents indicated that they paid no attention to campaign news or did not watch television.

Slightly less than one-third (30.5%) of the respondents reported listening to radio news "regularly," while 18.1 percent (N=41) indicated that they "sometimes" listened to radio news. Over half of the respondents (N=116 or 51%) said that they rarely or never listened to radio news. When asked to report how much attention was paid to radio or television talk shows, nearly 20 percent indicated that they "regularly" paid attention, while 28 percent reported paying attention "sometimes" (N=64). The largest percentage of the sample (40%) stated that they rarely or never paid attention to radio and television talk shows.

Regarding the question of how much attention was paid to news magazines, slightly more than one-third (38%) of the respondents in the sample reported either paying attention "regularly" (N=37) or "sometimes" (N=49). Slightly less than two-thirds of the respondents (62%) indicated that they paid either rare (N=35) or no attention (N=105) to news magazines. Approximately 85 percent of the sample (N=188) indicated that they had read a newspaper article about the presidential campaign. Slightly less than three-fourths of the sample (N=161) reported paying either "a lot" or "some" attention to newspaper articles about the presidential campaign, while the remaining one-fourth indicated that they paid either "a little" or "no attention."

Respondents were also asked to disclose their political partisanship and indicate their level of interest in the 1992 presidential campaign. Of the 226 respondents, 35 percent (N=79) identified themselves as Democrats, while 21.2 percent (N=48) identified themselves as Republicans. Ninety-nine respondents (44%) classified themselves as independent. Nearly two-thirds of the sample (64%) reported being "very much" interested in the 1992 presidential campaign, while slightly less than one-third (N=71) indicated that they were "somewhat" interested in the campaign. Only 11 respondents (5%) stated that they had "not much" interest in the election.

Over half (58%) of the respondents (N=131) reported watching or listening to three or all four of the presidential debates, while more than one-fourth (27%) reported seeing or listening to two debates. The remaining 15 percent reported seeing only one or no presidential debates. The reported time frame for making the candidate choice for president appeared to be unusually late according to traditional voting literature. However, 1992 was a most unconventional campaign with the third major candidate, Ross Perot, providing an on-again, off-again candidacy. Nearly one-third of the respondents (N=70 or 32%) indicated that they did not make their voting decision until the week before the election; 23 percent (N=49) indicated that their voting decision was made earlier in the fall campaign. Approximately 28 percent (N=60) of the respondents reported that they had made their voting decision during the summer while the remaining 17 percent (N=37) of respondents reported that their decision was made prior to the summer.

When respondents were asked if they had seriously considered voting for Ross Perot (N=183), 42 percent (N=77) stated "yes," while over half (N=106 or 58%) indicated "no." When reporting their actual voting behavior in the 1992 presidential election, 35 percent (N=74) reported voting for George Bush, 48 percent (N=102) for Bill Clinton, and 16 percent (N=34) for Ross Perot. Two respondents reported casting votes for other than the major candidates, and 13 respondents either refused or gave no response to the question.

Influential Commercial Recall

Respondents were asked, "Which television ad most influenced your thinking about the campaign?" Of the 224 valid coded responses, the results of the open-ended question fell into two broad categories (see table 8.1). First, there were responses on advertising influence that contained specific candidate and commercial information. The responses were candidate specific and traceable to a specific/group of advertisement(s) as the source of the information. Forty-six percent of the total unaided response (N=104) were categorized as *specific candidate, traceable commercial*. The responses in the second category (N=107 or 48%), while candidate specific, only recalled influential advertisements in general terms. A few unaided responses of advertising influence did not fall into the first two broad categories. The third category contained only thirteen responses (6%). These comments were responses about the campaign in general or campaign issues in general.

Table 8.1. *Advertising Influence by Typology of Recall*
"Which ad most influenced your thinking about the campaign?"

SPECIFIC CANDIDATE, TRACEABLE COMMERCIAL		(N=104)
Clinton Positive Ad	16.4%	(N=17)
Clinton Negative Ad	11.5%	(N=12)
Bush Positive Ad	11.5%	(N=12)
Bush Negative Ad	36.6%	(N=38)
Perot Positive Ad*	24.0%	(N=25)
	100%	
SPECIFIC CANDIDATE, UNTRACEABLE COMMERCIAL		(N=107)
Clinton Positive Ad	10.3%	(N=11)
Clinton Negative Ad	1.0%	(N=1)
Clinton Neutral Ad	24.3%	(N=26)
Bush Positive Ad	1.9%	(N=2)
Bush Negative Ad	19.6%	(N=21)
Bush Neutral Ad	9.3%	(N=10)
Perot Positive Ad	11.2%	(N=12)
Perot Neutral Ad*	22.4%	(N=24)
	100%	
NONCANDIDATE SPECIFIC, UNTRACEABLE COMMERCIAL		(N=13)
General Comments on Negative Ads	46.2%	(N=6)
General Issue Comments	53.8%	(N=7)
	100%	

*No respondent recalled Perot's advertising in negative terms.

Of the 104 responses in the *specific candidate, traceable commercial* category, the results were further broken down by candidate and by whether the respondents' recollection of the ad was stated in positive, negative, or neutral terms. In this category, 16 percent of the responses regarding campaign advertising that influenced thinking about the campaign were about Clinton's positive advertisements. Clinton's negative commercials were recalled (12%) as influential in thinking about the campaign by 12 respondents. Bush specific positive advertising was recalled as influential by 12 percent, while 36 percent (*N*=38) reported that Bush's negative commercials influenced their thinking about the campaign. Twenty-four percent stated that Perot's positive advertisements influenced their thinking about the campaign.

Of the 107 responses in the *specific candidate, untraceable commercial* category, Clinton's positive ads were mentioned by 10 percent as influencing campaign thinking, but only one respondent reported that a Clinton negative ad was influential. Twenty-four percent claimed that Clinton's ads, stated in neutral terms, influenced their thinking about the campaign. Only two respondents mentioned that Bush's positive ads influenced their thinking, whereas 20 percent indicated that Bush's negative ads influenced their thinking. Bush's ads stated in neutral terms were mentioned by 9 percent as influential. Perot's positive ads were reported as influential by 11 percent, while Perot's ads recalled in neutral terms were mentioned by 22 percent.

The smallest category of responses is termed as *noncandidate specific, untraceable commercials*. Only 13 responses comprised this category. These comments fell into two areas: general comments about negative commercials (*N*=6) and general issue comments (*N*=7).

Examples of Respondents' Comments

Actual examples of the open-ended responses that were coded in the *candidate specific, traceable commercial* category were:

- "Bush's variety of citizens talking about how you couldn't trust Clinton."
- "[the] *Time* magazine one that Bush did about Clinton."
- "Bush in the Oval Office, 'when the next term comes up, who [do you] want to see sitting in this chair?'"
- "Clinton ad—where it was a music video, showed images of working people, bus tour."
- "Perot's letter from a veteran ad."
- "Clinton—Read my lips."
- "Guy sent Perot a Purple Heart, and he told him to keep on in spite of insurmountable odds."

- "One effective Clinton commercial in which Bush was denying there was an economy problem."
- "Bush's ad where the grandchildren were walking through the woods."
- "Bush ad with nuclear winter in Arkansas after Clinton's election."
- "Bush ad with the buzzard over Arkansas."
- "Bush ad on Arkansas with the vulture in tree."

These responses about political advertising's influence on thinking about the 1992 presidential campaign can not only be traced to a specific ad sponsor, but to a particular commercial or specific group of thematic commercials. The specificity of the responses often made it possible to precisely pinpoint the framing within the commercial. For example, in the Bush negative commercials recalled, the terms "nuclear winter," "a buzzard over Arkansas," "on Arkansas with the vulture in tree" all refer to the same commercial in vivid and accurate terms. As one examines the comments, many of the commercials recalled as influential have vivid visual imagery cues such as "Perot's letter from a veteran," "grandchildren walking through the woods," and "the *Time* magazine one."

Examples of the second category of responses, *candidate specific, untraceable commercials*, included:

- "Bush's, none specifically, no specific one, just that Bush's were all negative."
- "Perot's, being outspoken particularly on the issue of paying off the national debt."
- "Perot's ads were really robust and grabbed my attention."
- "Clinton's commercials in general" [note from interviewer—no specific could be given—except she was drawn to the patriotism expressed in each of them]
- "The ads that Clinton ran."

These responses appear to suggest that in the unaided recall situation some respondents are only able to associate a specific candidate with a general direction of emotionality or a broad piece of campaign information. The comments in this typology have far less specificity than the previous examples in the first category.

When asked, "Which television ad most influenced your thinking about the campaign?" examples of the third and smallest category of responses, referred to as *noncandidate specific, untraceable commercials*, included the following:

- "I tried to ignore them [the ads] because I hate them. If it [political advertising] had any effect it would be negative."
- "None. Considered most of them [ads] hype."

- "All [ads] started getting ridiculous."
- "I'm turned off by all negative ads."
- "The one [ad] about abortion."
- "Ads for taxes and lowering them."

This small category appears to contain the two most emotionally charged words in the total group of responses, "hate" and "ridiculous." A few responses in this category are about a specific issue.

Advertising and Its Direction of Influence

After the question on which ad influenced respondents' thinking about the campaign, the next two questions concerned the direction of the ad's influence. Respondents were asked, "Did the ad make you feel more favorable toward Bush, Clinton, Perot, or none of the candidates?" Then a second question asked, "Did the ad make you feel less favorable toward Bush, Clinton, Perot, or none of the candidates?"

Of the 63 respondents who recalled Clinton's advertising as influencing their thinking about the campaign, 67 percent felt more favorable toward Clinton, 24 percent reported no influence from the ad, 5 percent more favorable toward Bush, and 5 percent felt more favorable toward Perot (see table 8.2). Of the respondents who reported Clinton ads as influencing their thinking about the campaign, 44 percent recalled positive Clinton ads, 37 percent recalled the ads in neutral terms, and 19 percent recalled negative ads as influential. However, of those who reported that Clinton's negative ads (which were anti-Bush) influenced their thinking about the campaign, the ads rarely appear to have created a backlash against the sponsor. In other words, the negative Clinton ads made viewers feel more positive toward Clinton (50%), had no influence (42%), or made viewers feel more positive toward Perot (8%). Only three respondents (17%) of those who recalled a negative Clinton ad as influential also reported that the ad made them feel less favorable toward Clinton. Fifty-eight percent said that the ad made them feel less favorable toward Bush and 25 percent expressed no influence.

Of the 79 respondents who recalled Bush advertising as influencing their thinking about the campaign, 43 percent felt more favorable toward Bush as a result, 34 percent expressed no influence, 19 percent said the ad made them feel more favorable toward Clinton, and 4 percent felt more favorable toward Perot. But Bush's negative ads, unlike Clinton's negative ads, sometimes backlashed against him. Respondents stated that Bush's negative ads influenced their thinking about the campaign much more (70%) than did the positive (18%) or neutral (13%) ads. Of those who reported influence of Bush's negative ads, more than one-third (36%) felt more favorable toward Bush or at

Table 8.2. *Recall of Candidates' Ad Influence by Direction of Favorability*
"Did the ad make you feel more favorable toward
Bush, Clinton, Perot, or none of the candidates?"

OF THOSE WHO RECALLED A CLINTON AD AS INFLUENTIAL		(N=63)
More favorable toward Clinton	67%	(N=42)
More favorable toward Bush	5%	(N=3)
More favorable toward Perot	5%	(N=3)
No influence on any candidate	24%	(N=15)
	100%	
OF THOSE WHO RECALLED A BUSH AD AS INFLUENTIAL		(N=79)
More favorable toward Bush	43%	(N=34)
More favorable toward Clinton	19%	(N=15)
More favorable toward Perot	4%	(N=3)
No influence on any candidate	34%	(N=27)
	100%	
OF THOSE WHO RECALLED A PEROT AD AS INFLUENTIAL		(N=59)
More favorable toward Perot	71%	(N=42)
More favorable toward Bush	5%	(N=3)
More favorable toward Clinton	3%	(N=2)
No influence on any candidate	21%	(N=12)
	100%	

least reported no influence (38%). But of those who indicated Bush negative ads as influential, 22 percent actually reported feeling more positive toward Clinton. Moreover, of those who recalled the Bush negative ads, 54 percent said that the ad made them feel less favorable toward Bush, while only 35 percent reported that the Bush negative ad made them feel less favorable toward Clinton.

Of the 59 respondents who recalled Perot ads as influencing their thinking about the campaign, 71 percent felt more favorable toward Perot as a result, 20 percent indicated no influence, 5 percent felt more favorable toward Bush, and 3 percent felt more favorable toward Clinton. Perot aired ads that could be considered negative, but none of the respondents' open-ended responses indicated that Perot's ads were negative. Due to the limitations of the sample size, further sophisticated analysis controlling for the influence of partisanship was not possible.

CONCLUSIONS

The results of this study suggest that respondents report political advertising's influence in candidate specific terms. Nearly 90 percent of the responses to an open-ended question were candidate specific. When asked, "Which ad most influenced your thinking about the campaign?" the study suggests that respondents recall influential ads in two distinct ways: either as a gestalt of general impressions or in visually vivid detail. The findings from the *specific candidate, untraceable commercial* group of responses support the arguments of Graber (1972) and Jamieson (1992) that bits and pieces of information are woven together over the course of a campaign to form the candidates' images. Conversely, the *specific candidate, traceable commercial* group of responses support Burns, Biswas, and Babin's (1993) notion that visual imagery shapes impressions. The researchers concluded that visual imagery vividness has the potential to help explain mental reactions to certain advertising strategies, including attitudinal and intentional consequences. Graber and Jamieson argue that candidates' impressions are formed in macroterms, while Burns et al. suggest a microlevel impression formation. Although the studies appear contradictory the results of both are supported in this study.

The intended effect of Bush commercials more often resulted in unintended consequences. Bush's negative commercials frequently impacted more negatively on Bush (the sponsor) than on the target(s) (Clinton and Perot). Of those who recalled a Bush ad as influential in thinking about the campaign, less than half (43%) reported that the ad made them feel more favorable toward Bush. This contrasts sharply with those who recalled a Clinton ad as influential and felt more favorable (67%) toward Clinton, or those who reported a Perot ad as influential, with 71 percent reporting more favorability toward Perot.

Popkin (1994) sheds additional insight to the question of why the Bush backlash occurred, writing that "given the difficulty of raising his own [Bush] ratings [approval], a good part of his campaign was devoted to lowering the ratings of Clinton and the Democratic party" (p. 257). In choosing this strategy, the Bush campaign purposefully executed a strategy that had a high potential for backlash. The results of this study illuminate voters' reactions to the Bush campaign's strategic approach. The results support the research findings of Johnson-Cartee and Copeland (1991) that direct attack ads have the greatest potential backlash effect. While voters may have viewed Clinton's character as an important campaign issue, the results of this study support Johnson-Cartee and Copeland's findings that voters are less tolerant of vicious personal attacks on the opponent. While Clinton's negative ads directed at Bush were hard-hitting (i.e., "Read My Lips"), they were anchored to the issues of taxes and the economy. Similarly, the study supports Roddy and Garramone's (1988) research that negative advertising based on issues will evoke more positive evaluations of the ad's sponsor. Clinton's issue-based negative ads rarely backlashed against him. Noteworthy is Perot's use of the implied comparison advertising strategy. Johnson-Cartee and Copeland argue that the implied comparison is the least likely format to produce backlash effects due to the opportunity for viewers to generate their own counter-arguments. The respondents who recalled Perot ads as influential did not perceive them as negative. The Perot thirty- and sixty-second commercials often used a single vivid visual (children's faces, a clock face, a Purple Heart) covered by a scrolling script of the announcer's narrative. The results of this study suggest that Perot successfully launched implied comparisons without creating a negative backlash, and important message points were seen as well as heard for greater memorability (Lang and Lanfear, 1990).

Lang and Lanfear (1990) suggest that negative ads are better recalled than positive ads. While this finding is well supported in political advertising research, this chapter has sought to examine a political advertisement's influence when thinking about the campaign, not just ad recall. Thus, the overall results of this study of postelection respondents' (N=224) recollection of an influential political advertisement appear to be more balanced among negative (35%), positive (35%), and neutral (30%) contexts. Future research should examine the differences in candidate favorability between ad recall and ad influence. Furthermore, this chapter suggests that vivid visual imagery when placed in a negative personal attack appeal may increase both an advertisement's memorability and the potential for sponsor backlash effects.

The use of the exploratory question, "Which ad most influenced your thinking about the campaign?" has produced, at least in this study, responses from voters as to the importance of a particular ad or group of ads on voters' thinking about the campaign. How one recalls an ad's influence—whether in terms of a gestalt (Graber, 1972; Jamieson, 1992) or as words or vivid images of specific ads (Burns, Biswas, and Babin, 1993)—leave rich research questions yet to be examined. The study suggests that there are two ways that people think about political advertising as influential. Why does one voter recall a political advertisement's influence in broad macroterms compared to one who recalls a micro visual detail as influential?

It is noteworthy that in a postelection survey, at least one-fourth (N=224) of the larger study's respondents (N=931) were able to retrieve, without any prompting whatsoever, information about the campaign's ads. While this chapter does not attempt to schematically map voter responses of advertising influence and its direction of favorability, the descriptive findings alone appear to suggest that this is a promising direction to pursue. The study also implies that political advertising, although sometimes memorable, may not have the intended effect. Little research exists on the impact of repeated exposure on candidate favorability. Much of the current body of research on political advertising's backlash effects has been conducted in experimental laboratory settings. These findings suggest that more sophisticated research techniques must be developed in order to incorporate the real intermedia and integrated dynamics that shape voters' impressions of candidates during the various phases of a campaign. In this chapter, a typology of citizens' responses to the open-ended question about political advertising and its influence suggests interesting research opportunities in schematic processing.

NOTE

This study was a portion of the Cross-National Election Study Project (CNEP). Principal investigators were Paul Allen Beck of The Ohio State University, Russell J. Dalton of the University of California at Irvine, and Robert Huckfeldt of the State University of New York, Stony Brook. The local study in Franklin County, Ohio, was funded by National Science Foundation Grant SES-9123578.

REFERENCES

Biocca, Frank (1991a). Some limitations of earlier "symbolic" approaches to political communication. In Frank Biocca, ed., *Television and political advertising, Volume 2: Signs, codes, and images.* Hillsdale, N.J.: Erlbaum, pp. 11–16.

Biocca, Frank (1991b). Viewers' mental models of political messages: Toward a theory of the semantic processing of television. In Frank Biocca, ed., *Television and political advertising, Volume 1: Psychological processes.* Hillsdale, N.J.: Erlbaum, pp. 27–89.

Biocca, Frank (1991). Looking for units of meaning in political ads. In Frank Biocca, ed., *Television and political advertising, Volume 2: Signs, codes, and images.* Hillsdale, N.J.: Erlbaum, pp. 17–25.

Bowes, John E., and Herbert Strentz (1978). Candidate images: Stereotyping and the 1976 debates. In Brent Ruben, ed., *Communication yearbook 2.* New Brunswick, N.J.: Transaction.

Boydston, John, and Lynda Lee Kaid (1983). An experimental study of the effectiveness of NCPAC political advertisements. Paper presented to the Political Communication Division of the International Communication Association convention, Dallas, Tex.

Burns, Alvin C., Abhijit Biswas, and Laurie A. Babin (1993). The operation of visual imagery as a mediator of advertising effects. *Journal of Advertising, 22*(2), 72–85.

Devlin, L. Patrick (1993). Contrasts in presidential campaign commercials of 1992. *American Behavioral Scientist, 37*(2), 279–90.

Faber, Ronald J., Albert R. Tims, and Kay Schmitt (1993). Negative political advertising and voting intent: The role of involvement and alternative information sources. *Journal of Advertising, 22*(4), 67–76.

Garramone, Gina M. (1986). Candidate image formation: The role of information processing. In Lynda Lee Kaid, Dan Nimmo, and Keith Sanders, eds., *New Perspectives on political advertising.* Carbondale, Ill.: Southern Illinois University Press, pp. 235–47.

Goffman, Erving (1974). *Frame analysis.* New York: Harper and Row.

Graber, Doris (1988). *Processing the news: How people tame the information tide.* 2nd. ed. New York: Longman.

Graber, Doris A. (1972). Personal qualities in presidential images: The contribution of the press. *Midwest Journal of Political Science, 16,* 46–76.

Hahn, Dan F., and Ruth M. Gonchar (1972). Political myth: The image and the issue. *Today's Speech, 20,* 57–65.

Hill, Ronald Paul (1989). An exploration of voter responses to political advertising. *Journal of Advertising, 18*(4), 14–22.

Iyengar, Shanto (1991). *Is anyone responsible? How television frames political issues.* Chicago: University of Chicago Press.

Jamieson, Kathleen Hall (1992). *Dirty politics: Deception, distraction, and democracy.* New York: Oxford University Press.

Johnson-Cartee, Karen, and Gary A. Copeland (1991). *Negative political advertising: Coming of age.* Hillsdale, N.J.: Erlbaum.

Kaid, Lynda Lee, and John Boydston (1987). An experimental study of the effectiveness of negative political advertisements. *Communication Quarterly, 35,* 193–201.

Kaid, Lynda Lee, and Dorothy K. Davidson (1986). Elements of videostyle: Candidate presentation through television advertising. In Lynda Lee Kaid, Dan Nimmo, and Keith R. Sanders, eds., *New perspectives in political advertising.* Carbondale, Ill.: Southern Illinois University Press, pp. 184–209.

Kern, Montague (1989). *30-second politics: Political advertising in the eighties.* New York: Praeger.

Krock, Arthur (1960, Oct. 16). The man who—not the issue which. *New York Times,* 19.

Lang, Annie (1991). Emotion, formal features, and memory for televised political advertisements. In Frank Biocca, ed., *Television and political advertising, Volume 1: Psychological processes.* Hillsdale, N.J.: Erlbaum, pp. 221–43.

Lang, Annie, and Patrick Lanfear (1990). The information processing of televised political advertising: Using theory to maximize recall. *Advances in Consumer Research, 17,* 149–58.

Lau, Richard R., and David O. Sears (1986). Social cognition and political cognition: The past, the present and the future. In Richard Lau and David Sears, eds., *Political cognition.* Hillsdale, N.J.: Erlbaum, pp. 347–66.

Lippmann, Walter (1922). *Public opinion.* New York: Macmillan.

McLeod, Jack M., and Lee B. Becker (1981). The uses and gratifications approach. In Dan Nimmo and Keith R. Sanders, eds., *Handbook of political communication.* Beverly Hills, Calif.: Sage, pp. 67–99.

Merritt, Sharyne (1984). Negative political advertising: Some empirical findings. *Journal of Advertising, 13*(3), 27–38.

Neuman, Russell W., Marion R. Just, and Ann C. Crigler (1992). *Common knowledge: News and the construction of political meaning.* Chicago: University of Chicago Press.

Newman, Bruce I. (1994). *The marketing of the president: Political marketing as campaign strategy.* Thousand Oaks, Calif.: Sage.

Nimmo, Dan, and Robert L. Savage (1976). *Candidates and their images.* Pacific Palisades: Goodyear.

Pan, Zhongdang, and Gerald M. Kosicki (1993). Framing analysis: An approach to news discourse. *Political Communication, 10,* 55–75.

Patterson, Thomas E., and Robert D. McClure (1976). *The unseeing eye: Myth of television power in politics.* New York: Putnam.

Popkin, Samuel L. (1994). *The reasoning voter: Communication and persuasion in presidential campaigns.* Chicago: University of Chicago Press.

Roberts, Marilyn (1991). Political advertising: Applications for political symbolism. In Rebecca Holman, ed., *The proceedings of the 1991 American Academy of Advertising Conference,* Orlando, pp. 122–28.

Roberts, Marilyn, Ronald Anderson and Maxwell McCombs (1994). 1990 Texas gubernatorial campaign: Influence of issues and images. *Mass Comm Review,* 21 (1 and 2), 4–19.

Roddy, Brian and Gina Garramone (1988). Appeals and strategies of negative political advertising. *Journal of Broadcasting and Electronic Media, 32*(4), 415–27.

Rumelhart, David E. (1980). Schemata: The building blocks of cognition. In Rand J. Spiro, Bertran C. Bruce, and William F. Brewer, eds., *Theoretical issues in reading comprehension: Perspectives from cognitive psychology, linguistics, artificial intelligence and education.* Hillsdale, N.J.: Erlbaum, pp. 33–58.

Rumelhart, David E. (1983). Schemata and the cognitive system. In Robert S. Wyer Jr. and Thomas K. Srull, eds., *Handbook of social cognition.* Hillsdale, N.J.: Erlbaum, pp. 161–88.

Rumelhart, David E., and Andrew Ortony (1977). The representation of knowledge in memory. In Richard C. Anderson, Rand J. Spiro, and William E. Montague, eds., *Schooling and the acquisition of knowledge.* Hillsdale, N.J.: Erlbaum, pp. 99–135.

Shapiro, Michael, and Robert Rieger (1989, May). Comparing positive and negative political advertising. Paper presented to the Political Communication Division of the International Communication Association, San Francisco.

Tuchman, Gaye (1978). *Making news.* New York: Free Press.

Weaver, David, Doris Graber, Maxwell McCombs, and Chaim Eyal (1981). *Media agenda-setting in a presidential election.* New York: Praeger.

Weigold, Michael F., and Vivian Sheer (1993). Negative political advertising: Effects of target response and party-based expectancies on candidate evaluations. Paper presented at the 1993 annual conference of the American Advertising Academy, Montreal.

NINE

Rhetorical Strategies for a Culture War

Abortion in the 1992 Campaign

RICHARD B. GREGG

The presidential election of 1800, like the election of 1992, turned on important domestic issues. Following the custom of the day, Jefferson and Adams did not actively campaign but "stood" for office in line with the desires of the founding fathers that elections not be decided by entreaties or promises but by character traits of "virtue" demonstrated publicly by the candidates over the course of their lives. While Adams and Jefferson obeyed the wishes of the founders, the fray of the campaign swirled around them as their supporters engaged in the politics of attack and defense and dispensed liquor on behalf of votes, a practice referred to as "swilling the planters with bumbo" (Troy, 1991, p. 9).

In 1800, as now, negative attacks on positions often blurred into personal attacks. Jefferson looked like the certain winner the voting would prove him to be, so desperate Adams supporters unleashed charges that make a good many contemporary attacks pale in comparison. Falling in league with forces of the Religious Right that had been busily spinning rumors of a worldwide conspiracy against Christianity initiated by the Illuminati in Europe, they smeared Jefferson by labeling him a coward, an adulterer, and an atheist. Timothy Dwight, president of Yale University, declared that if Jefferson won, "We may see the Bible cast into a bonfire, the vessels of the sacramental supper borne by an ass in public procession, and our children, either wheedled or terrified, uniting in chanting mockeries against God." Reverend William Linn of New York proclaimed that "the election of any man avowing the principles of Mr. Jefferson would . . . destroy religion, introduce immorality and loosen all the bonds of society." The *Connecticut Courant* joined the chorus by predicting that a Jefferson election would mean that "Murder, robbery, rape, adultery, and incest will be openly taught and practiced" (Hackler, 1993, p. C-3).

The attacks upon Jefferson in the campaign of 1800 display personal characteristics in a way that often occurs in negative campaigning. They expand the dimensions of persona beyond the individual person. They refer to values that have an impact on whole communities, translate impugned individual preferences into holistic philosophical perspectives, and imbue concrete symbols with emotional valences that are inclusive rather than exclusive. Their sweep transcends both person and moment. In our day, we might refer to such attacks as being symptomatic of a "culture war."

The presidential campaign of 1992 bears certain similarities to that of 1800. In 1992 domestic economic issues occupied center stage. Negative attacks were made of course; negativity is always present in political affairs as in all meaning whatsoever, for as Kenneth Burke (1966) has so ably argued, there can be no meaning without it. To borrow an example from him, we must realize that one of the most hallowed positive terms of American political life, "freedom," can only be understood in its fullest power when one asks the accompanying question, "Freedom from what?"

In 1992 the typical American voter perceived the issues of the day to congeal around economic problems. Unemployment, budgetary imbalances, deficit reduction, and the soaring costs of health care became dominant issues for discussion. The sign that hung in James Carville's campaign office had it right: "The economy stupid." As *USA Today*'s Bob Minzesheimer said, "Most voters believed that Bill Clinton dodged the draft and lied about Gennifer Flowers. They also believed that George Bush has lied about Iran-Contra. And the response was: 'So what? What are you going to do about the economy?'" (Freedom Forum Media Studies Center, 1993, p. 119). It is not surprising, then, that during the campaign negative attacks were launched within the context of economics. The honesty and trustworthiness of opposing candidates were questioned and doubts and fears were raised about the consequences of their proposed economic policies. Such efforts reached their highest intensity in the weeks immediately prior to Election Day when a Clinton ad, produced for television by the Clinton–Gore creative team, featured Bush repeatedly admonishing each of us to read his lips, with each iteration followed by an instance of his raising taxes on the middle class, and a Bush ad, produced by the November Group, voicing an enumeration of economic woes suffered by citizens of Arkansas under Governor Clinton while picturing a bleak, gray, windblown landscape presided over by a lone buzzard. The outcome of the election was largely determined by the economy. One remembers an observation of an earlier time that public opinion began to turn against the Vietnam War when enough body bags had come home to register in the personal experience of a critical mass of citizens. In 1992 the dislocations and disorders of a weak economy were profuse enough to give a significant edge to Clinton's call for change.

While the economy appeared most important to the majority of voters, there was another noticeable pattern interwoven in the fabric of campaign rhetoric. One can find it manifested at the level of personal character attack, and the more fundamental level of individual being and selfhood. One sees it focused on the singular attitudes and values of a particular candidate, and on the existential patterns and lifestyles of larger societal groups. It is a pattern comprised of rhetorical symbols that operate synechdochally to evoke and induce holistic perspectives on "reality." The phrase "family values" was the covering term for "hot button" issues in the culture war; the issue of abortion was the ugliest button pushed by true believers on the Radical Right.

A culture war, as James Davison Hunter (1990) points out, is about matters that are perceived to be of fundamental importance and about issues that need to be addressed in ultimate terms. Therefore, partisans in a culture war launch diatribe, ridicule, and invective in terms of high passion. "The end to which these hostilities tend," says Hunter, "is the domination of one culture and moral ethos over all others" (p. 42).

Major issues of the culture war had emerged in the years prior to the 1992 presidential campaign. They shaped concerns over gay rights, flag burning and other desecratory acts, sexual harassment, AIDS, euthanasia, and political correctness. Shortly before the 1992 campaign got underway, a cultural hot war erupted over the National Endowment of the Arts funding of what was called "pornographic art," and specifically photographs of Andres Serrano and Robert Maplethorpe. Foremost among those attacking the NEA was Senator Jesse Helms, who charged that the endowment had become "captive to a morally decadent minority which delights in ridiculing the values and beliefs of decent, moral taxpayers" (1990, p. 322). As chair of the National Endowment of the Arts, John Frohnmayer came to personify evil in the eyes of right-wing cultural conservatives. Frohnmayer was finally dumped by President George Bush, who, looking ahead to the coming election campaign, believed that he dare not alienate the Radical Right. It had become clear that ultraconservative political commentator Patrick Buchanan would challenge Bush for the presidential nomination, and Buchanan made clear that NEA funding of "filthy art" would be part of his attack on Bush in the Georgia primary. Georgia was a good target for Buchanan. Hard-core Republicans there were conservative. Furthermore, Georgia allowed crossover voting, presenting the possibility of a heavy turnout of evangelical Christians who, according to polling data, comprised some 60 percent of the vote in the

Republican primary in 1988. But Bush and his campaign captain's worries extended beyond Georgia. Jim Lake, Bush's campaign communications director, said, "There was a real concern about the right, not just in Georgia—[The firing of] Frohnmayer was a symbolic gesture to the right that needed to be done" (Germond and Witcover, 1993, p. 232). The strategy did not deter Buchanan, who unleashed an ugly thirty-second spot showing black men dancing in chairs and leather harnesses as a voiceover said: "In the last three years, the Bush administration has wasted our tax dollars on pornographic and blasphemous art too shocking to show. This so-called art has glorified homosexuality, exploited children and perverted the image of Jesus Christ" (Germond and Witcover, 1993, p. 233). The culture war was off to a virulent start in the 1992 campaign.

During the campaign, the negative rhetorical symbols of the culture war ran the gamut from the level of humor to the level of horror. On the humorous level, Vice President Dan Quayle in serious tone asserted that Hollywood was out of step with traditional family values and exemplified by referring to a fictional single parent, Murphy Brown. Quayle's comments resonated nationally and guaranteed a full audience in the fall when "Murphy Brown" premiered for the new season. The hour-long special ended by recalling a Quayle spelling gaffe when it showed a dump truck unloading a full complement of potatoes at the front gate of the vice presidential residence. The level of horror was experienced in a hotel lobby during the Democratic national convention when a pro-life advocate thrust a dead fetus at Bill Clinton.

This chapter focuses on the issue of abortion because it evoked intense emotions at the center of the family values dispute. The family values complex of issues involves policy decisions as well as lifestyle perspectives, and as Alan Abramowitz points out, "no issue in recent years has had a greater potential to produce policy-based voting than abortion" (1993, p. 2). He suggests three reasons for giving attention to the abortion issue. First, since 1980 both major political parties and their presidential candidates have adopted fundamentally different positions on abortion policy. Republican Party platforms, influenced by Christian evangelicals and "right-to-life" activists, have advocated a ban on abortion, while Democratic platforms, in response to the influence of "pro-choice" and feminist activists, have endorsed the 1973 Supreme Court decision legalizing abortion. Second, abortion is a highly symbolic and emotional issue easily understood by voters. Third, research on voting behavior uncovers evidence of the impact of the abortion issue on a number of recent gubernatorial and senatorial campaigns, providing strong reason to believe attitudes toward abortion have influenced voter decisions in recent presidential elections (p. 2).

A fourth reason must be acknowledged. In their newly published study on women in politics, Witt, Paget, and Matthews (1994, p. 16) point out that whereas abortion was an issue to be finessed or ignored in the 1970s, by the end of the 1980s it came to the fore in campaigning, and candidates at all levels were forced to announce their positions on the issue. The resulting controversy over abortion "has also meant that gender based issues have been front and center in American public life in the recent past—as opposed to their previous invisibility or marginalization" (p. 47). Abortion is clearly an issue with national impact, radiating emotional pressures and valences back and forth between local and presidential levels of campaigning. It was particularly important in the 1992 context of Republican Party politics, serving as a measure of the strength of moderates versus hard-line social conservatives. Germond and Witcover (1993) state that "If there was one issue likely to define their concept of 'family values,' it was abortion." In addition, "the issue was intriguing because it was one on which George Bush had pushed himself into an extremist corner with a position potentially damaging in a close election" (p. 404).

The problem of abortion played out on the level of presidential campaigning in 1992 by influencing the larger rhetorical strategies of both Clinton and Bush regarding the complex of family values issues. I shall begin with an overview of those strategies, narrowing the focus to the specific issue of abortion. I shall then pause to undertake a more in-depth analysis of the rhetorical power of the "dead fetus" image that surfaced in the 1992 campaign. As noted above, the fetus thrust at Clinton in the convention hotel lobby was real. The fetus image was more prevalent in video political advertising shown in various regions of the nation. If the abortion issue was the synechdochic representative of "family values" perspectives for many voters, I suggest that the "dead fetus" image was the concrete synechdochic representative of intense emotions evoked in the abortion issue. Understanding the rhetorical power of the fetus image can provide insight into the mind-set of "true believers." Finally, I shall widen my perspective to discuss the impact of the abortion issue on the 1992 presidential campaign, and the potential impact of political forces favoring the denial of abortion rights and pro-choice values in the immediate future.

THE ABORTION ISSUE IN THE CULTURE WAR

From the beginning of the campaign, Bill Clinton's position on abortion was clear. His stated view was that he regretted that abortion was used so often and would work to implement strategies leading to decreased reliance on abortion. But he was firmly committed to the legality of abortion under certain conditions and to the right of a woman's choice. The Clinton campaign's position paper (Clinton–Gore Campaign, White House Campaign File, Internet) underlines the significance of the issue: "May be the decisive issue of the campaign (predictably so for a number of Congressional races, second perhaps only to the economy in the Presidential race), certainly central factor in intensification of identifiable 'gender gap' in recent and projected electoral behavior." Further, "The role of the President in appointing Justices to the Supreme Court, and the present slim margin of opinion of the Court on the Constitutionality of statutory prohibition of abortion, makes the current campaign a critical one for both sides of this controversy." In a campaign video widely distributed by Clinton campaign workers in New Hampshire prior to that state's primary vote, one of the montage segments showed Clinton speaking on matters of choice, declaring that the Republicans had talked for twelve years in favor of choice without really believing in it. Republicans, he said, were willing to support school choice, even if it meant bankrupting the public schools, but "they were more than willing to make it a crime for a woman to exercise her right to choose ("The New Covenant,: 1992). The Democrats' convention was consistent with Clinton's brief video statement:

> *Choice.* Democrats stand behind the right of every woman to choose, consistent with Roe v. Wade, regardless of ability to pay, and support a national law to protect that right. It is a fundamental constitutional liberty that individual Americans—not government—can best take responsibility for making the most difficult and intensely personal decisions regarding reproduction. The goal of our nation must be to make abortion less necessary, not more difficult or more dangerous. We pledge to support contraceptive research, family planning, comprehensive family education, and policies that support healthy child life education, and policies that support healthy childbearing and enable parents to care most effectively for their children. (p. 10)

Two happenings at the Democratic convention gave further evidence of Clinton's pro-choice stance. Pennsylvania Governor Robert Casey, a staunch anti-abortionist, was denied an opportunity to address the convention. And on the day the Democratic platform was passed by the delegates, Clinton reaffirmed his pro-choice position in a public appearance before the National Women's Political Caucus. That night, six Republican women who supported abortion choice were featured at the podium.

While emphasizing issues regarding the economy throughout the campaign, the Clinton forces affirmed the broader complex of family values issues directly and indirectly. At the convention a filmed campaign biography featured Clinton family members who narrated the story and described the character of the man born in Hope, Arkansas. Throughout the campaign, handlers arranged and rearranged Hillary Clinton's hair to help her project the image of a young, intelligent woman who had time to handle a profession, work with a husband to achieve a stable marriage, and manage an environment in which her daughter could have a natural childhood. By word and visual deed, Bill Clinton stood foresquare in favor of family values. Evidence that he would continue to be harassed on such matters turned up in the form of a sign found on the floor of the Republican convention that read, "Woody Allen, Clinton Family Adviser." It is important to note that Clinton's stated view that he regretted the frequent use of abortion and would work to implement programs leading to decreased reliance on abortion, but remained committed to the legality of abortion, matched the views of his most important audiences.

Bush had a more difficult problem. A Bush–Quayle campaign press release of September 10, 1992 (Bush–Quayle, "President Bush on the Right to Life," Internet) began with a Bush quote: "Faith, family—these are the values that sustain the greatest nation on Earth. And to these values we must add the infinitely precious value of life itself. Let me be clear: I support the right to life." Many conservatives distrusted him on the abortion issue, finding him hypocritical because he had reversed his earlier pro-choice position as a condition for being nominated vice president on the ticket with Ronald Reagan in 1980. There was an irony to the Bush "conversion." His mother was a founder of the Planned Parenthood League in Connecticut. In addition, Bush's first speech in Congress was a statement of support for family planning. Furthermore, during the 1992 campaign, both Bush and Vice President Quayle wobbled in their unqualified condemnation of abortion when, in responding to interview questions on the matter, they said they would support their daughters if they chose to abort. Additionally, Mrs. Bush, the more publicly beloved of the pair, was suspected of being pro-choice, a suspicion she did not deny. The Bush campaign ducked a direct discussion of the abortion issue whenever possible, choosing instead to attack Clinton on other matters of family values, alluding to sexual infidelity, charging that Hillary Clinton had written in favor of allowing children to divorce their parents, and alleging that Clinton's policies would destroy traditional families and any proper sense of social responsibility. The best hope of the Bush campaign was to attack Clinton in ways that would negatively define him within the general framework of family values because Bush was in no position to hold himself up as pure on the anti-abortion stance. Even if he could, by doing so he would alienate swing voters tired of movement conservatives who placed social issues ahead of economic concerns.

At the Republican National Convention in Houston, more controversy was stirred up by abortion rights than any other single issue. During his two terms in the White House, Ronald Reagan had embraced the support of such rightist movements as Jerry Falwell's Moral Majority and Pat Robertson's

Christian Coalition. The Republican Party platforms of 1984 and 1988 explicitly rejected the legalization of abortion for *any* reason. As vice president, George Bush fell in loyally behind his president. Despite evidence that moderate Republicans favored some loosening of attitudes toward and restrictions on abortion, the so-called Christian Right firmly held the levers of power in the party platform processes and refused to budge in 1992. Bush, seeking to shore up a conservative base that had never fully trusted or accepted him, offered no challenge.

Thus the first section of the Republican platform (1992) was titled, "Uniting Our Family." Proclaiming that "personal responsibility, morality, and the family" were the pillars of civilized society, the platform writers charged that "Elements within the media, the entertainment industry, academia, and the Democratic Party are waging a guerrilla war against American values. They deny personal responsibility, disparage traditional morality, denigrate religion, and promote hostility toward the family's way of life" (p. 17). Addressing the issue of abortion directly, the platform announced: "We believe the unborn child has a fundamental individual right to life which cannot be infringed. We therefore reaffirm our support for a human life amendment to the Constitution, and we endorse legislation to make clear that the Fourteenth Amendment's protections apply to unborn children. We oppose using public revenues for abortion and will not fund organizations which advocate it" (p. 24).

The "family values" package, with the issue of abortion firmly imbedded in it, was showcased in the convention speeches of Marilyn Quayle, Pat Robertson, and Patrick Buchanan. Convention planners hoped to assuage the differences between moderates and conservatives by allowing voices for both to present major speeches, but at different times. Marilyn Quayle spoke on Wednesday night, family night at the convention, just before the statement of Barbara Bush and the introduction of the Bush family. Though the tone of the evening was to be warm and reassuring, there was no mistaking Quayle's attack on the values of the Democratic Party and its candidates. At the beginning of her presentation, she referred to the "boomer generation" label being applied to Clinton and Gore, and pointed out that she and Dan were also boomers. "But remember, not everyone joined the counterculture. Not everyone demonstrated, dropped out, took drugs, joined in the sexual revolution or dodged the draft." Continuing in the same vein, she said "most of us went to school, to church and to work. We married and started families." A few paragraphs later she declared "Our generation's social revolution taught us that family life needs protection. Our laws, policies and society as a whole must support families. As we have matured and assumed the responsibilities of parenthood and community leadership, most of my generation has recognized that our parents were wise in ways we did not appreciate. We learned that commitment, marriage and fidelity are not just arbitrary arrangements." Finally, as she moved to the end of her statement she said:

> Because leadership has everything to do with character and an unwavering commitment to principle, Dan and I have been deeply honored to serve these four years with President and Mrs. Bush. America loves Barbara Bush because she exemplifies our ideal of a strong and generous woman, dedicated to her husband, her children and her nation. She is a model for all generations—a woman I am proud to call a friend and our nation is proud to call First Lady." (*Washington Post,* Aug. 20, 1992, p. A-34)

Barbara Bush appeared next and after a brief speech produced twenty-two members of the Bush family, climaxed at the end by the appearance of "Poppy" Bush himself.

The themes struck on this third night of the convention stressed family values in the most traditional ways. Marilyn Quayle and Barbara Bush portrayed themselves as wives of prominent husbands. The former reminded her audience that she was a trained professional woman who gladly gave up her career to rear children. The latter physically centered her presence among a flock of children and grandchildren. Neither challenged conventional mores. Convention planners hoped to achieve a broad moderating tone that would override divisiveness. They failed. At the end of the evening, noted columnist and political commentator George Will summed up his observations on television while talking with Peter Jennings:

> Peter, what we saw tonight is symptomatic of a very strange transformation of American politics. Time was, not long ago, when we talked about what were recognizably public goods and government actions. Social Security, rural electrification, defense. Tonight, we talked about hugging your children and it's all right to cry. This was a prolonged sensitivity session, but it had a very hard political edge to it. Tonight was a sustained innuendo against the Democratic Party that they don't like marriage, families, women in the kitchen, or children. This is the heart of the question, "Can you be one kind of man and another kind of president?" They're saying Bill Clinton— and generically Democrats—are bad people. (Rosenstiel, 1993, pp. 225–26).

The hard political edge Will referred to came earlier in the week in the words of Pat Robertson and Patrick Buchanan. Robertson (1992a CRTNET), minister, contender for the Republican nomination in 1988, and leader of the Christian Coalition, announced that an "insidious plague has fastened itself upon the families of America." He spoke against high taxes, wasteful spending, and the liberal welfare state. "The tax-and-spend, check-kiting Democrats in Congress have undermined the family." Turning the attack on Clinton, Robertson said, "He told People magazine that he wouldn't let his 13-year-old daughter get her ears pierced, but he wants to give your 13-year-old daughter the choice without your consent to destroy the life of her unborn baby." Buchanan (1992b CRTNET) sharpened the vitriol and gave it shape:

> My friends, this election is about more than who gets what. It is about who we are. It is about what we believe and what we stand for as Americans. There is a religious war going on in this country for the soul of America. It is a cultural war as critical to the kind of nation we shall be as the Cold War itself, for this war is for the soul of America.

The adamant positions expressed by the fundamentalist Right during the convention troubled a number of other conservative and moderate Republicans, who feared the harsh and narrow rhetoric they were hearing would backfire among the public at large. They waited for the Bush forces to shift direction and strike a milder tone, but the shrill moralism remained etched in memory. Some disturbed delegates left the convention disappointed and determined not to campaign actively for the Bush team. As Germond and Witcover (1993) reported,

> This moral element was something new at this level of American politics. In the past, extremists on both ends of the ideological spectrum had demonstrated hard edges of hostility and anger; no one who was there could forget the Barry Goldwater delegates shouting their rage at the press at the 1964 Republican convention in San Francisco. But the argument had always centered on who was "right" and "wrong" in their approach to government. It had usually been possible for conservatives and liberals to behave with civility and even good humor toward those with whom they totally disagreed; indeed that was still the case where they came together regularly—in Congress for example. But the delegates of the religious right were a different breed of activists who believed those who disagreed with them were not just wrong, but evil. (pp. 412–13)

THE RECURSIVE RHETORIC OF THE FETUS IMAGE

A most powerful symbol of evil was the dead fetus, presented in the form of televised imagery never seen before in the context of political campaign advertising. As synechdochic representative of a deeply emotional complex of values, opinions, and feelings resonating among issues of gender, family, and morality, the dead fetus image is what Murray Edelman (1985) calls a condensation symbol, arousing threat. Because its meaning comes only partly or not at all from objective consequences that the public cannot know, "the meaning can only come from the psychological needs of the respondents; and it can only be known from their responses" (p. 7).

In the spring of 1992 advertising executive Michael Bailey won the Republican primary in the 9th Congressional District in Indiana. It was not the victory that won Bailey national attention, but the visuals of apparently aborted fetuses that aired on television. Bailey referred to himself as a right-wing Christian candidate who did not believe in the separation of church and state. He was an obsessed anti-abortionist who said he had been trying for years to air television advertising showing "the true horror of abortion." When he discovered that an FCC ruling prohibiting the censorship of political advertising would allow him to do it, he became a candidate. His purpose in running was not to win the election, but to secure airtime for his visuals. Just showing the ads, he said, was a victory for his cause. After winning the primary, he expressed pride in two ads he had already produced that he would use against Democratic incumbent Lee Hamilton. One ad interspersed photographs of Nazi swastikas, Holocaust victims, aborted fetuses, and American flags with filmed sequences of a ranting Adolf Hitler. The other showed a pair of tweezers picking through parts of an aborted fetus with a female voice saying, "It's my body" and "It's a woman's choice." "I'm talking ripped-apart arms and legs and torso, absolutely disgusting," Bailey said. "It's just sick, it's just sick. That's our point" (Booth, 1992, pp. A1–A7). Lee Hamilton defeated Bailey, winning 70 percent of the vote, but following his lead, fourteen other candidates asked for and received Bailey's permission to run the ads as part of their campaign. Images of the aborted fetuses thus appeared in Georgia, North Dakota, Tennessee, Missouri, Colorado, California, Illinois, Montana, Wisconsin, and Idaho.

The presentation of a visual image of an aborted infant is clearly an attempt to project a powerful symbol. Some immediate observations are in order. We know that visual presentations of children can be emotionally gripping. We also know that, all things being equal, visual presentation is likely to be more potent from the standpoint of symbolic inducement, that is, involvement from the various stages of identification to a partisan reaction of acceptance or rejection, than any other presentational mode. Given normal neurophysical development, the visual sensory system will override all others, even to the point of transforming them, and thus is profoundly significant in guiding knowing, valuing, and action (Gregg, 1984, pp. 38–49). We further recognize that the images shown in this case were carefully selected. The so-called aborted infants that were pictured were in the third term of development so that their human physical characteristics could be clearly perceived.

In every way, then, the Bailey type of political advertising was purposely and intensely rhetorical, in the fullest negative sense.

Among contemporary rhetorical theorists, Kenneth Burke has written most systematically about rhetorical negativity (1966, pp. 419–79). With some adaptation, Burke provides a useful way to critically unravel the anti-abortion ads. First, the image of the aborted fetus is meant to be both positive and positively negative. That is, the visual imagery featured is to be positively taken as an aborted infant. The infant is positively dead; indeed, in the context of the ad, it has had its life extinguished. It has been murdered. The image then moves beyond itself into the realm of value laden ideas—ideas of life and death, of power over life and death, of the positive act of nourishing life and the negative act of taking it away. It is a realm of ideas grounded in fundamental principles. The principles call forth an ultimate negative stance, the beginning and the end of negativity, the hortatory no, the thou shalt not. The command, "thou shalt not," is meant to stop an act in its incipient stage (Burke, 1962, pp. 183–89).

The sketch of rhetorical negativity just outlined follows a hierarchical path, from images, to ideas, to principles, to ultimate terms. To achieve a more comprehensive understanding of the negative potential of the anti-abortion ads, to get another view of the multilevel inducement evoked by the ads, let us briefly follow that rhetorical negativity in a recursive fashion. Recursive meaning is not circular, nor is it properly called reductive, though at times it may seem to be either or both. As I use the term, I follow the principle discovered by mathematician Kurt Godel. A recursive definition defines a phenomenon in terms of simpler versions of itself. It reduces to the most basic forms, values, and moods, shedding ambiguities and superfluities along the way. By way of exemplifying in a manner pertinent to this discussion, we note that perspectives of broad cultural scope can be reduced through human processes of subspeciation to issues salient for particular segments of the public, which may be further reduced to problems for more intimate social groups, and finally to matters of individual tension and concern. The reductive principle can be reversed, of course, so that phenomena can expand from problems of individual idiosyncrasy to those of cultural psychosis. I propose now to examine the manifestations of rhetorical negativity that can be evoked by the Bailey type of political advertising in a recursive fashion. The examination must be brief here; it can only bring together some insights about human symbolic behavior from such areas of study as history, mythology, anthropology, cognitive psychology, politics, sociology, and rhetoric.

Many of the individuals who march under anti-abortion banners share common orientations on a cluster of issues regarding pornography, gay rights, education, and family values. Their sheer numbers, their shared outlook on life and lifestyles, and the organized efforts they support attract our attention to the social movement character of their existence. We have seen such movements before in our history, movements both broad and narrow in their scope. In *Virgin Land* (1950), Henry Nash Smith chronicles the way many individuals in various walks of life employed mythologies of the frontier, the American West, and the agrarian lifestyle to avoid facing the constant industrializing and urbanizing of our nation in the nineteenth and early twentieth centuries. Whereas mythical conceptions of the agrarian frontier formulated by Jefferson, Franklin, and others gave impetus to exploration, settlement, and development of new lands early in our country's history, such myths were later employed to protect human psyches from the buffeting of a rapidly changing environment. In the years following the Civil War, and into the twentieth century, the rhetoric of sophisticated literature, poetry, academic essays, and dime novels induced attitudes that turned away from the implications of a rapidly changing agrarian lifestyle. The misdirected act of symbolic affirmation in reality cloaked psychological processes of denial. Thus, mythology provided stability in the midst of changing technology and corresponding lifestyle.

Closer to our interest is the Temperance movement that gained momentum in the middle of the nineteenth century and coalesced around attempts to assert old rural middle-class values. Joseph Gusfield (1986), employing a rhetorical-symbolic perspective, illustrates how the Temperance movement actually clothed a struggle over class status and respect (p. 7). Of particular interest is Gusfield's characterization of the Populist wing of that movement, which engaged in coercive reform. As Gusfield shows, the Populist supporter of the Temperance cause could no longer assume that or his or her way of life was dominant in American society. The chosen way to fight back politically was to try to inflict his or her morality on the larger society by coercing a public definition of morality and respectability (p. 19). The moralizing of issues rigidifies positions, decreases possibilities for compromise and common ground, and transforms those with differing viewpoints into enemies beyond redemption. A strong component of such a cause becomes an emphasis on rhetorical expression (p. 19), on announcing one's position, pronouncing one's values, proclaiming one's being, one's selfhood. It can lead to coercive demonstration, to offensive confrontation, to the casting down of symbols, like an aborted fetus, to affront horribly. What a fetus symbolizes is fundamental. It is a body bearing the capacity for life. Used as an important marker by persons within the anti-abortion movement, it represents the potential for individual selfhood enlarged to social dimensions. For those in the movement who resonate to the fetus-form as shown in the televised messages, that potential is extinguished in the imagery of a lifeless body.

Anthropologist Mary Douglas (1982) recursively turns our attention to the relationship between the human body and social relationships. While social relations are variable, the human body is common to all of us. It should not surprise us to find that natural conditions of our environment and being provide much of the material with which we structure our symbolic reality. Our own bodies are central to processes of natural symbolizing. Our bodies occupy space and provide the center from which we locate and understand physical others, forces, and relationships that constitute our environment. Douglas finds it useful to consider social structures, with bodies as the central locus, transformed into relationship and control phenomena. She maps our social and cultural relationships into schemata of grid and group. A coercive reformer clearly falls in the schema of group, characterized by a concern for clearly demarcated borders around one's environment to be protected against contamination from external sources, by an asceticism constrained by moral judgment, and by strict controls "set on bodily enjoyment and the gateways of sensual experience" (pp. 140–55). In this perspective, the issues and tensions of status become recursively transformed into matters of group identification and safety, with self in close-knit identification with others of similar bent, and identified against others of different perspective and value in an environment characterized by fluidity. In a strongly group oriented perspective, we note Douglas's conclusion that "The idea of self is surrounded with prickly moral contexts in which it has to operate" (p. 142).

Douglas brings us to our last recursive move, to the intellectual and physical center of selfhood where body and mind join to produce "reality." An illuminating study by Mark Johnson (1987) leads us to appreciate how dependent our cognitive structuring of reality is upon the knowledge we gain from our bodies. As infants, we discover ourselves, learn our limits, and explore our potentialities by processes of decentering that radiate from our physical being. We formulate such cognitive schema as containment, force, pressure, release, dimensionality, verticality, partiality, and other mental structures to organize our perceptions and knowledge. The schema of boundary, so directive of the emotions of coercive reformers, is absolutely fundamental to a concept of selfhood. Johnson corroborates as follows:

> Our encounter with containment and boundedness is one of the most pervasive features of our bodily experience. We are intimately aware of our bodies as three-dimensional containers into which we put certain things (food, water, air) and out of which other things emerge (food and water wastes, air, blood, etc.) From the beginning, we experience constant physical containment in our surroundings. —We move in and out of rooms, clothes, vehicles, and numerous kinds of bounded spaces. We manipulate objects, placing them in

containers (cups, boxes, cans, bags, etc.). In each of these cases there are repeatable spatial and temporal organizations. In other words, there are typical schemata for physical containment. (p. 21)

We are led to conclude that the coercive reformer of any historical period is an individual who perceives the process of fundamental change to be threatening to the boundaries of selfhood. The boundaries for such an individual are not flexible, not imbued with the kind of elasticity conducive to growth, nor permeable in the kind of productive way that allows fresh experiences to enter one's personal domain. Rather they stiffen, ready for defensive response.

Our recursive rhetorical journey began with the thrusting of an aborted fetus on the political scene as a condensed symbol of threat, thrust to open an offensive wedge against an offensive environment. Along the way, it engaged layers of meaning from status and legitimacy at its outermost surface to the threat of ego existence at its core. The image of the fetal body is powerful negative rhetoric imbued by true believers with a force that partakes of a kind of primitive magic.

We are now witnessing a struggle that some call a culture war, wherein an extremely anxious minority struggles to remain somehow viable in the midst of profound change, where respectability and status become ambiguous, and where individual psyches rise or fall according to forces that seem encouraged by alien others and menacing institutions. The old universe of discourse is changing, traditional values are being called into question, clusters of familiar terms are being redefined. Murphy Brown, the fictional single parent who sparred with a real vice president, was the tip of the family value iceberg, symbolic of the changes. Following the third presidential debate in a post-debate discussion, William Buckley attempted to frame the issues at stake in terms of the old liberalism and the old conservatism. But Bill Moyers corrected him, saying the swing was not from "conservative" to "liberal" as we now define them, but to a place beyond all labels and definitions currently in use—to a place beyond traditional political nostrums (C-SPAN, Oct. 19, 1992).

IMAGES OF LIFE AND DEATH:
THE ISSUE OF ABORTION IN THE FUTURE

In his study of the 1992 American National Election Study, Alan Abramowitz (1993) was able to track the vote pertinent to the abortion issue in the presidential election. His analysis reveals that abortion was a more salient issue for Republicans than for Democrats. In general, for all Bush and Clinton voters, national economic conditions, party identification, and ideology exerted the strongest influence on the voters' choice of candidate. But among the subset of voters for whom abortion was a salient issue, and who were aware of the major candidates' positions, the data shows otherwise. "In fact, among these aware and concerned voters, the influence of abortion attitudes far outweighed that of any other variable except party identification, including evaluations of national economic conditions. For this group of voters, which included approximately one-fourth of the electorate, a more accurate slogan would have been, 'it's abortion, stupid'" (pp. 6–7). Abramowitz found that Clinton was largely unaffected by defections of pro-life Democrats. Bush, however, did suffer a substantial number of defections from pro-life Republicans who tended to vote for Perot rather than Clinton (p. 7). Abortion, more than any other policy issue, made its presence felt in the presidential election of 1992.

The election of Bill Clinton does not signal an end to the culture war. For many, traditional notions of family values will continue to provide a center around which defenses against change can be erected as the nature of "family" undergoes fundamental transformation. Various public activist groups continue to mount symbolic and physical activity against abortion rights. Since the election, abortion clinics in various parts of the nation have been blockaded and picketed by anti-abortion advocates. Some clinics have been sprayed with chemicals, and others fire bombed. Some doctors who continued to engage in abortion practice have been bombarded by harassing phone campaigns. They have had their houses placed under surveillance and small white crosses planted in their yards. One physician, Dr. David Gunn, was shot to death by a pro-lifer in Florida. Anti-abortion spokespersons said that Gunn's death was unfortunate, but some activist anti-abortion groups raised funds to support the family of the killer, not the family of Gunn. Organized anti-abortion activities, under the auspices of such groups as Rescue America, Pro-Life Action Network, Operation Rescue, American Family Association, and others, have occurred in such states as California, Louisiana, Florida, Texas, Kansas, Oregon, Colorado, Minnesota, Wisconsin, Virginia, and Michigan.

Large numbers of anti-abortion believers find a comfortable home for their agenda among the causes championed by Pat Robertson's Christian Coalition. Though Robertson's bid for the presidential nomination of the Republican Party in 1988 was unsuccessful, Robertson and his followers did not back out of the presidential ring, but vowed to work harder. Operating on the idea that the typical American citizen does not bother to get involved in political and social problems at the local level, the Christian Coalition urged members to organize and attend meetings of school boards and PTAs to influence and perhaps eventually gain control of them. The coalition has also been working at the local and state levels to gain positions of influence in the Republican Party. The success of coalition efforts was revealed in the fact that three hundred of its members were delegates at the 1992 Republican convention and exerted an influence beyond their numbers. Following the convention, in September, candidate George Bush made an appearance at the side of Pat Robertson at Virginia Beach for the coalition's "Road to Victory" conference.

If public statements spoken and written by Pat Robertson recently are to be taken seriously, they reveal a conspiratorial view of the culture war, and echo the election campaign of 1800. The conspiracy to overturn "traditional values" began, according to Robertson, with the founding of the Order of Illuminati in Europe in 1776, an atheistic, Satanic society dedicated to placing a "new world order" in the hands of a chosen few. Over the years the Illuminati managed to infiltrate such groups and organizations as the Masons, the Council on Foreign Relations, the English Round Table, the Trilateral Commission, the Communist Party, and the Federal Reserve Board. Ever mindful of the need to solidify his conservative base, the Bush campaign began to drop the phrase "new world order" from its rhetoric from the middle of July to Election Day (Isikoff, 1992, p. C-3).

The Christian Coalition is reported to have raised 13 million dollars to elect pro-family Christians to Congress and to gain working control of the Republican Party by 1996. They actively campaign at local, state, and national levels against gay rights, equal rights amendments, and feminist issues. They are enthusiastically charged by the kind of exhortation Robertson wrote in a fund raising letter: "America is at a crossroads—Either she returns to her Christian roots—or she will continue to legalize sodomy, slaughter innocent babies, destroy the minds of her children, squander her resources and sink into oblivion" (Isikoff, 1992, p. C-3).

Thomas Edsall (Sept. 10, 1993, p. A-4) reports that the Christian Coalition and allied organizations appear to be growing in power; they have either gained majority status or domination of the Republican Party in Oregon, Iowa, Virginia, Washington, South Carolina, Alaska, and Louisiana. They also wield "powerful force" in Texas, California, Minnesota, Colorado, and Pennsylvania. Referring to the efforts of Ralph Reed, director of the Christian Coalition, Edsall concludes that "he raised from the ashes of Robertson's failed 1988 presidential bid an organization that within the Republican Party has influence that rivals, if not eclipses, that of the United Auto Workers or the National Organization for Women within the Democratic Party" (p. A-4).

In the months since the 1992 presidential campaign was over, the Christian Right and its core of anti-abortion forces give evidence of its intention to be a force in future elections. At its national meeting held in the nation's capitol in September, Senators Bob Dole of Kansas and Phil Gramm of Texas, both candidates for the Republican nomination in 1996, were among the speakers invited to address the two thousand gathered activists. Both spoke in tones of broad moderation and appeal. Both were overwhelmed by the powerful emotional response evoked by Pat Buchanan, who issued a clear threat to moderate Republicans: "We cannot raise the white flag in the culture war because that war is about who we are—Culture is the Ho Chi Minh trail of power; you surrender that province and you lose America." If the Republican Party abandons its anti-abortion stand, "then it's time to found a new party" (Edsall, 1993, p. A-8). Whether the ultimate objective of the coalition is subversion of the Republican Party or establishing a new political organization, the coalition clearly intends to have national impact. Currently, it is working to identify support groups throughout the country. Spiritual leader Pat Robertson, appearing on ABC's "Nightline" (Nov. 4, 1993), said the lesson he learned from the 1988 presidential campaign was that all politics are local, and that the coalition will work with issues where they find them, hoping someday to stitch them all together to form a national organization. The September 1993 *Harper's Index* notes that since November, 1992, three hundred thousand persons have enrolled in Robertson's Christian Crusade (p. 11).

They are a force to be reckoned with. A recent segment of CNN's "Inside Politics" (Jan. 23, 1994) revealed that Christian conservatives comprised 15 percent of the total electorate in the 1992 election. Looking ahead to upcoming campaigns, Brookings Institute political scientist Thomas Mann said that the Republican Party had to broaden its appeal without alienating the Christian Right. And commentator John Zarella stated that the Christian Right was increasingly viewed as the base of the Republican Party and would be a force in the 1994 and 1996 campaigns.

Robertson's outrageous claims will surely not win the day, though they may serve to rally some ideologues in this age of transition. A number of individuals will undoubtedly continue to rally around the image of a dead fetus, taking that rhetorical symbol to establish a leverage point against change. *Harper's* (Nov. 1992) refers to an advertisement carried in *Life Advocate*, a pro-life publication placed by Museum Replicas of Urbana, Illinois, for a replica of a fetus in a bottle that could be purchased for $16.25 (p. 14). The emotions surrounding the fetus image are beyond the means of direct engagement by a larger majority of the public, for there are no common grounds for engagement. For the true believer, the image is a fundamental and final statement, an impregnable metaphor of belief. For others troubled by the general idea of abortion, the image may rub against deep seated chords of value and emotion. The metaphor will not be argued away, but in time it may be overwhelmed by an apposing metaphor that strikes emotions more congenial to the larger environment. One such metaphorical candidate was launched by President Clinton's surgeon general, Joycelin Elders, who suggested it was time to end the love affair with the fetus and focus on the quality of life for children. Should an apposing metaphorical image gain dominance, and hence rhetorical power, the contexts for valuing life and death will have changed significantly. At this moment in time, however, for many, the image of an aborted fetus is a synechdochic symbol of resistance for a coalition of forces on the Radical Right that promise to influence presidential campaign rhetoric for the foreseeable future.

NOTE

This essay was originally written for this book. It has also been published in *Communication Quarterly* 42, No. 3 (Summer 1994), 229–243.

REFERENCES

Abramowitz, A. (1993). It's abortion, stupid: Policy voting in the 1992 presidential election. Paper presented at the annual meeting of the American Political Science Association, Washington D.C., Sept.

Booth, W. (1992, July 20). Antiabortion TV ads catch on in campaigns. *Washington Post.*

Burke, K. (1962). *A rhetoric of motives.* Berkeley: University of California Press.

Burke, K. (1966). *Language as symbolic action.* Berkeley: University of California Press.

Bush–Quayle, Sept. 10, 1992, campaign press release, Internet.

Clinton for President (1991). The new covenant. Little Rock, Ark. Great American Media.

Clinton–Gore, White House Campaign File, Internet.

CNN (1994, Jan. 23). Inside Politics.

CRTNET (1992a). PSUVM (Computer Program).

CRTNET (1992b). PSUVM (Computer Program).

The Democratic platform. (1992). Washington, D.C.: Democratic National Committee.

Douglas, M. (1982). *Natural symbols.* New York: Pantheon Books.

Edelman, M. (1985). *The symbolic uses of politics.* Urbana and Chicago: University of Illinois Press.

Edsall, T. (1993, Sept. 12). Buchanan warns GOP of schism on abortion. *Washington Post.*

Edsall, T. (1993, Sept. 10). Christian political soldier helps revive movement. *Washington Post.*

The finish line: Covering the campaign's final days (1993). New York: The Freedom Forum Media Studies Center.

Germond, J., and J. Witcover. (1993). *Mad as hell: Revolt at the ballot box, 1992.* New York: Warner Books.

Gregg, R. (1984). *Symbolic inducement and knowing: A study in the foundations of rhetoric.* Columbia, S.C.: University of South Carolina Press.

Gregg, R. (1993). Kenneth Burke's concept of rhetorical negativity. In J. Chesebro, ed., *Extensions of the Burkean system*. Tuscaloosa: The University of Alabama Press.

Gusfield, J. (1986). *Symbolic crusade*. 2nd ed. Urbana: University of Illinois Press.

Hackler, T. (1993, Mar. 28). God and man at Monticello. *Washington Post*.

Harpers (1993, Sept.).

Helms, J. (1990). Tax paid obscenity. *Nova, 14*.

Hunter, J. (1990). *Culture wars: The struggle to define America*. New York: Basic Books.

Isikoff, (1992, Oct. 11). The Robertson Right and the grandest conspiracy. *Washington Post*.

Johnson, M. (1987). *The body in the mind: The bodily basis of meaning, imagination, and reason*. Chicago: University of Chicago Press.

Nightline (1993, Nov. 4). God and the grass roots.

Quayle, Marilyn. (1992, Aug. 20). Our laws, policies and society as a whole must support our families. *Washington Post*.

The Republican platform. (1992). Washington, D.C.: Republican National Committee.

Rosenstiel, T. (1993). *Strange bedfellows*. New York: Hyperion.

Smith, H. (1950). *Virgin land*. Cambridge, Mass.: Harvard University Press.

Troy, G. (1991). *See how they ran*. New York: Free Press.

Witt, L., K. Paget, and G. Matthews (1994). *Running as a woman: Gender and power in American politics*. New York: Free Press.

TEN

Women's Issues, Women's Place

Gender-Related Problems in Presidential Campaigns

SUZANNE M. DAUGHTON

> Manhood and politics go hand in hand. . . . Everything
> that stands in contrast to and opposed to political life and
> the political virtues has been represented by women, their
> capacities and the tasks seen as natural to their sex.
> —Shanley and Pateman, 1991, p. 3

Although the year 1992 saw no woman on the presidential ticket of a major political party, it was heralded as "the year of the woman" in American politics.[1] Yet 1992, like 1972, 1988, 1990, and every other "year of the woman" before it (Salholz et al., 1992, p. 20), actually resulted in very little change in political representation for the gender that constitutes over half the population. American women have been struggling for equal rights for well over a century now—making gains, then losing ground, over and over, raising themselves up by increments. What was it about 1992's political campaigns that fed the image that this year would somehow be different? Did presidential candidates, those most visible of political campaigners, deal with gender-related issues any more frequently, or in more depth? Or were American feminists (men and women) so battered by what Susan Faludi (1991) characterizes as the 1980s "backlash" against feminism that they eagerly grasped any token of support for women's rights as symbolic of real commitment? These issues will be the focus of this chapter.

Ironically, the label itself, "The Year of the Woman," was indicative of the lack of potential for dramatic change. Designating *one* year as "the year of the woman" explicitly limits and confines women's achievements and expecta-

221

tions to a twelve-month span; in reality, social change takes far longer. For its retrospective on the "year of the woman," *Newsweek* asked Faludi to evaluate the promise and accomplishments of 1992. She wrote:

> The other day, a male friend and I were talking about that now shopworn phrase, "The Year of the Woman." How would it feel to have the tables turned? "The Year of the Man?" he said, dubious. "Ugh. It sounds like—well, like a death sentence. Like the doctor just walked in and said, 'I'm sorry, sir, you have a year to live.'"
>
> It doesn't feel much different for women, except for a macabre twist. We are supposed to be grateful, jubilant even, when the media doctors bring us the bad news. (1992, p. 31)

As Faludi notes, "The Years of Women have come and gone and come again" (1992, p. 31). But 1992 did see some landmark changes: After a decade of discussion of "the gender gap" in American politics, the results finally showed up at the polls. In a *Newsweek* article entitled "Did America 'Get It'?" Eloise Salholz et al. (1992) write, "Judging the meaning of '92 merely in terms of winners and losers or dollars and cents, however, may ultimately be another way of not *getting it.* The fact is, women's issues dominated political discourse in a dramatic new way" (p. 20). While some important changes did, of course, occur, 1992 was more of a turning point toward eventual parity than a major achievement in and of itself. The *Newsweek* authors' congratulatory tone tells us more about the media than about the political events of that year: Faludi demonstrates that the media habitually exaggerate the significance of small gains for women.[2] This media focus on how far women have come can serve to placate many women, preventing them from seeing how much farther they have yet to go, and keeping them from realizing the necessity of organizing for further group benefit. "You've *arrived,*" say the media. "Congratulations. Now *be quiet.*" So, yes, in "the year of the woman," the number of women in the Senate did triple, going from two to six. But six out of one hundred is still fairly dismal when one considers that women are a technical majority of the American population. Those who focus on the miracle of the six are ignoring the imbalance of the ninety-four, and vice versa.

But Salholz et al. (1992) ask that we focus on communication rather than on the numbers of winners and losers. So, statistics aside for a moment: Did public communication about gender-related problems (women's issues, women's place) change significantly during the 1992 campaign? Did women's issues in fact "dominate political discourse in a dramatic new way," as Salholz et al. claim? Did the presidential campaign during the "Year of the Woman" differ from its predecessors in its discourse about women's roles? If so, in what ways and with what implications?

Communication scholars have yet to focus systematically on how political candidates discuss women's issues and women's roles in society.[3] This chapter represents a first effort to address that topic, specifically, from a feminist rhetorical perspective. The analysis will center on national convention addresses, focusing particularly on how presidential candidates handle the gender-related problems that recur in campaigns. Although I will emphasize the 1992 campaign in my analysis, I have chosen to place it in historical perspective by examining it in the context of a broad range of previous addresses. For the sake of comparison, I examined thirty-nine speeches delivered at the Democratic and Republican National Conventions of the past two decades, a time period chosen to coincide roughly with the contemporary women's movement and hence with the potential rise in public consciousness about gender issues.[4] Although I have included some nominating speeches, vice presidential acceptance speeches, and selected other convention speeches in the sample, the majority of the discourse under consideration consists of keynote addresses and the acceptance speeches of presidential candidates.[5] These are the speeches that can expect the largest audiences, and they represent the candidates' and parties' main chance to convey their social and political agendas to the American people. Hence, if an issue appears in such an address to a national audience, it is an attempt to appeal to a significant portion of the voting population and constitutes an implicit, if not explicit, promise and forecast of leadership. And if an issue is ignored in such an address, that lack of attention is also significant.

Under the heading of "gender-related problems," I included the candidates' treatment of topics typically considered "women's issues": the Equal Rights Amendment, reproductive freedom, organizational flexibility, including parental leave and child care in the workplace, and so on. I also included broader questions concerning gender roles in society and politics, including debates over the role(s) appropriate to the "first lady" and the predisposition to link the role of president to some primitive concept of *machismo*. Many of these complex and recurring social policy concerns have challenged successive generations of political leaders and show no indication of easy resolution. Accordingly, I focus on how political candidates situate themselves rhetorically, in relation to these questions of gender identity, potential, and rights, as well as what such strategies tell us about the rhetoric of presidential campaigns.[6] Informed by the work of rhetorical theorist Kenneth Burke and feminist critics Kate Millett, Susan Brownmiller, Susan Faludi, and others, I will discuss the patterns in the candidates' rhetorical handling of women's issues, their discussion of women's appropriate roles and place in the social and political realms, and finally their discourse on men's roles.

FEMINIST CRITICISM AND RHETORICAL THEORY:
BRIEF BACKGROUND NOTES

In 1970 Kate Millett published *Sexual Politics*, which quickly became a classic of the women's movement. Millett defines politics broadly as "power-structured relationships, arrangements whereby one group of persons is controlled by another" and argues that "sex is a status category with political implications" (1970/1990, pp. 23–24). Patriarchy, the system by which male dominates female and elder male dominates younger male, permeates our society and relies on social conditioning (and the barely submerged threat of force) for its perpetuation (pp. 25–26). "Patriarchy's chief institution is the family," she writes, noting the "essentially feudal character" of the patriarchal family, in which the wife/wives and children were the property of the husband/father (p. 33). Her analysis of the historical and contemporary system of patriarchy corresponds to Kenneth Burke's (1966) characterization of human beings as "goaded by the spirit of hierarchy" (p. 15).[7] Burke's analysis of the competitive, classist impulse applies equally well to the sexist impulse of sexual politics. Where Burke uses "king" and "peasant," one could easily substitute "[Man] and [woman] are 'mysteries' to each other," and the same reasoning applies: One is lower in the hierarchy than the other, and neither can ever completely understand, or identify with, the other's experience. Both experience guilt and alienation as a result. Burke uses the terms "identification" and "consubstantiality" to discuss the ways in which persons who share a common interest are bound together, and "division" to connote the essential singularity of each individual and the opposition of groups.[8] Hierarchies, including patriarchy, ensure division between groups as well as allow identification within them.

Millett's analysis of the sexual politics of patriarchy was reinforced in 1975 by Susan Brownmiller's *Against Our Will: Men, Women and Rape*, a detailed study of the causes and effects of rape in society. Because of "man's structural capacity to rape and woman's corresponding structural vulnerability" (1975, p. 4), Brownmiller hypothesizes that the human female first agreed to submit to one man, in return for his protection from all others. Thus, biological differentiation made the creation and maintenance of patriarchy possible (pp. 7–8), for marriage "reduced [woman's] status to that of chattel" (p. 7). Rape, Brownmiller argues, is the threat of force that keeps women in their place in patriarchal society (p. 5).

More recently, Susan Faludi has documented a more sophisticated version of this age-old process of intimidation. Contemporary American women, she argues, are encouraged to stay within traditional boundaries by the phenomenon of antifeminist backlash that accompanies every perceived gain by women (1991, p. xix). The twist that makes this most recent (1980s) backlash especially ironic is that it often appropriates the language of feminism to encode its antifeminist attack. The 1980s backlash congratulates women on their "success" in achieving equality, but it simultaneously sends a more negative message: "You may be free and equal now . . . but you have never been more miserable"—and feminism is the cause of that distress (Faludi, 1991, p. ix–x). In Burke's terms, feminism had become the scapegoat for the social, economic, and political uncertainties and suffering of the 1980s, problems that had actually been caused by the patriarchy's resistance to women's equality.[9] When feminism, the chief vehicle by which women as a group can seek to remedy injustice, becomes a scapegoat, many women feel they must deny the feminist label. Instead of uniting to solve their problems as women, they focus on their individual problems (Faludi, 1991, p. 57), blaming themselves rather than the patriarchy, embracing the hierarchical guilt Burke described. Women are encouraged to identify with men, especially the men in their families, rather than with one another; thus they are divided from their potential political strength as a majority. In this way, women are consigned to the margins of politics; once that is accomplished, those questions of public policy identified as "women's issues" are automatically marginalized along with the women.

WOMEN'S ISSUES

One prominent rhetorical strategy for dealing with certain issues is to designate them "women's issues" and let them languish from neglect. Of course, the very idea of "women's issues" is problematic, for it effectively marks fully half the population as a "special interest group"—and therefore, in political parlance, as a selfish minority, a group to regard with suspicion, a group that does not seek the common good.[10] (Imagine the outrage that would ensue if "Caucasian males over forty" were so described!) Of course, men as well as women are hurt by such labeling, for these issues of human rights and welfare concern all of us by definition. The ways in which they are discussed or avoided can tell us a great deal about the social and political climate, as well as the ideology and rhetorical strategy of the speaker.

My analysis shows that the overall pattern for dealing with the gender-related problem of "women's issues" was to avoid it.[11] In effect, those issues most closely identified with the female half of the species were either systematically ignored or downplayed. The mentions became increasingly subtle here: For example, many candidates, especially during the 1970s and early 1980s, spoke about the evils of "discrimination" but did not specify whether they included discrimination based on sex as well as race in that category. "Women's issues" received only the briefest, vaguest attention from politicians, conveying a clear message that childcare in the workplace was not necessary for the majority of workers (i.e., men), that children's welfare was not a national concern, that sexual harassment and violence against women were not serious health and crime issues, and that reproductive freedom only concerned half the population—the half with less political representation. Most tellingly, the discussion of equal rights and opportunities was incredibly short-lived. Speakers at only two national conventions dared mention support for women's rights explicitly: Democrats Jimmy Carter in 1980 and Walter Mondale, Geraldine Ferraro, and Mario Cuomo in 1984.[12] Both Democratic candidates lost to Republican Ronald Reagan, the first president to oppose ERA since Congress passed it, and neither party brought up equal rights again.[13]

In 1992 the silence surrounding most women's issues continued and deepened. One major irony of the so-called Year of the Woman is that it was almost completely devoid of any discussion of women's rights in the conventions of the two major parties.[14] These changes in convention speakers' treatment of the issues most closely identified with American women mirrors the social trends of the time, characterized by Faludi as the 1980s backlash. But if they were not talking about women's rights, or even women's issues, what *were* politicians talking about that gave the media the idea that this was the "Year of the Woman"?

WOMEN'S PLACE

In a year when the Equal Rights Amendment was not even a whisper on the national scene, public furor over women's place and women's roles (and by implication, men's roles as well) was intense. However, while these topics undoubtedly served as distractors from other issues crucial to women's and men's lives (ERA, and so on), they are relevant to presidential campaigns. As Mary Lyndon Shanley and Carole Pateman (1991) explain, the very way in which our society defines politics is based on the assumption of sexual difference: By definition, politics is a male arena (pp. 1, 3). And in her classic work, *Man's World, Woman's Place*, Elizabeth Janeway (1971) explains how the myths of a society shape conceptions for proper behavior through the creation of roles (p. 96). It is a fact of contemporary American life that women populate the workforce, but no matter how commonplace it becomes for women to work, during a backlash some still insist on viewing working women as "nontraditional." How are those working women portrayed by the media and treated in society?

Once again, in the late 1980s and early 1990s, as they have been in earlier periods of backlash, "individual" women are suddenly "sick"—*lots* of them. Elaine Showalter (*The Female Malady: Women, Madness, and English Culture, 1830–1980*, 1985), Sandra Gilbert and Susan Gubar (*The Madwoman in the Attic*, 1979), and more recently, Susan Faludi (1991) and Carol Tavris

(1992), tell the same story. Historically, women who perform nontraditional roles, such as that of author, or who simply wish to live with some measure of independence, pose a threat to the established patriarchy and are therefore labeled with "the name of the symbolic female disorder" of that period; hysterical, schizophrenic, depressed, neurotic, and so on (Showalter, 1985, p. 4). But women who perform traditional roles "too well"—who care too much about others and are self-effacing—do not escape society's judgments either. As Tavris points out, while women are discouraged from enacting "male" (independent) roles, women who enact traditional female roles can then be judged deficient by comparison to a male standard of emotional health (1992, p. 197). In other words, *there is a diagnosis for every female condition.* For example, the contemporary "traditional" woman can be diagnosed as codependent, or as suffering from "self-defeating personality disorder" (a modernized version of that old, formerly discredited "feminine" trait, "masochism") (Tavris, 1992, pp. 179–86). In the 1980s American women who came together in groups no longer engaged in consciousness-raising, but in self-helping. This change, Tavris notes, was part of

> the larger cultural shift away from collective political action to an individualizing mental-health movement. . . . The feminist rallying cry of the 1970s, "the personal is political," meant that personal experience can be used to illuminate the darker corners of society's closets. Today that slogan has been reversed: The political is personal, and only personal. (1992, pp. 315, 328)

So instead of recognizing that if many women experience the same frustrations, a systemic problem may exist, society insists on telling thousands of women that they (each of them, alone) are the source of their own dissatisfaction, unhappiness, mental illness. Although no convention speaker has labeled women as mentally ill, the ramifications of the societal propensity to do so are all too relevant here. In the nineteenth century, slaves who rebelled or sought to escape were diagnosed as mentally ill (Tavris, 1992, pp. 176–77). In this century, the same reasoning is applied to women who seek freedom and control over their own lives. The presumption is that the status quo is just fine; the burden of proof lies heavily on those who would seek to change the conditions of their lives. In each case, the diagnosis of mental illness represents a refusal to recognize that oppressive social conditions are responsible for human misery and that protest is a rational and healthy response; instead, people insist that the problem belongs to those who are unhappy with their stations in life.

So how are women portrayed in presidential campaign discourse? What is the range of their appropriate roles? How far can they venture into "male" territory (i.e., politics) before they become "abnormal"? Isolated Democrats—

Barbara Jordan in 1976 and 1992 (quoted below), Jimmy Carter in 1980, Ann Richards in 1988 (quoted below)—have treated women as a group with a measure of respect in their convention discourse, acknowledging that women do exist in the public realm (business and politics), that they are there because they deserve to be, and that they have the right to make their own decisions about balancing career and family responsibilities.

In 1992 Bill Clinton exemplified the subtle change of that year's campaign, a focus on individual women's accomplishments. He spoke of his admiration for his mother, a working woman who sacrificed for her family, and for his spouse, who worked for education reform for children (Clinton, pp. 642–43).[15] Both women are praised less for professional accomplishments than for managing to fulfill the traditional role of nurturer. This trend supports Tavris' conclusion that the political is now *only* personal; Clinton's mother and spouse are admirable because they are *exceptional*, not because they are *representative* of working women and the ways in which they can successfully meet their challenges. In times of backlash, it is far less controversial to praise the actions of one woman than to praise women's generalized advances, for the same reason that we advise speakers addressing a hostile audience to rely on an inductive rather than a deductive approach. Ronald Reagan's success with the focus on individual "heroes" in his speeches of the 1980s made the strategy extremely popular among politicians. If the speaker feels safe (that is, if the audience is likely to be favorably disposed toward the speaker's position), he or she can draw out the political implications of those praiseworthy individuals' actions. But if the audience may be hostile or divided, one leaves those implications undiscussed, knowing that favorable listeners can read political significance into the choice of individuals to praise, and hostile listeners will have less concrete reason to feel threatened. Additionally, narrative, anecdotal (even fabricated!) evidence is far more "human" and "real" than statistics, and so can even serve to outweigh or negate the impact of studies that show, for example, that women and minorities lost ground during the Reagan years.[16]

My analysis shows that Republicans have tended to downplay, ignore, or even condemn women in nontraditional roles.[17] Pat Buchanan sneered at Hillary Rodham Clinton's advisory role during her husband's campaign, bringing up her profession as if it were an indictment: "Elect me, and you get two for the price of one, Mr. Clinton says of his lawyer-spouse" (1992, p. 713). The closest thing to Republican support for working women was George Bush's comment in his 1992 acceptance speech that "I meet parents, some working two jobs with hectic schedules, *who still find ways to teach old values* to steady their kids in a turbulent world" (my emphasis, p. 710). In other words, women may be grudgingly permitted to work as long as they still manage to perform their nurturing function in appropriately traditional style.

Both parties glorify the "political wife," especially the Republicans, who value her above any "career woman." In fact, she is the only woman in the public realm who receives any positive recognition from Republicans. She is praised for being an appropriate (which usually means *silent*) appendage to her husband's campaign. In 1992 Hillary Rodham Clinton was too much a participant for Republican tastes. Joanna Gillespie, in her essay on the phenomenon of the public wife, describes the female political spouse as "'morality' symbol": The political wife's job is to serve as public proof that the politician maintains control within his own family (1980/1990, p. 380). In light of her analysis, it is clear why it was so crucial for Mrs. Clinton to appear on the television show "60 Minutes" with her husband in early 1992 when they assured the American public that their marriage, which had had problems in the past, was now stable. "If that man can't run his own family," the reasoning goes, "how will he run the country?" Of course, this use of *a fortiori* reasoning is fallacious. As anyone who reflects on his or her own family knows, people are not pawns on a chessboard, to be kept in orderly rows by the chessmaster's hand. (And, of course, as every world leader can testify, countries do not work that way either.) But that "logic" is insidious. It assumes that "dominant husband, submissive wife and children" is the single workable norm for family life and the necessary role model for the entire nation (or else, homes will erupt in rebellion!). Of course this is not the case, but politicians, both male and female, still maintain the pretense.

In 1992, for example, Republican vice presidential spouse Marilyn Quayle's praise for another political wife tells women what they should aspire to *be*, not *do*, and implicitly criticizes Mrs. Clinton's divergence from the appropriate role:

> America loves Barbara Bush [applause] . . . because she exemplifies our ideal of a strong and generous woman dedicated to her husband, her children and her nation. She is a model for all generations—a woman I am proud to call a friend and our nation is proud to call First Lady. (1992, paragraph 14)

Quayle illustrates that in her own indoctrination into Public Wifery, she has come to know chapter and verse. Gillespie confirms: "The most conspicuously required public wife characteristic is that she appear as if there is nothing in the world she would rather be or do" (1980/1990, p. 386). Once their husbands are elected, "first ladies" are expected to have "projects" (not unlike Victorian ladies' "accomplishments") to which they devote their energies, but those projects are almost always of a "womanly" (nurturing or decorative) nature, such as Lady Bird Johnson's highway beautification program and Barbara Bush's work with literacy. (Hillary Rodham Clinton's assignment to head health care reforms was therefore risky in some respects, but safe in that it was still nurturing.)

The rare female politician or spouse who speaks at a convention displays more diversity. If she wishes to promote women's equality, she will often actually say so. In her keynote speech at the 1976 Democratic National Convention, Barbara Jordan celebrated her own achievement as symbolic of the achievements of others (p. 645). In 1992 she was even more explicit: She praised the long overdue entrance of greater numbers of women into politics, and looked forward to the day when "we meet in convention to nominate . . . Madame President" (p. 652). Of course, Jordan, who has become a sort of "elder stateswoman" for her party, had very little to lose by being so outspoken.

Geraldine Ferraro (1984) was also quite explicit about equal pay, equal opportunity, and the Equal Rights Amendment: "It isn't right that a woman should get paid 59 cents on the dollar for the same work as a man. If you play by the rules, you deserve a fair day's pay for a fair day's work" (p. 645). Ann Richards' 1988 keynote address was marked in its restraint, which was probably due to the male Democratic leaders' extreme lack of support for women that year. The closest Richards came to advocating equal rights was the conditional promise that "if you give us [women] a chance, we can perform" (p. 647). And Lynn Martin was a lone, pathetic voice at the Republican National Convention in 1992. She seemed to be trying hardest to convince herself, as she projected onto George Bush her own desire "to shatter the glass ceiling" (p. 725). The following year, after Martin had left her post at the Department of Labor, she would confess her discouragement about the terrible discriminatory atmosphere on Capitol Hill.

Karlyn Kohrs Campbell (1973) has written of the "oxymoron" of women speaking in public, traditionally a man's realm. If the female convention speaker does not wish to promote women's rights, she has several options by which she can try to overcome the paradox of a woman enacting power by speaking in public, and yet *not* advocating women's equality. She can downplay her own importance, denying her right to speak even as she speaks, as Barbara Bush did in 1992: "But there is something not quite right here, speeches by President Ronald Reagan, President Gerald Ford, Secretary Jack Kemp, Senator Phil Gramm and—Barbara Bush?! But I am not here to give a speech, but to have a conversation" (p. 718). Notably, Mrs. Bush does not mention Secretary Lynn Martin, nor her own "title" of "First Lady," both of which would have validated a woman's right to speak.

Another option of the nonfeminist speaker is that she may imply or even assert that her identity as a woman is not relevant. In other words, her own professional accomplishments have not impacted her definition of what women in general can or should do: She is a hardworking exception, a credit to her sex, rather than proof that the feminists are right. Katherine Davalos Ortega's keynote address at the 1984 Republican convention includes this kind of self-contradictory disclaimer: "I believe in our President not because I am a woman. Not because I am of Hispanic heritage. But above all because I am an American" (p. 712).

Most insidiously, she may imply or assert that other women's complaints are unfounded and that their goals are not worthwhile, in other words, that they do not know best which choices should be available to them. Marilyn Quayle's infamous speech at the 1992 Republican convention typifies this option:

> Dan and I are members of the baby boom generation, too. . . . But . . . not everyone believed that the family was so oppressive that women could only thrive apart from it. . . . Believe me, having a profession is not incompatible with being a good mother or wife. But it isn't easy. Women's lives are different from men's lives. We make different trade-offs. We make different sacrifices. And we get different rewards. Watching and helping my children as they grow into good and loving teenagers is a source of daily joy for me. There aren't many women who would have it any other way. . . . I sometimes think that the liberals are always so angry because they believed the grandiose promises of the liberation movements. They're disappointed because most women do not wish to be liberated from their essential natures as women. Most of us love being mothers or wives, which gives our lives a richness that few men or women get from professional accomplishments alone. (paragraphs 5, 7–8, 11)

Quayle's speech provoked quite a reaction, with its mix of the obvious, the uncontroversial, and the outrageous. It is emblematic of the rhetorical contortions that women speaking to a national audience must perform if they wish to validate and celebrate *only* traditional women's roles (as wives and mothers). But discussion of women's roles does not take place in a vacuum. As Carol Tavris points out (1992, p. 20), and as Mrs. Quayle's speech suggests, women and men are seen as dialectical opposites, even if quite a bit of shuffling has to occur to ensure their "natural" opposition.

MEN'S ROLES

Part of the contemporary myth about gender roles is that women's roles may be changing, but men's roles stay the same. Since the status quo of masculinity is supposedly just fine, no one needs to talk publicly about men's roles—except for one special case. Most presidential candidates are men and as it turns out, they define the role of president in exclusively, definitively masculine terms. In each presidential campaign, several candidates fervently audition for the role of Leading Man, and each must prove that he is "a natural" for the part. Therefore, the roles appropriate to *one particular man*, the president, become central issues in the campaign. And as Faludi notes, not only is masculinity defined as dialectically opposite from femininity; it must also continually prove itself superior (1991, pp. 61–62). No wonder it is such a strain!

There was a steady trickle of discussion about manhood in the convention speeches of the 1970s, and then the floodgate burst open in 1980 with Ronald Reagan, the cowboy, the Western movie hero, and has continued ever since. The consensus among the candidates and other convention speakers is remarkable. Both parties, across all six elections, manage to comment on these issues of manly qualifications for the office of the president.

My analysis of these speeches reveals that first and foremost, the president is the national patriarch, the paradigmatic American Man. Joanna Gillespie notes the strength of such a "family" identification, and the need for the president to "have fatherlike concern and be responsible for the maintenance of the social order" ever since the nation's founding (1980/1990, p. 381). The patterns of discourse under examination here indicate that the paradigmatic American Man is a strong leader: decisive, fit, visionary, and competent. The president's duties (roles) involve being the *guardian of moral values* (hence the scandals when candidates are accused of infidelity), the *protector of hearth and home* (including defense against international foes, fighting domestic crime, and more recently, protecting the environment), and, most significantly, *a good provider for his national "family."* Faludi notes that for the past twenty years, a nationwide poll asking its subjects to define masculinity has listed being a "good provider for his family" as the single most significant characteristic (1991, p. 65). (This finding also explains why women's small economic gains are so threatening to many men.) Therefore, it is no surprise that the president's reelection fate is often tied to the economy, if there is no immediate foreign foe.

Ronald Reagan perfectly embodied all the qualities of the national patriarch: he mentioned women's rights not at all, and talked almost incessantly about the economy, defense, and moral values. He was, in effect, proving his manhood and condemning the impotence of his rivals, Jimmy Carter and Walter Mondale:

> Never before in our history have Americans been called upon to face three grave threats to our very existence, any one of which could destroy us. We face a disintegrating economy, a weakened defense and an energy policy based on the sharing of scarcity.
>
> The major issue of this campaign is the direct political, personal, and moral responsibility of Democratic Party leadership—in the White House and in Congress—for this unprecedented calamity which has befallen us. . . .

I will not stand by and watch this country destroy itself under mediocre leadership that drifts from one crisis to the next, eroding our national will and purpose. (1980, pp. 642–43)

Of course, it is not hard to tell which strong leading man has been cast as the hero in this melodrama.

Individuals have tried at times to lower the testosterone-level requirements of the presidential role. In 1984 Mario Cuomo condemned Reagan's "macho intransigence" in resisting efforts to reduce the nuclear arsenal (p. 647). And in 1992 Bill Clinton's version of a more compassionate leader, and a government that would be "leaner, not meaner" (p. 644), drew both praise and criticism. Salholz et al. write, "Arguably, the person who did the most to feminize political rhetoric in '92 was Hillary's husband. Bill Clinton became the Oprah of presidential politics, embracing not only women's issues but womenspeak" (1992, p. 21). But his election win cannot be definitively interpreted as a validation of his less macho presentation of self, since the three-way race involved so many options of voting for and against Bush, Clinton, and independent candidate H. Ross Perot. Clinton also made plenty of statements to demonstrate that he had the strength required for the office. He described his vision for the nation, ticking off the required presidential duties as if they were on the TelePrompTer:

An America with the world's strongest defense, ready and willing to use force, when necessary. An America at the front of the new global effort to preserve and protect our natural environment, and promoting global growth. An America that will never coddle tyrants, from Baghdad to Beijing. (1992, p. 645)

Clinton not only demonstrates his willingness to use force, but criticizes George Bush for not being "man enough" to stand up to oppressive governments around the world. So despite all the media excitement about the changes in 1992, the role of president remains insistently male, making the idea of a female president a paradoxical vision of political cross-dressing.

CONCLUSIONS

In 1992 the presidential candidates had learned the lessons of the past. Antifeminist attitudes are still deeply embedded in popular culture. And since the central feature of most campaign speeches is an attempt to build coalitions for political power, politicians are justifiably anxious about including as many potential voters as they can, and offending as few as is humanly possible. Therefore, any position that is controversial will be embraced with the delicacy of a porcupine hugging a cactus.

As a result, contemporary (mostly male) politicians respond to gender-related problems in presidential campaigns in similar ways, regardless of party. Even if they ostensibly want to forward the goals of women's rights, they follow certain strategies guaranteed to provide a sort of ideological "plausible deniability," allowing them the possibility of later claiming not to be feminists. The strategies that have evolved form a sort of "presidential candidate's guide to convention etiquette during a backlash" and could be summarized as follows: (1) Remain vague in discussing women's roles. Praise individual women who exemplify traditional and nontraditional achievement, but do not spell out the generalizable implications, if any, of their accomplishments. (2) Reinforce the vision of the president as a strong male figure, the ultimate patriarch in a strong patriarchy. If you insist on also being sensitive, you will have to work even harder to prove your manhood. (3) Discuss "women's issues" only rarely, by implication and indirection. (4) Finally, discuss the concept of equal rights not at all. Women are so starved for validation during a backlash that they will accept even the smallest hint of support as "forward-thinking" and vote accordingly.

But in response to the dramatic rightward swing of the political pendulum, women are waking up to the backlash and beginning to fight it. One advertisement for the National Women's Political Caucus sought to capitalize on the mixed messages and results of the 1992 campaign: "THEY CALLED 1992 THE 'YEAR OF THE WOMAN.' DO WE ONLY GET ONE? Not if you get involved. You can help make every year the Year of the Woman. . . . MAYBE SOME DAY, THEY'LL HAVE TO DECLARE THE 'YEAR OF THE MAN' " (1993, p. 11).

As long as gender constructs remain contested and inequality based on gender exists in our society, gender-related problems will continue to surface for presidential candidates. The ways in which candidates react to such pressures will serve as a national as well as a personal test of the level of comfort with flexible gender roles. The degree of heat that such discussions generate (and the length of time that the debates occupy the public consciousness) are a rough measure of social upheaval. Although Geraldine Ferraro's rough treatment by the press and the Republicans during the 1984 campaign discouraged and intimidated many women (Ferraro included), Faludi points to some hopeful polling data that show that for many Americans, Ferraro's presence on the campaign trail made the idea of a female candidate more acceptable (1991, p. 269). As more and more women enter politics, their public presence may therefore gradually come to seem more familiar and less threatening. Then perhaps the ultimate gender-related problem of presidential campaigns, that the successful ones are limited to males only, will be solved at last.

NOTES

This essay was originally written for this book. It has also been published in *Communication Quarterly* 42, no. 2 (Spring 1994), 106–119.

1. A typical magazine article in the spring of that year began, "Will 1992 be the Year of the Woman? American women are poised to stamp an emphatic mark on the politics of 1992. More of them are running for office, contributing to campaigns and voting as a cohesive group than ever before" (Roberts and Cohen, 1992, p. 37).

2. Faludi (1991) also notes the tendency of the media to create "social trends," or the convincing appearance of them, by echoing each other's stories without checking facts (pp. 9–19, 80–89).

3. Several relevant rhetorical analyses have recently been published or presented: see, for example, essays by Bonnie Dow and Mari Tonn (1993), Patricia Sullivan (1993), Ann House (1993), and Lori Montalbano (1994). Each of these forays into the gendering of contemporary politics takes a unique and valuable approach; none examine public discussion of "women's issues" or women's roles systematically. Dow and Tonn examine Texas Governor Ann Richards' rhetoric, focusing particularly on her 1988 keynote address at the Democratic National Convention, and conclude that Richards incorporates feminine style in her discourse, ultimately modeling a form of political judgment based on traditionally feminine values and concerns. Sullivan takes a similar approach to the recent (1987–92) public discourse of congressional representative and former presidential candidate Patricia Schroeder, arguing that "Schroeder's political discourse reflects a gendered approach to decision making that manifests prototypic characteristics of women's culture" (1993, p. 530). House examines closely the 1992 acceptance speeches of presidential candidates George Bush and Bill Clinton, focusing on how each candidate used gendered language differently in order to appeal to women voters. And Montalbano's analysis of media images (1984–92) reveals that the media consistently presented female political players as if they must belong to one of three stereotypical roles: traditional wives and mothers, "men," or members of a lunatic fringe.

4. See the appendix for a list of speeches examined.

5. With the exception of Marilyn Quayle's address at the 1992 Republican National Convention, I relied on *Vital Speeches of the Day* as a reliable (and uniformly available) source for the selection of the messages. *Vital Speeches* always printed the acceptance speech of the presidential candidate, usually printed the keynote address from the convention, and often printed other speeches as well. I selected speeches for consistency as well as variety; in other words, I always examined the presidential nominee's address and the keynote address (if available). I also sought and examined speeches from different ideological perspectives, genders, and roles within the party.

6. I examined each speech and marked each mention or discussion of women's issues, women's roles, and men's roles. After reading through the speeches the first time, I used a combination of thematic brainstorming and informal content analysis to develop the categories of "women's issues," "women's roles," and "men's roles." In the category of "women's issues," I included any mention of (1) the Equal Rights Amendment and pay equity, (2) revaluing and compensating "women's work," (3) sex discrimination, (4) sexual harassment, (5) reproductive freedom, (6) child welfare, (7) educational improvement and opportunity, (8) child care, (9) parental leave, (10) organizational flexibility, (11) health insurance, and (12) "family values." Discourse about "women's place and roles" centered around two topics: (1) the relationship between career and family, and (2) women in the public realm (business and politics). And I counted as discussion of "men's roles" talk about the president as (1) the national patriarch, the paradigmatic American Man, (2) the guardian of moral values, (3) the protector of hearth and home (including defense, at home and abroad, as well as protecting the environment), and (4) the national provider. Interestingly enough, while the speakers discussed women's roles in society in general terms, they talked about men's roles almost solely in terms of what it meant to be the ideal president (or to fail at being so). In the discussion that follows, I collapse some categories together when they overlap or do not seem to be sufficiently differentiated in the analysis; although each category arose from the data to some extent, not every category proved to be equally useful. After coding each mention, I then recorded its location and valence on a chart, noting, in other words, whether and when a candidate spoke in favor of a topic, against that topic, against the opponent's support of that topic, or against the opponent's opposition to that topic. This enabled me to recognize trends of positive and negative concentration of attention, as well as patterns of silence, for each topic.

7. Burke (1966, p. 15).

8. Burke (1969b, pp. 20, 22).

9. Burke (1969a, p. 406).

10. See Tavris (1992, pp. 16–17) for a discussion of "women's issues" versus "important issues."

11. For a fuller discussion of the patterns of discourse about women's issues, see Daughton (1994).

12. Gerald Ford mentioned the concept of "equality" briefly in 1976 and 1980, but did not specify whether he meant gender or racial equality.

13. Faludi (1991) notes that 1980 marked "the first time since 1940 that the ERA failed to receive the GOP's endorsement" (p. 236).

14. The closest any speaker got to mentioning equal rights was conservative Republican Pat Buchanan, who railed against "women in combat units" (p. 713).

15. Subsequent citations of speeches will be made parenthetically in the text.

16. Faludi (1991, pp. 229–80).

17. Faludi (1991) points out that the New Right is composed of "pseudo-conservatives" (Theodore Adorno's term). "Unlike 'classic conservatives,' [they] . . . perceive themselves as social outcasts rather than guardians of the status quo. They are not so much defending a prevailing order as resurrecting an outmoded or imagined one" (p. 231). Unfortunately, the Republican Party during the 1980s embraced these pseudoconservatives with little regard for their mainstream Republican constituents; the resulting disjunct was clearly evident in the discourse and the results of the 1992 campaign, which disgusted many who formerly identified with the Republican Party.

REFERENCES

Brownmiller, S. (1975). *Against our will: Men, women and rape.* New York: Bantam.

Burke, K. (1966). *Language as symbolic action.* Berkeley: University of California Press.

Burke, K. (1969a). *A grammar of motives.* Berkeley: University of California Press.

Burke, K. (1969b). *A rhetoric of motives.* Berkeley: University of California Press.

Campbell, K. K. (1973). The rhetoric of women's liberation: An oxymoron. *Quarterly Journal of Speech, 59,* 74–86.

Daughton, S. (1994). Silencing voices by celebration: The paradox of "The year of the woman." *Iowa Journal of Communication, 26,* 44–65.

Dow, B. J., and M. B. Tonn (1993). "Feminine style" and political judgment in the rhetoric of Ann Richards. *Quarterly Journal of Speech, 79,* 286–302.

Faludi, S. (1991). *Backlash: The undeclared war against American women.* New York: Anchor/Doubleday.

Faludi, S. (1992, Dec. 28). Beyond the slogans. *Newsweek,* 31.

Gilbert, S. M., and S. Gubar (1979). *The madwoman in the attic: The woman writer and the nineteenth-century literary imagination.* New Haven: Yale University Press.

Gillespie, J. B. (1990). The phenomenon of the public wife: An exercise in Goffman's impression management. In D. Brissett and C. Edgley, eds., *Life as theater: A dramaturgical source book.* 2nd ed. Hawthorne, N.Y.: Aldine de Gruyter, pp. 379–97. (Original work published 1980.)

House, A. (1993). Language and gender in political speeches: An analysis of the Bush and Clinton acceptance addresses. Paper presented at the Organization for the Study of Communication, Language and Gender convention, Phoenix, Ariz.

Janeway, E. (1971). *Man's world, woman's place: A study in social mythology.* New York: William Morrow.

Millett, K. (1990). *Sexual politics.* 2nd ed. New York: Touchstone/Simon and Schuster. (Original work published 1970.)

Montalbano, L. (1994). Performing politics: Media performance aesthetics for women in political campaigns. Paper presented at the Central States Communication Association convention, Oklahoma City.

National Women's Political Caucus (1993, Aug. 16). They called 1992 the "year of the woman." Advertisement. *Newsweek,* 11.

Roberts, S. V., and G. Cohen (1992, Apr. 27). Will 1992 be the year of the woman? *U.S. News and World Report,* 37–39.

Salholz, E., L. Beachy, S. Miller, P. Annin, T. Barrett, and D. Foote (1992, Dec. 28). Did America 'get it'? Women's gains in '92: A glass both half empty and half full. *Newsweek,* 20–22.

Shanley, M. L., and C. Pateman, eds. (1991). *Feminist interpretations and political theory.* University Park, Pa.: Penn State University Press.

Showalter, E. (1985). *The female malady: Women, madness, and English culture, 1830–1980.* New York: Penguin.

Sullivan, P. A. (1993). Women's discourse and political communication: A case study of Congressperson Patricia Schroeder. *Western Journal of Communication, 57,* 530–45.

Tavris, C. (1992). *The mismeasure of woman.* New York: Simon and Schuster.

Appendix: List of Speeches

Note. All speeches, unless otherwise noted, were published in *Vital Speeches of the Day* on the date indicated.

Agnew, S. T.	(1972, Sept. 15).	Acceptance speech. Pp. 710–11.
Askew, R. O. D.	(1972, Aug. 1).	Keynote address: The dreams of Americans. Pp. 612–14.
Bradley, B.	(1992, Aug. 15).	Keynote address. Pp. 655–56.
Buchanan, P.	(1992, Sept. 15).	The election is about who we are. Pp. 712–15.
Bush, B.	(1992, Sept. 15).	Family values. P. 718.
Bush, G.	(1980, Aug. 15).	Acceptance speech. Pp. 646–47.
Bush, G.	(1988, Oct. 15).	Acceptance speech. Pp. 2–5.
Bush, G.	(1992, Sept. 15).	A new crusade to reap the rewards of our global victory: Acceptance speech. Pp. 706–10.
Carter, J.	(1976, Aug. 15).	Acceptance speech. Pp. 642–44.
Carter, J.	(1980, Sept. 15).	Acceptance speech. Pp. 706–10.
Clinton, B.	(1992, Aug. 15).	Acceptance speech. Pp. 642–45.
Cuomo, M.	(1984, Aug. 15).	Keynote address. Pp. 646–49.
Cuomo, M.	(1992, Aug. 15).	Nominating address. Pp. 648–51.
Dukakis, M. S.	(1988, Aug. 15).	Acceptance speech. Pp. 642–45.
Ferraro, G.	(1984, Aug. 15).	Acceptance speech. Pp. 644–46.
Ford, G. R	(1976, Sept. 15).	Acceptance speech. Pp. 706–8.

Ford, G. R.	(1980, Aug. 15).	Let's talk about the future. Pp. 651–53.
Goldwater, B.	(1984, Sept. 15).	Freedom. Pp. 714–15.
Gore, A.	(1992, Aug. 15).	Facing the crisis of spirit: Acceptance speech. Pp. 646–48.
Gramm, P.	(1992, Sept. 15).	Had the Congress said yes. Pp. 721–23.
Hart, G.	(1984, Aug. 15).	Unity speech. Pp. 649–51.
Jackson, J. L.	(1992, Aug. 15).	The moral center. Pp. 652–54.
Jagt, G. V.	(1980, Aug. 15).	Wake up America: Keynote address. Pp. 647–51.
Jordan, B.	(1976, Aug. 15).	Who then will speak for the common good? Keynote address. Pp. 645–46.
Jordan, B.	(1992, Aug. 15).	Change: From what to what? Keynote address. Pp. 651–52.
Kean, T. H.	(1988, Oct. 15).	Keynote address. Pp. 7–10.
Kennedy, E. M.	(1980, Sept. 15).	Principles of Democratic Party. Pp. 714–15.
Martin, L.	(1992, Sept. 15).	We who have dared to dream. Pp. 723–25.
McGovern, G.	(1972, Aug. 1).	Acceptance speech. Pp. 610–12.
Mondale, W.	(1980, Sept. 15).	Acceptance speech. Pp. 710–13.
Mondale, W.	(1984, Aug. 15).	Acceptance speech. Pp. 642–44.
Nixon, R. M.	(1972, Sept. 15).	Acceptance speech. Pp. 706–9.
Ortega, K. D.	(1984, Sept. 15).	Keynote address. Pp. 712–13.
Quayle, D.	(1992, Sept. 15).	The family comes first: Acceptance speech. Pp. 711–12.
Quayle, M.	(1992, Aug. 19).	Speech at the Republican National Convention (prespeech release text). Available from CRTNet, an electronic newsletter. File #607.
Reagan, R.	(1980, Aug. 15).	Acceptance speech. Pp. 642–46.
Reagan, R.	(1984, Sept. 15).	Acceptance speech. Pp. 706–10.
Reagan, R.	(1992, Sept. 15).	America's best days are yet to come. Pp. 715–17.
Richards, A.	(1988, Aug. 15).	Keynote address. Pp. 647–49.

ELEVEN

Managing Perceptions of Public Opinion

Candidates' and Journalists' Reactions
to the 1992 Polls

SANDRA BAUMAN AND SUSAN HERBST

Now that polling has become an integral part of most national campaigns and the media reports about those campaigns, candidates and journalists have been forced to create a new language—a language that enables them to respond to survey results. Although polls have been a pervasive part of campaigns since the 1960s, an enormous number of surveys were published during the 1992 presidential campaign. A study of the print media revealed that over 130 national polls were published from early June 1992 through Election Day (Miller, 1993).[1] One interesting and understudied aspect of poll reporting concerns the way that political actors (candidates, their managers, and journalists) react to the public polls. What types of rhetorical approaches do candidates and managers take when surveys indicate that they are losing? And how did this discourse look in the specific circumstances of the 1992 campaign involving George Bush, Bill Clinton, and Ross Perot? This chapter attempts to answer these questions, and raises other questions about how polls are reported in the media. We begin with a brief discussion of some recent literature about polls. Next, we analyze how the "horse race" (presidential preference polls) was reported in five major daily newspapers during the last two months of the campaign. In our evaluation of media coverage, we focus on how candidates reacted to public polls, and how their managers tried to put a "spin" on survey results, as well as themes in journalistic discourse about polls.

241

CANDIDATES, POLLS, AND MEDIA

Polling has been a vital part of national American political campaigns since the early decades of the nineteenth century, when party activists, journalists, and citizens conducted numerous straw polls before elections (Herbst, 1993a). These unscientific polls were popular in the highly charged partisan atmosphere of the nineteenth century. Men took politics very seriously; voter turnout was high as was involvement in politics. Since those early years, communications technology has become more sophisticated, and computers have been introduced into the polling process. And these advances in technology, driven by a general trend toward increasing rationalization of the public sphere (Habermas, 1989), have made polls even more valuable and authoritative for candidates and journalists.

Bruce Altschuler (1982) predicted that all future presidential candidates would have pollsters as influential advisers, and his predictions have become a reality. Since Jimmy Carter's campaign in 1976, all major presidential candidates and presidents have relied upon pollsters to gauge the public sentiment. These men (and a handful of women) have come from the rather quiet world of social science research, but are now minor celebrities: Patrick Caddell, Robert Teeter, Richard Wirthlin, Peter Hart (Moore, 1992). During Reagan's White House years, Wirthlin stayed on the team, meeting regularly with the president, his aides, and Nancy Reagan (Honomichl, 1984; Moore, 1992). Perhaps the newest name on this all-star pollster list is Stanley Greenberg, President Clinton's pollster. Like Wirthlin, he moved from the campaign to the Clinton administration, in order to oversee polling, and meets personally with the president on a regular basis.

To give some idea of the amount candidates spend on polling, Greenberg estimates that the Clinton campaign spent a total of $125 million on the entire campaign, with a very large (but unspecified) portion of that money spent on polling and focus group testing (Greenberg, 1993). Clinton's team conducted national polls weekly from June through Labor Day, twice a week through September, and three times a week during October. Focus groups were conducted every couple of weeks until October, and were then run four nights a week with two groups each night. Polling was an integral part of the Clinton campaign, Greenberg notes, and "there was no limit to research spending."

Just as the number of private polls conducted by campaigns has increased with each presidential election, so has the number of public polls sponsored by the media. In 1972 two organizations conducted three polls; in 1980 seven organizations conducted 122 polls; and in 1988 eight organizations conducted 259 polls (Ladd and Benson, 1992). The *New York Times* alone conducted 80,000 interviews in 31 polls at a cost of $1.5 million in 1988 (Lavrakas, 1991; Mann and Orren, 1992). The *Los Angeles Times* conducted twice as many polls before the 1988 election as they did before the 1984 election, with 88 percent more respondents (Lewis, 1991).

Campaigns use media polls, in addition to their own surveys, and most pollsters acknowledge that they monitor as many public polls as they can. Greenberg and Fred Steeper, Bush's pollster, both maintained averages of media poll results during the Bush–Clinton campaign, and used them in conjunction with their private polls to make decisions and plot strategies. How candidates choose to react to public polls is a vital part of the campaign planning. According to Harrison Hickman (1991), candidates' reactions to public polls are a function of actual standings and expectations. Campaign strategy calls for a positive approach when results show the candidate doing better than the public expected. When exceeded expectations are combined with high candidate standing, the campaign usually seeks to disseminate the results widely and to defend the poll's validity. In these cases, the candidates attempt to take advantage of the good news through their comments to reporters. In addition, candidates stress that they are doing better than expected, and call attention to the positive trend in comparison with previous polls. Campaign strategy calls for a negative approach when candidates fare worse than expected. Candidates usually take a disconfirming approach and use a variety of tactics to undermine both the credibility of the poll and its significance. Those around a candidate try to put the results in the "best light" while attacking the poll's methodology—an ironic practice that is reversed if the results are in the candidate's favor. Another strategy is to ignore the results and hope that the poll does not get much media attention. Yet the media invest far too much money in polls to ignore them, so a more common strategy is for the candidate to limit comments to reporters and save significant campaign pronouncements and events for the next news cycle (Hickman, 1991). Regardless of where the candidate finds himself in the expectations game, he can usually "spin" some good news for his campaign and some bad news for an opponent's, argues Hickman. Generally, candidates' reactions can be seen as trying to exploit polls when results are favorable to them, and to distract the public's attention when the results are unfavorable (see also Kagay, 1991).

In this chapter, we focus on media polls published in newspapers, and also on campaign officials' references to private campaign polls. Using the 1992 campaign as a case study, we argue that a new form of political discourse about polls has emerged as polling becomes more central to American politics.

PARTISAN REACTIONS TO THE 1992 POLLS

In order to understand how candidates, consultants, and candidates' (or parties') pollsters react to published polls, we collected all articles that mentioned polls from September 1, 1992 through Election Day in five newspapers: the *New York Times,* the *Washington Post,* the *Chicago Tribune,* the *Chicago Sun-Times,* and the *Los Angeles Times.*[2] In some of these articles, poll results were simply mentioned by the journalists, while other articles were devoted to extensive analysis of recent surveys. Articles where polls were referred to but where no data were published were not included in the sample.[3]

While one could conceivably conduct a quantitative content analysis of these articles, a qualitative, interpretive analysis is far more appropriate and revealing. Polls are discussed in so many different ways, by so many different political actors, that a systematic coding scheme that truly captures the texture of polling discourse would have far too many categories with small entries. This study is intended to be a suggestive, not definitive, evaluation of one form of campaign rhetoric.

Reactions to polling, and discussions of survey data, produce a sort of "heteroglossia" (Bakhtin, 1981): There are a multitude of sublanguages *within* language about polling. Of most interest to students of political communication are the nature of these sublanguages, the reasons for their existence, and how they resonate with each other. The articles we collected were saturated with political rhetoric on the part of journalists, campaign managers, and candidates themselves. Yet we chose to focus on how a variety of actors, presented (usually by the journalist writing the article) with poll data, reacted to those data—the kinds of arguments they make in reaction to the numbers.

There were four particularly interesting themes in the reactions to polls, published in these five major urban dailies. Most of these reactions are from Bush campaign officials, who battled the polls constantly throughout the summer and fall of 1992. Candidates and managers who have the polls on their side, as Clinton did in the 1992 campaign, try not to appear smug in the light of their impending victory, so they often simply reiterate that the campaign is not over and that they are still working fervently in order to win. In contrast, Republicans were always "spinning," even when things looked bleakest. On October 18, for example, Republican pollster Linda DiVall said, "Right now I'd say the race is basically a flat line on the screen." Yet she followed up her negative comment by noting that Bush could still win the election (*New York Times,* p. A10).

The first reaction of candidates and campaign managers to negative poll results is the "it's still early" response. This reaction is nearly routine during campaigns, since it is the truth: Theoretically, anything could happen in the weeks or even hours before the polls open on Election Day. Regardless of their privately held beliefs about the election outcome, candidates and campaign officials try to emphasize the notion that the polls do not matter, despite the fact that they do. Robert Teeter, who was often quoted on polling matters, simply dismissed Bush's negative poll standing early in the campaign. On September 1, after both party conventions had ended, he told a reporter for Reuters that the "polls conducted to date had little significance" (*Chicago Tribune*, p. 4). Over a month and a half later, though, when things still looked grim for Bush, Teeter had to provide a more convincing reaction. On October 19, 1992 he told the *New York Times*, "We can win and will win. It's also going to be tough. . . . I think people decided they want to sit and watch the four debates and then begin to make up their minds. . . . The real trick is to get people focused on their choice and really drive that point home for two weeks" (p. A1). Up until the end, Republicans like Teeter argued that critical events could still turn the electorate around in a dramatic fashion. This sort of comment assumes that public opinion is not as stable as it might appear; that it is actually weak and malleable. It is always in the best interest of the trailing candidate's team to argue for a fickle view of the public mood, while those who lead in the race want to believe that public opinion is motionless and placid.

A more interesting sort of reaction to polls in 1992 was to attack the pollsters and journalists or pundits who reported survey results. This form of argumentation is as old as the sample survey itself, but Harry Truman perfected the rhetorical form in the days before the 1948 election. Although the major pollsters believed Truman would lose to Dewey, Truman refused to give in to the sentiment, and often poked fun at pollsters. He continued this practice as president (Herbst, 1993a). Even Michael Dukakis, who spoke very little about the polls during his 1988 bid for the presidency, attacked polls in the final days of the campaign. Following in this tradition, George Bush made repeated verbal assaults against pollsters and pundits during rallies and television appearances. Pollsters were, in Bush's view, alternatively "sorry" (*Chicago Tribune*, Oct. 24, 1992, p. 2) and "nutty" (*New York Times*, Oct. 23, 1992, p. A12).

Attacks on the pollsters are an effective form of rhetoric at campaign rallies, since survey researchers are an easy target: They are the bearers of bad news. It is nearly impossible for pollsters to answer these sorts of verbal assaults, since they are unspecific. Bush did not, to our knowledge, single out any pollsters to admonish, and never levelled specific charges about the logic or methodology of polling. To call them "nutty" makes pollsters sound unscientific, which undermines their legitimacy, since polling is a form of social science research. Attacking the pollsters seems a desperate form of argumentation, especially since it tends to come at the end of a losing campaign. It is the last resort, since little time remains for major policy speeches or events that might reverse public opinion.

Interestingly, attacks on pollsters, and on the practice of polling, are also implicit warnings about so-called bandwagon effects. Assaults on polling as a form of measurement are an attempt to distract people from the surveys, in hopes that they will not be influenced by them. Although empirical evidence for preelection bandwagon effects is scanty (Merkle, 1991), many public leaders, journalists, and campaign workers fear such movements of public opinion. In his "nutty pollsters" comments, Bush was trying to weaken the potential (or imagined) influence of polls on voters.

Another approach that candidates and their managers take when confronted with negative polls is to battle public polls with their own private polls. Rarely do campaign officials provide estimates from their private polls, or even hint at the methodology used in these surveys. Yet this secrecy does not stop campaign spokespeople from citing their private data, claiming that it is somehow superior to the polls we find in newspapers and television news broadcast reports. Jeb Bush, President Bush's son, often spoke to the news media about his father's campaign and the polls. He told the *New York Times* on September 17, 1992 that public poll data were simply wrong. He hinted at private poll data, although his comments were far less sophisticated than those of more experienced campaign managers: "Intuitively, I think we are ahead and in a close race. . . . That's my own feeling, but how does one really know? The good news for us is that our Republican base is back and we're doing well in conservative Democratic areas, and that is enough to win in [Florida]." He also made reference to the "it's still early" notion: "Whether we are up or down right now, we have a plan. . . . And that plan is not predicated by what the polls show in September" (p. A10). Campaign officials like Charles Black were more blunt, simply telling a *New York Times* reporter that the campaign's private polls showed Clinton slipping (Oct. 18, 1992, p. A1).

More interesting than vague references to their private surveys or research, though, is the sort of statistical dance that a losing campaign must do to save face and keep loyalists focused on victory. Although campaign officials are most likely to claim that Election Day is far off or that polls are unreliable, they must occasionally resort to quantitative arguments themselves. *New York Times* journalist Andrew Rosenthal reported on a particularly interesting example of statistical jousting, while he covered the final days of the campaign:

> On his way [to Montana and South Dakota] the President stopped off in Detroit, to focus on the sort of thing that Gov. John Engler of Michigan was calling "data bits"—ever-thinner slices of the voting public, modest policy proposals and the fine details of the electoral map. . . . Clearly uncomfortable, Mr. Engler acknowledged that internal Republican polls essentially reflect the results of published surveys, which show no movement for Mr. Bush. But he said that when the polls were dissected into "likely voters" and then into unspecified "competitive legislative districts," Mr. Bush had gained a point or two. Although such movements would be of no statistical

significance, Mr. Engler said that these "data bits" can be glued together into a national picture. "When we push that likely voter component, that's where we're seeing movement," Mr. Engler said.

Rosenthal, apparently unable to let Engler's nonsensical remarks stand without qualification, noted that Michael Dukakis had also claimed a "last-minute surge" at the end of the 1988 campaign. To this, Engler "snapped" that Dukakis did not really have a surge at all (Oct. 26, 1992, p. A12).

Engaging in hand-to-hand combat, using statistics as weapons, might seem to be a very compelling way to respond to poor poll standings. Surprisingly, though, candidates and campaign managers are not particularly interested in, or adept at, this sort of quarrel. In the nineteenth century, party leaders and loyalists were constantly engaged in a war of numbers during campaigns (Herbst, 1993a), yet this form of argumentation has declined instead of becoming more common. The reason has something to do with the rise of opinion polling as a profession. Pollsters, even if they are partisans working for campaigns, know that the campaign is short, and that they will be looking for other clients afterwards. Even the regular party pollsters, however, need to maintain their reputations for integrity and competence *within* the survey research community. These professionals are probably reluctant to engage in statistical arguments in public, when their colleagues in other firms have come to a consensus about the standings of the candidates. As a result, men like Teeter do not want to reveal details of their own polls, or engage in specific discussions of survey data. They are happy to make vague and often mysterious references to their own superior poll data.

Opinion polling is such a critical aspect of the campaign, and the reporting about campaigns, that survey numbers seem to have a life of their own: Public opinion becomes reified through the numbers, as candidates, campaign workers, and journalists speak of statistics "doing" things. It was Walter Lippmann (1925) who argued most eloquently that public opinion was itself a reification—a "phantom" invented by journalists. The reification of public opinion has become even more apparent with the rise of polling, however, since numbers seem to concretize the nebulous public mood.[4] In an effort to make themselves look rational and scientific, campaign officials and more objective commentators will react to poll data without ever referring to human beings: For the purposes of campaign polling, people area represented by statistics, so it is not necessary to refer to them at all. In a comment to the *Washington Post* on October 29, Robert Teeter said, "The key now is you've got to see continued movement [in the polls]. . . . That may or may not be dependent on Perot" (p. A10). We find a similar comment in a "Political Memo" from the September 7, 1992 edition of the New York Times: "Bush can't win without that [favorability] number moving," said Mr. Mahe, the veteran Republican strategist. "If the Clinton unfavorable doesn't move, then the result in the final analysis can't be a great deal different than it is now" (p. 8).

One might argue that this sort of talk about polls is simply a type of shorthand used by campaign analysts pressed for time. And that may be the case, since the discourse is very economical—no wasted words, just the numbers. But we believe that these types of comments echo what Baudrillard (1988), the postmodern theorist, has argued about polling: that polling distances citizens (or readers of a newspaper) from their own opinions. In other words, poll numbers are a "force" that seems unattached to people themselves. Baudrillard argues that we are "constantly confronted with statistical verification of our own behavior," but that the true nature of public feeling (if it exists at all), and real debate between factions with the public, becomes crushed in a sea of numbers with no human referents at all:

> We are no longer confronted with our own will. We are no longer
> even alienated, because for that it is necessary for the subject to be
> divided in itself, confronted with the other, to be contradictory. . . .
> Each individual is forced despite himself or herself into the undi-
> vided coherency of statistics. (p. 210, emphasis added)

One finds, in the coverage of the 1992 polls, that discourse about numbers is a sublanguage with a kind of "coherency." As a result, pollsters and journalists can speak of polls as actors, even if they are simply representatives of actors (citizens). Regardless of what campaign officials and journalists mean when they discuss survey data, their talk implies that numbers "do things." And if numbers can act as a force, only marginally connected to what real people think, they gain a certain amount of authority and legitimacy. It is this autonomy of numbers, implied by political actors, we believe, which makes polling feel so oppressive during campaigns.[5]

THEMES IN THE COVERAGE OF POLLS

Political communication scholars have long been interested in the ways that journalists report on and use polls (e.g., Paletz et al., 1980). And the poll reports from the five newspapers we studied do not differ very much from those of other recent presidential election campaigns. The polls are used in "horse race" style coverage, as a way to involve readers in the excitement of the race. At times, polls are briefly cited, while at others, a journalist engages in more sustained analysis of what the numbers mean. A common type of article evaluates state polls, in order to figure out who will win the electoral votes in those states (e.g., *New York Times*, Nov. 1, 1992, p. A1).

While each of the five newspapers we examined had its strengths and weaknesses when it came to reporting on the polls, journalists writing for the

New York Times tended to be the most cautious in their articles about surveys. The *Times* most consistently reported multiple poll results, from different pollsters, in order to give its readers some sense of the variance among surveys. While other papers published these sorts of reports on occasion, the *Times* did it consistently throughout the final weeks of the campaign. The effects of these reports, which demonstrated how professionals trained in the same social science methodologies could come up with different predictions, are unclear: What did readers take away from these reports? While difficult to explore empirically, since many citizens are already dubious about the reliability of polling data, it is likely that multiple, varying results increased the public's skepticism even further (despite the fact that the pollsters, with the exception of Gallup, were fairly accurate in their preelection predictions).

In trying to interpret poll results, journalists sometimes assume causality, connecting campaign events to movement in the polling numbers. The entrance, exit, and return of Ross Perot made fluctuating polls difficult to interpret, since he clearly had effects on a variety of survey results. While journalists at the *Times* were careful not to make authoritative statements about the reasons for moving poll numbers, on occasion they hinted at such reasons while trying to interpret polls. For example, in an October 31, 1992 "round-up" of the polls entitled "Surveys Vary," the *Times* noted that "Two new polls show Gov. Bill Clinton retaining his lead over President Bush, while two other polls show the race virtually even. Ross Perot's support has dropped since he accused the Bush campaign of threatening to disrupt his daughter's wedding" (p. A6). While it is entirely likely that Perot's accusation caused a drop in his support, the journalist really had no evidence of causality in this regard. This sort of theorizing is to be expected in poll reports, as journalists try to make sense of the constantly moving numbers—even when the changes are small and within the range of sampling error.

While the papers in this study carried a variety of editorials and op-ed pieces that favored one candidate or another, journalists were careful not to introduce much partisan bias into the reporting of polls. The *Chicago Tribune*, however, allowed the occasional mixing of editorial remarks with poll reporting, as in this front-page story by Charles Madigan:

> Arkansas Gov. Bill Clinton has a strong advantage over President Bush and Texas businessman Ross Perot in all the national polls, and individual state polls taken at various points over the past month give him far more than the 270 electoral votes he needs to push Bush from the White House. That is not to say Bush cannot still win in this unusual election year. Clinton's support has never been as solid as the polling numbers might indicate, with about half his backing coming from people who readily admit they are casting votes against Bush. (Oct. 25, 1992, p. 1)

In this excerpt, Madigan writes as though polling data are not firm, but provides little explanation of what he means. What do firm election polling data look like? Is he arguing that intended votes for Clinton are simply protest votes? If so, why does that make these votes *unstable?* It is likely that Madigan either allowed his partisanship to slip into the article, or was simply trying to keep the horse race alive, so the piece would be more engaging for his readers.

Flaws like the ones in Madigan's piece are not a serious problem in the journalistic discourse about campaign polling. The more significant and disturbing problem with poll reporting is that journalists are still both ambivalent and confused about how to use poll data, despite the fact that the sample survey has been available since the 1936 election. During the 1992 primary season and campaign, newspapers carried a variety of articles and opinion pieces about the problems associated with polls—the notion that polling is both an "art" and a "science." Such articles are an attempt to comfort readers, who may blame their confusion about varying poll results on their own lack of sophistication or education in these matters. A good example of this type of article was published in the *Washington Post* by Richard Morin. Morin introduced his technical explanation of sampling error this way:

> Poll-watchers might be forgiven if they felt whiplashed after reading the results of the latest two *Washington Post*–ABC News presidential preference polls. Last week, the poll was the toast of Little Rock after it found Democrat Bill Clinton with a 21-percentage point lead over President Bush. The latest survey might bring cheers at the White House, as it found the Arkansas governor with a nine-point advantage. A Clinton collapse? A Bush surge? Perhaps, but probably not. (Sept. 29, 1992, p. 6)

The *Chicago Sun-Times* also ran an article about confusing poll results in September, with the headline, "Pollsters Downplay Confusing Results" (Sept. 13, 1992, p. 18). As a "sidebar" to this piece, they also published a short article from the Gannett News Service, quoting a polling critic who called the confusion over survey results "a delightful development." While pollsters and journalists do the best they can, trying to explain why polls differ, they sometimes try to use statistical terminology that probably just confuses readers further. An example is this excerpt from the *Chicago Tribune*'s Jon Margolis:

> That trend [showing Bush closing the gap] was what statisticians call "'regression to the mean," with the top going down, the bottom going up, and the middle staying where it was, raising the possibility that each of the three candidates would soon have the support of about one-third of the electorate. (Oct. 26, 1992, p. 1).

"Regression to the mean" is undoubtedly meaningless to any reader who has not had a course or two in advanced statistics. It is not clear from this article that Margolis himself understood the concept, or knew how to write about it.

Among the many ironies of the 1992 campaign is that journalists recognized alienation and cynicism in the electorate, but rarely realized that surveys might contribute to that cynicism. And how does one measure or report on cynicism? By polling, of course. *New York Times* reporter Maureen Dowd reported in late September that

> According to a Time/CNN poll conducted last week, . . . sixty-three percent have little or no confidence that government leaders talk straight. Seventy-five percent believe there is less honesty in government than there was a decade ago. Forty percent say George Bush does not usually tell the truth, and 36 say that about Bill Clinton. (Sept. 29, 1992, p. A10)

In typical journalistic fashion, Dowd reports these data uncritically, and without putting them in historical perspective. At what point in time did Americans trust their leaders? Is the current lack of trust real, or are people in part mimicking what cynical journalists tell them? Dowd never raises such questions, even though they would enable her readers to interpret the poll more intelligently.

CONCLUSIONS

Polls have become so pervasive in American political campaigns that we have learned to live with them: We expect to see daily figures on the presidential race, in order to find out how our favored candidate is doing. Journalists find the polls very useful as well, and build stories around the horse race. Finally, candidates themselves have constructed a variety of rhetorical techniques to shape the statistical discourse of the campaign. The effect of these techniques is difficult to isolate empirically, and therefore hard to measure, but the art of discrediting the polls will probably become increasingly refined and sophisticated as survey research becomes more sophisticated: Rhetoric about polls must change to "keep up" with the quality of polls, so new discursive inventions are critical for candidates and their spokespeople.

Interestingly, in 1992, while Bush eventually attacked the pollsters himself, most of the rhetorical work with regard to "spinning" the polls was conducted by campaign professionals and not by the candidates themselves. Perhaps candidates prefer not to engage in messy statistical battles, leaving this dirty work to campaign operatives. If candidates spend too much time attacking the polls and the pollsters, they will appear to be distracted from the issues and the race itself. Attacks on polls are too technical and not emotionally compelling.

In terms of democratic theory, the most interesting thing about campaigns' reactions to polls is that they contribute to a relatively new (still evolving) form of political discourse. Since the early Greek democracies, people have debated about the nature of public opinion. But only recently has the debate over the character of public opinion been tied (at times, almost exclusively) to polling data. Fights over numbers began in the nineteenth century, but the nature of these disputes has changed somewhat in the twentieth century, becoming a bit more subtle and multifaceted. That such debates about assessing the national mood distract voters and journalists from issues is obvious. Yet this distraction is an inevitable outcome of our nearly obsessive concern with opinion measurement.

NOTES

* This essay was originally written for this book. It has also been published in *Political Communication* 11, No. 2 (April–June 1994), 133–144.

1. This is a very conservative figure, though, given how many state polls and unscientific straw polls one also found on the evening news and in newspapers.

2. These five papers were chosen because of their wide circulation, as well as the diversity of their editorial politics. Other newspapers with large readerships (e.g., the *Atlanta Constitution*) might have been included, but we feel as though the five studied here are reasonable "representatives" of the larger universe of important American dailies.

3. Counting the number of "articles" we analyzed is problematic, since brief mentions of polls and long articles devoted entirely to polls are very different types of news items. The total number of articles examined, including long and short pieces, was seventy-seven. To give a better idea of the nature of the sample, though, we can report that the *Los Angeles Times* and the *Washington Post* both published poll results of some sort on eight days during the sample period. The *Chicago Tribune* included poll data on sixteen days during the period, while the *Chicago Sun-Times* had fifteen. The *New York Times* published the most articles on polls during this period—on twenty-four days during the period of interest. Since this canvass of articles was done "by hand," it is possible that a few articles with very brief mentions of polling numbers might have been excluded from the sample. This is not problematic, for our purposes though, since we are most interested in *sustained* discussions of polling data.

4. On the reification of the public mood, see Bourdieu (1979), Blumer (1948), Ginsberg (1986), and Herbst (1993b).

5. On the reification of polls and the way they stifle public discourse (during and between campaigns), see Ginsberg (1986) or Herbst (1993a, 1993b).

REFERENCES

Altschuler, B. E. (1982). *Keeping a finger on the public pulse: Private polling and presidential elections.* Westport, Conn.: Greenwood.

Bakhtin, M. (1981). *The dialogic imagination.* Ed. C. Emerson and M. Holquist. Austin: University of Texas Press.

Baudrillard, J. (1988). *Selected writings.* Ed. M. Poster. Stanford, Calif.: Stanford University Press.

Blumer, H. (1948). Public Opinion and Public Opinion Polling. *American Sociological Review,* Vol. 13, pp. 242–49.

Bourdieu, P. (1979). Public Opinion Does Not Exist. In A. Mattelart and S. Siegelaub, eds., *Communication and Class Struggle.* New York: International General.

Gallup, G., and S. Rae (1940). *The pulse of democracy: The public opinion poll and how it works.* New York: Simon and Schuster.

Ginsberg, B. (1986). *The captive public: How mass opinion promotes state power.* New York: Basic.

Graber, D. A. (1989). *Mass media and American politics.* 3rd ed. Washington, D. C.: Congressional Quarterly Press.

Greenberg, S. (1993, May). Public opinion in the campaign and in the White House. Speech presented at the forty-eighth annual conference of the American Association for Public Opinion Research, St. Charles, Ill.

Habermas, J. (1989). *The structural transformation of the public sphere: An inquiry into a category of bourgeois society.* Cambridge: MIT.

Herbst, S. (1995). On the disappearance of groups: Nineteenth and early twentieth century conceptions of public opinion. In C. Salmon and T. Glasser, eds., *Public opinion and the communication of consent.* New York: Guilford.

Herbst, S. (1993a). *Numbered voices: How opinion polling has shaped American politics.* Chicago: University of Chicago Press.

Herbst, S. (1993b). The meaning of public opinion: Citizens' constructions of political reality. *Media, Culture and Society,* 15, 437–54.

Hickman, H. (1991). Public polls and election participants. In P. J. Lavrakas and J. K. Holley, eds., *Polling and presidential election coverage.* Newbury Park, Calif.: Sage, pp. 100–133.

Honomichl, J. J. (1984). *Marketing research people: Their behind-the-scenes stories.* Chicago: Crain Books.

Kagay, M. R. (1991). The use of public opinion polls by the *New York Times*: Some examples from the 1988 presidential election. In P. J. Lavrakas and J. K. Holley, eds., *Polling and presidential election coverage.* Newbury Park, Calif.: Sage, pp. 19–56.

Ladd, E. C., and J. Benson (1992). The growth of news polls in American politics. In T. E. Mann and G. R. Orren, eds., *Media polls in American politics.* Washington, D. C.: The Brookings Institution, pp. 19–31.

Lavrakas, P. J. (1991). Introduction. In P. J. Lavrakas and J. K. Holley, eds., *Polling and presidential election coverage.* Newbury Park, Calif.: Sage, pp. 9–18.

Lewis, I. A. (1991). Media polls, the *Los Angeles Times* poll, and the 1988 presidential election. In P. J. Lavrakas and J. K. Holley, eds., *Polling and presidential election coverage.* Newbury Park, Calif.: Sage, pp. 57–82.

Lippmann, W. (1925). *The phantom public.* New York: Harcourt, Brace.

Mann, T. E. and G. R. Orren (1992). To poll or not to poll . . . and other questions. In T. E. Mann and G. R. Orren, eds., *Media polls in American politics.* Washington, D. C.: The Brookings Institution, pp. 1–18.

Merkle, D. M. (1991, May). The effects of opinion poll results on public opinion: A review and synthesis of bandwagon and underdog research. Paper presented at the forty-first annual conference of the International Communication Association, Chicago.

Miller, P. V. (1993). The 1992 horse race in the polls. In W. Crotty, ed., *America's choice: The election of 1992.* Guilford, Conn.: Dushkin, pp. 139–48.

Moore, D. W. (1992). *The superpollsters: How they measure and manipulate public opinion in America.* New York: Four Walls Eight Windows.

Paletz, D. L., J. Y. Short, H. Baker, B. C. Campbell, R. J. Cooper, and R. M. Oeslander (1980). Polls in the media: Content, credibility and consequences. *Public Opinion Quarterly, 44,* 495–513.

TWELVE

Presidential Endings

Conceding Defeat

PAUL E. CORCORAN

Losing a presidential election is not a pretty sight. Dwelling on defeat in public contradicts a basic American commitment to success. Why not turn the public gaze to the triumphant winner, drawing a veil of silence over the despair, anger, shame, and crushed hopes of defeat? For a culture devoted to being "No. 1," there might have been a taboo, consigning defeat to the metaphysical nothingness it deserves: Winning is not everything, it is the *only* thing.

On the contrary, in American presidential politics losing is an elaborate ritual. Conceding defeat is a theme composed in a minor key, sounding the tragic undertones of high political drama.[1] Yet a rite of capitulation acknowledges that electoral politics survives as a restaging of mortal combat, in which military virtues and heroic victory necessarily involve a worthy sacrifice, the conquest of a noble enemy. Where is the glory in extinguishing an ignoble foe?

THE RHETORIC OF VICTORY AND DEFEAT

Winning

A victorious presidential election campaign is a triumph, but hardly an end to the campaign. For the winner and his[2] supporters, there is euphoria, as near to ecstasy as politics can be. Military and athletic metaphors reciprocate in celebration of an outcome that an hour before was a one percent margin. So the victory speech is inevitably a continuation of the strutting and posturing of battle, the winner's *spolia opima*.[3]

In victory, the campaign continues, not only to wage the wars of office but to commence immediately the campaign for reelection. The president has not been elected to retire from the field of battle. Thus electoral triumph is incomplete, penultimate, a prelude. The puffery and promises must continue. Public relations tactics survive unabated for the half-way house status of the "president-elect." Inauguration, with its artifice of pomp and circumstance, is months away.

On Election Night the winning candidate may *experience* the end of his toil, but in the moment of triumph this cannot be truthfully spoken. What he *feels*, the imagination easily supplies. He is overwhelmed by a sweet flood of joy, an incomparable wave of relief, a surge of self-love. His profoundest desire for power and recognition is utterly satisfied. Yet winning has its terrors: fear of vast expectations, trepidation that his talents will be exposed as too weak for the task, that his character is too small for the legendary role he is now to enact. Is it unworthy even to have such feelings? Can he block out what he had to do and fail to do, say and fail to say, feel and pretend not to feel to win this prize? About these compelling truths one cannot, must not, give a speech.

The victory speech, then, is merely a continuation of all that has gone before: the campaigner's pretense of righteousness, omnipotence, and inevitability. Caution enters as the one new theme. Even on the feverish election night, candidates begin to speak anxiously of a "smooth transition." In the flush of victory, the winner will pay some final homage to charting a course to different coordinates, but financial markets and military complexes the world over will be reassured that America will chart a steady course.

By January, the victory will be transmuted into history. The inaugural[4] address, a prophetic ritual of "new beginnings," will gravely stress continuities. The ship of state plies ponderously on, barely deflected in its course by the democratic review in that long-ago November. The newly (re)elected president is no longer a celebrant, a mere possessor of a narrow margin in anything so serendipitous as a rough and tumble, gimmicky vote. The president-elect is already an icon, not a "winner" but The President. The "new" president now offers himself as a "renewal" of values centuries old. Momentum is all. Promises will, of course, be kept if Congress joins ranks as it has never done before. The "new beginnings" solemnly intoned at the inaugural are mere survivals of the campaign, a reminder that the battle continues. There are no endings here.

Losing

Amidst the noise and high-tech fakery of the modern political campaign there remains one quaint requisite harking back to blood sport and mortal combat. Conquest requires an anticlimactic scene, a final revelation of defeat. It has been long anticipated by pollsters, the general public, one's campaign organization, and even the candidate's sleepless dreams. Yet defeat—an unbearably public humiliation, a still unexpiated inner grief, anger, sorrow, and mortification—barely an hour old, must speak itself. On the heels of crushed hopes is a final ordeal, the concession speech.

It is not surprising that commonplaces have evolved for such a painful ceremony. Metaphorically, it is a fate worse than death: not simply to bow to the conquering foe, but to declare his triumph. Bloodied but unbowed, the conquered warrior must offer the wreath of victory to his sworn enemy. The concession speech also is an opportunity—he is, after all, a lifelong politician—to show that he has not gained the palm of martyrdom, but merely lost on points. Suddenly the metaphors of war, the bravado of mortal combat, give way to gallantry, sport. What was until hours ago a fateful struggle for national survival now suddenly is a test of chivalry: the loser's still ardent loyalty to Rousseau's queen of democracy, public opinion.

The rhetorical challenge is to portray one's own defeat as a chapter of honor in the nation's history, to put a brave face on failure, transforming defeat into a semblance of victory. To concede[5] is a means of preempting defeat, to yield the ground, grant victory to the opponent. Seize the initiative, make a "gracious" retreat; get it over with before the votes are officially counted.

With an unwonted tone of respect, the television anchor man informs the viewing public that the defeated candidate is about to concede. It is an unlikely setting for noble virtue, a scene of exhaustion and hollow joy at a "victory party" amidst the folly of a hotel "ballroom" and the clutter of television weaponry. Brought onto a veritable stage, the candidate responds in mock heartiness to the strained cheers arising from the pall of sorrow, anger, and exposed illusions. What he is about to announce the television networks projected in solemn finality hours ago. As silence falls, the candidate admits what he has for months denied. A year's declarations of certain victory must now in five minutes be transformed into a gallant fight against "the odds," a brave struggle for a worthy cause. Though doomed to failure on this day, the "fight" goes on. An opponent likened to a traducer, a hypocrite, an incompetent, must now be congratulated. Loyal supporters must be urged to join ranks with the enemy for a greater glory.

Until this moment, news reporters have pilloried him, scorning his optimism and trivializing his efforts. For months they have taunted him with unfavorable polling figures, condemning him to certain debacle at the polls. Why now the sudden deference, toleration, and fellow-feeling from the television troubadours and inky scribblers? Surprisingly, there are interesting answers to these questions. Presidential defeat is theater of a high sort. Its resonance with classical drama is more compelling than the rhetoric of victory. There is much to do here with death: its taboos and shame, its unspeakable finality, its inescapable public sorrow.

A presidential campaign needs a good ending, a desire extending beyond the defeated politician to all participants and witnesses. For a brief moment, democracy's reject is the center of attention. The loser, alone, can truly "congratulate" the winner and at the same time absolve the electoral process of its enormities. Only the loser can be "gracious." How could the winner—hoarse, drunk on the liquors of victory, proud, struggling to contain the gambler's delirium—possibly be gracious? Now, suddenly, the winning camp *needs* to have had a formidable adversary to ennoble its victorious achievement. The loser's benediction is solicited by the media-chorus, and eagerly awaited by the sequestered hero. Whatever the vanquished might say in the received formulas of surrender—he will certainly not "*concede defeat,*" but it will be said that he has done so—his concession will be reported as "very gracious indeed."

Analogy as Metaphor

The end of a drama is always a problem. Getting the lights out and the curtain down is the most difficult task facing a modern playwright. It is hard for the audience, too. Especially in contemporary theater, the end of a play—the final scene, the very last line—is a nuisance, fraught with unfashionable meanings most playwrights would positively like to avoid. Just as modern theater is emancipated from strict adherence to classical forms, so it often abjures any obligation to abide by classical rules of dramatic closure: the narrative resolved, emotional catharsis achieved, and a clear moral arising from the finale.

Getting the lights out is even more difficult when theater in the round or a thrust stage consciously intrudes the action into the audience. There *is* no curtain to bring down. Without a proscenium, the play has no physical *cum* metaphorical closure that separates and hides the world of illusion from the relinquished "real" world that is gradually restored to the audience by the house lights. Deprived of the proscenium stage, we are obliged to accept, in the modern democratic tradition, that *we* are the deus ex machina. Gangs of stage lights, sound technicians, and other instruments of illusion are crudely exposed for all to ignore. Purposefully, there is little to support a distinction between "the play" and "reality."

Modern drama in its loosely defined forms—realism, expressionism, the absurd—presents a slice of life in all its humdrum perversities, anxious rituals, and tedium. It concerns itself not with the cosmic or heroic, but with the mundane, the banal, the impenetrably trivial. The focus is not on actions that are larger than life or intentions whose meanings are illuminated by divine truths. Instead we are faced with aims and actions that are utterly physical, nonsensical, absurd. Heroic characters are invariably exposed as shams, hopelessly deluded, pathetic. A complex plot unraveled to a satisfying resolution, or a character evolving a heightened moral consciousness, is exactly contrary to modern and postmodern sensibilities. The idea that "real" stories have a beginning, middle, and end is inherently problematic; the notion that good will triumph—*must* triumph—over evil is scorned.

One classical tradition persists: The stage blacks out. There has to be an "end," and it is awkward when a play ends weakly. We no longer expect a happy, startling, astounding, clever, bittersweet, or shocking ending. Yet we feel a disturbing void if the final scene shifts abruptly to facile symbolism, self-mockery, or surrealism; if the actors' routine business simply continues while the stage lights gradually dim to black; if some sprightly but inconsequential dialogue is cut off in a sudden blackout. Did I miss something? Must I supply the ending? On reflection, we know that the playwright *is* sending us a message. Things do not simply resolve, characters do not really change. This is the way things and people are. Morals to the tale would be gratuitous, false, an insult to our intelligence. The playwright rubs our noses in it, but at the same time respects our intelligence enough not to foist on us a cheap and easy dénouement, the plot neatly resolved, everyone living happily ever after.

The reader will appreciate that I have, by analogy, "set the stage" for a consideration of concession speeches in presidential campaigns. Extending this analogy into a rather ludicrous psychological metaphor expresses my special theme. In the theater of modern election campaigns, the proscenium sits precariously upon a candidate's shoulders.[6]

The curtain rises for the final act, a defeated candidate entering before a cheering throng. Here is the stuff of classical drama, but no less fraught with the absurdist dilemmas of modern theater. Aristotle's types—tragedy, comedy, and epic—remain marvelously apt for what we are likely to see. Paradoxically, modern theater-goers expect *cinema verité*—but of the studio, shooting on location—the open-air rough and tumble of circus-in-the-round: clowns, spin doctors, p.r. trapeze artists, and other exotics. Thus a concession speech is a throwback. In this scene, no one wants *verité*. A bit of illusion will do nicely.

The proscenium sitting precariously upon the candidate's shoulders, only his mind is "backstage," with its unseen dimensions. Despite the intrusions of the electronic media, there is a secret, psychic enigma. What is behind the mask? Despite television "coverage" and the stylized theater of campaign artifice, a tenuous dramatic suspension survives. Perhaps there *is* something real going on in the candidate's mind. Is the "act" real? Does it portray (or betray) "character"? Is the campaign a genuine pageant of common values

and experience, or merely a "play"? These are fine distinctions, but they are
the crucial perceptual valences that determine how journalists write and how
voters cast their ballot.[7]

A CASE IN POINT

The drama of defeat is seldom reflected in the text of a concession speech.
On the evidence of the presidential races since 1952, this is not the moment
for singing phrases and the open hand of eloquence. Hands pressing against
the cheers of his supporters in an obviously impatient and irritated attempt to
silence them, President George Bush brought the 1992 presidential election
to a close with these words:

> Thank you very much.
> Thank you.
> Thank you very much.
> Hey listen, we gotta get goin'.
> Thank you. Thank you very much.
> Hey listen you guys.
> Thank you very much. Look.
> Thank you very much!
> Here's the way I see it.
> Here's the way we see it, and the country should see it, that the
> people have spoken and we respect the majesty of the democratic
> system. I just called Governor Clinton over in Little Rock and
> offered my congratulations. He did run a strong campaign. I wish
> him well in the White House.[8]

The speech rambled on for another five minutes, the syntax garbled and
broken, the delivery stumbling in every phrase.[9] One minute after the above
introduction, Bush said:

> Now, now I ask that we stand behind our new president, and
> regardless of our differences, all Americans shamed it—share the—
> same purpose to make this nation the world's greatest nation more
> safe and more secure and to guarantee every American a shot at the
> American Dream.

Two minutes later, the president had another Freudian *contre temps* with
an sh- word:

> But, uh, tonight is really not a, uh, night for speeches,[10] but I want to
> spare a, sare [sic] a special message with the young people of
> America.

The script in his hand appears to have provided him with the only singing phrase of the speech: "I remain absolutely convinced that we are a rising nation. We have been through an extraordinarily difficult period, but do not be deterred." This "difficult period" was not recession and unemployment in the United States, the collapse of the Soviet Union, or the abortive Gulf War. The difficulties he has in mind—perhaps interpolated extemporaneously[11]—are the "fire of a campaign year or the ugliness of politics." The address closes with a double Freudian slip:

> And again, my thanks, my resp . . . , my congratulations to Governor Clinton, to his running mate, Senator Gore and special thanks to each and every one of you. Many of you have been my side [sic] at every single political battle. May God bless. May God bless the United States of America. Thank you very much. Thank you so much. Thank you.

An hour later in Little Rock, Arkansas, Governor Clinton opens his victory speech by telling the nation that he has received a telephone call from President Bush: "It was a generous and forthcoming telephone call, of real congratulations and an offer to work with me in keeping our democracy running." Clinton went on to express his gratitude for "the grace with which he conceded the results of this election tonight, in the finest American tradition."[12]

The next morning, newspapers followed Clinton's lead: "Facing Bitter Crowd, Bush Exhibits Grace in Defeat." In the following article, the *New York Times* found a "gloomy and sometimes angry post-election gathering." The "mood had been ugly in the cozy ballroom festooned with balloons and Bush–Quayle banners," and "it was left to President Bush to sound a note of grace in defeat" (Wines, 1992, p. B5). The *Los Angeles Times* headline pours a soothing balm on the bloodied gladiator: "For Bush, a Sense of Relief Eases the Disappointment: Combative no more, he is gracious in defeat, urging nation to 'stand behind' successor." The accompanying article is even more imaginatively therapeutic.

> A combative politician no more, Bush turned gracious in defeat. His demeanor was that of an executive suddenly conscious of possibilities he could barely fathom[13] while fighting to keep a hard-charging challenger at bay. (Jehl and Gerstenzang, 1992)

Newsweek's frame for its coverage of the election was epic: "The Torch Passes." Bush's Election Night performance was an "Exit on the High Road," and the "president's weary smile did not betray the shock he must have felt" (McDaniel, 1992). The *National Review*, in the jaundiced euphuisms of William F Buckley Jr. (1992), saw no grace or heroism in the Election Night proceedings. Buckley refused to adopt the clichés of the daily press, finding

"Mr. Bush's congratulatory speech" neither a concession nor gracious, but rather a ritual of duplicity and self-deception.

> He had spent the better part of three months denouncing Bill Clinton as a draft-dodger, as a liar, as an inexperienced yuppie and an ideological menace. . . . [H]ow do you parse such a congratulation? "I want to congratulate Mr. Clinton on his extraordinary skill in disguising his lack of patriotism, his inexperience, his wretched job as governor of Arkansas, and his indifference to family values, sufficiently to seduce the majority of the American people into voting for him." . . . Mr. Bush was engaging in a formality. The whole thing was sad, grotesque, even.

Not all presidential concession speeches have been so garbled and distracted as Bush's. The speeches are rituals with very little scope for complex or expansive rhetorical aims. Nevertheless, the concession speech is a performance, an enactment of meanings and intentions arising less from the rhetorical text/strategy than from the cathartic expectations of large audiences and powerful witnesses.

THE FORMALITIES OF DEFEAT

The televised business of counting votes and projecting wins and losses to each camp is merely a technical skirmish, a suspenseful prelude. The dramatic dénouement comes in a challenge to the loser to "concede defeat," the middle gesture in a rhetorical triad of the press, a defeated candidate, and the winner.

1. The news media, a vicarious public chorus, serve as enforcers of custom and exponents of the public right. They demand a concession/confession of defeat.
2. The loser's concession converts loss into honor: a heroic sacrifice, not to fate, but to the popular will. The speech condones victory to the winning candidate as a noble act in a great epic of democracy and nationhood.
3. The winner acknowledges this concession as gracious, thus magnifying the prize by recognizing the loser as a worthy foe. The victory speech is an epilogue. The curtain is already down.

This rite of succession is not metaphor and dramaturgy, pure and simple. The concession speech is an institutionalized, public speech act integral to democratic life and the legitimacy of authority. It has its own etiquette and symbolism, but the yielding and taking of power is also a practical affair. As one sees throughout the world, the transition of power is a matter of life and death on a grand scale. The drama of concession transcends electoral defeat by translating the meaning of the campaign from the genuine language of combat (real interests in fundamental opposition) into metaphors of chivalry and sport. The concession speech's routine forms of congratulating the winning candidate and declaring this fact to a national audience are important instances of what J. L. Austin (1965, pp. 5–6; Martin, 1987, pp. 87–89) distinguishes as illocutionary and performative speech acts: "To utter the sentence (in, of course, the appropriate circumstances) is not to *describe* . . . or to state that I am doing it: it is to do it." We are painfully aware of the catastrophic consequences obtaining in societies lacking "the appropriate circumstances" for the routine, formulaic yielding of power. The concession speech, then, is not merely a report of an election result or an admission of defeat. It is a constitutive enactment of the new president's authority, and more conducive to the democratic process than the presidential "coronation"—for that is what *that* drama is about—three months hence.[14]

The defeated candidate's courage, in the ancient sense of virtue or manliness,[15] is in doubt until he congratulates his opponent. By the same token, the winner's *gravitas* and dignity are faulted if he claims victory before the loser concedes. There are thus antique moral dimensions in conceding defeat. A concession speech is a form of noble condescension.[16] The candidate publicly condones the vilification visited upon him by his opponent ("it was a hard-fought race") and the humiliations of defeat ("I respect the people's verdict"). By this symbolic condonation, he forgives the depredations of his private and public honor by journalists, comedians, media experts, the general public, and the party process as a whole.

It is remarkable that journalists—supreme exponents of postmodern cynicism—treat the "moment of truth" of the election campaign as a matter of honor, routinely framing these events as grace in defeat and generosity in victory. The concession also marks a brief time when participants in the drama, institutional and individual, Republican and Democrat, contritely acknowledge their complicity. Cynical journalists and partisan operatives momentarily recant their scorn, drollery, fear, prejudice, professional self-interest, and hatred. Now the candidate is portrayed—in the frame of a semiretired anchor man's perspective—as a valiant, worthy, hard-fighting opponent on the brink of oblivion, a tragically flawed leader whose broken dreams inspire sympathy. The vanquished candidate now has a proven will for sacrifice. He has paid the price.

CONCEDING DEFEAT AS GENRE

Presidential concessions of defeat, although delivered with a minimum of preparation by strong personalities in a time of great stress and emotional volatility, conform to a remarkably stable pattern. Institutional and formal consistencies, together with recurring, easily identified thematic elements, readily qualify concession speeches as a rhetorical genre.[17] The scholarly inattention to this tradition is surprising.[18]

Concession speeches are brief and shun grandiloquence. Opening the address by reading a telegram—an archaic gesture to tradition—helps the defeated candidate get past the hardest part. Disheartened attempts at scripted eloquence are interspersed with ex tempore sentiment. The syntax is often garbled. Standing behind the loser are brave but weeping wives and children.

Press reaction to these performances is as predictable as the speech. "Exits with grace" and "gracious in defeat" are the standard framing devices. What the reporter really means is that the candidate did show up to congratulate the winner; he was a "good loser" for doing so with a brave face and a kind word for his opponent; and his self-control was sufficient to avoid giving vent to his true feelings or breaking into uncontrollable sobs. Nothing the defeated candidate *says* or the press *writes* is very surprising, edifying, or interesting.[19] But the drama as a whole, including its unstated rules and regularities, is coherent. There is, indeed, a hidden grammar, a structure beneath the surface of what losers say and witnesses report.

The concession speech has become a public duty prescribed by an unwritten law, an integral, legitimating feature of a presidential election. It must be performed, at a requisite time, invoking key themes; and it must be gracious. More than a ceremonial gesture, perfunctory in content and performed at a time of devastating stress, the concession has evolved as an essential framing device, a prologue for the winning candidate's acceptance of victory. To enforce this law, news media representatives "duel" with the losing candidate's staff to observe the customary etiquette of elections (before the hotel bar service closes). Deny the network projections, or concede: clear the way for a victory speech during West coast prime-time.

Journalists routinely rely on the formality of the speech setting to report that losing candidates "concede defeat." Yet the words "concede" or "concession" are never uttered by defeated candidates; "defeat" and "loss" are virtually banished. What occurs is an elaborate circumvention and denial: The winner is to be congratulated; his own candidature has been gloriously exonerated; his supporters were loving and the campaign staff brilliant; voters across the country have reconfirmed his faith in the majesty of democracy (had it been in doubt?); we will have the smoothest transition in the history of the world; it has been the greatest moment of my life; the party must reunite; the struggle must go on; the larger victory is assured, blah, blah, blah. But the message everyone *hears* is, "I lost!"

An analysis of presidential concession speeches since 1952 reveals four main elements of the rhetorical genre. They occur in each speech roughly in this order.

1. The *periphrasis of defeat* is a congratulatory declaration of the winner and an acceptance of the electoral verdict. The candidate introduces this as a fait accompli by reading a telegram or noting a telephone call to the winner. This key performative element circumvents defeat by seizing the initiative to declare the winner.
2. A *call to unite* behind the winner extends de loser's initiative.
3. The *paean to democracy* implicitly exonerates and legitimizes the losing campaign.
4. A plea to *continue the fight* converts defeat into a trooping of colors for the just cause and the future victory.

Perfunctory themes typically set the tone of the speech: expressions of gratitude and love to family members, staff, and supporters; a tribute to the vice presidential running mate; invocations of God's blessing to the audience and nation. There are also common subsidiary themes: a special appeal to young people; references to physical fatigue. The election campaign is often evocatively described as injurious to the body politic. It is, after all, a kind of civil war, symbolically rupturing and sundering the nation. Election Day is a break in the continuity of its life. To some the campaign is not just bitter and divisive, but repulsive—ugly, as George Bush described it, or dirty. Restored health will require everyone's united help to heal this wound, to mend the break that has been exacted as the tribute to democracy. This healing is presumed to begin with conceding defeat. It is the loser's privilege to cease hostilities, declare peace, and make the first gesture in restoring the nation to its common labor.

Defeat as Psychodrama[20]

Given the dogged adherence to periphrasis and denial in concession speeches, a deeper understanding of the rhetoric of defeat requires attention to what is veiled and unspoken. Such an interpretive inquiry proceeds from two propositions:

1. Although a highly conventionalized rhetorical practice, a concession speech is nevertheless expressive of the speaker's psychological landscape. The speech text is a map of a certain terrain. Maps, too, are highly conventional, but they take you to different places, and they have to be read.
2. The concession speech, as a dramatic performance, is expressive of public meanings, but as theater often does, it strives to hide what is obvious, render invisible what is seen. But theater also potentially renders visible what is unseen.

However routine its words, a concession speech is emotionally charged, a melodrama in the penultimate act of democratic politics at the highest level of power. An emotional high-wire act before a national audience, it is unquestionably an *act*, a naked example of political theater at its most unsettling. Now the suspense is not whether the candidate *can* convey his character, but that he just *might!* Psychologically, the speech is inescapably ambivalent and inherently unstable, emotionally fraught. Yet in virtually every case, the speeches are prosaic—and false, and hypocritical,[21] and embarrassing.

The protagonist of the ceremony must declare the campaign over and cast a public verdict against himself. Will the speech—anywhere in the candidate's psychological landscape, in the deep and silent structure of his utterances—reveal, illuminate, or communicate anything about his experience of defeat? That *is* what the speech is about. He has an audience almost uniquely attentive and engaged: supporters, opponents, admirers, haters, obituarists, and comedians both professional and amateur. All are in some way interested in what might *happen.* More than in a carefully rehearsed play, there is suspense.

The concession speech has great dramatic potential precisely because of its existential instability—can he play this new role?—and the partly sadistic fascination of the audience. Parallels with Greek tragedy, and with the comedies, are not far-fetched. The concession speech also calls to mind the annual ceremony of paying homage to Athenian soldiers slain that year in the Pelopponesian Wars.[22] This ceremony, too, was a marking of the end of a campaign, in winter, at the cessation of hostilities until the new year.

PRESIDENTIAL CONCESSION SPEECHES, 1952–1992

1952: Adlai Stevenson

Stevenson's poetically concise concession to Dwight Eisenhower is a classic, as is the news report (Blair, 1952) of the speech: "Stevenson Concedes the Victory as Weeping Backers Cry 'No, No.'" It begins with the periphrasis:

> My fellow-citizens have made their choice and have selected General Eisenhower and the Republican party as the instruments of their will for the next four years. The people have rendered their verdict and I gladly accept it. (Stevenson, 1952)

The periphrasis is completed near the end of thirteen short paragraphs:

> I have sent the following telegram to General Eisenhower at the Commodore Hotel in New York.
> "The people have made their choice and I congratulate you. That you may be the servant and guardian of peace and make the dale of trouble a door of hope is my earnest prayer."

Stevenson's nearest reference to defeat is a closing anecdote of Abraham Lincoln's comment on an "unsuccessful" election: "it felt like a little boy who had stubbed his toe in the dark. He said that he was too old to cry but it hurt too much to laugh."

The paean to democracy is combined with the continuing struggle.

We vote as many, but we pray as one. With a united people, with faith in democracy, with common concern for others less fortunate around the globe, we shall move forward with God's guidance toward a time when his children will grow in freedom and dignity in a world at peace.

The plea for unity is invoked with the authority of tradition.

It is traditionally American to fight hard before an election. It is equally traditional to close ranks as soon as the people have spoken. . . . That which unites us as American citizens is far greater than that which divides us as political parties.

General Eisenhower's victory speech was also brief, but for him it is clear that yet another battle is underway:

Recognizing the intensity of the difficulties that lie ahead, it is clearly necessary that men and women of goodwill of both parties forget the political strife through which we have passed and devote themselves to the single purpose of a better future.

He seems constrained by the formal requisites of the speech: "Now, my friends, it is trite to say that this is a day of dedication rather than of triumph. But I am indeed as humble as I am proud of the decision that the American people have made." His thanks to those who "worked so hard to make this crusade a success thus far" implies continued struggle. Eisenhower's only solecism is a reference to the telegram "that I sent to my late rival."

1960: Richard Nixon

The 1960 election was very close. Nixon was reluctant to yield, just as Kennedy deferred any declaration of victory. From Los Angeles, after midnight, the *New York Times* reported "Nixon Virtually Concedes" (Schumach, 1960), but Nixon's speech transcript was cautiously labeled a "Statement of Result." Nixon's periphrasis was extremely convoluted. He used the third person to depersonalize his statement, but conceding defeat was obviously on his mind.

As all of you know, as all of you in this room know and as all of you millions who are listening on television or radio realize, it is normally the custom for a candidate for the Presidency or for any other office not to appear until after the decision is definitely known and all the votes are counted beyond doubt.[23] (Nixon, 1960)

Six paragraphs later Nixon reaches the point:

And I—as I look at the board here; while there are still some results still to come in—if the present trend continues, Mr.—Senator Kennedy will be the next President of the United States.

Nixon has not yet telegraphed his congratulations to Kennedy, but presumes "that he probably is listening to this program" at 3:00 A.M. on the East coast. Making no admission of defeat, he emphasizes the uncertainty of the voting tally. His congratulations to Kennedy and appeal to unity are banal, garbled, and conditional.

one of the great features of America is that we have political contests, that they are very hard-fought as this one is hard-fought and once the decision is made we unite behind the man who is elected.
    I want all of you to know, I want Senator Kennedy to know and I want all of you to know [sic] that certainly if this trend does continue, and he does become our next President, that he will have my wholehearted support and yours too.
    My friends, with that, I want to say again: My deep thanks to all of you who are here; to those who have listened on television and radio, and again my congratulations [sic: there was no previous mention] to Senator Kennedy for his fine race in this campaign.

Nixon's paean to democracy struggles to incorporate themes of unity and future challenges.

I have great faith about the future of this country; I have great faith that our people—Republicans, Democrats, alike—will unite behind our next President in seeing that America—in seeing—that they will unite our next President [sic] in seeing that America does meet the challenge which destiny has placed upon us.
    And that challenge is to give the leadership to the whole world, which will produce the world in which all men can have what we have in the United States—freedom, independence, the right to live in peace with our neighbors.

The next morning, Nixon's press secretary read Nixon's telegram to Kennedy:

I want to repeat through this wire the congratulations and best wishes I extended to you on television last night. I know that you will have the united support of all Americans as you lead the nation in the cause of peace and freedom in the next four years.

The *New York Times* report (Becker, 1960) of this press conference declares that "Vice President Nixon conceded today . . . " but betrays an uneasiness about the claim.

The telegram was read to newsmen by Mr. Nixon's press secretary. . . . The Vice President did not make a personal appearance. . . . It was obvious [to whom?] that the Vice President had considered his remarks late on election night a virtual concession. . . .

How did Mr. Nixon take his first political loss?

"I have never seen a man take such a defeat with so much grace," Mr. Klein replied. "Even in defeat Mr. Nixon goes down in history as one of the truly great champions of our country."

. . . The Vice President had not heard from President Eisenhower by concession time [sic]. . . .

In his television appearance shortly after midnight [the previous] morning Vice President Nixon extended "my congratulations to Senator Kennedy for his fine race in this campaign." But no where [sic] did he use the word "concede."

The account of Kennedy's victory speech (Bigart, 1960) also probed the issue.

Senator John F. Kennedy accepted in solemn mood today his election as president. He pledged all his energy to advancing "the long-range interests of the United States and the cause of freedom around the world."

He made his pledge . . . an hour after Vice President Nixon . . . had conceded defeat.

His wife, Jacqueline, stood at his side as the 43-year-old President-elect faced 300 newsmen and massed batteries of TV cameras and gave his victory statement to the nation. . . . The Kennedys showed no evidence of jubilation. All wore expressions of solemnity. Mr. Kennedy's margin of victory was too slender to stir much elation. . . .

Mr. Kennedy, after responding to applause with a diffident bow and a smile, first read the telegram from Mr. Nixon conceding defeat [sic] and extending congratulations. The Senator had stayed up until 3:50 A.M. awaiting this concession and had gone to bed disappointed when the Vice President withheld it.

Kennedy's victory statement, brief and low key, was largely devoted to reading the full text of congratulatory telegrams from Nixon and President

Eisenhower, and his own telegrams in reply. In effect, Kennedy allowed his
opponent to declare the victory. After this ritual, Kennedy (1960) read five
perfunctory paragraphs, appealing to "all the citizens of this country, Democrats, independents, Republicans, regardless of how they may have voted,"
claiming "the next four years are going to be difficult for us all."

Nixon's actions on Election Day also expressed a foreboding. Having
returned to California after 1:00 A.M. for a final preelection appearance at an
airport hangar, he arose on election Tuesday "less than three hours after he
had gone to bed. He had cast his ballot by 7:35 A.M." in his hometown, East
Whittier.

> After posing for pictures and casting his vote, the Vice President
> predicted it would be late tonight before the outcome of the elec-
> tion would be known.
>
> He then drove away, accompanied by a Secret Service agent, a
> military aide and a driver. His press secretary, Herbert G. Klein, said
> Mr. Nixon wanted "to get away from it all for a little while."
>
> Mr. Nixon was driven to Tiajuana, Mexico, about 100 miles
> away. He had lunch there with the Mayor of Tiajuana, Xicotencatl L.
> Alemán. (Schumach, 1960, p. 20)

No one reported what Mrs. Nixon, having accompanied her husband at
the final rally and voting with him in East Whittier, did for lunch that day as
the candidate, hoping to be elected president of the United States, left the
country.[24]

1964: Barry Goldwater

Barry Goldwater also refused to make a concession speech on the night of the
election, despite the televised reports of an unprecedented majority for
President Johnson. At a news conference in Scottsdale, Arizona, the next
morning, Goldwater's concession speech began in an orthodox fashion, but
he refused to withdraw from party struggle.

> I know many of you expected me to make some statement last night
> but I held that off. I sent the President the following wire. . . .
>
> "Congratulations on your victory. I will help you in any way that
> I can toward achieving a growing and better America and a secure
> and dignified peace. The role of the Republican party will remain in
> that temper but it also remains the party of opposition when
> opposition is called for" (Goldwater, 1964).

Goldwater's appeal for unity is pointedly qualified, assuring President
Johnson that "all Americans will join with you," but only if he has "honest

solutions" to a host of problems: Vietnam, Cuba, law and order, the economy, and communism. His disclaimer of ill will is unusually candid.

I have no bitterness, no rancor at all. I say to the President as a fellow politician that he did a wonderful job. He put together a vote total that's larger than has ever been gained in this country. However, it's interesting to me and very surprising to me that the latest totals I can get do not reach the totals of the 1960 election. I am disappointed in this because I thought that the American people would have turned out in greater numbers. . . . But he did a good job and I have to congratulate him on it.

The remainder of Goldwater's speech avoids the standard sermon on unity and the majesty of democracy. Rather, he emphasizes a commitment to "the Republican philosophy" and strengthening the party.

There is a two-party system in this country and we're going to keep it.[25] We're going to devote our days and the years ahead to strengthening the Republican party . . . and I feel that the young people coming along will provide the army that we need. . . . This effort . . . turns out to be a much longer effort than we thought. It's not an effort that we can drop now nor do we have any intentions of dropping it now. . . . I want to just ask the people in this country who worked so hard in this election not to be despondent, that we have a job to do and let's get along with it, because there are many questions that have to be answered.

After the formal statement, reporters successfully invited Goldwater to break the taboo: "Have the Republican voters not shared in repudiating this philosophy you say the party must cling to?" Goldwater replied: "Well, unfortunately I think you're right—that my defeat to some degree . . . was occasioned by Republicans in this country who would not vote for . . . the top of the ticket." Another reporter asked, "was there any single factor . . . which you think most substantially contributed to your defeat yesterday?" Goldwater replied "No . . . I can't think of any major mistake that we made," but he went on to make an astute observation.

it's growing increasingly difficult to upset a man who is in the White House with his tremendous base to start with of Federal employees . . . the power of investigation, the power of news and his ability to control news.
I think that the Republicans have to realize that they're up against something that we have seen developing in this country for many years but never have seen it in the nature and proportion we

saw this time. It's not—we're not running elections any more as we used to, and I think we have to study new techniques. We have to get closer to the news, closer to you fellows who handle the news. We have to be constantly on television, and so forth and so on, to build over four years some kind of a machine that can cope with this vast power of the federal machine.[26]

Johnson gave his victory speech on Election Night despite Goldwater's refusal to concede. Otherwise, Johnson adopted the formula of humility, gratitude, and a plea for unity. He also employed a metaphor of injury and rupture as a consequence of the rigors of the election.

Now, tonight, our purpose must be to bind up our wounds; to heal our history and to make this nation whole. . . .

I ask all those who supported me and all those that opposed me to forget our differences because there are many more things in America that unite us than divide us and our nation. And these are times when our nation should forget our petty differences and stand united before all the world.

1968: Hubert Humphrey

Considering Humphrey's prolix habits, his concession speech was relatively brief. The *New York Times* front-page headline—"A Loser Concedes and Tries to Smile"—captures the pathos (Apple, 1968). Even though he was devastated by the defeat,[27] his concession begins with a classic periphrasis and other generic elements.

I am sure you know that I have already called Mr. Nixon to express to him our congratulations, and I have sent the following telegram just a few moments ago. . . .

"According to unofficial returns, you are the winner in this election. My congratulations. Please know that you will have my support in unifying and leading the nation. This has been a difficult year for the American people. I am confident that if constructive leaders of both our parties join together now, we shall be able to go on with the business of building the better America we all seek in a spirit of peace and harmony."

After two paragraphs of gratitude for his supporters, and a rare admission that he has "lost," Humphrey seems to close his speech with the theme of continuing the struggle.

I intend to continue my dedication to public service and to the building of a responsive and vital Democratic party. I shall continue my personal commitment to the cause of human rights, of peace and to the betterment of man. If I have helped in the campaign to move these causes forward, I feel rewarded. I have done my best. I have lost. Mr. Nixon has won. The democratic process has worked its will, so now let's get on with the urgent task of uniting our country. Thank you.

The end of the speech? Not for the Happy Warrior. The remaining half of his concession speech is an impromptu coda, meandering by turns reflective and maudlin—even incoherent.

Now, go have some fun. It has been a lot of hard work. I don't want anybody to have any extra sympathy. As a matter of fact, what I'd like to have you do is just redouble your efforts to do what you thought you were doing and what I thought I was doing and maybe we can make an even greater contribution to the things that are important in this country.

I really don't feel very badly. I actually feel that we've done a heck of a job.

I don't want you to think we'll continue to campaign right away, but I—I just thought you ought to know you maybe ought to have a little rest. We intend to take some. We're not quite sure just what we're going to do in the next few days. . . . I haven't mowed the lawn for some time. . . .

As a matter of fact, I feel a great sense of both release and relief, and I hope and pray that all of you will feel the same way. I want you to be of good cheer. I'd like to have you feel a little happy. It's not easy, but quite frankly, this was an uphill fight all the way. . . . We've got a President-elect. He's going to have my help. Cheers.

Richard Nixon's victory speech (Nixon, 1968) uncannily echoes his 1960 concession speech and has ironic portents for what would become of his presidency. The speech, twice as long as Humphrey's concession, begins with a limp joke: "Ladies and gentlemen, I didn't realize so many of you would stay up so late."[28] As in 1960 he seems to depersonalize and distance himself from his audience.

I want to express first my grateful appreciation to all of those in this room, but more than that, through the medium of television and radio, to the thousands, and, I understand, millions across the country who worked for our cause.

I know that many that I will never have the chance to speak to personally gave hours and days of time, and we will always be grateful for what you did.

Nixon confides to the millions that he has "received a very gracious message" from Humphrey "congratulating me for winning the election." Then he veers off into a long meditation—not on victory, but defeat—with an elaborate message of condolence to those he has beaten. Celebrating victory with his own supporters is not on his mind.

> I have also had a telephone conversation with him, and I thought I might share with you and also our television audience some of the thoughts that I expressed to him in that telephone conversation.
>
> I congratulated him for his gallant and courageous fight against great odds. I admire a fighter, and he proved himself to be one. He never gave up and he gave us a good fight.
>
> I also told him that as he finished his campaign that I know exactly how he felt. I know exactly how he felt. I know how it feels to lose a close one. Having lost a close one eight years ago and having won a close one this year, I can say this—winning's a lot more fun.
>
> But I would like to express to him and also to the thousands who worked for him—because he, like myself, had a great corps of volunteer workers, many young people as well as others—a bit of philosophy that has guided me through the years of defeat toward victory.
>
> It is this: A great victory is never won without defeat. It is always won without fear. What is important is that a man or a woman engage in battle, be in the arena, participate, and I hope that all those who supported Mr. Humphrey will continue their interest in politics. They will perhaps be in the other party; we may be contesting again. Who knows? But the important thing is that our process in this country works better when we have devoted, dedicated people giving their all in battle for a cause that they believe in.
>
> And I would urge particularly the young people who supported him and lost not to be discouraged but to continue their interest and to go on to other areas of public service.

Taking up fully a third of the speech, Nixon concludes with expressions of gratitude to Mr. and Mrs. Eisenhower, President Johnson, and the Nixon family. Conspicuous by its absence is any mention at all of the Republican Party. Nixon's only rhetorical fancy is "one final thought that I would like to leave with regard to the character of the new Administration."

> I saw many signs during the campaign. Some of them were not friendly and some were very friendly . . . but a teenager held up a sign, "Bring Us Together." And that will be the great objective of this Administration at the outset, to bring the American people together.

This will be an open Administration, open to new ideas, open to men and women of both parties, open to the critics as well as those who want to support us.

This objective seemed understandable in the light of Edmund Muskie's observation the day after the election that Nixon "appeared to have received the smallest percentage of the popular vote accorded a victorious Presidential candidate since Woodrow Wilson prevailed over the divided Republicans in 1912" (Bigart, 1968).

1972: George McGovern

The pendulum had swung again, and the close election of 1968 was followed by a lopsided result, this time against a Democrat in favor of the incumbent. The newspaper accounts were predictable: "Senator George McGovern conceded defeat of his Presidential candidacy here tonight" (Naughton, 1972). His concession begins routinely, but the reference to "peace abroad" echoes a divisive campaign theme.

I have just sent the following telegram to President Nixon:
"Congratulations on your victory. I hope that in the next four years you will lead us to a time of peace abroad and justice at home. You have my full support in such efforts" (McGovern, 1972).

In a near breach of the taboo, McGovern recalls Stevenson's 1952 anecdote about the boy who stubbed his toe.

It does hurt all of us in the auditorium and many others across the country to lose, but we're not going to shed any tears tonight about the great joy that this campaign has brought to us over the past two years. . . . The Presidency belongs to someone else, but the glory of those devoted working friends and their dedication to the noble ideals of this country sustains us now and it will sustain our country.

Turning to a central issue of the election, McGovern declares that his opposition to the Vietnam War is a benchmark of success for the campaign.

There can be no question at all that we have pushed this country in the direction of peace, and I think each one of us loves the title of peacemaker more than any office in the land. We will press on with that effort until all the bloodshed and all the sorrow have ended once and for all.
I want every single one of you to remember and never forget it that if we pushed the day of peace just one day closer, then every minute and every hour and every bone-crushing effort in this campaign was worth the entire effort.

McGovern subordinates the theme of unity to the theme of opposition, and his reference to a loyal opposition recalls Goldwater's insistent partisanship.

Now, the question is to what standards does the loyal opposition now rally? We do not rally to the support of policies that we deplore. But we do love this country and we will continue to beckon it to a higher standard.

McGovern does not call for unity and a common effort with President Nixon, nor does he offer a homily on the majesty of America democracy. Instead, he alludes to the "McGovern reforms" that democratized and broadened the basis of representation in the Democratic Party's state primaries and national convention.

So I ask all of you tonight to stand with your convictions. I ask you not to despair of the political process of this country, because that process has yielded too much valuable improvement in these past two years. The Democratic party will be a better party because of the reforms that we have carried out. The nation will be better because we never once gave up the long battle to renew its oldest ideals and to redirect its current energies along more humane and hopeful paths.

President Nixon's 1972 victory speech, a third example of his effort to distance himself from election night festivities, takes the final step by preempting the victory celebration.

Before going over to the Shoreham Hotel to address the victory celebration there, I wanted to take a moment to say a word to all of you in this very personal way [sic] from the Oval Office. I first wanted to express my deep appreciation to every one of you, the millions of you who gave me your support in the election today. (Nixon, 1972)

Preferring the dignified political vacuum of the nation's highest sound studio, Nixon paradoxically concentrates on the great and noble battle of "the game of politics." As in 1968 he speaks more of defeat, in empathy with the losers, than of celebrating victory with his supporters. Again there is the paradoxical psychological interiority juxtaposed to Nixon's obsession with the outward appearance of his own conduct: an obsessive narcissism, but from an external, self-regarding, third-person perspective. He does not *express* his feelings but invites us to join him in *looking* at the image of his accomplishments. "I tried to conduct myself in this campaign in a way that would not divide our country—not divide it regionally or by parties or in any other way." In a pseudosympathetic, banal philosophizing on politics as the "great game of life," Nixon offers his "respect" to the McGovern supporters, then shifts quickly from the first person.

I want to express my respect for millions of others who gave their support to Senator McGovern. I know that after a campaign, when one loses he can feel very, very low; his supporters as well may feel that way. And when he wins, as you will note when I get over to the Shoreham, people are feeling very much better.

The important thing in our process, however, is to play the game. And in the great game of life, and particularly the game of politics, what is important is that on either side more Americans voted this year than ever before.

And the fact that you won or you lost must not keep you from keeping in the great game of politics in the years ahead, because the better competition we have between the two parties, between the two men running for office—whatever office that may be—means that we get the better people and the better programs for our country. (Nixon, 1972)

If this reflection on competition and "better people" is not a preposterous and tasteless boast, then it must be Nixon's intention to assuage the losers' disappointment. The next five paragraphs, warming to his theme of greatness, attempt to enlarge his empathy into a theme of unity: the "great goal," "great tasks," "greatest generation of peace," "great country," and "great political victories" are "bigger than whether we're Democrats or Republicans."

Toward the end of the speech, Nixon combines the themes of greatness, unity, and victory with another striking reflection on his "conduct" as an external, historical artifact.

I had noted in listening to the returns a few minutes ago that several commentators have reflected on the fact that this may be one of the great political victories of all time. In terms of votes, that may be true. . . . I would only hope that in these next four years we can so conduct ourselves in this country and so meet our responsibilities in the world in building peace in the world that years from now people will look back to the generation of the nineteen seventies and how we've conducted ourselves and they will say, God Bless America.[29]

1976: Gerald Ford

Ending the 1976 campaign with laryngitis, Gerald Ford enlisted his wife, Betty Ford, to read a concession "statement" (Ford, 1976): "The President asked me to tell you that he telephoned President-elect Carter a short time ago and congratulated him on his victory." This report and subsequent reading of the text of a telegram to Jimmy Carter distance and depersonalize the periphrasis as a fait accompli: "It is apparent now that you have won our long and intense struggle for the Presidency." Ford makes no specific admission of defeat, nor does he issue a paean to democracy. His appeal to unity only hints at a future partisan struggle.

> I believe that we must now put the divisions of the campaign behind us and unite the country once again in the common pursuit of peace and prosperity. Although there will continue to be disagreements over the best means to use in pursuing our goals, I want to assure you that you have my complete and wholehearted support as you take the oath of office this January.

The press described Ford as "red-eyed" and noted that his

> immediate family stood with him in a brief and emotional ceremony, exchanging embraces, kisses and stricken looks. The President himself appeared uncommonly drawn but composed. Mrs. Ford . . .held back tears as she read. . . . Their three sons . . . seemed silently shattered. Susan Ford, 19, looked as if she had cried all night. She was still inconsolable. (Lydon, 1976)

1980: Jimmy Carter

President Carter's concession speech began with an unusually direct expression of pain: "I promised you four years ago that I would never lie to you, so I can't stand here tonight and say it doesn't hurt." He is unable to bring himself to say what "it" is. The periphrasis occurs in his report of telephoning the winner.

> About an hour ago I called Governor Reagan in California and I told him that I congratulated him for a fine victory. I look forward to working closely with him during the next few weeks. We'll have a fine transition period—I told him I wanted the best one in history. (Carter, 1980)

Carter also sent Reagan a telegram that reiterates the periphrasis:

> It's now apparent that the American people have chosen you as the next President. I congratulate you and pledge to you our fullest support and cooperation in bringing about an orderly transition of government in the weeks ahead.

Apart from a reference to leaving office, Carter does not mention defeat. Rather, the struggle will continue:

> I've not achieved all I set out to do, perhaps no one ever does, but we have faced the tough issues. We've stood for and we've fought for

and we have achieved some very important goals for our country. These efforts will not end with this Administration. The effort must go on. Nor will the progress that we have made be lost when we leave office. The great principles that have guided this nation since its very founding will continue to guide America to the challenges of the future.

Carter's appeal to unity is unqualified.

This has been a long and hard-fought campaign, as you well know. But we must now come together as a united and a unified people to solve the problems that are still before us, to meet the challenges of a new decade. And I urge all of you to join in with me in a sincere and fruitful effort to support my successor when he undertakes this great responsibility as President of the greatest nation on earth.

The paean to democracy follows, with a brief homily upon problem solving and moral responsibility.

Ours is a special country because our vast economic and military strength give us a special responsibility for seeking solutions to the problems that confront the world. But our influence will always be greater when we live up to those principles of freedom, of justice, of human rights for all people.

Carter's closing words admit to disappointment, but not defeat. "I've wanted to serve as President because I love this country and because I love the people of this nation. Just one more word. . . . I am disappointed tonight but I have not lost either love."

1984: Walter Mondale

In 1984, trailing badly in the polls, the Democratic candidate had plenty of time to contemplate defeat. This may account for the unusual length of the speech, and its focus upon the end of Mondale's political career. His periphrasis and congratulation to President Reagan are typical and unqualified, as is the paean to American democracy.

A few minutes ago I called the President of the United States and congratulated him on his victory for re-election as President of the United States. He has won. We are all Americans. He is our President, and we honor him tonight. . . .

Again tonight, the American people, in town halls, in homes, in fire houses, in libraries, chose the occupant of the most powerful office on earth. Their choice was made peacefully, with dignity and majesty, and although I would have rather won, tonight we rejoice in our democracy, we rejoice in the freedom of a wonderful people, and we accept their verdict. I thank the people for hearing my case.

I have traveled this nation, I believe, more than any living American . . . and if there is one thing I'm certain of, it is that this is a magnificent nation, with the finest people on earth. (Mondale, 1984)

Claiming that he "would rather have won," Mondale makes a reluctant and convoluted admission that he has lost in every state except his own.

We didn't win, but we made history and that fight has just begun. And once again, here I am in Minnesota. In over 24 years, never once have the people of Minnesota turned me down. They voted tonight. Minnesotans, this is a special state—a remarkable state with a special spirit. And time and again in the past, Minnesota has led the way for our nation, and I think you did it again tonight.

. . . I want to say a special word to my young supporters tonight. I know how you feel because I've been there myself. Do not despair. This fight didn't end tonight. It began tonight. I have been around for a while, and I have noticed in the seeds of most every victory are to be found the seeds of defeat, and in every defeat are to be found the seeds of victory. Let us fight on. Let us fight on.

My loss tonight does not in any way diminish the worth or importance of our struggle. . . . Let us continue. Let us continue.

This quickly, the campaign begins anew. "Let us fight for jobs and fairness. Let us fight for these kids. . . . Let us fight for our environment." *Fight* occurs eight times, and is his concluding plea: "I am confident that history will judge us honorably. So tonight let us be determined to fight on." His claim that "we made history and that fight has just begun" is a nicely coordinated allusion to what was labeled Geraldine Ferraro's "talk" immediately following from New York.[30]

even though he did not win this race for the Presidency, in 1984 he waged another battle, a battle for equal opportunity, and that battle Walter Mondale won.

For two centuries, candidates have [never] asked a woman to be [their] running mate until Walter Mondale. When he asked me to campaign by his side, he opened a door which will never be closed again. This is a victory of which every American can be proud. Campaigns, even if you lose them, do serve a purpose. (Ferraro, 1984)

Ronald Reagan also stuck to the script. His victory speech in Los Angeles concluded: "You know, so many people act as if this election means the end of something. To each of you I say, it's the beginning of everything. You ain't seen nothin' yet" (Raines, 1984).

1988: Michael Dukakis

Dukakis also had time to prepare a long speech. However, all the generic elements—the periphrasis, the call of congratulation, the plea for unity, and a hint of continued struggle—are combined in his second paragraph.

> Just a few minutes ago, I called Vice President Bush and congratulated him on his victory. I want to, and I know I speak for all of you and for all the American people when I say that he will be our President, and we'll work with him. This nation faces major challenges ahead, and we must work together. (Dukakis, 1988)

Dukakis's repeated use of the Boston marathon as a metaphor invokes heroic endurance as well as local color. His paean to American democracy is an extended reminiscence of memorable places and people during his campaign-marathon.

> As I think back on this marathon, I'll never forget the beauty of this magnificent land, from those beautiful colonial villages of New Hampshire to the farmland of Iowa to the magnificence of Yellowstone and the California coast. But most of all I'll remember the people I've met: their strength, their values, their generosity.

But the scenic imagery leads to a renewed campaign.

> And it is very important that we continue to fight for them and for families all across America. We've got to fight for that young family in Levittown. . . . We've got to fight for that family in Sioux City. . . . We've got to fight for those high school students in Los Angeles. . . . We've got to fight to end the shame of homelessness. . . . We've got to fight for those unemployed steel workers.

Dukakis had a special message for the young people involved in his campaign, a theme echoed four years later, less confidently, by George Bush. "I want you to be encouraged by what you have done in this campaign. I hope many of you will go into politics and public service. It is a noble profession, a noble profession."

Ross Perot: 1992

Having begun with George Bush's 1992 concession speech as a counterpoint to Adlai Stevenson's eloquent reserve, we come full circle to Ross Perot's chaotic, plebeian excess. Both eccentric and innovative, appealing to a jaded electorate, he was an anticandidate running the first "postmodern campaign" (Turque, 1992). Refusing to abide by the rules, Perot attracted a massive, predatory media coverage. He unapologetically used his personal wealth to finance an amateurish but canny electronic campaign. He suspended his campaign in July,[31] then reentered and received a large proportion (19%) of the popular vote. Yet his concession speech—despite its folksy, new age populism, crisp managerialism, and pep rally atmosphere—observed the rules. He had even rented a hotel ballroom for a "victory party."

Journalists imposed the standard framing devices, only hinting at the strangeness. The *New York Times*, headlining "Perot Exits Dancing," notes that he had "delivered a poignant and gracious concession speech tonight" (Sack, 1992). *Newsweek* told its readers that "Perot ends his campaign on a grace note" (Turque, 1992). The *Los Angeles Times* played the same tune.

> Ross Perot conceded defeat in his independent bid for President Tuesday night with grace and generosity. . . . The highly competitive and unconventional tycoon, never famous for magnanimity in his many business triumphs, graciously urged his supporters to give three cheers for President Bush's many years of public service. (Broder, 1992)

The published "excerpts" (Perot, 1992c) of the speech are reasonably routine. The periphrasis of defeat implies a victory and declares a continuing struggle.

> Starting last February you did something that everybody said couldn't be done. Millions of you came together to take our country back. You gave Washington a laser-like message to listen to the people. . . . The American people have spoken. They have chosen Governor Clinton. Congratulations. [*Boos and jeers.*]—Wait a minute—oh. No, no. Whoops. Wait a minute. Wait a minute. The only way we're going to make it work if it's [sic] all team up together. So let's give Governor Clinton a big round of applause. He's won. Thank you.
>
> Now, let's forget, forget the election. Forget the election. It's behind us. The hard work is in front of us. And we must all work together to rebuild our great country.

Concession speech transcripts often seems *less* coherent than the speech itself. As above, digressions and broken sentences fail to convey instances of spontaneity and adroit shifts by the speaker in response to cheers and jeers. But the Perot (1992c) transcript gives an impression of greater coherence than is evident when viewing a videotape of the performance. Perot's actual performance on this occasion is much more complicated. He arrives to an ovation, but instead of a speech he announces a delay for the networks and asks the band to play "When the Saints Go Marching In." After this, he returns to the microphone: "Ed, you've got to play our campaign song, *Crazy*. . . . Let's sing it! Everybody!" After *Crazy*, Perot seems to begin his "speech" with a series of pep squad questions:

> Are you more dedicated than ever to puttin' this country back to work? [*Yes!*] "Anything wrong with . . . ? [*No!*]. . . . O.K. We'll keep on going as long as you want to keep on going. . . . I really don't like this, but there's still time to kill. Ed, how about *Way Down Yonder in New Orleans?* That's where the voodoo comes from.

The *New York Times* transcript of Perot's speech (1992c) "begins" four minutes and ten seconds later, sounding the standard themes of renewed struggle and national unity.

> This is no time to get discouraged. This is no time to throw in the towel. This is the time to redouble our efforts and work with the new Administration and to make sure our country is a beacon to the rest of the world, to make sure that our cities, our alabaster cities that gleam undimmed by human tears.

For the C-SPAN viewer, network delays, fragmented pep talks, and musical interludes undermined any certainty that Perot would deliver a formal speech. After a second pep-talk, Perot farewells his audience repeatedly—"thank-you," "God bless you"—and the band plays "United We Stand, Divided We Fall." Suddenly Perot introduces his running mate, James Stockdale, who *does* give a speech. Then Perot recommences with the lustiest effort of all: a classic of its genre, one might say, in every respect but form, style, and content.

> Now then! . . . I don't want any bitterness in our crowd, I don't want any negativism, I want you to join me now in thanking President George Bush for years and years and years of service to our country. . . . I propose three cheers for George Bush in his years of service to our country. . . . [*Cheers and applause.*] . . . Now to Governor Clinton, you're to be our next President. The people have given you a strong mandate. Our organization pledges to help and support any programs that are good for this country. Fair enough? . . . Now then, we always got the safety valve, right? . . . You can bring that ol' stray dog

out from the dog pound again. [*Prolonged cheers.*] Well, now, just a minute now, there's more than one way to skin a cat, right? . . . Is there anybody here tonight that's discouraged or down in the dumps? [*No!*] No! Hell no! There you go. Anybody going to go home tonight and suck his thumb? No! We're gonna get up tomorrow and say, O.K. suckers let's just go build it . . . right? [*Right!*] O.K.! O.K.! That all that matters, it doesn't matter who does it, it doesn't matter how it gets done, it does matter that it gets done, and it matters that it gets done right! We can make enormous progress in this country, and we don't have four years to waste, right? [*Right.*] So let's just pick up a shovel in the morning and start cleaning out the barn! O.K. O.K. Great. God bless you all. You're the greatest. [The band strikes up *God Bless America*, the singing led by Mrs. Perot.] (Perot, 1992b)

This is coarse and bracing stuff. The crowd loved it, but *New York Times* readers missed it. In the pep rally atmosphere the periphrasis is complete: a mandate to the winner, three cheers to the loser (Bush), and the "ol' stray dog" is still on the scent. Not a hint of defeat; discouragement is literally sworn away.

CONCLUSIONS

The simple concession speech involves complex spiritual concerns: catharsis, confession, and forgiveness. Although a requisite affair of state, it is a perversely public invasion of privacy, a recanting of one's most private dreams and ambitions. At its most elemental, the concession speech is a rhetorical enactment of failure in the face of civic triumph: a ritual sacrifice in which the individual tragedy attests to the legitimacy of the public right. It is thus a quintessential narrative of democratic action. This supremely painful personal resignation is symbolic of a public moral drama, a disarming revelation of the price of seeking the nation's highest office.

A modern election campaign often appears to be little more than an entertainment market for public illusion and P. T. Barnum fakery. Yet this is also an arena in which private delusions and self-deceptions must, in the end, be accounted for. Presidential campaigns are orchestrated as a theater of combat. They are depicted by both journalists and scholars in a romantic language of cinematic lyricism: strategic themes, a plotting out of a year's grand strategy by weeks and days, marshaling a great army, professional and volunteer, and of course a cast of millions. It is a conjuring of cinematic landscapes, surging momentum, color, heat, and noise. The reality, of course, is otherwise: a rush of press releases, regional airports, buses, stock speeches keyed to the day's slogan, another hotel, pandering dinners with overdressed, distracted people. The only thing cinematic about the process is achieved at editing benches surmounted by batteries of video monitors in tacky little film studios or in hastily convened interviews on regional television. The lyricism and grand scale, the epic "book" of the campaign give way each day to maneuvering the candidate to a "pic fac" where he will utter a sound bite of numbing inanity to a crush of cynical reporters and scruffy cameramen.

For these public deceits and so many more private ones—about money, cosmetics, theatrics, and exploiting or redressing negatives—the defeated candidate's final duty, another ritual, is to offer forgiveness to all those who have forced deception upon him: his family, aides, best friends, the media, the opposing party. Small wonder that the concession speech rises to that otherwise archaic form of noble obligation: condescension. The campaign organization, the media teams high and low, the party, the networks, and in a sense the entire nation require the loser's forgiveness.

Yet the losing candidate must also seek a moral dispensation. He has been complicit at every step. Quite apart from the deeds forced upon him by others, he requires exoneration for his willing engagement in public deceit and private venality. For many months he has groveled for praise, adoration, and other people's money. He has been pliant to public relations flaks, cosmeticians, hair dressers, fashion consultants, speech coaches, sloganeers, and advertising executives—and all of this with much success, and in absolute secrecy. Passion of all kinds has swept him to heights of self-deception in the face of certain defeat. And this stark reality is certain as he approaches, with a dread of finality, a gaggle of microphones in a hotel ballroom. He has in his hand a script for the worst, the saddest, the most pathetic speech he has ever given in his life.

NOTES

This essay was originally written for this book. A shorter version has been published in *Political Communication* 11, No. 2 (April–June 1994), 109–131.

1. The theatrical, dramatic, and ritualistic character of politics, and of political campaigns in particular, is an ancient interpretive device and the subject of study in numerous disciplines. An introductory discussion and bibliography of communication research in his area is Swanson and Nimmo (1990, pp. 197–207, 364). Gronbeck (1984) illustrates a dramaturgical analysis of presidential elections. Burke (1966) is a seminal discussion of rhetoric as symbolic action.

2. Male pronouns will be used in reference to presidential candidates, reflecting the fact that only men have been nominated by a major political party in America.

3. The spoils of honor a Roman general could win only by killing the opposing leader himself [*spoliare*, to plunder]. (Livy, *Histories*, IV). Democracy triumphant on election night postpones this issue.

4. In Latin, *augurare*, divination by omens; to portend or foresee. An augur was a Roman religious official who foretold events by observing the behavior of birds, the weather, etc.

5. The Latin *cedare*, yield, is tantalizingly chose to *celare*, hide or conceal.

6. The image is a fairly exact description of a "talking head" on a television screen.

7. An interesting case is when Nixon and the GOP in 1972 promised "a new American Revolution," a phrase that caused not a ripple in the press or the electorate. Had McGovern's antiwar campaign used this phrase, it would have brought McGovern's candidature to a sensational halt.

8. This is my own transcription of C-SPAN's live broadcast of President Bush's speech in Dallas, Texas, late on the night of Nov. 3, 1992.

9. A few days later, in a radio address to the nation from Washington, Bush and his speech writers had regained coherence, humor, and self-possession: "Having known the sweet taste of popular favor, I can more readily accept the sour taste of defeat. . . . Winston Churchill [whose government was voted out of office after World War II] said: 'I have been given the order of the boot.' And that is the exact position in which I find myself today. I admit this is not the position I would have preferred, but it is a judgment I honor" (Lippman, 1992).

10. At this very moment Bush looks down at a typescript, picks it up, and begins reading his speech.

11. Bush's delivery falters when he attempts to read his script, but gains articulacy and conviction when he appears to interpolate ad lib.

12. Clinton dryly reports, "I heard tonight Mr. Perot's remarks and his offer to work with us."

13. Presumably this is a condescending reference to Bush's facetious statement in his speech: "I plan to get very active in the grandchild business."

14. Campbell and Jamieson (1986, pp. 204, 219) describe the inaugural address as "a rite of passage, a ritual of transition," a "rite of investiture." These priestly concepts implicitly distinguish between election to office and confirmation in it. Campbell and Jamieson miss the *celebratory* nature of the ceremony, a feature that is more evident in the victory speech, where illusions, danger, and the euphoria of combat have not been suppressed.

15. For the Greeks, his *heart*; for the Romans, his *virility*.

16. Between social superiors and inferiors, the virtue of noble condescension—perhaps an oxymoron in egalitarian society—requires special notice, kindness, civility, respect, or generosity toward one's servants or inferiors. Condescension is related to the French idea of noblesse oblige—not a special privilege, but special obligations and responsibilities.

17. Rhetorical genres are defined, illustrated, and critically evaluated in Bitzer (1968), Campbell and Jamieson (1978, 1985), and Simons and Aghazarian (1986).

18. Weaver (1982) is the unique exception I have noted; Chesebro and Hamsher (1974) take an oblique interest. An enormous literature is devoted to presidential rhetoric. Studies of inaugural addresses predominate, but State of the Union messages, party convention acceptances, keynote speeches, campaign oratory and debates, and press conferences have received wide attention. Numerous studies have been devoted to a distantly related topic, the *apologia.* A closer parallel is the presidential farewell address, discussed in detail by Campbell and Jamieson (1990, pp. 191–212) as "a ritual of departure" occurring at a rhetorically "privileged time." They argue that "leave-taking rhetoric" most clearly exhibits "the links between the various presidential genres" (pp. 193, 212), but concession speeches are nowhere mentioned. For basic concepts, recent literature on presidential rhetoric as a genre, and a bibliographical orientation, see Swanson and Nimmo (1990, pp. 233–41, 364–69, 379–86). For a methodological discussion of rhetorical genres and presidential inaugurals as a paradigm, see Simons and Aghazarian (1986). Studies with a dramaturgical perspective focus exclusively on either campaign/ convention rhetoric or presidential rhetoric as isolated (generic?) phenomena. Here I argue the "twain" *does* meet. What has been overlooked is the transitional suspense on Election Night, the *commedia* itself: the verdict as rhetorical enactment. Of all nights, of all speeches, should victory and defeat be ignored because they produce predictable, boorish, maudlin, *generic* speeches?

19. Does this account for the paucity of scholarly interest? Apparently not, considering the burgeoning literature on press conferences, campaign ad spots, television news, and other ephemera.

20. By *psychodrama* I mean the special interiority of *self*-enactment as distinct from rhetorical *enactment* in ceremony and ritual on an occasion that is, far from laudatory, communal, and harmonious, a recognition of personal exclusion and failure.

21. *Hypocrite* derives from the Greek word for actor.

22. Pericles' great Funeral Oration was given on this occasion. Thucydides (1960) describes the ceremony in Book II, ¶ 34; Pericles' speech is at ¶¶ 35–46.

23. It seems especially apposite for Nixon to begin with this statement, since of course it is not true.

24. News coverage of the Nixon campaigns has reflected a fascination for his strangely abstracted conduct. In 1972 the *New York Times* reported (Semple, 1972, p. 34) that when Nixon appeared at his polling place to vote, "he admitted that he did not know his own address at his house some two blocks away."

25. Goldwater's combative tone may have been a response to Johnson's claim of support from "men of independent views and men and women of both parties who put their country before their party" (Johnson, 1964).

26. Note that Goldwater conflates the federal machine with television and the news. Is he confusing separate issues: the power of incumbency as distinct from the power of the television news media to frame issues and images and to set agendas? Or is he offering a subtler insight: the "presidential machine" and the news media are, for all intents and purposes (especially to a challenging candidate), the same thing?

27. Immediately after the speech, Humphrey returned to his hotel room, but stood alone for some minutes in the hallway. A close friend then stood with him silently for some time. When he put a hand on his shoulder, Humphrey said: "I have a lot of thinking to do. Jesus, I think I would have done a good job in the White House." Humphrey later said of the concession speech: "It was the most difficult assignment of my private or public life. What made it so difficult was that I knew we could have won it—and that we should have won it" (Solberg, 1984, p. 406).

28. Affecting surprise to find another enthusiastic audience waiting to listen to him, Nixon repeats the coy pretense he used to begin his 1960 concession speech: "Well, you know . . . I thought we'd had the last rally of the campaign, but here we go again!"

29. Nixon's presidential "conduct" was the exclusive focus of national interest, but only for two-and-a-half years. Senate and media investigations of the Watergate burglary by employees of Nixon's reelection committee, "dirty tricks" by White House "plumbers," and the tape-recorded coverup led inexorably to Nixon's resignation in 1974.

30. Ferraro followed the classic format of concession speeches: congratulations to President Reagan; telephoned "best wishes" to Vice President Bush; the theme of unity. "This is not a moment for partisan statements. It is a moment to celebrate our democracy and to think of our country."

31. Counting his withdrawal from the race on July 16, Perot (1992a) in effect gave two ending speeches.

REFERENCES

Apple, R. W., Jr. (1968, Nov. 7). A loser concedes and tries to smile. *New York Times*, 1, 22.

Austin, J. L. (1965). *How to do things with words.* New York: Oxford University Press.

Becker, Bill (1960, Nov. 10). Nixon wire gives his "best wishes." *New York Times*, 1, 42.

Bigart, Homer (1960, Nov. 10). Winner's pledge. *New York Times*, 1.

Bigart, Homer (1968, Nov. 7). Muskie in defeat, bars bitterness. *New York Times*, 22.

Bitzer, L. F. (1968). The rhetorical situation. *Philosophy & Rhetoric, 1*, 1–14.

Blair, William M. (1952, Nov. 5). Stevenson concedes the victory as weeping backers cry "No, no." *New York Times*, 1.

Broder, John M. (1992, Nov. 4). Perot says movement will remain a force for change. *Los Angeles Times*, A11.

Buckley, William F., Jr. (1992, Nov. 30). Bush congratulates Clinton. *National Review*, 62.

Burke, Kenneth (1966). *Language as symbolic action*. Berkeley: University of California Press.

Campbell, Karlyn Kohrs, and Kathleen Hall Jamieson (1985). Inaugurating the presidency. *Presidential Studies Quarterly, 15*, 394–411.

Campbell, Karlyn Kohrs, and Kathleen Hall Jamieson (1986). Inaugurating the presidency. In Herbert W. Simons and Aram A. Aghazarian, eds., *Form, genre, and the study of political discourse*. Columbia, S.C.: University of South Carolina Press, pp. 203–25.

Campbell, Karlyn Kohrs, and Kathleen Hall Jamieson (1990). *Deeds done in words*. Chicago: University of Chicago Press.

Campbell, Karlyn Kohrs, and Kathleen Hall Jamieson, eds. (1978). *Form and genre: Shaping rhetorical action*. Annandale, Va.: Speech Communication Association.

Carter, Jimmy (1980, Nov. 5). Transcript of the president's concession statement. *New York Times*, A18.

Chesebro, James W., and Caroline D. Hamsher (1974). The concession speech: The MacArthur–Agnew analog. *Speaker and Gavel, 11*, 39–51.

Clinton, Bill (1992, Nov. 4). Excerpts from the victory speech by President-elect Clinton. *New York Times*, B3.

Dukakis, Michael (1988, Nov. 5). Excerpts from the speech by Dukakis conceding the election. *New York Times*, A27.

Ferraro, Geraldine (1984, Nov. 7). Excerpts from Ferraro's talk. *New York Times*, A21.

Ford, Gerald (1976, Nov. 4). Transcripts and the statements of the president and Mrs. Ford and Carter. *New York Times*, 23.

Goldwater, Barry (1964, Nov. 5). Transcript of Goldwater's concession and news conference. *New York Times*, 20.

Gronbeck, Bruce E. (1984). Functional and dramaturgical themes of presidential campaigning. *Presidential Studies Quarterly, 14*, 468–99.

Humphrey, Hubert H. (1968, Nov. 7). Transcript of the Humphrey concession statement. *New York Times*, 22.

Jehl, Douglas, and James Gerstenzang (1992, Nov. 4). For Bush, a sense of relief eases the disappointment. *Los Angeles Times*, A10.

Johnson, Lyndon Baines (1964, Nov. 4). Johnson victory speech. *New York Times*, 22.

Kennedy, John F. (1960, Nov. 10). Kennedy remarks at news conference. *New York Times*, 36.

Lippman, Thomas W. (1992, Nov. 8). Taking "full responsibility" for loss. *Washington Post*, A1.

Lydon, Christopher (1976, Nov. 4). President concedes defeat and offers support to rival. *New York Times*, 1, 23.

Martin, Robert M. (1987). *The meaning of language*. Cambridge, Mass.: MIT.

McDaniel, Ann (1992, Nov.–Dec.). Exit on the high road. *Newsweek*, 12.

McGovern, George (1972, Nov. 8). Transcript of the speech by McGovern. *New York Times*, 3.

Mondale, Walter (1984, Nov. 7). Statement of concession by Mondale. *New York Times*, A21.

Naughton, James M. (1972, Nov. 8). McGovern to back moves for peace. *New York Times*, 1.

Nixon, Richard M. (1960, Nov. 9). Text of Nixon's statement of result. *New York Times*, 20.

Nixon, Richard M. (1968, Nov. 7). Transcript of the statement by Nixon pledging to "bring America together." *New York Times*, 21.

Nixon, Richard M. (1972, Nov. 8). Transcript of Nixon's victory speech. *New York Times*, 34.

Perot, Ross (1992a, July 17). Excerpts from Perot's news conference on decision not to enter election. *New York Times*, A16.

Perot, Ross (1992b, Nov. 3). Transcription of concession speech from C-SPAN2, broadcasting from the Grand Kempinksi Hotel, Dallas, Tex.

Perot, Ross (1992c, Nov. 4). Excerpts from Perot's concession speech to his supporters in Dallas. *New York Times*, B5.

Raines, Howell (1984, Nov. 7). Mondale concedes loss. *New York Times*, A1, A20.

Sack, Kevin (1992, Nov. 4). Leaving door open, Perot exits dancing. *New York Times*, B5.

Schumach, Murray (1960, Nov. 9). Nixon virtually concedes; Kennedy defers statement. *New York Times*, 1, 20.

Semple, Robert B., Jr. (1972, Nov. 8). Nixon issues call to "great tasks." *New York Times*, 1, 34.

Simons, Herbert W., and Aram A. Aghazarian, eds. (1986). *Form, genre, and the study of political discourse*. Columbia, S.C.: University of South Carolina Press.

Solberg, Carl (1984). *Hubert Humphrey, a biography*. New York: W. W. Norton.

Stevenson, Adlai E. (1952, Nov. 5). Statements by the loser and the winner. *New York Times*, 16.

Swanson, David L., and Dan Nimmo, eds. (1990). *New directions in political communication: A resource book.* Newbury Park, Calif.: Sage.

Thucydides (1960). *The history of the Peloponnesian War.* Ed. and trans. Richard Livingstone. New York: Oxford University Press.

Turque, Bill (1992, Nov.–Dec.). We'll keep on going. *Newsweek,* 13.

Weaver, Ruth Ann (1982). Acknowledgment of victory and defeat. The reciprocal ritual. *Central States Speech Journal, 33,* 480–89.

Wines, Michael (1992, Nov. 4). Facing bitter crowd, Bush exhibits grace in defeat. *New York Times,* B5.

THIRTEEN

Conclusions

The Struggle for Interpretive Dominance

CRAIG ALLEN SMITH

The twelve preceding chapters contribute significantly to our understanding of presidential campaigns. This chapter tries to connect their contributions with an overarching theoretical framework based on the premise that the process of developing and sustaining electoral coalitions unavoidably entails a struggle for interpretive dominance.

The consistent theme of this book is the struggle for interpretive dominance: The candidates, journalists, and voters struggled to define the story of the election; Democrats, Republicans, and Perot struggled to define the issues with their visions; advocates of "women's issues" and candidates like Larry Agran struggled to get on the political agenda; and the Religious Right fought a culture war over the perception that their traditional vision was losing its grip on American life.

THE STRUGGLE FOR CONTROL
OF THE ELECTORAL PROCESS

The chapters by Kendall, Meyrowitz, Owen, Bauman and Herbst, and Corcoran all help illuminate the interactive struggle for interpretive dominance among the politicians, the public, and the press. Kendall's analysis of campaign materials, speeches, debates, and news coverage shows that the candidates attempted to address public needs and policy issues that related directly to the question of who should govern, only to have their words reinterpreted by journalists interested in the question of who could win. The implications of this interpretive conflict are profound. Conventional wisdom holds that mass communication has facilitated candidate-citizen communication, but that is hardly the case when discussions of values, priorities, and governance are hijacked and transformed into horse race stories by the very news organizations that purport to serve the public interest. Indeed, several chapters invite us to conclude that the watchdogs of the fourth estate themselves have become an important source of public dissatisfaction with government.

Meyrowitz's account of Larry Agran's candidacy is especially unsettling. Nothing Agran did—including catching Tom Harkin and Jerry Brown in the polls—could get the press to treat him as a significant candidate. Although the Democratic Party's 1972 reforms opened the nomination process with primaries and proportional allocation of delegates, Meyrowitz implies that this very opening of the process compelled news organizations to assume the function of winnowing the field because contemporary journalism is conducted in the economic logic of scarce resources. The press might want to cover all the candidates, but they cannot afford the personnel, the equipment, the time, or the space to do so. The "Super Tuesday" primaries were instituted to keep northern primaries from winnowing the field before southern voters could participate, but Meyrowitz's research suggests that the press is now winnowing that field well before the first New Hampshire voters cast their votes. That might be acceptable if they used their audience's criteria to winnow, but journalists' ask "Who will win?" while the public wants to know "Who can govern best?"

Owen's discussion of debates reveals how earlier candidates adapted to the demands and logic of news organizations and thus relinquished control over these potentially valuable forums. The concept of televised candidate debates before an audience of citizens was hijacked by the journalistic community, which insisted on framing debates, transforming them into joint press conferences, and reporting on "who can win." Owen also shows that waning voter satisfaction with debates was revived with the town hall format of 1992. Clearly, the journalistic community won the struggle for control of presidential debates from 1960 to 1988, but they lost ground in 1992. We should now watch carefully to see whether journalists, citizens, or candidates gain control of political debates.

Bauman and Herbst suggest a third way that the journalistic community has distanced voters from the process. Campaign reporting has increasingly relied on public opinion polls that are typically reported in a way that disembodies the opinions from the public, ignores historical contexts, and assumes causal relationships. We might add that they frequently misuse their polls and thus mislead voters, as when they discuss the closeness of the election in terms of aggregate national opinion rather than individual state polls and projected electoral vote totals. In combination, journalists' use of polls dehumanizes the electorate and misleads them on important factual matters.

Finally, Corcoran observes that press coverage of concession speeches is so formulaic that it is common for journalists to report a "gracious concession" that is neither gracious nor a concession. This matters because, as Corcoran insightfully notes, democratic legitimacy is contingent not upon the winner but upon the loser. For it is the losers who must help reinterpret their story as one of success, efficacy, and ultimate loyalty to the system and its new president, whom they despised only an hour before.

Taken together, these studies suggest that the journalistic community intervenes in candidate-citizen communication by (1) redefining the story of the election from "who should govern" to "who can win," (2) winnowing the field of primary candidates even before the first primary, (3) framing public expectations of candidate debates, (4) asking the questions at candidate debates, (5) framing the outcome of debates and their electoral (but not governing) implications, (6) dehumanizing public opinion, (7) reporting polls in ways that are inaccurate and misleading, and (8) proclaiming the gracious concession and loyalty of losing candidates, even when the candidates do not do so themselves. Such is the behavior of our watchdogs of the democratic process. Why has this happened?

The eight press behaviors all make sense in the logic of journalism that is grounded in the journalistic code and reporters' needs. The journalist tells a story to a regularly attentive audience. A story requires dramatic tension and a regular audience needs to be kept interested. These imperatives have combined to shape the melodramatic requirements of news in America:

> Moral justice is at the heart of most melodrama—trials of the virtuous, calumny of the villainous, good rewarded, evil punished. Suspense is the key—from certain death to miraculous safety, disgrace to vindication, paradise lost to paradise regained, vanquished to victor. Anxiety is provoked—unrelenting dangers, unexpected threats, hairbreadth escapes. And characters are clearly labeled—good are good, bad are bad. Finally, happy endings are preferred but not essential. . . . Tragic endings suffice. (Nimmo and Combs, 1990, p. 16)

This melodramatic logic simply does not permit its users to prefer dispassionate discussion of problems and solutions to stories of characters and their actions in surprising plots. Contrasting the melodramatic logic of journalism and the empirical logic of social science in the 1988 primaries revealed that several familiar journalistic truths are empirically illogical. For example, no winner of the Iowa caucuses has ever been elected president, and victory there does not predict meaningful gains in either New Hampshire or the Super Tuesday states (Smith, 1992). But in the journalistic logic of campaigns there is little disincentive to be mistaken, for misguided expectations often result in exciting plot twists that pique audience interest.

Thus, future studies of American presidential elections might devote even more attention to the struggle among journalists, candidates, and citizens over control of the story. There are important subcultures to follow. Meyrowitz found important differences between the national and local journalistic communities, and we expect that incumbents and challengers, Democrats and Republicans, liberals and conservatives are interpretive communities. The struggle among these interpretive communities for control of the ways that new communication technologies will be used in election campaigns is bound to have a profound impact on democratic practice.

THE STRUGGLE TO MOBILIZE A WINNING COALITION

The most familiar interpretive struggle in election campaigns seeks to mobilize a coalition sufficient to win the election, and all of the chapters suggest factors that contributed to the interpretive outcome of the 1992 presidential campaign. We turn next to those reasons. Because incumbents enjoy the benefit of presumption, and especially because George Bush enjoyed 90 percent public approval nineteen months before the election, we shall concentrate on the factors contributing to Bush's loss of that presumption, the factors that enabled Clinton to capitalize on Bush's difficulties, and the factors that contributed to Perot's unique fate. We shall strive for clarity in this synthesis by extrapolating points from the chapters, generally without regard to authorship of those points, on the assumption that the reader will recall the chapters.

George Bush Loses His Advantage

President Bush approached the campaign confident of renomination and reelection. But as the Trents note, Bush lacked support among bedrock conservatives. The Buchanan wake-up call hurt Bush in several respects. First, he was perceived as less of a fighter (and more of a wimp?) than Buchanan, Tsongas, and the other Democrats. Second, the local press had difficulty reporting a positive Bush story in New Hampshire. And third, the national press was left to amplify Bush's aloofness and his critics' accusations. Press attention to his critics' campaigns and to Bush's inevitable decline from his unprecedented 90 percent popularity encouraged reporters to infer a causal relationship. Bauman and Herbst's "it's still early" disclaimer did not quite fit the president's predicament. As Buchanan continued to send his message the Bush campaign apparently began to worry about the nomination and Bush altered his approach in order to curry favor on the right.

Bush's strategic shift was particularly precarious because, as Wendt and Fairhurst contend, his was a transactional rather than transformational or charismatic presidency. Trent and Trent found that Bush did not establish the importance of his foreign policy expertise in the post-cold war era, running away from his strength because of voters' economic concerns. However, John Sununu's advice that he adopt a laissez-faire posture toward the economy left Bush with no cogent economic rhetoric either.

Deprived of cold war rhetoric, economic prosperity, a cogent economic rhetoric, the image of a fighter, positive press coverage of his rhetorical agenda, a transformational style of leadership, personal charisma, and personal skill with either metonymy or synecdoche, George Bush lost the presumption of incumbency. And as Bush's critics gained credence, his incumbency became an albatross. He tried to capitalize on this populist anti-incumbency in his commercials, but Roberts' respondents perceived them as negative and he suffered substantial backlash perhaps, as Stuckey and Antczak suggest, because he had come to epitomize the very sort of Washington insider that his messages attacked. Bush was reduced to attacking Clinton and Perot, but in doing so he failed to erase doubts about his own character and leadership.

Clinton Combines Strategy, Vision, and Style

The Buchanan, Tsongas, and press critiques of Bush's presidency contributed to a climate in which any challenger who could appeal to Bush's opponents would be taken seriously. Trent and Trent suggest that Clinton went about this by positioning himself as neither liberal nor conservative, but centrist. Stuckey and Antczak point to Clinton's rhetorical form that combined traditional values with liberal solutions. Their view is consistent with the position that Clinton's campaign was framed in the logic of his "New Covenant" jeremiad. He frequently argued that America had always been the greatest country in the world because (1) Americans have always believed that tomorrow would be better than today and (2) that each American has a personal moral responsibility to make it so. Clinton argued that Bush had exercised false leadership by dividing Americans and by being afraid to change in a changing world. Thus the logic of Clinton's campaign was that the path to future success was to be found in a return to traditional values of responsibility, concern for the "forgotten middle class," and pragmatic policies (Smith, 1994). Rhetorically, Clinton's jeremiadic "New Covenant" vision enabled him to use metonymy to advantage by suggesting that he, more than Bush, had lived the American Dream and that he, unlike Bush, had detailed multipoint programs that could fulfill his personal moral responsibility to make tomorrow better than today.

Clinton's style of campaigning also proved to be an asset. The Gennifer Flowers episode that occasioned his appearance on "60 Minutes" helped establish him as a fighter, and his frequent use of the town hall format enabled him to interact with skeptical voters. On the day of the "60 Minutes" broadcast, for example, the national press was preoccupied with the Flowers drama and its implications for the "who will win" story, but Clinton talked for hours with New Hampshire voters who questioned him about his analysis and prescriptions for the nation's problems (Nimmo, 1994). Had he dealt only with the scandal that interested the press, he could not have addressed the concerns that interested those who would cast the votes that decided the distribution of delegates.

Unlike Bush, who seemed to remain aloof, Clinton dramatized his communitarian themes by interacting with citizens and by "feeling their pain." Thus, the Trents conclude that Clinton capitalized on prevailing conditions and executed challenger strategies more effectively than his competitors, and more skillfully than Bush was able to execute the incumbent strategies. Moreover, Kern's research shows that Clinton's ads nurtured the image of a caring candidate, and Roberts found that Clinton's ads created little backlash. Their findings are consistent with the aggregate profile reported by Pomper (1993). He found that Clinton's national coalition of 43.7 percent of the electorate was built by supplementing his core of 23.5 percent Democratic loyalists with 12.2 percent whom he converted from Bush and 8 percent whom he recruited from the ranks of the previously nonvoting public, in contrast to Bush's larger core of 32 percent loyalists whom he could supplement with only 1.5 percent converts from Dukakis and 3.2 percent new recruits. Moreover, Clinton's conversion and recruitment of 20 percent of the electorate far surpassed the 4.9 percent of Dukakis voters that he lost to Perot (3.4%) and to Bush(1.5%).

Overall, Clinton strategized to win delegates and electoral votes rather than aggregate personal popularity by executing effectively the traditional challenger strategies and by framing his critique in the powerful logic of the jeremiad rather than in the ideology of the Democratic Left. By thus transforming the election into a referendum on George Bush as an agent of change, his campaign drew momentum from Perot's arguments for change and from Bush's own attacks on gridlock in Washington. He also merged traditional values and liberal policies to retain Democratic votes, to convert some erstwhile Bush voters, and to recruit marginal voters. But the Clinton electoral coalition made it difficult for him to claim a broad interpretive mandate, and this has complicated his task of forming an effective governing coalition (Smith, 1995).

The Perot Paradoxes

The 1992 campaign of H. Ross Perot was a campaign odyssey, with "odd" being the operative syllable. Perot was coaxed into running on a talk show but ran as a strong leader with experience. Perot was a self-proclaimed servant of the people who quit the race just when within striking distance, and who reentered the race after public interest had waned. Perot was a candidate dedicated to discussion of the issues rather than personalities, whose reentry increased coverage of personalities and decreased the news space devoted to issues (Sims and Giordano, 1993). And Perot was a candidate dedicated to the will of the people who won 19 percent of the popular vote and no electoral votes, and who then declined to support "the people's choice" for implementing change. How can we explain such a campaign? The authors of the preceding chapters provide several clues about these paradoxes of the Perot candidacy.

First, it is helpful to view Perot as a product of the candidate-journalist struggle over control of the election story. The pressures impelling the journalistic community to narrow prematurely the field of "major" candidates to a handful of front-runners ran directly counter to their need to justify audience interest in the campaign marathon. By March, with four months to go until the convention and eight until the election, campaign coverage was reduced to news of the waning Buchanan challenge, Clinton's personal foibles, and Jerry Brown's 800 number. But as Bush and Clinton drew closer to nomination neither tried very hard to court public favor. Thus, news coverage turned to voter dissatisfaction with the available candidates—a story that might never have unfolded had the press been less hasty to winnow the field of candidates.

The resulting interpretive climate was conducive to an independent candidacy, and Perot was particularly appropriate for the role. Because he was so rich he had little need to court wealthy contributors. Because he did not seek any party's nomination he had no need to debate other challengers to detail a platform, or to win convention delegates. Because he had considerable name recognition and an ill-defined political ideology he was able to benefit from everyone else's attacks on professional politicians. Because he was persuaded to run by Larry King he was less vulnerable than most others to suspicion of ambition and personal gain. And because so little was known about his politics he could quickly personify "none of the above" for disaffected voters.

Kern's analysis of Perot's narratives of heroic sacrifice is enlightening. Perot's populist stories conveyed the benefits of the individual standing up for principle and the innate goodness of people, and sought to downplay his heroism. However, the narrative form of his messages served to elevate the narrator, enhance audience dependency, minimize the appetite for propositions and data, and foster identification that enhanced ethos. The fact that Perot's narration dominated his infomercials should not be ignored because it gave him the spotlight in which to dramatize his humility.

THE STRUGGLE FOR ACCESS
TO THE AGENDA-SETTING PROCESS

The third interpretive struggle was the contest for access to the agenda-setting process. Daughton's chapter illuminates many of the subtle problems inherent in the so-called Year of the Woman. Underlying her analysis is the familiar dilemma that faces every marginalized interpretive community that seeks political access. Put simply, the melting pot dilemma is this: Any interpretive community will be accorded access to the majority if it melts, but if it melts it loses the very identity that it has just come to value. Women, of course, constitute a numerical majority; but females do not all prefer feminist positions, nor are feminist positions preferred only by females. Enactment of the feminist agenda will require the support of a majority of those in positions of power, and they still are so disproportionately male that the appropriate persuasive appeals must be diverse. But diversification of the rhetorical repertoire contributes to the perception that women are being disenfranchised by new means.

This melting pot dilemma faced Martin Luther King Jr. and his handling of it in his "I Have a Dream" speech may prove instructive. The genius of King's speech is that he argued for fair treatment of all Americans, not solely African Americans, and that he did so not with the rhetoric of the black experience but with the rhetoric of the white middle class. Unlike Malcolm X, Stokely Carmichael, and H. Rap Brown, King did not advance the reasons that energized African Americans. Perhaps the choice for women, too, will entail a close examination of individual and collective needs: Is it more important to have "women's issues" as a source of community identification, or to secure enactment of policies that address positively their concerns?

As marginalized interpretive communities strive for access to the agenda-setting process, other interpretive communities struggle to preserve their access. Gregg's chapter on the culture war of the Religious Right illustrates this phenomenon. From their perspective, the traditional American way of life is under attack on several fronts. The loss of something is normally felt more keenly than a delay in the attainment of something new, and this deprivation is likely to be especially painful and disorienting when it is perceived in moral terms. Thus it should not be surprising that the rhetoric of a culture war would be a powerful vehicle for reaching, mobilizing and energizing a variety of interpretive communities who feel threatened.

The Religious Right is unlikely to go quietly into the night because the type of rhetoric associated with the culture war is so ego-involving that it draws strength from external attacks. We can expect the rhetoric of the culture war to be an effective vehicle for social conservatives, but this may pose more problems for Republicans than Democrats because the 1992 campaign left the Republican coalition in the same sort of interpretive disarray as that experienced by the Democrats in 1980. In both elections an incumbent president representing the moderate wing of his party (Bush and Carter) was challenged in the primaries by an ardent voice from his party's more extreme wing (Buchanan and Edward Kennedy), defeated that challenge, lost supporters to an independent candidate (Perot and John Anderson), and lost the presidency to the opposition party's candidate, who won less than 51 percent of the popular vote.

Will the Republican coalition coalesce more quickly than did the Democrats? A recent 1994 Times-Mirror Center poll indicates a significant increase in the number of moral conservatives, such that they now outnumber the economic conservatives by almost two-to-one. In addition to that split, the potential problem for Republicans is that the "moralists'" agenda alienates the third group of likely Republicans, "libertarians," who are laissez-faire on social issues. Thus, culture war rhetoric may expand the very segment of the Republican coalition that will complicate their mobilization of a winning electoral coalition (Kohut, 1994). Of course, that hardly appears consistent with the Revolution of 1994 that gave Republicans control of the House, the Senate, and the national agenda. If their "revolution" produces popular changes and a viable candidate for president by the end of the first quarter of 1996 they will be well along the road to the White House. But if their Contract with America falls prey to the same set of constraints that undermined Clinton's leadership of a Democratic Congress, if no Republican candidate emerges who is able to take the center from Clinton, or even if the 1992 presidential voters who did not vote in 1994 emerge in 1996, the Republican majority could prove tenuous. If Republicans plan to defeat "big government, tax and spend, liberal" Bill Clinton they might well reconsider their responses to his crucial 1995 State of the Union Address, a vintage Clinton New Covenant speech that deviated little from his standard message since the 1970s. Christine Todd Whitman's response said that it could have been given by George Bush, Dan Quayle told CBS that it could have been given by Ronald Reagan, and Speaker Newt Gingrich said that the President had heard the voters' message. By glorying in the dominance of Republicanism these three important spokespersons have overlooked Clinton's claim to represent the reasonable, moderate center.

The chapters on women's issues and the culture war highlight the problems of developing and sustaining interpretive coalitions that can win presidential elections. Communities seeking access to the coalition face the melting pot dilemma, but coalition builders can alienate those communities by appealing to them in the wrong way. On the other hand, interpretive communities that feel threatened can generate a culture war rhetoric that is a powerful vehicle for recruiting, consolidating, and mobilizing supporters even as it complicates the process of mobilizing an electoral majority.

CONCLUSIONS

The twelve chapters in this book suggest the presence of three kinds of interpretive struggles in presidential campaigns. First, the studies suggest a possible trend away from journalistic control of the process—a trend that could profoundly influence future campaigns. Second, we saw the struggle among candidates Bush, Clinton, and Perot to mobilize electoral and governing coalitions. The studies suggest that President Bush lost the advantages of incumbency, that Clinton executed the challenger strategies well enough to win the election without creating a foundation for an effective governing coalition, and that Ross Perot undermined Clinton's ability to forge a governing coalition without threatening to win any state. Finally, the studies illuminate struggles by women and the Religious Right to gain and to maintain, respectively, their access to the agenda-setting process. In both cases, their rhetorical choices will likely have profound effects on the ability of future candidates to forge electoral and governing coalitions.

REFERENCES

Kohut, Andrew (1994, Sept. 21). Remarks at the Washington Journalism Center. Washington, D.C.: C-SPAN.

Nimmo, Dan (1994). The electronic town hall in campaign '92: Interactive forum or carnival of Buncombe? In Robert E. Denton Jr., ed., *The 1992 presidential campaign: A communication perspective.* Westport, Conn.: Praeger, pp. 207–26.

Nimmo, Dan, and James E. Combs (1990). *Mediated political realities.* 2nd ed. New York: Longman.

Pomper, Gerald M. (1993). The presidential election. In Gerald M. Pomper, ed., *The election of 1992.* Chatham, N.J.: Chatham House, pp. 132–156.

Sims, Judy R., and Joseph R. Giordano (1993). 1992 presidential campaign issues: A content analysis of character/competence/image versus platform/political issues. Paper presented at the annual convention of the Speech Communication Association.

Smith, Craig Allen (1992, Summer). The Iowa caucuses and Super Tuesday primaries reconsidered: How untenable hypotheses enhance the campaign melodrama. *Presidential Studies Quarterly, 22,* 519–30.

Smith, Craig Allen (1994). The jeremiadic logic of Bill Clinton's policy speeches. In Stephen A. Smith, ed., *Bill Clinton on stump, state, and stage: The rhetorical road to the White House.* Fayetteville: University of Arkansas Press, pp. 73–100.

Smith, Craig Allen (In press). "Rough stretches and honest disagreements": Is Bill Clinton redefining the rhetorical presidency? In Robert E. Denton Jr. and Rachel Holloway, eds., *The emerging Clinton presidency: A communication perspective.* Westport, Conn.: Praeger.

Contributors

Frederick J. Antczak is Associate Professor and Chair, Department of Rhetoric, University of Iowa. He studies and teaches about rhetoric's relation to the development of character, and about the standing accorded to rhetoric and character in liberal polity. His book *Thought and Character: The Rhetoric of Democratic Education* (Iowa State University Press, 1985), won a Phi Beta Kappa book award. Among other honors have been a Thomas Jefferson teaching award at the University of Virginia, and the University of Iowa's Certificate of Teaching Excellence, 1994.

Sandra Bauman is a Ph.D. student in the Department of Communication Studies, Northwestern University, and Project Director at Roper Starch Worldwide, New York.

Paul E. Corcoran, Associate Professor of Politics at the University of Adelaide, Australia, is the author of *Political Language and Rhetoric* (University of Texas Press, 1979; published concurrently by Queensland University Press, St. Lucia, 1979), and *Before Marx: Socialism and Communism in France, 1830–1848* (London: Macmillan, 1983; published concurrently by St. Martin's Press, New York, 1983), and numerous essays and articles in the fields of language and political philosophy. He is the recipient of a 1995 Australian Research Council grant to study victory and concession speeches in Australian parliamentary elections since 1941.

Suzanne M. Daughton is Assistant Professor of Speech Communication, Southern Illinois University at Carbondale. Her research interests involve the study of gender, processes of empowerment, and rhetorical style in public discourse. She has published in the *Quarterly Journal of Speech*, *Communication Quarterly*, *The Iowa Journal of Communication*, and *Human Communication Research*. She is the past recipient of the Karl R. Wallace Memorial Award, given by the Speech Communication Association to promote the research of a promising new scholar in rhetoric and public address, and the Central States Outstanding New Teacher Award.

Gail T. Fairhurst is Professor and Chair, Department of Communication, University of Cincinnati. Her research interests revolve primarily around discourse approaches to the study of leadership. She has published in *Communication Monographs, Human Communication Research, Communication Yearbooks* 8, 9, & 10, *Academy of Management Journal, Academy of Management Review,* and *Organizational Behavior and Human Decision Processes,* among others. She is on the editorial board for *Communication Monographs* and *Journal of Communication,* and has received a number of grants, including one to support a sabbatical at Procter and Gamble.

Richard B. Gregg is Professor of Speech Communication, The Pennsylvania State University. His research focuses on contemporary rhetorical theory and criticism, and contemporary American political rhetoric. He is co-author of *Speech Behavior and Human Interaction,* and author of *Symbolic Inducement and Knowing: A Study in the Foundations of Rhetoric,* winner of the 1984 James A. Winans, Herbert A. Wichelns Award for Distinguished Scholarship in Rhetoric and Public Address.

Susan Herbst is Associate Professor of Communication Studies and Political Science, Northwestern University. Her research interests include public opinion, political theory, and social change. She has published *Numbered Voices: How Opinion Polling Has Shaped American Politics* (University of Chicago Press, 1993), and *Politics at the Margin: Historical Perspectives on Public Expression Outside the Mainstream* (Cambridge University Press, 1994).

Kathleen E. Kendall is Associate Professor of Communication, University at Albany, State University of New York. She is author of articles on political communication in journals such as *Quarterly Journal of Speech, Presidential Studies Quarterly, American Behavioral Scientist,* and *Communication Quarterly,* and is Chair of the Political Communication Division of the International Communication Association. She regularly assists the Albany-area media with political ad watches and presidential campaign analysis.

Montague Kern is Assistant Professor of Journalism and Mass Media, Rutgers University. She is the author of *Thirty-Second Politics: Political Advertising in the Eighties* (Praeger-Greenwood, 1989), the first author (with Patricia W. Levering and Ralph Levering) of *The Kennedy Crises: The Press, the Presidency, and Foreign Policy* (University of North Carolina Press, 1983), and co-author of a forthcoming book, *Crosstalk: Citizens, Media, and Candidates in a Presidential Election.* Professor Kern has published articles in such journals as *Political Psychology, Political Communication,* and *Argumentation and Advocacy,* as well as many book chapters. She has been a research fellow at the John Shorenstein Barone Center, Harvard University, John F. Kennedy School of Government, and often assists the media with analysis of political advertising.

Joshua Meyrowitz is Professor of Communication at the University of New Hampshire. He is the author of *No Sense of Place: The Impact of Electronic Media on Social Behavior* (Oxford University Press), which has won several awards including the Speech Communication Association's Golden Anniversary Book Award. Professor Meyrowitz has published numerous articles in scholarly journals and anthologies as well as in general-interest magazines and newspapers.

Diana Owen is Assistant Professor of Government at Georgetown University. Her research is focused on the political behavior of the mass public, and she has published scholarly and popular articles on topics relating to elections and voting behavior, public opinion, political socialization, the mass media, and political culture. Currently, she is working on projects that examine the role of the "new media" in American politics, and the political socialization of Generation X. She is the author of *Media Messages in American Presidential Elections* (Greenwood, 1991), and has consulted for NBC News and the Times Mirror Center for the People and the Press.

Marilyn S. Roberts is Assistant Professor of Advertising, College of Journalism and Communications, University of Florida, Gainesville. Her research interests include the effects of political message strategies, the use of visual symbolism, and the intermedia agenda-setting influence of campaign advertising. Roberts' articles have appeared in *Political Communication, Journalism Quarterly, Mass Communication Review,* and the *Proceedings of the American Academy of Advertising.* She currently serves as editor of the joint newsletter of the political communication divisions of the International Communication Association and the American Political Science Associations. She has served as a media consultant to a United States Congressman for twelve years, and owned her own advertising and public relations firm.

Craig Allen Smith is Professor of Communication Studies at the University of North Carolina, Greensboro, where he teaches courses in political communication, rhetorical theory and criticism, and speechwriting. His books include *Political Communication* (Harcourt Brace Jovanovich, 1990), *The White House Speaks: Presidential Leadership as Persuasion* (with Kathy B. Smith, Praeger, 1994), and *Persuasion and Social Movements* (3rd edition, Waveland, 1994; 1989, 1984, with Charles J. Stewart and Robert E. Denton, Jr.). He served as the initial chair of the Speech Communication Association's Political Communication Division, and has chaired SCA's Task Force on Presidential Communication as well as the Communication Theory and Rhetoric and Public Address Divisions of the Southern States Communication Association. He often analyzes campaign communication for media in North Carolina.

Mary E. Stuckey is Associate Professor of Political Science, University of Mississippi. Her research interests include: the presidency, political rhetoric, and political communication. She has published *The President as Interpreter-in-Chief* (Chatham House, 1991), *Theories and Methods of Political Communication* (State University of New York Press, forthcoming), and *Strategic Failures in the Modern Presidency* (Hampton Press, forthcoming), as well as numerous essays on the rhetorical presidency.

Jimmie D. Trent is Professor of Communication, Miami University, Oxford, Ohio. He has published in the areas of political communication, communication theory, interpersonal communication, argumentation, and public relations. His current research involves media treatment of political candidates.

Judith S. Trent is Professor of Communication and Associate Vice President of Research and Advanced Studies, University of Cincinnati. She teaches courses in political campaign communication, has written and spoken widely on presidential campaigning and women in politics, and is co-author (with Robert V. Friedenberg), of *Political Campaign Communication: Principles and Practices* (Praeger, 1991). She is Second Vice President of the Speech Communication Association, and will become the Association's president in 1997.

Ronald F. Wendt is a Ph.D. student, Department of Communication, Purdue University. His research focuses primarily on organizational communication, including management strategies, power dynamics, and corporate rhetoric. He has been a researcher for an executive search firm, and a political activist.

Index

309